Dear John

TONIGHT AT THE
TARRAGON

With love

From Your Tarragon

TONIGHT AT THE

TARRAGON

A CRITIC'S ANTHOLOGY

EDITED BY KAMAL AL-SOLAYLEE

HALF LIFE • JOHN MIGHTON
RUNE ARLIDGE • MICHAEL HEALEY
THE OPTIMISTS • MORWYN BREBNER
I, CLAUDIA • KRISTEN THOMSON
MOTEL HÉLÈNE • SERGE BOUCHER,
   ADAPTED BY JUDITH THOMPSON FROM A
   TRANSLATION BY MORWYN BREBNER
IT'S ALL TRUE • JASON SHERMAN

PLAYWRIGHTS CANADA PRESS
TORONTO

PLAYWRIGHTS CANADA PRESS
The Canadian Drama Publisher
215 Spadina Ave., Suite 230, Toronto, ON Canada M5T 2C7
phone 416.703.0013 fax 416.408.3402
info@playwrightscanada.com • www.playwrightscanada.com

Playwrights Canada Press acknowledges the financial support of the Government of Canada through the Canada Book Fund and the Canada Council for the Arts and of the Province of Ontario through the Ontario Arts Council and the Ontario Media Development Corporation, for our publishing activities.

Canada Council Conseil des Arts   ONTARIO ARTS COUNCIL
for the Arts   du Canada   CONSEIL DES ARTS DE L'ONTARIO

Cover by BFdesign
Interior design by Blake Sproule

LIBRARY AND ARCHIVES CANADA CATALOGUING IN PUBLICATION
Tonight at the Tarragon : a critic's anthology / edited by Kamal Al-Solaylee. -- 1st ed.
Includes bibliographical references.
ISBN 978-1-77091-025-6

1. Canadian drama (English)--Ontario--Toronto. 2. Canadian drama (English)--21st century.
3. Tarragon Theatre. I. Al-Solaylee, Kamal

PS8315.7.T67T65 2011   C812'.60809713541   C2011-905564-3

First edition: October 2011
Printed and bound in Canada by Marquis Book Printing, Montreal

TABLE OF CONTENTS

ALTERNATIVE TO THE ALTERNATIVE: A SHORT AND (MOSTLY) UNBIASED CRITICAL HISTORY OF THE TARRAGON THEATRE

Contradictions are not unusual in a city that has followed eight years of a progressive, left-leaning mayor with a move to the political right of Rob Ford and the Tea Party North of his "Ford Nation." Torontonians often hold two opposing views on the same issue and defend both vigorously. Listen to the various conversations in which multiculturalism is discussed as the boom *and* doom of this city or how art funding is sometimes cast as a pursuit of the elites and, when politically expedient, Toronto's claim to fame as a world-class city. Once described by its own artistic director, Urjo Kareda, as a "220-seat house on the wrong side of the tracks,"[1] the Tarragon Theatre is yet another one of the city's bewildering contradictions.

It's a relatively small but hugely bankable theatre that, since its early years, has built a reputation as a de facto national theatre—or at the very least the unofficial Home to the Canadian Playwright. It put Toronto on the Canadian theatrical map in the 1970s and, in doing so, placed Canadian drama on the world stage, mainly but not exclusively through productions of its signature playwrights in the United States. Despite such a stellar reputation—and until Soulpepper Theatre Company's brash debut in 1998 with its well-heeled sponsors—the Tarragon enjoyed the bragging rights to the "The Theatre Artists Love and Hate Equally" Crown. Theatre history books[2] place it in the continuum of alternative theatres in Toronto (alongside Theatre Passe Muraille, the now-defunct Toronto Free Theatre, and what was then called the Factory Lab) that rode a new wave of American counterculture and Canadian nationalism in the late 1960s and early 1970s.

The same historians generally agree that the establishment of the Canada Council for the Arts in 1957 and the centennial celebrations in 1967 mark the true beginnings of a distinctly Canadian self-expression onstage. Regional theatres— the Manitoba Theatre Centre in Winnipeg in 1958 first among them—provided

---

1   Urjo Kareda, "A Former Life," in *Theatre Memories*, 72. Kareda was discussing the fluidity and "marvellous turnabouts" in Canadian theatre since the 1970s that would allow a stage veteran like Martha Henry to star in a production of *Pal Joey* at the Tarragon.

2   I'm indebted to three in particular for vital historical and analytical content: Denis W. Johnston's *Up the Mainstream: The Rise of Toronto's Alternative Theatres*; Renate Usmiani's *Second Stage: The Alternative Theatre Movement in Canada*; and Don Rubin's: *Canadian Theatre History: Selected Readings*.

home for professional local and touring productions across the country. But even there, the programming tilted in favour of local productions of Broadway and West End hits as well as picks from the touring circuits. That and the establishment of the Stratford Festival as a colonial outpost in southern Ontario in 1953 ignited the alternative theatre movement in Toronto. Theatres like Factory and Passe Muraille made it their business to stage works by Canadian playwrights in the case of the former and to follow more collaborative aesthetics in the search for and development of Canadian stories in the case of the latter.

The movement has been mythologized, interpreted, and reinterpreted enough to cast some doubt on the accuracy of its histories, but what remains uncontested is the fact that it has produced "one of the most exciting phenomena ever to appear on the cultural scene of this country."[3] The same books also point out that Bill and Jane Glassco established the Tarragon in 1971 as an alternative to the alternative houses that came before it. Its very name—Glassco's favourite herb for dressing salads and a symbol of coziness because of its family-kitchen association—was a reaction against the string of alternative new spaces with words like workshop, lab, or studio. This would be a theatre in the more traditional sense—and deliberately so. A certain emphasis on production standards, house-management policies, and audience relationship-building gave it a degree of professionalism that contrasted with the daredeviling of, in particular, Ken Gass's Factory Lab or Paul Thompon's Passe Muraille, the two perceived edgier venues. Unlike Gass, writes Denis W. Johnston, Glassco "would not compromise the theatrical effectiveness of one production for the sake of more numerous productions."[4] And unlike Thompson, "he had no wish to redefine the traditional tasks of director, playwright, and actor, nor did he seek out a new audience."[5] Unfairly, this has cast the Tarragon as a "safe" company: home to the well-made naturalism of, say, David French, even if it simultaneously introduced Toronto to the best of groundbreaking Quebec theatre, including, of course, the early works of Michel Tremblay.

Much of its past and current legacy can be attributed to its geographical (and in part accidental) location. Sandwiched between the splendour of Forest Hill mansions and the bourgeois homes (and frat houses) of the Annex, and on the borders of the main campus of the University of Toronto, the theatre has travelled between two worlds—privilege and bohemia, old and young—with admirable ease since it opened its doors in October 1971 in the renovated warehouse on Bridgman Avenue it still occupies.[6]

---

3   Usmiani, vii.

4   Johnston, 140.

5   Ibid.

6   For an analysis of the Tarragon Theatre's physical location from the critical perspective of cultural materialism, see Richard Paul Knowles and Jennifer Fletcher, "Towards a Materialist

Fast forward about forty years and two artistic directors—the late Kareda and the current Richard Rose—and the Tarragon still occupies the same place not just physically but in the collective perception of Canadian theatre artists and critics. Toward the end of my tenure as a theatre critic for the *Globe and Mail*, I could describe it as the most consistently reliable and artistically grounded theatre in Canada without fear of contradiction or accusations of being Toronto-centric. It remains a lofty ambition for many young playwrights to land a production there. Theatregoers and artists continue to talk about the Tarragon as a healthy and prosperous, if sometimes staid, institution while Passe Muraille and Factory—theatres that have traded on the discourse of risk and edginess—have slipped in and out of so many comas over the years that pulling a plug on them feels more like an act of mercy than maliciousness.

The Tarragon's endurance, however, belies its turbulent early years and its many brushes with box-office and critical disasters. The opening season (1971–'72) may have been bookended by the now-legendary remount of David Freeman's *Creeps*—it debuted at the Factory Lab in February 1971—and the premiere of French's *Leaving Home*, the first in his Mercer trilogy, but in between there were several critical and financial disappointments. So much so that, as Johnston points out, had *Leaving Home* failed to connect with audiences and critics, Bill and Jane Glassco would have closed down the Tarragon for good.[7] Luckily, word of mouth and critical reception for French's brand of naturalism were glowing and the Tarragon lived to see another season (and thirty-nine more so far).

It's not hard to justify the "golden age" moniker given by theatre historians and artists to those early seasons at the Tarragon when you take a look at the production history. The third season, 1973–'74, for example, featured French's follow-up hit *Of the Fields, Lately*; *Sticks and Stones*, the first instalment of James Reaney's Donnelly trilogy (all of which premiered at the Tarragon); and Tremblay's cross-dressing dream of a play, *Hosanna*, as famous now for a breakthrough performance by the late Richard Monette in the title role as for its English translation by Glassco and John Van Burek. However, the exhaustion and continuous struggle of running a successful theatre got to the Glasscos, who put the Tarragon on hiatus for a full season, 1975–'76, in order to "assess what we have done and to think about where we want to and should be going."[8] The theatre was rented out to several companies during the hiatus, keeping the name and spirit of the Tarragon going even when its creators could not. When Glassco resumed normal Tarragon business in 1976–'77, audiences could immediately spot those new directions. The theatre now included more works by European

---

Performance Analysis: The Case of Tarragon Theatre," in *The Performance Text*, 205–26.

7   Johnston, 152.

8   Quoted in Johnston, 166.

and American writers in addition to its usual serving of Canadian plays. It also became the home of now-established playwrights along the lines of French and Tremblay and, as Johnston points out, of second and third plays by younger writers.[9]

One of the unabashed champions of the early Tarragon—and the new alternative spaces in Toronto in general—was Urjo Kareda, then the erudite and powerful theatre critic for the *Toronto Star*, a job he held for four years—1971–'75—until he joined the Stratford Festival as its literary manager at the invitation of its then-artistic director Robin Phillips. It's hard to imagine theatres as temperamentally different as Passe Muraille and the Tarragon surviving without his unqualified endorsement. By 1974, Kareda's support went beyond Toronto's (and Canada's) borders: as a regular arts commentator for the *New York Times* he championed the Tarragon as the most influential theatre in Canada.[10] When Glassco decided to step down from the Tarragon in 1981, he simply appointed Kareda as his successor, starting with the 1982–'83 season. As Mallory Gilbert—the legendary general manager of the Tarragon since 1978 and a member of the theatre staff since 1972—recounted his appointment, Glassco "chose Urjo to be the next artistic director—no search committee involved... It was unusual then and it would probably be impossible today."[11] Unlike Glassco and despite his many talents, Kareda didn't think of himself as a theatre director. His forte was dramaturgy and play and playwright development. From his new position as artistic director of the Tarragon, Kareda helped solidify the careers of such prominent Canadian playwrights as Judith Thompson, whose long association with the Tarragon began in 1984 with *White Biting Dog* and continued through *Capture Me* in 2004. Other writers strongly identified with the Kareda years include Jason Sherman, Morwyn Brebner (both of whom are included and discussed elsewhere in this anthology in more detail), and Joan MacLeod.

As different as the above-mentioned playwrights are from each other, they all fall into what can be justifiably described as Kareda's (and by extension the Tarragon's) twin pulls of literary work and variations of stage naturalism, including poetic naturalism.[12] Glassco drew this blueprint for the Tarragon in programming plays by French and Reaney but Kareda took it to complete fruition. The emphasis on poetic naturalism with its attendant focus on the psychological and personal and the shift from the social and political has, unfairly, shaped the Tarragon's reputation as a theatre that is

9   Johnston, 168.

10   Kareda, "Canada's new playwrights have found a home at home," *The New York Times*, November 23, 1974, NYTA 7.

11   Quoted in Robin Breon, "Tarragon Flavoured Memories," in *Canadian Theatre Review*, vol. 113 (2003), 5.

12   Knowles and Fletcher, 214–215.

at once in the city but removed from it. While the very mention of Sherman and Thompson with their interest in issues as varied as Jewish identity and underclass rage is enough to shoot down that proposition, elsewhere Kareda's programming privileged literary texts with a naturalist bent over other modes of theatrical expression.

No one can accuse Kareda of being inconsistent; his fearlessness as a theatre critic morphed into disarming forthrightness as a dramaturge. The letters he sent playwrights who submitted hundreds of unsolicited manuscripts—which he personally read—have become the stuff of legend among the theatre community for their wit and brutal honesty. When I wrote a story in 1999 for the *National Post* about the Tarragon's playwrights unit where he displayed his dramaturgical acumen year after year, many writers who were rejected from the unit or had an unhappy experience with it complained about what they saw as imperiousness and bias in Kareda's script analysis. He liked a certain kind of gay theatre but not working-class and certainly not lesbian, I was told. Hardly any playwright of colour made it to the unit, others carped. Still, just as looking at the production history of the early Tarragon years can be a surreal experience—so many classics in just a few years—the output of the playwrights unit during the 1980s and 1990s when Kareda ran it is staggering: Sherman's *Three in the Back, Two in the Head*; MacLeod's *Jewel* and *Toronto, Mississippi*; and Jonathan Wilson's *Kilt*, to name but a few that premiered at the Tarragon. Many more—Florence Gibson MacDonald's *Belle* and John Mighton's *Scientific Americans*—found homes elsewhere.

While the Tarragon's bourgeois reputation was further solidified during Kareda's reign, which continued until his premature death of brain cancer in December 2001, so too was its financial health. In 1987 the theatre finally purchased and renovated its Bridgman Avenue home for $1.3 million. It opened up the Extra Space, an intimate one-hundred-seat theatre that became home to a number of smaller (in scale) plays, most notably a string of one-woman shows (*I, Claudia*, anthologized here, is a prime example). The outpouring of grief over Kareda's death in 2001 suggested that his influence as an artistic director extended beyond the walls of the theatre itself. In fact, with so many plays in the unit receiving their premieres at other stages—and so many Tarragon premieres getting second and third productions across the country—the theatre became an official home to and supplier of Canadian theatre. The de facto national theatre reputation seems highly justified to me.

Any artistic director stepping into Kareda's giant shoes had his work cut out for him. But Richard Rose, already a celebrated director and dramaturge for over twenty-five years at the time of his appointment in 2002, stood as good a chance as any. As founder and artistic director of the Toronto-based Necessary Angel Theatre Company and with a long history at the Stratford Festival, Rose was well positioned to combine the intellectual rigour of the former with the wider appeal of the latter. After overseeing Kareda's last season in 2002–'03, Rose's tenure started in earnest and to mixed reviews in 2003–'04, which was also my first as a theatre critic for the *Globe and Mail*. The season launched with Sherman's ambitious but uneven *Remnants (A Fable)*, a retelling of the biblical story of Joseph; continued with an unnecessary remount of Karen Hines's futuristic musical *Hello...Hello*; and concluded with Peter Froehlich's befuddling *simpl*, an homage to Germany's Charlie Chaplin, Karl Valentin. Although I called that season "officially disappointing"[13] in my review of *simpl*, it gave birth to Michael Healey's *Rune Arlidge* and the Toronto premiere of Carole Fréchette's *Helen's Necklace*. While the former sank without a trace, the latter retuned the following season with a slight cast change but just as much impact.

The 2004–'05 season proved even more uninspiring and came close to tarnishing Rose's reputation as a director and, by extension, the Tarragon's as the solid home of Canadian drama. I began to wonder if the theatre had lost its way for good with poor fare in the form of personal diatribes from Oren Safdie—*Private Jokes, Public Places*—and David Macfarlane—*Fishwrap*—amidst mediocre offerings in David Gow's *Bea's Niece* and the adaptation of Alistair MacLeod's novel, *No Great Mischief*, directed by Rose himself. But the year was saved by one play that, arguably, counts among the best in Canadian theatre to date: John Mighton's *Half Life*, co-produced with Rose's former company Necessary Angel. Rose found his footing as artistic director in the 2005–'06 season, which included a great selection of plays that introduced new names to the Tarragon roster of talent (Rosa Laborde's *Leo*), revived long-standing associations with past masters (Tremblay's *Past Perfect*), and proved what the Tarragon could do to a mid-career playwright with a strong production of Morwyn Brebner's *The Optimists*, which premiered in Calgary in 2004.

Rose continues to provide his audiences (and Toronto theatre) with a judicious mix of new and tried-elsewhere Canadian plays. He kept the Tarragon mandate of a minimum of six previews and invested in developing a string of young playwrights including Brendan Gall, Laborde, and Hannah Moscovitch, whose debut plays grew out of the unit under his watch and represented a new wave of bold writing at the Tarragon. He also continued the theatre's tradition of introducing Quebec theatre to English audiences, finding success with the plays of Wajdi Mouawad, in particular *Scorched*. His most meaningful departure from the legacies of Kareda and Glassco lies in experimenting with alternative forms of storytelling onstage, including movement-based and collaborative theatre. In the 2008–'09 season he programmed *UBUNTU (The Cape Town Project)* created by members of the Theatrefront ensemble—a work that owes its narrative strategies to Theatre Passe Muraille's heyday of

---

13   Kamal Al-Solaylee, "German political comedy? That's about as funny as it gets," *Globe and Mail*, April 29, 2004, R7.

collective creation. It would have been unthinkable to see it at the Tarragon before Rose took over. To me, such subtle shifts represent the thrill of watching a theatre develop without changing its skin entirely as well as the logistical impossibility of encompassing its history in one representative anthology.

From the moment that I decided to work on this collection I wanted it to be something other than a sampling of six or seven texts from the literally hundreds that played on the Tarragon stages over forty years. Instead, and with the exception of *I, Claudia*, I selected plays that I reviewed or previewed (or both) during my years as a theatre critic and feature writer at *Eye Weekly* and the *Globe and Mail* (1998–2007). The time frame overlaps with the last years of Kareda's and the early ones of Rose. The anthology is therefore intended to represent my own journey as well as that of the Tarragon in and around the millennium and to capture the artistic and critical zeitgeist of Toronto. And while such hits as *Half Life* and *I, Claudia* are no-brainers for any editor, the other selections in this anthology emphasize my idiosyncratic editorial approach. Even Healey himself described the poorly received *Rune Arlidge* in an email to me as an "orphan of a play." I stand by my initial assessment of it as a stunning work and I'm delighted to give it a second life here. I reviewed the world premiere of *The Optimists* in Calgary in 2004 and its Toronto debut in 2005. It represents Brebner's wit and wisdom as much if not more than her relatively better known *Music for a Contortionist* or *Liquor Guns Karate*. Of the many Québécois plays that the Tarragon has introduced to Toronto going back to the early Tremblay, *Motel Hélène* is relatively unknown. However, its opening night, featuring performances by Jane Spidell and Tony Nappo, are imprinted in my memory as one of the most electrifying productions that I, as a relatively new critic in town, experienced. I knew I had to include it. Similarly, either *Patience* or *Remnants (A Fable)* would have made better representation of Sherman than *It's All True*. But I didn't see the first production of *Patience* at the Tarragon—although I reviewed its revival at Canadian Stage a few years later—and I don't think that *Remnants* captures the same zest and idealism of *It's All True*, which I reviewed in its remount at Buddies in Bad Times Theatre in the fall of 1999 and still consider to be among the playwright's finest; a play that imbues a sense of—and ends with the word—magic.

I can't think of a better tribute to the Tarragon and its forty years of creativity, successes, and failures than that one word. Acts of magic take place every night at the theatre thanks to its cast of administrative team, actors, directors, designers, stage managers, and volunteers. While I certainly mean the magic onstage, I have in mind other feats of wizardry that Tarragon artists perform: actually producing theatre in an environment where funding for the arts has reached yet another crisis point. As anyone who's been to the green rooms and administrative offices (including four where their resident playwrights work) know, they look like they've been furnished by dedicated scavenging of curbs on garbage nights complemented by some serious dumpster diving. Yet nothing is spared when it comes to giving the audience the best possible theatre experience. There's nothing anyone can do about the freight train that seems to make its way to the Tarragon vicinity at the quietest moments of any play, but a theatre that can rightfully claim the title of the "mother of English-Canadian drama" and whose playwright unit was described as "the womb of Canadian dramatists"[14] in the national paper of record deserves to be treated better by funding organizations that, paradoxically, sometimes punishes it for being financially stable.

As someone who either reviewed or previewed the majority of productions in Toronto in my ten years as a working critic and feature writer, it wasn't a stretch to choose the Tarragon as the first anthology of its kind in Playwrights Canada Press history—an anthology of plays that focuses on the artistic development of a single theatre at a certain point in its history. Not only was there more to choose from given its commitment to play development and Canadian playwrights, but the many contradictions—its perceived reputation being just one of them—that accompany the Tarragon make for a richer and more illustrative barometer of Canadian theatre in general and Toronto's in particular. As this one theatre goes, so does the performing arts in its city. But in many other ways, the Tarragon has fallen short of reflecting the full breadth of communities that share this multicultural landscape. Until the 2011–'12 season was announced in the spring of 2011, it would have been fair to charge its past and present artistic directors of keeping the theatre as a white fortress onstage and in the demographics of its audience. The 2011–'12 season makes up for lost time by featuring the work of two black playwrights and one South Asian. Factory Theatre has had more success in expanding its repertoire of plays to include the work of African Canadian and Asian playwrights and companies. Passe Muraille acted more aggressively in courting a multicultural agenda but often at the expense of its original subscription base. The Tarragon on the other hand remained defiantly unaffected by the demographic shifts happening in its own backyard. Its forays into the Middle East came mainly from French Canadian plays (*Scorched* and *Helen's Necklace*) and go more into its stellar track record of bicultural exchange within Canada's two official languages than the multicultural forces that have redefined what it means to be Canadian and how to live in Toronto. But, in yet another example of the Tarragon's many contradictory positions, it's probably this deliberate focus on the experiences of a traditional and middle-class Canadian audience that has allowed it to enjoy the financial and artistic stability it does today. This is a theatre that knows its audience—literally—as anyone who has seen its front-of-house staff interact with their subscribers knows.

---

14   Kate Taylor, "Twenty seasons at the Tarragon," *Globe and Mail*, September 15, 2001, R12.

But as it enters its over-forty stage, the Tarragon—like all other theatres in Toronto and possibly much of English Canada—must deal with a demographic time bomb. After years of attending opening-night performances as a critic, I began to develop an almost morbid fascination with the real audiences of Toronto theatres who buy tickets for the rest of the run. I wrote about this elsewhere[15] a few years ago but the passage of time only confirmed my worst suspicions: our theatres don't have a chance without some serious attempts at audience renewal. Not only are the largely old subscribers dying but there's little evidence that a younger or even middle-aged demographic is replacing them. It seems opportune that the Tarragon Theatre's fortieth birthday coincides with the first year of baby boomers' mass retirement (those born in 1946 turned sixty-five in 2011). This might provide the theatre with more subscribers with leisure time suddenly on their hands but it doesn't count as a long-term strategy. And in a city like Toronto where visible minorities are on the cusp of becoming the majority, it's obscene that many of our theatres, including the Tarragon, have but scant representation of those communities onstage or in the aisles. Add the continuing financial uncertainty and the triple whammy of Conservative politicians at the federal, provincial,[16] and municipal levels and the Tarragon's future may not look as certain as we like to think. One thing we can be sure of: it'll continue to inspire loyalty and envy and will build on its stable leadership and fiscal responsibility to survive. At this juncture of Canadian theatre history, survival is a goal in itself.

As I continue my professional relationship with the Tarragon—as a feature writer and editor after a decade of being a critic—I know that I won't always love what I see on its two stages or particularly enjoy walking under that tunnel off Dupont on bitterly cold evenings. Still, every visit to the Tarragon comes as close as any theatre can promise to deliver: the best in stage art and craft that money and time constrains can provide. There's no reason to believe that tonight or any other at the Tarragon will be different.

---

15   Kamal Al-Solaylee, "Too Poor to Send Flowers: The State of Canadian Theatre," *Best Canadian Essays 2009*, 3–6.

16   At the time of writing this, the Ontario Conservatives under the leadership of Tim Hudak had a shot at overthrowing the Liberals at Queen's Park. I'd be pleasantly surprised if this were to change by the time this anthology came out.

A NOTE ABOUT THE METHODOLOGY FOR THE CRITICAL INTRODUCTIONS

In discussing the plays in short critical introductions I created my own theoretical framework by re-exploring and building on a body of journalistic works—preview articles, profiles, reviews—that accompanied the original productions and revivals of each play in this anthology, including, when necessary, my own writing. In doing so, and from my vantage point as a journalism professor, I'm hoping to bridge the gap between the work of theatre journalists and academics. While this approach is determined in part by the lack of critical commentary in current Canadian theatre scholarship of the new plays collected here, it also echoes my own belief that if journalism is the earliest draft of history, then theatre journalism is the first (and most immediate) account of stage history. Not using it is inexplicable to this theatre journalist and academic.

HALF LIFE

JOHN MIGHTON

For my parents.

Half Life received its world premiere at the Tarragon Theatre in February 2005, co-produced by Necessary Angel Theatre Company and the Tarragon with the following company:

Anna .... Laura de Carteret
Agnes, First Scientist, Diana .... Barbara Gordon
Clara .... Carolyn Hetherington
Tammy, Second Scientist .... Maggie Huculak
Reverend, Stanley .... Randy Hughson
Donald .... Diego Matamoros
Patrick .... Eric Peterson

Directed by Daniel Brooks
Set & costumes designed by Dany Lyne
Sound designed by Richard Feren
Lighting designed by Andrea Lundy
Stage managed by Crystal Salverda
Assistant stage management by Kathryn Porter

Half Life was developed in residence with da da kamera through the support of the Ontario Arts Council Playwright Residency Grant and the Canada Council for the Arts Artist in Residence Program.

    Half Life was developed in partnership with the National Theatre School (Montreal, Quebec), the Royal Scottish Academy of Music and Drama/Tron Theatre (Glasgow, Scotland), and the Playwright Project (Mooresville, North Carolina).

    Half Life was further developed by Necessary Angel Theatre Company (Toronto) and received its first public presentation at Theatre Passe Muraille as part of Necessary Angel's 2003/2004 season.

John Mighton is a mathematician, author, playwright, and the founder of JUMP Math, a registered charity to enhance the potential in children by encouraging an understanding and love of math in students and educators. Mighton completed a Ph.D. in mathematics at the University of Toronto and is currently a Fellow of the Fields Institute for Research in Mathematical Sciences. He has also taught mathematics at the University of Toronto and lectured in philosophy at McMaster University, where he received a master's in philosophy. His national best-selling book, *The Myth of Ability: Nurturing Mathematical Talent in Every Child*, describes his successes with JUMP, and how anyone can learn and teach math. In May of 2007 John released a follow-up book called *The End of Ignorance*, the most up-to-date account of the JUMP philosophy and methods.

His plays have been performed across Canada, Europe, Japan, and the United States. He has won several national awards including the Governor General's Literary Award for Drama, the Dora Award, the Chalmers Canadian Play Award, and the Siminovitch Prize. His play *Possible Worlds* was made into a full-length feature film directed by Robert Lepage. In 2004, he was granted a prestigious Ashoka Fellowship as a social entrepreneur for his work in fostering numeracy and building young children's self-confidence through JUMP Math. Most recently John was the recipient of three honorary doctorates in recognition of his lifetime achievements. He is an Officer of the Order of Canada.

Even before its March 1, 2005, opening in a co-production with Necessary Angel Theatre Company, there were enough reasons to believe that *Half Life* would be a hit for its playwright John Mighton and the Tarragon. Not only did a public presentation as part of Necessary Angel's 2003–'04 season at Theatre Passe Muraille elicit enthusiastic responses, but Mighton himself had become a bit of a local hero since his last play, *The Little Years*, closed more than nine years before *Half Life*'s Tarragon run. This new status had nothing to do with theatre, however.[1] The mathematician-turned-playwright used the hiatus to complete his doctoral thesis and set up a volunteer-based educational charity to spread the word of math among students and teachers. JUMP (Junior Undiscovered Mathematical Prodigies) Math earned Mighton the kind of public accolades that, before *Half Life*, his plays never necessarily garnered. His book *The Myth of Ability: Nurturing Mathematical Talent in Every Child*, also written during those gap years, became a Canadian bestseller.[2] *Half Life*'s production files at the Tarragon also indicate a considerable media curiosity about this new play, aided in no small part by the casting of stage and TV veteran Eric Peterson in the role of Patrick.

The subtext of the critical responses to *Half Life* is a collective sigh of relief that in conducting his usual mix of science and drama, Mighton gave more weight to the latter this time, particularly when compared to his previous plays, including *Possible Worlds*, *A Short History of Night*, and the appropriately titled *Scientific Americans*. Indeed, while the play itself contains some of his most sustained reflections on such concepts as artificial intelligence and evolutionary necessities, Mighton himself sees the scientific content in it as "pretty secondary."[3] For all intents and purposes, *Half Life*'s power lies in its nature as a simple love story: two nursing home residents who may

---

1   It's not a coincidence that *Half Life* includes Mighton's cheekiest observation to date about the "character" of artists. As Donald tells Anna, a higher percentage of artists take their own lives than any other segment of the population because, he suspects, "Anyone who has time to dwell on their life for more than fifteen minutes is bound to be suicidal."

2   Kamal Al-Solaylee, "A drama about the power of forgetting," *Globe and Mail*, March 1, 2005, R3.

3   Sarah B. Hood, "A memorable play: Award-winning playwright explores the nature of identity," *Tandem/Corriere Canadese*, February 27, 2005: http://www.tandemnews.com/printer.php?storyid=4958.

or may not have crossed paths during the Second World War. ("Romeo and Juliet story in reverse," mused Peterson in an interview.)[4]

The biographical origins of the play may have helped this humanist thrust. *Half Life* grew out of Mighton's own experience caring for his mother in a nursing home for five years after she suffered a stroke. It's easy to see how some of the detailed observations about life in a nursing home have come from that personal experience, but its effects on the structure of the play is far more pervasive. As Mighton explained to me in an interview a week before the opening, seeing a spark in people who were facing adversity and maintaining communication with others who switched on and off mentally suggested a kind of structure where conversations and scenes would start and stop. "I couldn't organize my emotions or all the things I felt until I had a structure they would fall into."[5]

This structure of emotion became deceptively simple and noticeably complex in Daniel Brooks's ultra-tight production at the Tarragon, and it lost none of that quality when it transferred to the larger Bluma Appel Theatre at Canadian Stage two years later. Despite all the planned interruptions, the production sustained continuity throughout its ninety-five-minute run. That continuity manifested itself also in the range of ideas and philosophical propositions that act as guiding metaphors—or guiding angels, even—to the main characters. It begins with demystifying perceived notions of time five minutes into the play. When Anna, whose father is checking into the nursing home, complains that it's taking her an hour to complete admission forms and worries about the dog who's been home alone all day, Donald, the university chair of a psychology department, assures her that dogs have no keen sense of time between their owners' departures and returns. But rather than using this factoid (and let's assume for now it is a fact, at least within the world of the play) to elaborate a theory of time, Mighton connects it to his overarching theme of love. Anna's response to Donald's observation is that it explains why dogs are able to love unconditionally. "Every moment is a new moment for them. Their hurts are forgotten."

Forgetting, in fact, becomes another one of the play's connective tissues. A line from the play, "We wouldn't survive if we remembered everything," was used in much of the production's advertising and even as the tag line in the published edition of the text. The position is first tested in a clinical setting when Donald is officiating a contest to determine if he's speaking to a machine or a human. When the machine repeats a phone number with a random pattern, Donald confronts the scientists with his theory: "Our brains evolved to forget phone numbers for a reason. I'm afraid we'll never be able

---

4   Quoted in Jon Kaplan, "It's never too late," *NOW Magazine*, February 24, 2005, 70.

5   Al-Solaylee, "A drama."

to simulate human thought until we can simulate forgetting." And, in another example of the play's emphasis on the human experience, forgetting becomes the central mystery and emotional thread of the romance between Patrick and Clara. Had they met before Patrick began his WWII career as a code breaker? Were they once lovers?

It's not a mystery that Mighton even attempts to solve in *Half Life*. What matters in this context is not the past but the present moment. (That reference to a dog's life, again.) In an unexpected way, the play acquires a hedonistic tone through its relationship with time. When characters die or move on to other jobs—like Tammy, the nurse—it's deliberately undramatic. Their existences took place in the past. None of this is to say that Mighton represents memory and history as disposable or depressing human experiences. Note for example how the play ends on Clara's trip down a particular memory lane. It's a beautiful moment but one that marks the end of the play (and probably Clara's life).

The life of *Half Life*, of course, didn't end there. With several cast changes, Brooks's production went on to play on most major Canadian stages, including the Citadel in Edmonton, the Centaur in Montreal, and the Manitoba Arts Centre in Winnipeg. It become the hit that regional theatres reverted to when it came to filling the Canadian content quota of their programming, much like *The Drawer Boy* had been earlier in the same decade. Its successes further afield—Glasgow, Scotland, and Melbourne, Australia—also confirmed the validity of the playwright's emphasis on his characters' emotional life and theatre's role in exploring and sharing their humanity.

CHARACTERS

DONALD
ANNA
TAMMY
REVEREND HILL
AGNES
CLARA
PATRICK
DIANA
STANLEY
FIRST SCIENTIST
SECOND SCIENTIST

SCENE 1

DONALD and ANNA, two characters in their forties, sit in the common room of a nursing home for veterans and their families.

DONALD   I was telling a story once, about my father's experiences during the war—he spent four years in a prisoner of war camp—and right in the middle of my story, a man walked up and handed the woman I was talking to a drink. The man only spoke to the woman for a moment but while they were talking it occurred to me that she might already have forgotten my story. So when the man left, just to see what would happen, I started to talk about something else.

ANNA   Did she remember your story?

DONALD   No. So now, at parties, as an experiment, I won't continue telling a story when I'm interrupted, and sixty percent of the time the person I'm talking to will forget I was telling a story.

ANNA   Sixty percent? Does it really happen that often?

TAMMY enters and hands ANNA a form.

TAMMY   I need you to sign this.

ANNA   I hope Dr. Stevens has sent you his files.

TAMMY   Yes.

ANNA   My father hasn't eaten properly for months. He suffers from depression but he refuses to take his medication.

TAMMY doesn't respond.

Also... I'm not sure what he's told your social workers about me. He tends to make up stories. I've always been afraid that if he died under mysterious circumstances I would be arrested.

Anna hands back the signed form.

Thank you.

Tammy exits in a hurry.

She seems pleasant.

Donald   She's much better once you get to know her. My mother seems to like her.

Anna   Is your mother happy here?

Donald   My mother is always happy. But she's not often here. She's a little confused.

Pause.

I should wake her up now.

Donald doesn't move. Anna picks up a paper and starts reading.

Anna   Oh my God!

Donald   What is it?

Anna   Three hundred people died yesterday. In Nepal.

Donald   You should check the date on the paper. It's two years old.

Anna   Oh.

Anna puts the paper down and starts rummaging among the magazines.

Donald   You won't find anything more recent. I've read them all.

ANNA	*(looking at her watch)* It's taken her an hour to fill out a form. I have to get home.
DONALD	Is someone waiting for you?
ANNA	My dog. She's been alone all day.
DONALD	I don't know if this is any comfort to you, but dogs don't have a very keen sense of the amount of time that elapses between the moment their owner leaves and the moment they return. One hour or eight hours are pretty much the same to them.
ANNA	Are you sure about that?
DONALD	*(pointing to the pile of magazines)* I read it in one of those magazines.
ANNA	That must be why dogs are able to love people unconditionally.
DONALD	What do you mean?
ANNA	A dog isn't going to sulk or attack you for being late. Every moment is a new moment for them. Their hurts are forgotten.
DONALD	Are you married?
ANNA	Divorced.
DONALD	So am I.
	Pause.
	What do you do for a living?
ANNA	I'm an artist.
DONALD	That must be fulfilling.
ANNA	Yes, but it's hard to make ends meet. I make most of my money doing commerical work.
DONALD	What kind of work?

ANNA   I create designs for wallpaper, tiles, things like that.

DONALD   What did you say your name was?

ANNA   Anna.

DONALD   I'm sorry—I'm not very good with names.

ANNA   You have to take a moment when you meet someone to say
              their name to yourself several times.

DONALD   Anna, Anna, Anna...

              Pause.

ANNA   Are you sure it's sixty percent?

DONALD   What?

ANNA   The proportion of people that forget your stories at parties.

DONALD   More or less.

ANNA   It's depressing.

DONALD   I may not be a very good storyteller. I suppose it's natural. We
              wouldn't survive if we remembered everything.

              Pause.

ANNA   Where was your father stationed?

DONALD   The Pacific.

ANNA   Mine was in Europe. He was a mathematician, so he was re-
              cruited for intelligence in London. He never actually fought.

DONALD   Mine was captured in the first week of his posting.

ANNA   Where?

DONALD   Hong Kong. His regiment had just arrived from Canada. They
              were all from small towns in Ontario, with hardly a month of

training. The Japanese soldiers had been fighting together in China for three years. They would creep up at night and drop grenades down the ventilator shafts of the pillboxes. My father saw his best friend with his leg blown off. The second night of his posting the company commander had a breakdown and started drinking. He ordered my father...

TAMMY enters.

TAMMY   Your father's room will be ready tomorrow morning.

ANNA   Thank you. I don't mean to be annoying, but I just wanted to warn you—my father will likely try to escape. He has a serious problem with his liver but he insists on drinking. And he's addicted to cigarettes.

TAMMY   *(handing ANNA a card)* This is the code that unlocks the front door. He won't be able to leave the home unless he's with someone who knows the code.

ANNA   He worked as a code breaker during the Second World War.

TAMMY   If the staff and his doctor determine he's a danger to himself he'll be moved to a secure ward on the second floor.

ANNA   Thank you.

TAMMY exits. ANNA looks at the card with the code on it.

DONALD   I wouldn't lose that if I were you.

ANNA   Why not?

DONALD   I've been trapped in the lobby a dozen times waiting for someone to open the door. It's very hard to memorize... there's no pattern.

ANNA stares at the code.

I think I'll wake my mother up now. Otherwise she'll sleep all day... It was nice talking to you.

ANNA   You too.

DONALD   Good luck with your father. He sounds like quite a handful.

ANNA   Yes... he is. Thank you.

                DONALD turns to leave.

                Wait a minute.

                You didn't finish your story... Was that intentional?

DONALD   No. I only do that at parties. I just didn't think this was the right time for a story. You have other things to think about.

SCENE 2

                Two scientists stand in front of a curtain of the sort one sees in a hospital or nursing home. DONALD enters.

DONALD   Hello, Dr. Peters.

FIRST
SCIENTIST   Hello, Professor Reynolds. It's an honour having you offici-
                ate this year.

DONALD   Thank you.

FIRST
SCIENTIST   I expect you're familiar with the rules of the contest?

DONALD   Yes.

FIRST
SCIENTIST   You have five minutes to determine whether you are speak-
                ing to a human or a machine. Shall we begin?

DONALD   Yes.

                DONALD sits in front of a microphone.

                Hello. I'm Professor Reynolds.

A voice emanates from behind the curtain.

STANLEY   Hello, Professor Reynolds. I'm Stanley.

DONALD   I hope you don't mind if I ask you a few questions, Stanley.

STANLEY   That's what I was told to expect.

DONALD   I understand you're a mathematician, Stanley.

STANLEY   Who told you that?

DONALD   Dr. Peters.

STANLEY   No... I think there's some mistake. I'm an artist.

DONALD   Really?

STANLEY   A painter.

DONALD   Are you sure?

STANLEY   Well, I think I would know what I am.

DONALD   Yes, I suppose you would... Do you like patterns, Stanley?

STANLEY   What sort of patterns?

DONALD   Wallpaper designs, tilings...

STANLEY   Well, I am an artist.

DONALD   My phone number has a very unusual pattern in it.

STANLEY   What is it?

DONALD   314-159-2653.

        Pause.

STANLEY   I said I'm an artist, not a mathematician.

DONALD   You don't have to be a mathematician to appreciate it.

STANLEY   I'm afraid I can't see any pattern.

          Pause.

DONALD   What does your father do for a living?

STANLEY   My father is dead.

DONALD   I'm sorry. How long ago did he die?

STANLEY   He died when I was three.

DONALD   Do you remember him at all?

STANLEY   I remember a trip to the zoo.

DONALD   Can you tell me what you remember?

STANLEY   I remember walking between some cages with my father. I must have seen something that scared me because I started to cry. My father picked me up. I remember pressing my face against his chest. I felt very safe in his arms.

          Pause.

          That's all I remember.

DONALD   What's my phone number?

STANLEY   314-159-2653.

SECOND
SCIENTIST Shit.

DONALD   Thank you, Stanley. That will be all.

STANLEY   Aren't you going to ask me any more questions?

DONALD   No, Stanley.

STANLEY   Why not?

          A SCIENTIST pulls back a curtain to reveal a bank of computers.

DONALD	Because you're a machine.
STANLEY	A machine? Are you crazy?
FIRST SCIENTIST	All right. Turn it off.
STANLEY	I'm not a machine. I'm an artist!

The SECOND SCIENTIST turns off the computer.

FIRST SCIENTIST	Was that really your phone number?
DONALD	No—it was a completely random sequence. The first ten digits of pi.
SECOND SCIENTIST	Shit.
DONALD	Our brains evolved to forget phone numbers for a reason. I'm afraid we'll never be able to simulate human thought until we can simulate forgetting. The way information is lost is as important as the way it is retained. Good luck next year.

He exits.

SCENE 3

AGNES, who is eighty-five, and PATRICK, who is eighty-two, sit in the games room of the home.

CLARA, who is eighty, is asleep in a wheelchair between them. TAMMY pulls a chalkboard into position in front of them.

TAMMY	Would you like to play a word game today, Clara?
AGNES	Where's Mrs. O'Neill?
TAMMY	Mrs. O'Neill won't be joining us today.

AGNES	Why not?
TAMMY	She was taken to hospital this morning. Her food tube came out.
AGNES	At least she didn't have to eat what they served for lunch.
TAMMY	Before we begin, I'd like to introduce everyone to our newest resident. Agnes and Clara, this is Patrick.
CLARA	Hello, Patrick. It's nice to meet you.

PATRICK stares ahead and doesn't say anything.

TAMMY	Patrick only moved in here yesterday. I think he's still getting adjusted.
CLARA	Patrick, have you played hangman before?
PATRICK	No.
CLARA	It's a lot of fun.
TAMMY	I think Patrick will pick it up as we play. I've heard he's very smart. Is everybody ready? *(drawing a scaffold)* First I draw a scaffold. Then I draw some blanks. *(TAMMY draws six blanks for the word "animal.")* When it's your turn, Patrick, you try to guess a letter that's in the word. Clara, maybe you could try to help us start. Would you like to guess a letter?
CLARA	A.
TAMMY	That was a good guess. There are two As. One here, and one here. Would you like to guess again?
CLARA	Z.
TAMMY	No, Clara, there are no Zs. I'll put the Z here so you remember you guessed it.
PATRICK	E.
TAMMY	No, Patrick. I'm sorry, there are no Es. So I'll draw a head for Clara's Z and a stick for...

PATRICK	I.
TAMMY	Yes, there's an I. Very…
PATRICK	N.
TAMMY	Patrick, you'll have to give someone else a try. I can see we have a very serious player here… Agnes, would you like to play today?
AGNES	*(looking at* PATRICK*)* If I'm allowed to have a turn.
TAMMY	Of course you are. Everyone gets a turn.

AGNES stares at the chalkboard.

AGNES	At lunch they gave me peas again.
TAMMY	Oh. I'm sorry, Agnes.
AGNES	They can't seem to remember I don't like peas.
TAMMY	I'll remind them.

AGNES looks at the board.

AGNES	I was much better at this a few years ago. I was one of those children who would…
PATRICK	N.
TAMMY	Just a minute, Patrick. I think Agnes would like a turn.
AGNES	Who would disappear and find a hill just outside of town and climb to the top and spend the day writing stories in my head.
CLARA	Those children have personalities. Thinking… they're always thinking.

Pause.

The teachers always seemed to rush through fractions. But now they use decimals.

PATRICK	That's right.
CLARA	My father wanted to take me swimming. He had a good laugh at me. The beach was all pebbles. His feet were used to it but I could hardly walk it hurt so much. The waves were very irregular. They seemed to be coming from all directions. And you could feel the undertow... I guess I should let somebody else speak now.
AGNES	This is going to take all day.
TAMMY	Patrick, would you like to try again?
PATRICK	No.
TAMMY	Why not?
PATRICK	I already know what the word is. *(to CLARA)* I'll give you a hint. It's a living thing.
TAMMY	Clara, would you like to guess again?
CLARA	A.
TAMMY	We've already had that, dear.

       Pause.

       How about you, Agnes?

AGNES	I was much better at this when I was a child.

       Pause.

       My father took away my childhood. When I was eight, he decided I was the love of his life. I've never told anyone. *(She starts to cry.)*

TAMMY	I think we'll stop for today.

       Pause.

       Reverend Hill wanted me to remind you that a number of our residents, including Patrick, will be honoured at his

Remembrance Day service in a few weeks. Also, this is the year of the Older Person, so there will be a ceremony at the home Wednesday afternoon, which the mayor will attend.

CLARA   It's late. I'm cold. The boat will never get there.

SCENE 4

DONALD sits in a hallway of the nursing home. REVEREND HILL approaches.

REVEREND   Can I sit with you?

DONALD   Yes. I'm just waiting for my mother to be changed.

REVEREND   *(sitting)* I was supposed to be sitting in hospice with someone and he just died. One hundred years old... He was a crusty old gentleman... He used to drive everyone here crazy. He had an old typewriter and he would type his complaints. He wanted answers.

Pause.

I've seen this so many times and it's still an awesome experience... I won't visit your mother today. It's times like these I want to go home and have a good drink.

The REVEREND has tears in his eyes.

I've seen this so many times.

DONALD   Thank you for visiting my mother so often.

REVEREND   You don't have to thank me. Your mother was a devoted member of our congregation. I don't think she missed a single Sunday before she came here.

DONALD   I'm sorry I haven't been able to bring her to church. It takes me two hours to drive here. And I have other commitments on the weekend.

REVEREND	I understand.
DONALD	I know she enjoyed your sermons.
REVEREND	I think she liked the singing more. She loved the classic hymns.
DONALD	Yes. She used to take me to church every Sunday.
REVEREND	Do you still attend church?
DONALD	No.
REVEREND	I take it you didn't enjoy it as a child.
DONALD	No. It was a little scary.
REVEREND	Scary?
DONALD	Until I was thirteen, I was certain I was going to hell. I don't think they ever cleaned the stained glass in our church. You had to make your way down the aisle guided by the blue hair of the congregation. I don't know if you've ever heard a three-hundred-year-old Protestant hymn sung by a choir whose average age is seventy accompanied by a badly tuned organ. I'm sorry, but it was my idea of eternal damnation.
REVEREND	Churches have changed a great deal since then.
DONALD	I'm afraid I don't believe in Christ... Though I appreciate some of his teachings.
REVEREND	Your mother tells me you're a scientist.
DONALD	I study neural networks. They're a kind of computer that simulates the brain.
REVEREND	So you work in artificial intelligence?
DONALD	Yes.
REVEREND	And you believe the mind is a kind of program or machine?

DONALD   That's a bit simplistic. But close... We've learned a lot by modelling the nervous systems of simple organisms like flatworms and slugs. One day, possibly very soon, we'll create artificial life.

REVEREND   Do you think so?

DONALD   I'm absolutely certain.

REVEREND   Why call the things that science creates "life"? Surely they're only machines.

DONALD   Because these machines will one day think, reproduce, and evolve. Why call it a machine if you can't distinguish its behaviour from your own?

    Pause.

REVEREND   Have you ever seen a person die?

DONALD   No.

REVEREND   Before I came to the home this evening, I went and looked at the weeds by the train tracks. It seems to me that these plants only show their real beauty in dying. Some retain bright flowers while others whither into the most exquisite greys and browns. You could scarcely find more variety in hue and texture anywhere in nature—even on a coral reef. People on the verge of death also express their essences in very different ways—in the extent to which they open up or withdraw, are stoic or complain, even in the few phrases or sounds they are reduced to repeating. There's a subtle beauty and variety which one easily overlooks if one regards old people as having outlived their purpose—as weeds... Whenever she sees me, one woman at the home cries out "Dee, dee, dee, dee!" with the greatest joy. This would be beautiful in an infant—why is it merely tragic in an older person? Our feelings about this show the extent to which we judge adults by their function... Even when the mind fails there's something that shines through. For lack of a better word, I call it the soul...

DONALD   What you call the soul...

TAMMY enters.

TAMMY   Your mother is ready.

REVEREND   I guess we'll have to continue this conversation on another occasion.

DONALD   Yes.

SCENE 5

CLARA has fallen asleep in front of a card table. She holds several playing cards in her hand. PATRICK, who is seated at the table, watches her. She opens her eyes.

CLARA   I fell asleep. I just closed my eyes and fell asleep.

PATRICK   So you're feeling better?

CLARA   Oh yes. Sleep is the greatest protection. And when I think about what the pioneers had to do. There were some... they hadn't been in this country for too many centuries... and their old homes were heaven to them. I went to the Baptist church one night. He said, "What have you come for, just to look at us?" And I thought—he shouldn't worry, I wasn't making fun of them... So I went to the Anglican church. I had an aunt who went to the States and joined the Salvation Army and she loved the singing and spent her life there and never married. So you see, there's all kinds of people around—it keeps us guessing.

Pause.

You look familiar.

PATRICK   I'm Patrick... We were playing cards. It's your turn to bid.

CLARA looks at the cards in her hand.

CLARA   Oh for heaven's sake. I didn't get anything that looks vaguely like it should look.

PATRICK	So what are you making it?

CLARA looks at a card on the table.

CLARA	Whose card is that?
PATRICK	Yours.
CLARA	I could have picked it up but I didn't.

She leaves the card on the table.

PATRICK	What are you making trumps?
CLARA	What did you say your name was?
PATRICK	Patrick.
CLARA	I knew a Patrick once. During the war. He used to take me dancing.
PATRICK	I was never much of a dancer.
CLARA	Neither was he... Is it my turn?
PATRICK	Yes.
CLARA	Whose card is that?
PATRICK	Yours.

CLARA picks up the card.

CLARA	I always loved to dance. Ever since I was a little girl. I could have been a professional dancer. But my parents couldn't afford to give me lessons. Of course, Dad was on the railroad. He was a good Presbyterian. He had three nuns in the waiting room... Oh my life is... I've done the best with what I had.

Pause.

You don't say much about yourself, Patrick.

PATRICK   There's not much to say.

CLARA   Do you enjoy playing hangman?

PATRICK   Yes.

CLARA   You seem to be very clever. What did you do for a living?

PATRICK   I was a mathematician.

CLARA   Are you a veteran?

PATRICK   Yes. I worked for Special Services.

CLARA   What did you do?

PATRICK   I've never told anyone what I did.

CLARA   Why not?

PATRICK   For a long time I couldn't. Now I can, but nobody cares.

CLARA   You could tell me.

             CLARA looks at her cards.

             Is it my turn?

             TAMMY enters with a hospital trolley and a gift for CLARA.

TAMMY   How are you two getting along?

CLARA   Very well, thank you.

TAMMY   How was the punch?

CLARA   Very good. It was nice of you to make it for us.

TAMMY   Who's winning?

PATRICK   We haven't finished a hand.

TAMMY	I hope you're being nice to Clara, Patrick. She's my angel. Aren't you, Clara?
CLARA	Yes.
TAMMY	She never complains. She's the only one here who doesn't. I only have to see her smile and it changes my day. I bought you something, Clara.

TAMMY takes a blue shawl out of tissue wrapping.

CLARA	Oh my.

TAMMY puts the shawl around CLARA's shoulders.

TAMMY	Look. Isn't she beautiful?

Pause.

You're not too old to notice a beautiful woman are you, Patrick?

PATRICK	*(looking at CLARA)* There are some things I can't do anymore. But there are others I can.
CLARA	I think I went to the bathroom.
TAMMY	I'm sorry, Clara—I'm on a busy shift. I'll change you after lunch. Can you wait till then?
CLARA	Yes. Of course.
TAMMY	Thank you, dear... You look so beautiful. I'll save a table for the two of you.

TAMMY exits.

CLARA	Whose turn is it?
PATRICK	Yours. What are you making trumps?
CLARA	Spades.

PATRICK   *(looking at his hand)* Are you sure?

CLARA   Yes.

She lays down a card.

PATRICK   I'm going to trump it.

He lays down a card and takes the trick.

CLARA   I knew a Patrick once. During the war. He used to take me dancing. In his spare time he made models out of sticks and plasticine. I believe he called them polyhedra.

PATRICK   Polyhedra?

CLARA   Is that a word?

PATRICK   Yes.

CLARA   The only problem was... they were very confusing.

PATRICK   Yes, they can be.

CLARA   He said they were shadows of something... in the fourth dimension. I didn't understand how they could be shadows of anything.

PATRICK   *(holding up his cup)* This cup is three dimensional—but its shadow... this circle... is two dimensional.

CLARA   Yes. That's what he said. He held up his cup just like that.

Pause.

We would walk... in the shadows. By the river. Do you remember those days, Patrick?

PATRICK   Barely.

Pause.

Are you going for lunch?

CLARA   I don't think there's any point... Are you staying?

PATRICK   Yes.

SCENE 6

> DONALD *sits in front of a curtain identical to the one in Scene 2. We hear a female* VOICE *from behind the curtain.*

DONALD   Were you close to your father?

VOICE   He died when I was five.

DONALD   I'm sorry. Do you remember him at all?

VOICE   I remember the rug in his bedroom.

DONALD   The rug?

VOICE   My father was a heavy smoker. After he died I found dozens of little holes in the rug where his ashes had fallen... That's all I remember.

DONALD   Do you enjoy your work?

VOICE   I enjoy helping people. When they're worth helping.

> *Pause.*

That's it. Stand up so I can pull up your pants.

> *We hear the sound of* CLARA *being helped to her feet.*

I'm getting too old for all the lifting.

> TAMMY's *hand pulls back the curtain to reveal* TAMMY *and* CLARA.

TAMMY   Here she is. As beautiful as ever.

> TAMMY *exits.*

CLARA	Hello, dear.
DONALD	Hello, Mom... How are you feeling?
CLARA	Wonderful.
DONALD	Did you do anything special today?
CLARA	No. Not that I can remember.
DONALD	Did you go to the ceremony this afternoon?
CLARA	Yes.
DONALD	How was the mayor's speech?
CLARA	Very interesting.
DONALD	What did he say?
CLARA	They've dug up a soldier in France.
DONALD	What for?
CLARA	They're going to bury him again.
DONALD	In a different place?
CLARA	Probably.
DONALD	Well that's good... The Copes sent you a postcard, Mom. Look—it's from Florida. Would you like me to read it?
CLARA	Yes.
DONALD	*(reading)* "Dear Clara. Florida is very cold for this time of year. Will return on the fifteenth. Hope you are well. Love Marjorie and Jim..." Isn't that nice. Very informative... Where would you like me to put it?
CLARA	In my drawer.

DONALD opens a drawer in CLARA's dresser.

DONALD It's getting very crowded in here, Mom. We'll have to go through your things and decide what you want to keep.

> DONALD *puts the card in the drawer and closes it. He opens a bag and takes out a toy car made of recycled materials.*

Nina wanted you to have this. It's her science project. She made it out of materials that would have ended up in the garbage. See... the wheels are spools from old computer ribbons. The headlights are little tinfoil plates. And the driver is a cork. It actually runs—she put an elastic band inside. Look.

> DONALD *puts the car on the floor and it moves a few inches.*

She designed it herself. Isn't that amazing?

> *Pause.*

Where should I put it?

CLARA On my dresser.

DONALD I brought you Nina's report card too. She did very well. *(showing the card to CLARA)* Straight As.

> CLARA *stares at* DONALD, *not noticing the card.*

I'll put it in your drawer too.

CLARA You were the dearest, sweetest little thing.

DONALD What?

CLARA You were such a good cartoonist. Why don't you send your cartoons to the *New Yorker*?

DONALD My cartoons?

CLARA Yes.

DONALD I don't draw cartoons anymore, Mom.

CLARA That's too bad.

DONALD   And publishing in the *New Yorker* isn't something you just decide to do.

CLARA   You could do anything if you put your mind to it. You have so many talents.

> *DONALD puts the report card in the drawer. He notices CLARA's blue shawl and pulls it from the drawer. He unfolds it and shows it to his mother.*

DONALD   Is this new?

CLARA   Yes... You can put it in my drawer.

DONALD   It was in your drawer. *(taking CLARA's change purse from her drawer)* Did Tammy buy it for you?

CLARA   Yes.

DONALD   *(counting the money in CLARA's purse)* There's eighty dollars missing. Did she get a receipt?

CLARA   I don't know.

DONALD   She's not supposed to buy you things.

CLARA   I needed it.

DONALD   What for?

CLARA   So I could look my best.

DONALD   I'll have to talk to her again.

CLARA   Today was a special day. This morning from my window I saw a pair of Canada geese. Flying south. I've only ever seen them in flocks. Even though they were a couple, they looked so alone.

> *TAMMY enters.*

TAMMY   The nurse says you're not drinking enough fluids, Clara. You have to remember to drink your juice.

DONALD	Did you happen to keep a receipt for the shawl you bought my mother?
TAMMY	I'll look for it if you want.
DONALD	Yes. Please. I like to keep a record of her expenses.
CLARA	My son has money. He'll give you some money.
TAMMY	That's all right, Clara. I've taken an extra job. I clean the Clarksons's house on weekends.
DONALD	Is that the couple who bought the mansion on Crown Hill?
TAMMY	They like to go on about the way the government wastes their money. But they don't mind wasting money on themselves. One of her bracelets would pay for my son's education. She wouldn't even notice if I took it.
DONALD	So you believe in redistributing money from the rich to the poor?
TAMMY	I believe in giving people a hand up, not a kick in the ass. Sorry, Clara.
CLARA	My son is rich.
DONALD	Mom, please stop saying that.

TAMMY exits.

	How's Mrs. O'Neill?
CLARA	She's in the hospital again.
DONALD	I hear there's a new resident.
CLARA	Yes. Patrick.
DONALD	I met his daughter.
CLARA	He has a daughter?

DONALD	Yes. Anna.
CLARA	Does she look like her mother?
DONALD	I didn't know her mother.
CLARA	How long was he with her? I don't mean what year is this.
DONALD	I'm sorry, Mom. I don't know what you're talking about.

Pause.

CLARA	How's Susan?
DONALD	Fine, I think.
CLARA	Why don't you bring her to see me?
DONALD	We're divorced, Mom.
CLARA	I worry about you.
DONALD	I'm fine.
CLARA	One day you'll find someone who will make you happy.
DONALD	I'm happy being single.
CLARA	Don't you get lonely?
DONALD	Sometimes. But it's nice to wake up and know that no one can ruin your day... My work is going extremely well. And Nina is a constant joy. I'm very happy right now.
CLARA	So am I.
DONALD	Why are you so happy?

TAMMY enters.

TAMMY	It's time for your physiotherapy, Clara.
CLARA	All right.

DONALD   Work hard for me, Mom.

CLARA   I will.

SCENE 7

> *ANNA and DONALD sit reading in the common room of the nursing home.*

DONALD   Do you know what time it is?

ANNA   Seven.

DONALD   I should wake my mother up.

> *DONALD yawns.*

I'm a little sleepy myself. I almost fell asleep at the wheel tonight.

ANNA   How long does it take you to drive here?

DONALD   Two hours.

ANNA   But you come here almost every day.

DONALD   Yes.

ANNA   How do you find the time?

DONALD   I don't have many commitments. I have a daughter—but I only see her on weekends.

> *DONALD tilts his head to one side.*

ANNA   Is something the matter?

DONALD   My neck.

ANNA   Is it sore?

DONALD   No.

He tilts his head to one side.

But I can barely move my head in this direction. I used to be able to touch my head to my shoulder.

ANNA   Why don't you try stretching?

DONALD I think it's too late. There's a whole range of motion I'll never recover.

ANNA   It's hardly irreversible. You should stretch several times a day.

DONALD I try. But I keep forgetting. And it takes so much effort. I know I could look better and feel better if I joined a health club and worked out three times a week. But I don't really care anymore. You start to die the day you lose your vanity. Gradually I'll just stiffen up. I'll put on weight. I'll become weaker and weaker.

ANNA   How old are you?

DONALD Forty-five.

ANNA   You're really not that old.

DONALD Yes. I am.

ANNA   I'm forty-two and I feel like I'm entering the prime of my life.

DONALD Do you get depressed very easily?

ANNA   Why do you ask?

DONALD A higher percentage of artists take their own lives than any other segment of the population... I suspect that has nothing to do with the character of artists. Anyone who has time to dwell on their life for more than fifteen minutes a day is bound to be suicidal. Most people are kept alive by the relentless distractions of the working world. When I'm driving here I have a lot of time to think. Maybe that's why I've been so depressed lately.

ANNA   I'm actually very happy. That may be why I'm not very successful.

Pause.

DONALD   Would you pay eighty dollars for a shawl?

ANNA   Is this some kind of personality test?

DONALD   No. I just wondered if that was a reasonable price.

ANNA   It seems a little expensive.

DONALD   That's what I thought.

ANNA   Are you planning to buy a shawl for your mother?

DONALD   No. She already has one.

Pause.

How's your father adjusting?

ANNA   Very well, thank you.

DONALD   You were concerned about him escaping.

ANNA   He seems to love it here. I've never seen him so happy.

DONALD   Maybe he's having an affair.

ANNA   If he is, I pity the poor woman he's seduced.

DONALD   Is he really that bad?

ANNA   My father is such a good liar, he's even able to fool himself.

DONALD   Then he's not a liar. He's just deluded.

ANNA   But there's a part of him that knows the things he says aren't true.

DONALD   What did he do during the war?

ANNA   I'm not sure exactly. When I was growing up, he always had a different story. I think it was all a cover for his affairs.

Pause.

DONALD   How long ago were you divorced?

ANNA   Five years ago.

DONALD   Are you with someone now?

ANNA   Not at the moment... I've become a little burdened with the things I want to avoid.

DONALD   Yes, I know what you mean.

ANNA   For once, I'd like something to just happen to me. Without my anticipating it, or chasing after it, or manipulating the situation. Something that just crept up on me without my noticing. Like an adventure, or a romance.

DONALD   Yes. Like something that happened to people in our parents' day.

Pause.

Do you like to dance?

ANNA   I love to dance.

DONALD   I haven't been dancing in years.

ANNA   I wouldn't think so. Not at your age.

DONALD laughs.

DONALD   You seem like such an easygoing person.

ANNA   Are you checking off your list?

DONALD   What list?

ANNA   Your list of qualities that you like in a person.

DONALD   I'm not that calculating.

ANNA   Would you settle for someone who had less than half the quali-
                ties on your list?

DONALD   At my age, yes.

ANNA   You'll never fall in love that way.

DONALD   Why not?

ANNA   Love isn't a matter of one quality more or less. That's why
                it can last when a couple grows old, even when most of the
                qualities that brought them together are gone... Because it's
                a union of souls.

DONALD   You must have been talking to Reverend Hill. He's always
                lecturing me about the soul.

                        ANNA *laughs.*

ANNA   I can't explain it... but whenever Reverend Hill talks I have
                an uncontrollable urge to laugh.

DONALD   Why?

ANNA   I don't know.

DONALD   I don't find him all that funny.

ANNA   He reminds me of you.

DONALD   What?

ANNA   You're both very serious.

DONALD   I don't think I'm anything like him.

ANNA   I suppose not. He's always on the verge of crying. I don't think
                he's suited for his job.

DONALD   I'm very emotional too.

ANNA   Yes... you are. You're very protective of your mother... You
                must love her very deeply.

Pause.

How long ago did your father die?

DONALD   Six months.

ANNA   Were you close?

DONALD   My father was the moral centre of my life. He endured things that would have broken my spirit. The world doesn't have heroes like my father anymore... I miss him.

ANNA   The other day you were telling me a story. About something that happened to your father during the war.

DONALD   Oh yes.

My father was only nineteen years old when he was sent to Hong Kong. His company was assigned to defend a bridge on the outskirts of the city. Sometimes I try to imagine how he must have felt. Ten thousand miles from his home. Huddled in the dark with the other men... boys really... they could hear the Japanese soldiers creeping along the far side of the river. The company commander ordered my father to set up a mortar and fire it in the dark. The first shell hit a branch and...

                TAMMY enters carrying a garbage pail. She shows ANNA the contents of the pail.

TAMMY   Your father's been smoking in his room.

ANNA   Where did he get the cigarettes?

TAMMY   He says you bought them for him.

ANNA   He must be leaving the home somehow. I'll come and speak to him. *(to DONALD)* I'm sorry.

DONALD   That's all right. I should wake my mother up. Before it's time for her to go to bed.

SCENE 8

CLARA and PATRICK are making crafts with modelling clay and Popsicle sticks. AGNES sits at a separate table, in front of a jigsaw puzzle.

TAMMY   You should start by finding all the pieces with a straight edge.

AGNES   Why should I do that?

TAMMY   Those are the ones that go around the outside.

TAMMY picks up several pieces.

They make the border of the picture. See?

Pause. AGNES stares at the pieces TAMMY has put together.

AGNES   I'd like to go to my room now.

TAMMY   Then you'll say you want to come back.

AGNES   I'm sick and tired of these games. I'm a senior citizen and I'd like to be treated like one.

TAMMY moves to CLARA's table.

TAMMY   *(to CLARA)* How's my angel this morning?

CLARA   Very well, thank you.

TAMMY   Has Patrick been behaving himself?

CLARA   No.

TAMMY   I'm very disappointed in you, Patrick.

CLARA   I told him he would have to be patient. With someone like me there's less to tell. So it takes me longer to open up.

TAMMY   *(to PATRICK)* Patrick, if anyone finds out you've been going out to buy cigarettes, they'll lock you upstairs.

PATRICK	I'll stop smoking. *(to CLARA)* For you.

REVEREND HILL enters.

REVEREND	Good morning, everyone!
CLARA	Hello, Reverend Hill.
REVEREND	I can see everyone is hard at work today. Tammy keeps you very busy.
CLARA	Yes, she does.
REVEREND	What's that you're making, Patrick?
PATRICK	A tesseract.
REVEREND	Pardon me?
PATRICK	A four-dimensional cube.
REVEREND	I was never much good at mathematics. Although it's all part of God's intricate design. I'm glad to see you're working in clay again, Clara.
CLARA	It's like when you were little. And you could put your hands in the mud.
REVEREND	*(to PATRICK)* Has Clara shown you any of her creations?
PATRICK	Not yet.
REVEREND	I've offered to be her agent. And I explained to her that an agent gets ninety percent.

REVEREND HILL laughs at his joke.

TAMMY	*(to AGNES)* Why don't you try putting these two pieces together?
AGNES	Why don't you go to hell?
REVEREND	It's so important to have a hobby as you grow older. One of my parishioners became seriously depressed after he retired. He

tried everything—therapy, medication... nothing seemed to help. One day he developed an interest in history and it's made all the difference. He's deeply engaged in his research on the Holocaust now and I think that's made him a lot happier.

CLARA That's wonderful.

REVEREND Don't let me keep you from your work.

AGNES Where's Mrs. O'Neill? Why isn't she here?

TAMMY She died last night.

CLARA Oh. That's terrible.

AGNES How did she die?

REVEREND She died very peacefully and quietly in her sleep.

AGNES At least she doesn't have to do crafts anymore.

REVEREND There will be a memorial service for her in the common room on Friday. Her friends and family will share some stories and memories if you'd like to participate.

CLARA I didn't know her very well, but she was very pleasant.

REVEREND *(with tears in his eyes)* Yes. She was an extremely pleasant woman... How are you getting along with your puzzle, Agnes?

AGNES Terrible.

REVEREND It looks like you've made a very good start.

AGNES I've been here all morning. Too long.

REVEREND You've assembled quite a few pieces.

AGNES I need you to get me out of here.

REVEREND Is it a mountain scene?

AGNES I have no idea what it is.

REVEREND   Have you looked at the picture on the lid?

AGNES   There is no lid.

TAMMY   It's right in front of you, Agnes.

TAMMY turns over the lid and shows it to AGNES.

AGNES   I was much better at this when I was a child.

REVEREND   I expect you were a very clever child.

AGNES   I was one of those children who would disappear and find a hill somewhere just outside of town. I'd spend the day writing stories in my head... My father would call me. When it was time to come home.

AGNES looks at her feet.

My socks keep falling down. I told them I like the ones with elastics. They can't seem to remember anything here. I'm sick and tired of these games.

AGNES knocks the puzzle box off the table.

TAMMY   I'll take you to your room, Agnes.

AGNES   I'd like to finish my puzzle.

TAMMY picks up the pieces of the puzzle. DONALD enters.

DONALD   Hello, Mom.

CLARA   Hello, dear? Is it time for bed?

DONALD   Not yet. It's 11:30 in the morning.

CLARA   Why are you here so early?

DONALD   I didn't have to teach today. So I thought I'd surprise you. I'm taking you out for lunch.

REVEREND   Isn't that wonderful, Clara.

DONALD	I've already made a reservation for two at your favourite restaurant.
CLARA	For two?
DONALD	Yes.
CLARA	Isn't Patrick coming?
DONALD	Not today, Mom.
CLARA	Do you have other plans, Patrick?
PATRICK	No.
CLARA	Then why don't you come?
PATRICK	I wasn't invited.

Pause.

DONALD	*(to TAMMY)* Is my mother ready to go?
TAMMY	Yes. *(to CLARA)* I'll get your coat, Clara.

TAMMY exits.

REVEREND	Isn't this a wonderful surprise, Clara? Your son is taking you out to lunch. *(to DONALD)* I thought I should let you know, this Sunday I'll be paying tribute to your father.
DONALD	Thank you.
REVEREND	I've often wondered how I would stand up in the face of the things he endured. As Pericles said, "The man who can most truly be accounted brave, is he who knows best the meaning of what is sweet in life and of what is terrible, and then goes out determined to meet what is to come." Of course you see exactly the same kind of heroism right here in this room. If I was suddenly crippled and had to live in constant pain, I'd think I'd suffered the fate of Job. But old people endure worse things with hardly a complaint.

CLARA	Will you be coming to the ceremony, Patrick?
PATRICK	No.
CLARA	Why not?
PATRICK	There's nothing I care to remember.
REVEREND	Were you a combatant during the war?
PATRICK	No.
REVEREND	But you're a veteran... You must have had some experiences that you'd like to share with our congregation.
CLARA	That's right, Patrick.
REVEREND	The outcome of the war wasn't entirely decided on the field of battle. On Remembrance Day I also honour the men and women who played their part behind the scenes. You may not have risked your life as a soldier, but every clerk and factory worker was a hero in their way. You should be proud of your role in the war, no matter how insignificant it might seem to you.
PATRICK	My role wasn't insignificant.
REVEREND	I'm sorry. I didn't mean to imply that it was.
PATRICK	I broke an important code.
REVEREND	Really?

TAMMY enters with CLARA's coat.

I think our congregation would be very keen to hear about the part you played in the war. Thanks to mathematicians like you, the Allies knew what the Germans were planning throughout the second half of the war. You may well have saved thousands of lives.

PATRICK	*(looking at CLARA)* Yes. But I lost my own.

REVEREND	What do you mean by that?

PATRICK takes CLARA's hand.

DONALD	We should go, Mom.
CLARA	I'd like Patrick to come.
DONALD	He'll be here when you get back.
CLARA	Will you wait for me, Patrick?
PATRICK	Yes. I'll be waiting.
CLARA	Do you promise?
PATRICK	Yes.
AGNES	She's only going for lunch.
PATRICK	Goodbye, my darling.

SCENE 9

TAMMY is getting CLARA ready for bed. She holds up a blue dressing gown.

TAMMY	What do you think? It's your favourite colour.
CLARA	It's beautiful... Whose is it?
TAMMY	Yours.
CLARA	Is it new?
TAMMY	Yes.
CLARA	I don't remember buying it.
TAMMY	I picked it up this afternoon... It was on sale.

CLARA   Why did you do that?

TAMMY   So you can look your best.

CLARA   Is my son coming?

TAMMY   No, not this evening.

               *TAMMY helps CLARA into her dressing gown. REVEREND HILL
               enters.*

REVEREND   Knock, knock. I hope everyone is decent.

CLARA   Hello, Reverend Hill.

REVEREND   Hello, Clara.

TAMMY   *(looking at her watch)* I'm just putting Clara to bed.

REVEREND   I won't stay long. I'd like to sit down if you don't mind. You
               look beautiful, Clara. How was your bath?

CLARA   I've been scrubbed from top to bottom.

REVEREND   Is that a new dressing gown?

CLARA   Yes. So I can look my best.

REVEREND   Is your son coming this evening?

CLARA   No.

REVEREND   He visits you almost every day.

CLARA   I don't know what I did to deserve so much attention.

REVEREND   You don't have to do anything to earn the love of your child.
               You can be a miserable failure in the estimation of the public,
               but in the eyes of your child you're still the most important
               person in the world... Not that you're a miserable failure,
               Clara. .

TAMMY   Have you been drinking?

REVEREND	I've just come from Mrs. O'Neill's wake.

TAMMY starts straightening CLARA's bed.

My goodness, Clara, your bed is a mess. Have you been having an affair?

CLARA	I don't believe in sex before marriage.
TAMMY	Then you'll have to get married.
CLARA	Aren't I too old to be married?
TAMMY	Reverend Hill has married dozens of couples older than you.
REVEREND	I'm not sure that Clara is ready for marriage quite yet. She would have to ask permission from her son. He has power of attorney.
TAMMY	It's past Clara's bedtime.
REVEREND	Yes, I should go. Into the dark, cold night.

TAMMY continues to straighten CLARA's bed.

Watching you make Clara's bed has given me an idea for a sermon.

TAMMY	Don't you ever relax?
REVEREND	No. I'm afraid I'm condemned to find a moral in everything.

Pause.

There's only one way to make a bed. The pillow goes at the head. The sheets go under the blankets. And then, inevitably, the blankets and sheets are pulled up to meet the pillow. I'm not sure why, but apparently there's no comparison between order and disorder... there are just so many more ways... I think almost an infinite number of ways... for the world to be a complete and utter mess.

TAMMY	No wonder you're losing your congregation.

PATRICK enters.

REVEREND   Hello, Patrick. What are you doing here? Are you lost?

PATRICK   It's nine o'clock.

REVEREND   Yes. And you're in Clara's room.

PATRICK   We have an appointment.

REVEREND   An appointment? But it's time for you and Clara to go to bed.

PATRICK   That's why I'm here.

REVEREND   Come along, Patrick. I'll take you back to your room.

PATRICK   I'd like to stay.

TAMMY   Why don't we leave them alone?

REVEREND   Do you think that's a good idea?

TAMMY   They're adults.

REVEREND   But the rules of the home are quite strict.

TAMMY   Let them have a little time together.

REVEREND   All right. But I think we should stay too.

Everyone sits uncomfortably.

Why don't you tell us about the code you broke, Patrick? You must have known Alan Turing?

PATRICK   Yes.

REVEREND   I expect he would have overseen your work. What was he like?

PATRICK   Why do you want to know?

REVEREND   One of my hobbies is collecting stories about the war.

PATRICK   I'm not a hero.

TAMMY   I have a surprise for you, Clara.

               TAMMY takes a tape of old dance music from the forties and a small tape deck from her bag. She shows CLARA the tape.

               I'm afraid it's a little worn. I hope it doesn't break.

               TAMMY puts the tape in the deck.

REVEREND   When I like a song I'll play it over and over for three weeks. And then I can't hear it in the same way anymore.

               TAMMY pushes the play button.

               Oh my... that's lovely. Does that bring back memories, Clara?

CLARA   Yes. Do you remember this song, Patrick?

PATRICK   Yes. Of course.

CLARA   It was my favourite song.

PATRICK   Yes. I know.

TAMMY   Why don't you ask her to dance, Patrick?

PATRICK   I'm not much of a dancer.

TAMMY   *(taking PATRICK's hands)* It's easy. You just have to step like this... *(TAMMY begins to dance with PATRICK.)* Pretend I'm your date. That's it... you're getting the hang of it. You look very dashing in your officer's uniform. *(looking at CLARA)* And suddenly, across a crowded room, you catch her eye... the woman you've been waiting for your entire life... Here, Clara. I'll help you up.

               TAMMY helps PATRICK hold CLARA.

               You'll have to hold her tight.

               PATRICK and CLARA dance, with TAMMY supporting them. ANNA enters and watches CLARA and PATRICK dance.

REVEREND   There was a time, a hundred years ago, when people had to wait a long time to hear their favourite song. Sometimes they would wait several years between one performance and another. And sometimes they might only hear a song once.

Pause.

Imagine how well you would listen if you thought you were hearing a song for the last time. All the cares and resentments of your daily life would seem so unimportant. You'd let go of any thoughts that might distract you from the song. You would almost forget who you were.

AGNES enters.

AGNES   Would you mind keeping the noise down in here? I'm trying to sleep.

TAMMY turns off the music.

REVEREND   *(seeing ANNA)* Yes, I think it's time for everyone to go to bed.

SCENE 10

ANNA and DONALD sit in the common room of the nursing home.

ANNA   Is something the matter? You seem very preoccupied.

DONALD   No. I'm fine.

ANNA   Is your mother sleeping?

DONALD   She wasn't in her room. She must be having a bath.

ANNA looks at her watch.

Where's your father?

ANNA   He wasn't in his room either... *(laughing)* Maybe we should try to find our parents.

DONALD	Yes.

Pause.

ANNA	My father seems to have taken quite a liking to your mother.
DONALD	Yes.
ANNA	I hope that doesn't bother you. I know your father passed away recently.
DONALD	I'm sure it's not very serious. My mother isn't really herself. Sometimes she thinks my father is still alive and that they're still living in their old house. You might warn your father to be a little cautious. He may be hurt if he gets too attached.
ANNA	My father seems to think he knew your mother during the war.
DONALD	Where was he stationed?
ANNA	Near Toronto. Before he was sent overseas.
DONALD	I don't know how they would have met. My mother lived on a farm near Windsor. She and my father were married a week before he was shipped to Hong Kong. During his imprisonment he lost over forty pounds. He contracted rickets and malaria. And he was beaten mercilessly by the guards. But he wrote in his diary, "We are determined to bear our humiliation without a murmur." My mother didn't receive a letter from him for two years. She didn't know if he was alive or dead. But she never lost hope.
ANNA	They must have been deeply in love.
DONALD	Yes. They were. Their marriage was the most consistent thing in my life.

TAMMY enters. She walks past DONALD and ANNA and is about to exit.

Hello, Tammy. Have you seen my mother?

TAMMY	She's in the basement.

DONALD	What's she doing in the basement?
TAMMY	Dancing.
DONALD	With who?
TAMMY	Patrick.

TAMMY exits.

ANNA	Well, at least they're having fun.
DONALD	I think Tammy is stealing money from my mother.
ANNA	What makes you think she's stealing money?
DONALD	She buys things with my mother's money, but she never keeps the receipts. And everything she buys is twice as expensive as you'd expect.
ANNA	You should tell the director. There may have been other complaints.
DONALD	But my mother loves her. What if they let her go? It's terrible not knowing what kind of a person she is... I'm a terrible coward.
ANNA	Why do you say that?
DONALD	I spend half of my visits sitting in this chair. I find it hard to see my mother in the condition she's in.
ANNA	But she seems quite healthy.
DONALD	She can tell you which dress she was wearing the day my father came home from war. But not what she did yesterday.

Pause.

Do you remember the saddest day of your life?

ANNA	There've been so many.

DONALD   But if you had to choose.

ANNA   I suppose it was the day my daughter stopped talking out loud when she played.

DONALD   Your life is hardly the stuff great tragedies are made of.

ANNA   Yes, but it was very sad.

DONALD   This happened on a particular day?

ANNA   Yes. And the worst thing is, I think I caused it.

DONALD   How?

ANNA   My daughter and I had just come home from her cousin's fourth birthday party. She said her cousin was so cute because she always did the voices for her dolls and animals when she played. I said, "Just like you," and she looked stunned. It was the first time she was aware that she spoke out loud when she played. After that she always played with her toys in complete silence. I couldn't hear what she was thinking anymore.

           Pause.

DONALD   This summer, at the cottage, I was aware that I was having fun, but my enjoyment was always overshadowed by so many concerns—worries about the future, about my daughter Nina, my work, even worries about the way our activities were affecting the lake—there were huge boathouses springing up everywhere—all part of the relentless development of the north. But looking back, a few weeks later, I cried—I felt the pure joy of watching Nina jump into the water over and over. I remembered the way she and her friends named every dive— "the pencil," "the chair," "the dead man"—even though every dive was essentially the same, but the way they laughed, the way they shouted out the names, the anticipation... it was so simple... they will never be happier—I cried for that, because it was so simple and so hard to reproduce—because it would never happen again... People should be put to death at age ten... What purpose does growing old serve?

ANNA   Maybe the purpose of life isn't ultimately to be happy or to suffer, but to do both at the same time. Children can never experience the incredible bittersweetness of joy and pain at the same time, of life lived in retrospect, the awareness of things passing—for that you need memory—you need to grow old.

                Pause.

                My father would like to marry your mother.

DONALD   You're not serious, are you?

ANNA   I think it's something we should consider.

SCENE 11

                DONALD paces back and forth in front of a door with a small stained-glass window. He opens the door a crack. We hear organ music. DONALD closes the door. AGNES approaches.

AGNES   Am I late?

DONALD   The service just started.

AGNES   Aren't you going in?

DONALD   No. Not at the moment.

                Pause. AGNES looks at the door.

AGNES   Is it safe?

DONALD   Safe? Oh... yes. I'm just stretching my legs.

                AGNES continues to look at the door.

                There's nothing wrong. It's just a service. Just a bunch of people sitting in pews.

                AGNES opens the door to the church. We hear the REVEREND's voice.

REVEREND   Rats as big as dogs, gorging themselves on human flesh in no man's land...

AGNES enters the church. DONALD continues to pace. A few moments later AGNES opens the door to the church.

Six million Jews, twenty million Russians, fifty million Chinese...

AGNES glares at DONALD and leaves the church. ANNA and PATRICK enter. PATRICK is wearing his uniform.

DONALD   Hello, Patrick. You look very dashing. My God, look at all those medals. What's this one for?

PATRICK   Keeping my mouth shut.

ANNA   Why don't you go in, Dad? I'll join you in a minute.

PATRICK opens the door and enters the church.

REVEREND   ...Every day is like an endless trip to the laundromat, we can never get all of our chores done...

ANNA   Where's your mother?

DONALD   Inside.

ANNA   Why aren't you with her?

DONALD   I find it hard to listen to Reverend Hill's sermons. I guess it reminds me of my childhood.

Pause.

ANNA   My father was very hurt by your decision. He doesn't understand how you could object to their marriage... Haven't you seen them together? They're like little children.

DONALD   Yes. They are. And I find it extremely sad.

ANNA   But your mother is so happy.

DONALD	That's because her mind is barely functioning.
ANNA	Functioning?
DONALD	Yes.
ANNA	You talk about her like she's a machine. What percent of her would you say is still operating?

Pause.

DONALD	Even if my mother was more herself, I'm afraid I couldn't allow her to marry your father.
ANNA	Why not?
DONALD	Your father is hardly a suitable match.
ANNA	Why do you say that?
DONALD	He's an alcoholic and a womanizer.
ANNA	A womanizer?
DONALD	Yes.
ANNA	He's eighty-two.

Pause.

He's taking his medication regularly for the first time in his life. He hasn't tried to escape or go drinking since he came here. He's even started to talk to me. He's told me stories about his childhood and the war that have made me see him differently.

DONALD	Why is he so determined to marry my mother?
ANNA	He wants to walk down the aisle with his bride. To wake up every morning beside her. To cherish and care for her. Until the day he dies. You may not understand it, but it means something to them. It's his last chance to share a life with someone.

DONALD   I'm sorry, but my mother is far too vulnerable.

                *ANNA turns and opens the door to the church. We hear an el-
                derly congregation singing. ANNA enters the church.*

CONGREGATION   A thousand ages in thy sight
                Are like an evening gone;
                Short as the watch that ends the night
                Before the rising sun.

                *The music fades slowly as the door closes. Moments later ANNA
                comes rushing out through the door.*

ANNA   My father is gone.

SCENE 12

                *PATRICK is tied to a chair with restraining straps. He is still
                wearing his uniform. He has a large bruise on his face.
                DONALD enters.*

DONALD   Hello, Patrick. Where did they find you? *(noticing PATRICK's
                face)* Did you have a fall?

PATRICK   *(indicating the straps)* Would you mind cutting these?

DONALD   I think I should ask a nurse.

PATRICK   It's all right.

DONALD   Where do you want to go?

PATRICK   I don't want to go anywhere. I just don't like being tied up.

                Pause.

DONALD   Listen, Patrick... I'm sorry... about my decision... but if I al-
                lowed you to marry my mother, I wouldn't be living up to my
                responsibilities as a son. She's not fully herself.

PATRICK   We made love.

DONALD   What?

PATRICK   She asked me to. So I put her on the bed and straightened her
            out. She...

DONALD   I don't think I need to know the details.

PATRICK   We're adults... We know what we want. I'm the only person
            she ever loved.

DONALD   Do you think so?

PATRICK   Yes.

DONALD   I'm afraid that's not true, Patrick. My mother loved my father.
            They were married before he went to war.

PATRICK   She thought he was dead.

DONALD   Your daughter says you tend to make up stories.

PATRICK   This one's true.

DONALD   Then why didn't you come back for her after the war?

PATRICK   I couldn't.

DONALD   Why not?

PATRICK   My superiors wanted me to stay overseas. They needed me.

DONALD   What for?

PATRICK   I served my country. I don't have to tell you the details.

DONALD   My mother lived on a farm with her parents, you weren't sta-
            tioned anywhere near her. How could you...

            Anna enters.

ANNA   Hello.

DONALD   Hello.

Pause.

(very uncomfortable) I was just talking to your father. *(indicating PATRICK's straps)* He wants someone to remove his straps.

ANNA   I don't think so.

PATRICK   Why not?

ANNA   They don't want to lose you again.

DONALD   They can't keep him tied up forever.

ANNA   *(to DONALD)* He's being moved to the second floor this afternoon.

DONALD   Why are they doing that?

ANNA   *(looking at her father)* They've decided he's a danger to himself.

DONALD   But surely that's up to you to decide.

ANNA   It's not up to me. If he drinks again it could kill him.

              Pause.

Don't worry. It's not your fault... if that's what you're concerned about. It was an impractical idea. I'm sorry I encouraged it.

SCENE 13

REVEREND HILL and DONALD sit in the common room of the home.

REVEREND   I enjoy our conversations. I feel a little out of place in this town. The deciding issue in the last election was snowmobile trails.

              Pause.

DONALD   How do you know when God is talking to you?

REVEREND   God doesn't talk to me. Not personally. As Paul said, "We only see him through a glass darkly."

DONALD   But then he only sees us through a glass darkly.

REVEREND   No. I believe he sees us as we truly are.

Pause.

DONALD   Have you seen Patrick?

REVEREND   Yes. I saw him this morning.

DONALD   How is he?

REVEREND   I think he's adjusting.

DONALD   Do you think I'm a terrible person?

REVEREND   Why would I think that?

DONALD   I've made a lot of people unhappy.

REVEREND   I'm sure that wasn't your intention.

DONALD   No. But I don't think Anna will ever forgive me.

REVEREND   Patrick is an adult. He made a decision to go drinking. In the end only God can understand or forgive a person's motivations.

DONALD   That's a convenient way to ease your conscience. What if there is no God?

REVEREND   A Russian novelist—I believe it was Dostoevsky—said that if there is no God then everything is permitted. But I think it's even worse than that. Because if there is no God then everything will be forgotten.

DONALD   Yes. I agree. But that's simply the way the world happens to be. There's no point inventing an omniscient God to console yourself. Even the most powerful computer has to clear its memory when it's full. You can't have consciousness without constant loss.

REVEREND So what do you live for? What will survive of the things you devoted yourself to? I couldn't live without the faith that there's something more permanent than us. Something that watches and remembers.

DONALD To be honest, I don't know what I'm living for. I used to think it was my work. But I'm too old to do anything remarkable now. And when people do finally understand the mind they'll build computers or neural implants that will make us all look like Neanderthals. Then there's my daughter. But she barely has time to see me anymore.

REVEREND How old is she?

DONALD Ten. And then there's my mother. But unfortunately she's dying. And when she's dead, no one will ever think of me the way she did again... Not even God.

Pause. TAMMY enters.

REVEREND How's Agnes?

TAMMY Dr. Stevens thinks you should see her.

REVEREND I'll be right there.

TAMMY exits.

If you need someone to talk to, I would be happy to talk. I won't try to convert you.

DONALD You won't be able to help it. What else do you have to offer besides faith?

REVEREND Just my friendship.

SCENE 14

DONALD watches CLARA sleeping.

DONALD   Hello, Mom.

CLARA   Hello, dear.

DONALD   Sorry I'm late. The traffic was bad.

CLARA   It was nice of you to come.

DONALD   How was your day?

CLARA   Wonderful.

DONALD   Did you do anything special?

CLARA   No... Not that I can remember.

DONALD   How are you feeling?

CLARA   Fine.

DONALD shows CLARA a postcard.

DONALD   Another postcard from the Copes. There's a picture of a cave on the front. They're in Southern California now. Would you like me to read it?

CLARA   Yes. Please.

DONALD   "Dear Clara, hope you are well. We visited the Carlsbad Caverns today. Look forward to seeing you when we return on the fifteenth. Love, Jim and Marjorie..." I'm sure they'll have lots of news when they get back.

DONALD opens CLARA's drawer and puts the postcard inside.

We really have to organize this drawer, Mom. Maybe on the weekend... I have a meeting with the president of the university tomorrow morning. I think he's going to ask me to be the head of the psychology department.

CLARA   That's good. You can change all those crazy things the first years have to do.

DONALD   What crazy things?

CLARA   All those pranks.

DONALD   They're not going to put me in charge of orientation, Mom. I'll be the youngest chair at the university. It's something I'm really proud of.

CLARA   On the first day of school you were so frightened. All the other children were running and screaming. You wouldn't let go of my leg. The teacher couldn't pull you away.

DONALD   I don't remember that.

CLARA   I had to take you home again.

               Pause.

DONALD   How are you feeling?

CLARA   A little sleepy.

DONALD   But you're all right?

CLARA   Yes. Of course. Why shouldn't I be? Why do you keep asking me how I am?

               Pause.

DONALD   You didn't drink your juice, Mom.

CLARA   I don't want it.

DONALD   The nurse said you should drink more.

CLARA   I'll have it at home.

DONALD	This is your home.
CLARA	I mean at my house.
DONALD	We sold your house.
CLARA	Why?
DONALD	You needed help taking care of yourself.
CLARA	I've always taken care of myself.
DONALD	Your memory's not very good anymore, Mom.
CLARA	I can still remember my phone number.
DONALD	What is it?
CLARA	705-635-2063.
DONALD	That's very good, Mom.

> *Pause.*

How was dinner?

CLARA	I didn't go.
DONALD	Why not?
CLARA	My date didn't show up.

> *Pause.*

DONALD   *(shaken)* Why don't you have some juice?

> *DONALD reaches for the juice and knocks it over.*

I'm sorry, Mom. I've made a terrible mess... I'll get something to clean it up with.

> *DONALD exits. He returns a moment later with a mop and pail.*

(mopping the floor) There. At least you won't slip on it.

CLARA   You always take such good care of me.

DONALD   I try my best.

　　　Pause.

You must be starving. I'll go and see if I can get you something to eat. I'll be back soon.

CLARA   All right.

　　　DONALD hugs CLARA. He holds her for several seconds.

Goodbye, dear.

　　　DONALD exits. CLARA sits starting ahead. DONALD re-enters.

DONALD   I forgot my coat.

　　　DONALD picks up his coat.

See you soon.

　　　He exits.

　　　A nurse, DIANA, enters.

DIANA   Hello, dear. I've come to get you ready for bed... My goodness—your bed's a mess. Have you been having an affair?

CLARA   Yes.

DIANA   Good for you.

　　　DIANA continues tidying the bed.

CLARA   I don't remember you.

DIANA   I don't usually work on this floor. I'm usually upstairs.

CLARA   I'd like to go there.

DIANA	Oh, I don't think so, dear.
CLARA	Why not?
DIANA	It's very sad up there. There's one old gentleman who stands by the door all day asking if he can go out.
CLARA	Do you think he'll get out?
DIANA	No. He's a drinker. No one will let him out...

Pause. DIANA helps CLARA into bed.

Tammy asked me to say hello.

CLARA	Tammy?
DIANA	She said you were like a second mother to her.
CLARA	Where is she?
DIANA	She has another job.
CLARA	What's she doing?
DIANA	I'm not sure. I think she's in sales.

Pause. DIANA picks up a picture on CLARA's dresser.

Is this your son?

CLARA	Yes.
DIANA	He's very handsome.
CLARA	He's gone.

Pause. CLARA stares at the mop.

He was the dearest, sweetest thing.

DIANA	Oh... I'm sorry.

Diana notices that Clara is staring at the mop.

Someone forgot to put away the mop. I'll get this out of your way, dear.

CLARA   *(indicating the logo on the bucket)* What does this mean?

DIANA   Rubbermaid? It's just the name of the company that made the mop and pail.

CLARA   Oh.

Pause.

DIANA   I have to get your medicine, dear.

Diana exits. Clara closes her eyes and falls asleep. Patrick enters and sits by her bed. Clara opens her eyes.

CLARA   I fell asleep. I just shut my eyes and fell asleep.

PATRICK   So you're feeling better?

CLARA   Oh yes. Sleep is the greatest protection.

Pause.

And when I think about what the pioneers had to do.

Pause.

It wasn't like it is now... But the water was clear.

Pause.

I missed you, Patrick.

PATRICK   I missed you too.

Pause.

CLARA   Today was a special day. We had a visit from a children's choir.

PATRICK   I'm sorry I missed it.

CLARA   The children said we could sing along. For the last song.

Pause.

I hope they didn't get tired from standing so long.

PATRICK   There's always a danger in that.

CLARA   Isn't it funny, children can never walk. They have to run.

Pause.

You don't really remember me do you, Patrick?

PATRICK   Yes. I do.

CLARA   But I didn't mean anything to you.

PATRICK   You meant everything.

Pause.

CLARA   Do you remember when we first met?

PATRICK   Yes. I was on leave.

CLARA   But you were wearing your officer's uniform.

PATRICK   You were in a blue dress.

CLARA   You were another person's date.

PATRICK   I didn't care about my date. You were so beautiful.

Pause.

CLARA   A week later you were gone.

PATRICK   I'm sorry. I had to.

CLARA   And I never heard from you again.

Pause.

You'll find people never do what you think they should do.

PATRICK   I'm sorry. For everything.

CLARA   I forgive you... Now we can start over.

DIANA enters and stares at PATRICK.

DIANA   Hello, Patrick. What are you doing here? You're on the wrong floor.

Pause.

How did you get down here?

PATRICK   I broke the code.

DIANA   You're very naughty. Now we'll have to change it.

She takes PATRICK's arm.

Come along now, dear. We'll find a nurse to take you upstairs.

PATRICK   I'd like to stay.

DIANA   It's time for Clara to go to sleep.

PATRICK   She asked me to stay.

DIANA   Oh, I couldn't leave you two alone without a chaperone.

Pause.

Come along, Patrick. It's time to go. I'm on a busy shift.

DIANA leads PATRICK away. CLARA closes her eyes. DIANA enters.

I'm sorry, Clara. I don't know how he got down here. He seemed very disoriented.

DIANA gives CLARA her medicine.

CLARA   I didn't mind. We're married.

DIANA   Oh, are you? Is he a good husband?

CLARA   Yes.

DIANA   You're lucky then. I wish I could say the same... Mine has his moments.

               DIANA pulls CLARA's blankets up.

               Do you like your covers up under your chin?

CLARA   Yes.

DIANA   Just like a little girl... There, you're all tucked in. I hope you have a beautiful sleep.

CLARA   Thank you.

DIANA   Would you like me to draw the curtain?

CLARA   Yes.

               DIANA draws the curtain. We hear CLARA's voice from behind the curtain.

               What did you say your name was?

DIANA   Diana.

CLARA   I'll try to remember that.

               Pause.

               Will I see you again tomorrow?

DIANA   I'll be on Patrick's floor tomorrow.

               DIANA exits.

CLARA   I knew a Patrick once during the war... You would be too young to remember.

Pause.

Apparently he has a daughter now.

Pause.

Of course Dad was on the railroad... We had a lot of miles to walk down the track. But he was good company.

Pause.

I enjoyed the morning. There were quite a few there. Not as many as last year. But there were some good singers.

The lights fade.

RUNE ARLIDGE

MICHAEL HEALEY

Rune Arlidge premiered at the Tarragon Theatre, Toronto, in March 2004 with the following company:

FRANCES ....Fiona Reid
TOM, TOM JUNIOR...John Dolan
RUNE ARLIDGE ....Jane Spidell
MICHELLE ....Julie Stewart
MATTHEW..Rick Roberts
HARVAR..Ari Cohen
LILLIAN .... Severn Thompson

Directed by Leah Cherniak
Set and costumes designed by Charlotte Dean
Lighting designed by Andrea Lundy
Sound design by Kirk Elliot
Stage managed by Arwen MacDonell

Rune Arlidge received workshops at the Tarragon Theatre in 2002, and at the Shaw Festival in 2002 and 2003. My thanks to both companies and to the actors who read those drafts.

Ari Cohen wrote the fat-in-your-new-pants line, and I remain eternally in his debt.

Originally trained as an actor at Toronto's Ryerson Theatre School, Michael Healey began writing for the stage ten years after graduation. His first play, a solo one-act called *Kicked*, was produced at the Fringe of Toronto Festival in 1996. He subsequently toured the play across Canada and internationally, and in 1998 it won the Dora Mavor Moore Award (Toronto's annual theatre prize) for best new play. *The Drawer Boy*, his first full-length play, premiered in Toronto in 1999, has been produced across North America and internationally, and has been translated into German, French, Hindi, Portuguese, and Japanese. His other plays include *The Road to Hell* (co-authored with Kate Lynch), *Plan B*, *The Innocent Eye Test*, *Generous*, and *Courageous*. He has adapted Chekhov and Molnár for Toronto's Soulpepper Theatre Company. Michael's plays have, in the last fifteen years, won the Governor General's Literary Award, the Chalmers Canadian Play Award, five Dora Awards, as well as awards across Canada and internationally. He is a playwright-in-residence at Tarragon Theatre.

It was just as well that Michael Healey followed his runaway 1999 hit *The Drawer Boy* with *Plan B* (2002) and not *Rune Arlidge*, the latter two at the Tarragon Theatre. The predominantly lacklustre-to-vicious reviews of *Rune Arlidge* by most of the city's theatre critics—Jon Kaplan of *NOW Magazine* and myself in the *Globe* were the exceptions—would have added the "How do you follow *The Drawer Boy*?" stigma to a play that had enough problems to deal with already. Imagine the awkward conversations and the headlines: Playwright follows triumph with disaster!

A narrative of awkwardness, stunted growth—emotionally and physically—and disappointments, however, makes an excellent companion to *Rune Arlidge*. Healey himself approached the play as a study in "long-term disappointment," he said. "A question became interesting to me: What happens to someone over a long period of time in their life, if they are somehow thwarted, emotionally? . . . How do people bear up under that, over the long term?"[1]

This long term is represented in the play over three acts and a stretch of twenty-five years, from 1994, to the present day of the play's premiere in 2004, to the future of 2019. The setting remains the same: a cottage somewhere in southern Ontario, overlooking a lake that seems to be particularly leech-infested. But while Healey had set *The Drawer Boy* in rural Ontario, there were significant differences between the two plays, most noticeably its gender balance. *The Drawer Boy* was a three-person, three-man play. And to a large extent *Plan B*, with its focus on politics in Ottawa, featured more men than women. *Rune Arlidge* is unabashedly a play about the lives of women: the matriarch Frances and her two daughters, Michelle and the titular Rune Arlidge. Men are either dead when the play opens or flown in and out of the action to bring the inner workings of these women's lives to a sharper focus.

But don't let the family part of the drama or its cottage setting fool you into thinking this is a play about a clan torn apart and then brought together by trauma. Connections and healing play no part here. What makes *Rune Arlidge* a stunning but difficult play rests on Healey's ultimately determinist reading of love and blood relations. There's little to no emotional growth borrowed from that beloved self-improvement cult of North America. Neither Rune nor her sister—and they are different creatures on the page and in the performances of Jane Spidell and Julie Stewart onstage—seem capable

---

1   Quoted in Allan Gould, "Drawer Boy author brings new play to Tarragon," *Post City Magazine*, March 2004, np.

of learning from their mother's mistakes or their own. Nowhere does this become more obvious than in their encounters with love and sex. Rune in particular strikes out with no less than two eligible suitors for, it becomes clear, reasons that she both can and can't control. Even when she makes her own decisions, she seems helpless.

Helpless but not a victim, it's crucial to point out. While trapping his women in the cottage for what literally counts as a life sentence, Healey avoids casting them in the victim roles. He accomplishes this partly through giving all of them variations of the gift of gab. Critics have pointed out that the characters' wicked tongues constitute part of the script's problems. John Coulbourn of the *Toronto Sun* wrote that "Healey's penchant for the wise-crack leads the ensemble into too many emotional cul-de-sacs," while Richard Ouzounian in the *Toronto Star* complained that after a while "everyone starts to sound like playwright Healey."[2]

However, I think neither has taken the women's need to speak into full consideration. And it's not just the women. When Harvar, Rune's suitor in Act 2, expresses his discomfort about Lillian, Michelle's ten-year-old daughter, he follows the women's example: "I feel like I have to keep talking or she'll do something." If the women can talk—and shout and curse—they can at least fight the inevitable entropy. Frances especially seems to revert to this strategy in Act 1 and brings to mind Samuel Beckett's Winnie in *Happy Days*. But instead of being buried in a mound, she's let loose in a cottage that's literally sinking into the ground. Part of her ongoing tragedy is a series of strokes that leave her without speech as Act 2 begins. The only sounds coming from her are crying and grunting incomprehensibly. Rune, on the other hand, speaks on several levels. It's not a coincidence that she happens to be a newspaper columnist, even if her opinions get her a fair share of hate mail and physical threats.

Those threats are the closest the play comes to physical violence. Most of the violence in *Rune Arlidge*—and it's been described by some critics as a modern tragedy, albeit a flawed one   is emotional, and self inflicted at that. The characters insist on swimming in the lake despite the blood-sucking leeches and the physical pain of rubbing salt on the wounds. Despite all of this, it's not difficult to agree with director Leah Cherniak's first impressions of the script as a "fable or fairy tale"[3] or with the naturalistic feel she and set and costume designer Charlotte Dean gave the production. *Rune Arlidge* meets all of the requirements for each narrative genre and mood of theatrical presentation mentioned above, but does so primarily because of its painfully

---

2   John Coulbourn, "Play leaves family in Rune," *Toronto Sun*, March 4, 2004, np; Richard Ouzounian, "Cottage tale makes merry and drowns," *Toronto Star*, March 3, 2004, F4.

3   Quoted in Jon Kaplan, "Rune's tune," *NOW Magazine*, February 27, 2004: http://www.nowtoronto.com/stage/story.cfm?content=140493&archive=23,26,2004

recognizable story. This may explain why, unlike *The Drawer Boy*, it failed to find a life outside of its one Tarragon production. It's possible that Healey has stretched the limit of cynicism to the point of nihilism here. Admitting to seeing ourselves in his characters counts as an invitation to years of therapy and personal reckoning. As audiences (and critics), we've embraced a view that characters must be likeable and relatable before declaring a play—or any other narrative-based art form—a success. Aside from the fact that this yardstick would render most of world literature a failure, it elevates the theatre of affirmation above that of confrontation by denying darker and more unsettling works the kind of popular appeal they deserve. In film, that's the role of so called "art house" releases; in theatre, it's the independents who have to accept that the price of confrontation is marginalization—or, as is the case here, critical drubbing.

I stand by my original review[4] of this play as both a beautiful and wise work. In fact, I've revisited it over the years at points of sadness and elation in my life and grew to admire it more with each reading, faults and all. The real tragedy of *Rune Arlidge* is that its women's rambling voices were never heard again. In theatrical terms, a cross-section of Canadian actresses were denied a chance to play powerful and flawed women who will draw as much admiration as ire from the audience. The Tarragon took a risk with this production and for that I, for one, am grateful.

---

4   Kamal Al-Solaylee, "Generational journey tries to fill in gaps," *The Globe and Mail*, March 4, 2004, R3.

CHARACTERS/SETTING

Act One: A cottage, 1994

RUNE ARLIDGE, 20
MICHELLE, her sister, 26
FRANCES, her mother, 58
MATTHEW, her boyfriend, 23
TOM, the handyman, 59

Act Two: The same, ten years later

HARVAR, 38
LILLIAN, almost 10

Act Three: The same, fifteen years later

TOM JUNIOR, 50
TOM and TOM JUNIOR are played by the same actor

NOTE

Because playgoers can't be counted on to look at their program, we decided in the first production to include briefly projected slides at the top of each act. They read:

August, 1994;
Ten years later;
and
Fifteen years later.

ACT ONE

The porch of a cottage in southern Ontario, 1994. Late summer. Dawn. We hear TOM's truck pull up, the door open and shut. TOM enters and bangs on the cottage door. Eventually, FRANCES comes to the screen.

TOM   Morning.

FRANCES   Is that Tom?

TOM   Missus Arlidge, you can see it's me.

FRANCES   What are you accusing me of? I can't see it's you. Not necessarily. You're backlit.

TOM   It's Tom.

FRANCES   And also, there's the filthy screen between us. So maybe I can't see it's you. Maybe you're just some shapeless grey hulk, there on the other side of this not particularly useful door, this filthy door. I mean why does everyone—

RUNE   *(from within)* Mother, shut up.

FRANCES   —everyone is so ready to accuse me of something. Do you know how early it is? I was seconds ago asleep just over there, and now I'm standing here, and I don't even remember how I got here.

TOM   Missus Arlidge, it's Tom. Sorry. I'm here—

FRANCES   I can't see anything. I can't see anything. What time is it?

RUNE   *(from within)* Mother, shut up.

FRANCES   Good Lord, it's—what time does that say? I will not shut up. We're being accosted probably. It's—what?

TOM   It's early.

FRANCES   Good Lord. What does that—is that six o'clock?

TOM   Rune said I should—

FRANCES   Tom—if that's who it is—no offence now, but, are you out of your mind?

TOM   Rune said—

FRANCES   Why on earth would you come out here and knock at this time of the morning? You can't be Tom. He wouldn't do this. Tom Ilesic is a sweet man. A helpful and useful—

MICHELLE   *(from a different part of the cottage)* Mother, SHUT THE FUCK UP.

FRANCES   Yes, very nice, that's fine, sorry to disturb you ladies, but a man has come to rape and kill us all.

RUNE   *(appearing behind her mother)* In which order.

TOM   I could come back.

RUNE   Hi, Mr. Ilesic. No. Come on in. Move it, Mother.

FRANCES   Wait! How do you know it's—

> RUNE opens the door and steps outside. She is in her pyjamas, as is her mother. And when MICHELLE emerges, she'll be in pyjamas, too.

Oh. Hello, Tom.

TOM   Missus Arlidge. Hey Rune.

RUNE   Thanks for coming.

TOM   It's okay.

FRANCES   Hello, Tom. Why is Tom here?

RUNE   I called Mr. Ilesic to come and fix the water.

FRANCES   Yes. What's the matter with the water?

RUNE   Nothing. The water's perfect. It just doesn't come out of anything.

FRANCES   Oh, the pump. Your fucking father—Tom, would you like some coffee?

TOM   Sure.

FRANCES   God. Me too.

            FRANCES steps onto the porch, throws herself into a chair. TOM heads inside. A pause.

            (of the landscape) Pretty.

            A pause.

            Michelle!

MICHELLE   *(from within)* Mother?

FRANCES   Get up and make some coffee. *(to RUNE)* How are you, um, feeling today?

            A pause.

            You and your sister have to race today. Don't forget.

RUNE   The race is today?

FRANCES   Nobody in this family listens. Yes. Today. One o'clock or something. It's on the thing.

RUNE   I'm not going today. I have to stay here.

FRANCES   Don't even start.

RUNE   I'm not going anywhere. I have to stay here.

FRANCES   You have to— Now listen. There are a dozen pennants in there. Hanging proudly in there, singles and doubles and under thirteens and father-daughter things, and whatnot, in there. You and your sister and your father earned every one of them. It's one of the only joys of my summer, watching for you to return with another pennant. It's one of the few things that makes this place tolerable, mainly because it meant that the summer was almost over. And there is a four-year gap now, in there, a four-year pennant gap. And I do not judge, I mean, of course you would go to school, and your sister had all the things to do she did, and other sometime family members developed other, obscure priorities unrelated to those parental and matrimonial ones he had already fucking acquired—

RUNE   How do you speak in paragraphs? It's barely light out.

FRANCES   Never mind me. Never mind attacking my syntax. Today is the day the pennant drought ends for this family. End of story.

RUNE   No. I'm... No.

FRANCES   I'll get a shoehorn, we'll fit it into your incredible schedule. Between the sleeping twenty hours a day and the staring at the inside of the refrigerator.

              MICHELLE comes out carrying a bottle of red wine, a corkscrew, and a tumbler.

              Good morning. Don't make any plans for later. You and your sister are paddling.

MICHELLE   Anybody I know?

FRANCES   You're going to win another pennant for your mother.

MICHELLE   Oh. Okay.

FRANCES   Really?

MICHELLE   Why not? My stroke isn't what it was, but I'm sure I'll—*(struggling with the cork)* motherfucking—what time is this?

FRANCES   One o'clock. So you'll do it?

MICHELLE   Sure. If I'm conscious. Why not. C'mon, you stupid— Is it at the thing?

FRANCES   See, Rune? Your sister, who's normally the cunt about these things, is willing to paddle for me.

RUNE   I don't want to.

FRANCES   Frankly, young lady, what you want is of no concern to— *(noticing MICHELLE and the wine)* What in the hell are you doing?

MICHELLE   *(the bottle between her legs)* Motherfucking Niagara piece of—

FRANCES   I believe I asked for coffee.

MICHELLE   Can't—make—coffee.

TOM comes outside.

TOM   It's the pump.

FRANCES   Is it the pump? That comes as absolutely no surprise to me.

TOM   Have to go down below.

MICHELLE   Mr. Ilesic? Can you get that?

TOM   Sure.

TOM takes the bottle, pulls on the corkscrew.

Boy. That's in there, eh? You know, if you store this on its side, the cork won't dry out.

FRANCES   Now what am I being accused of? Improper wine storage? That's the limit. For your information, that bottle of wine was never meant to be drunk. It was brought here by some guests, many years ago, and I left it prominently displayed as an example of an unacceptable bottle of wine to bring to someone's cottage.

The fact that this one has decided to open it at this disgustingly early hour and disgustingly late date means I now have to take advice about how to keep wine, from a man, a nice man, to be sure, but a man who nonetheless drives to Penetanguishene for a cosmopolitan experience. Which is beyond the limit. You're a nice man, Tom. But, I mean, come on.

TOM   No, I understand.

Tom has opened the bottle and he hands it to Michelle. He then steps off the porch and removes some of the lattice fronting the crawl space below. He crawls under the porch with a flashlight and tools. Michelle drinks the wine: a quick first glass and then nurses the refill.

FRANCES   *(She's looking out over the lake.)* It's what time of the day, and I've already reached the limit. Did your father ever teach you to fish?

RUNE   No.

MICHELLE   Yes.

FRANCES   That's nice. Did you enjoy it?

MICHELLE   No.

RUNE   Yes.

A pause.

FRANCES   Did I ever tell you the story of how your father and I found this place?

Michelle and Rune immediately rise and disappear inside.

We found it in a canoe. We had a cabin rented across the lake, that little place that called itself a resort. We howled with laughter at that when we pulled up. A half-dozen shacks on the water and a couple of leaky canoes. Howled with laughter. Of course, a couple of nights there and it stopped being funny. After one night in the bed, your father woke with a red lump on his stomach, which we later learned was where the spider had chosen to burrow in to lay her eggs. It was two weeks later, and he was at his doctor, who told him he had inadvertently become a spider-egg host. The doctor had him look away while he lanced the bump, but your father glanced back in time to see all the baby spiders spill out of his skin.

But oh, God, the sex. That cabin, for that week, 1960-something; probably only because there was no television. There were no televised sports. Which, incidentally, is how you got your name. His love of televised sports. Did you know that?

So, one day we took a canoe and paddled out onto the lake, and sort of got drifted all the way across here, and your father shouted and swore at me, but a blister's a blister and so that was the paddling over, as far as I was concerned. Drifting. The view was wonderful, all that green and all that blue, the sun getting lower; your father screaming behind me.

We wound up here, in this bay, and this place had a for-sale sign on it and we argued about whether or not he should break in here and use the phone to call someone from the resort to come and pick us up. He was standing down there, in the water, up to his ankles, holding the canoe, and when he finally stepped out of the water to do what I'd told him, he saw the leeches. He had cut his foot on one of the sharp stones in our bay and they had just come running for him. And when he fainted, he was just like one of those inflated dolls you punch: he hit the dock with his head and sprung right back up into place. He broke that window and found a box of salt and took care of the leeches. And he was so embarrassed at the mess he made, he put in an offer on the place, just to be polite. It was absurdly low. It took them forty minutes to accept.

A pause.

All the absent men.

A pause. TOM backs out of the crawl space.

Why, here's one now. Tom. Tell me something.

TOM   Any idea what this is?

FRANCES   Let me see?

He brings it to her. It's a piece of wadded-up tinfoil.

Well, I suspect you'd have to ask Rune. She was down there last. She's convinced she knows how to fix the pump because her father dragged her under there once and showed her what to do. Except as we know, he was really quite clueless when it came to the plumbing. In fact, he was worse than that: he was clueless and deluded. About plumbing. Anybody's plumbing. If you take my meaning. Would you like some coffee?

TOM   Not falling for that one again.

FRANCES   No, I'll get one of the girls to boil some water from the lake.

TOM   No thanks. I gotta go. Thomas Junior and I are putting up the new place across the way. He'll be waiting. Tell Rune she had the right idea with this, but that it's gonna take an actual part at this point. I'll pick it up at the end of the day and put it in tomorrow morning.

FRANCES   Same time?

TOM   'Fraid so. But at least you'll only have to go a day without.

FRANCES   Hmm. Tell me something.

TOM   All right.

FRANCES   You left the missus, correct.

TOM   *(who is too old to be embarrassed by the likes of her)* Correct.

FRANCES   After how many years?

TOM   Moved out two days before the thirty-first anniversary. It was pointed out to me. Several times.

FRANCES   And, if I'm not, could you tell me why?

TOM   Well, Frances, I guess I don't know exactly. I just, I don't really know. It was a long time to be married.

FRANCES   That must have been incredibly difficult for her. There not being a reason.

TOM   I guess so.

FRANCES   Yes.

TOM   Did Mr. Arlidge have a reason?

FRANCES   Not as such. No serious reason.

TOM   Huh. Men.

    A beat.

    Girls all right?

FRANCES   Hmm? Yes, thanks. Far as I can tell.

TOM   That's good.

FRANCES   They hate me.

TOM   No.

FRANCES   Genuinely. I pretend it rankles. Do you love your children?

TOM   Just got the one. And he's no child these days. I can just about stand his company all day long if there's something to busy us, like this monster cottage.

FRANCES   Yes.

TOM   Yesterday we put in the hot tub. Today it's a free-standing sauna combination goddamn smokehouse. So this guy can spend his summers making his own bacon. And sweating.

    A pause.

    Maybe I can come back some evening, play some cards.

FRANCES   Oh. Tom. Oh. You're not my type at all.

TOM   Jesus, lady, you think you're mine?

FRANCES Well.

     A pause.

     God. It never, ever gets any easier, does it.

TOM   I guess not.

     A pause.

     Okay.

FRANCES Yes.

TOM   See you in the morning.

FRANCES Yes.

     He exits. The truck starts and leaves. MICHELLE comes out of the cottage with the bottle, the glass, and a roll of toilet paper. She puts down the bottle, takes the last slug out of the glass, and puts it down. As she disappears around the side of the cottage:

     Yes, sorry. Just till tomorrow.

     A beat. RUNE comes out.

     (handing her the tinfoil) Tom says nice try, but unfortunately you've inherited your father's delusional plumbing condition.

RUNE   Why'd you scare him off?

FRANCES Good Lord. I didn't scare anyone off. That was flirting.

RUNE   That was flirting? Jesus Christ. One of us has no idea what the hell they're doing.

FRANCES That's right, dear. How is your fellow. What was his name?

RUNE   Matt.

FRANCES	That's right. How is he?
RUNE	He's fine.
FRANCES	I see. Do you want to tell me about it, dear?
RUNE	I don't think so.
FRANCES	Thank God. Did you make some coffee?
RUNE	No, Mother, I didn't.
FRANCES	Do you not know how?
RUNE	I don't want any.
FRANCES	Oh, you don't. Don't you. Well, young lady, the question of your needs, what you want any of or not want, is not the issue here. Perhaps this is the root of your problem with this fellow. Not being able to appreciate the needs of others because of the apparent enormity of your own is a big problem. It's crippling. It's fundamentally a lack of empathy. Which is the glue of the world, my dear. The glue of the world.
RUNE	No, I'll tell you what my problem is—
FRANCES	Your problem, if I may, is that you haven't made any frigging coffee. You know, I blame myself. An ability to empathize is probably a mother's job to impart. Another in the long list of failures. I tried with you girls, I really did, but somehow, I was always trying at the wrong thing.

MICHELLE enters, smoking a joint. To RUNE:

MICHELLE	Want some of that?
RUNE	Not really.

RUNE takes the joint.

FRANCES	Once I spent God knows how long making you a motherfucking flying saucer suit, don't ask me why, school probably, all I knew was here was my chance to behave in a motherly

fashion. And I gave it everything. You have no idea. Nights, sitting up, developing new ways to attach tinfoil to cardboard so it wouldn't fall off. Tinfoil attachment methods DuPont would take years and billions to develop. Until your father pointed out no one had eaten a decent meal for weeks. The house was a wreck. You children were filthy.

MICHELLE   So? Is he coming up today?

RUNE   No.

FRANCES   God only knows what I looked like. And it was that moment the real estate agent began bringing young couples through the house.

MICHELLE   Why not?

FRANCES   Your father had neglected to mention we were selling the house.

RUNE   I don't know. But it was yesterday.

MICHELLE   He was supposed to come up yesterday?

RUNE   That's what we said.

FRANCES   One of you, I forget which, actually came down with actual scurvy. From all the poor nutrition. First case in two hundred years, they said. What?

RUNE   I can't say I'm sorry, actually.

MICHELLE   Why.

FRANCES   What?

RUNE   He's been very weird lately. I think he's trying to figure out how to dump me. He's being nice.

MICHELLE   He is nice. He's big and nice.

FRANCES   You've invited people out here?

RUNE   No, he's being nice.

MICHELLE   He's too nice, if you ask me.

FRANCES   Have you invited people out here?

MICHELLE   And probably too big.

RUNE   He's being shifty and secretive and nice. He wants to make sure I see his carefully concealed agony.

FRANCES   Unbelievable. What are these people supposed to eat?

RUNE   I'm supposed to appreciate his bravery during this very difficult period of his trying to figure out how to dump me.

MICHELLE   Are you sure that's what he's doing?

RUNE   Of course not. I get to guess.

FRANCES   Honest to God.

RUNE   But his not showing up at all is a pretty solid indicator, I think.

FRANCES   I thought we had agreed that this—

MICHELLE   Mother, you can stay, but you've got to shut the fuck up.

             A pause. FRANCES stands and goes indoors. MICHELLE and RUNE look at each other. Eventually, from inside:

FRANCES   You people don't treat me properly.

MICHELLE   Yeah, well...

             RUNE looks at her.

             All right. I'm sorry. I'll come in in a second and poach some eggs.

FRANCES   *(at the screen)* If you want. Don't make one for me, though. Your poached eggs are dreadful. They're all over the place. Your poached eggs can't concentrate. I'm going back to bed.

MICHELLE   Capital idea. But go to bed. Don't just fall asleep on the couch again.

FRANCES I find that bed slightly nauseating, I don't know why. Oh, yes. Your father slept in it.

MICHELLE Go sleep in mine, then.

FRANCES Yes. That's bound to be a much more wholesome experience. All right, then. Good night.

A pause. Rune gets up and looks inside. She nods to Michelle; the coast is clear.

MICHELLE Is she worse, lately?

RUNE That's a really interesting question. We should examine that.

MICHELLE Yeah, let's get right on that.

RUNE Yeah.

A pause.

MICHELLE Did I tell you?

RUNE What.

MICHELLE I got offered a job the other day. I forgot if I told you that.

RUNE No you didn't. Like a real job?

MICHELLE Oh, fuck, no. Bobby, that, you know, guy? From the gas station bathroom? Calls up and asks if I want to be the sous chef in his new restaurant.

RUNE What's a sous chef?

MICHELLE No idea. I ask him if he knows I've never cooked anything in my life. Says he doesn't care. Asks if he can come over and talk about it. I more or less say no. While he's on his way, I figure out he's married. Which he at first denies.

RUNE You're getting better.

MICHELLE   Yes I am. I can spot 'em a mile off, me. Anyway, we're having sex, which is kind of weird because his penis has a definite curve to the left.

RUNE   Really.

MICHELLE   Really. It's like he was constantly nudging me over toward the door. Like he was trying very subtly to get me out of the room.

RUNE   His left or your left?

MICHELLE   Well, darling, it depends which way I'm facing, doesn't it? At the end, I told him that based on his technique as a lover, I didn't think I'd want to ever eat at his restaurant. And so I wouldn't want to work there, either.

RUNE   You total bitch.

MICHELLE   I was trying. But he said he found my comments interesting. Said I had a head for marketing. Completely impervious to insult. In some ways, the perfect man. Well, no, you've got the perfect man.

RUNE   Christ. You think so?

MICHELLE   I suppose. If he dumps you, then he will absolutely become the perfect man. He will in retrospect become the perfect, mysterious guy who you let get away. It's how these things work. If he doesn't dump you, then you have God knows how long to figure out he's not the guy you thought he was. Time plus proximity equals, well, grossness. Time plus separation equals, uh, the opposite of grossness; whatever, you know, whatever that is. And if I'm going to continue to dispense wisdom, I need another fucking drink.

RUNE   Are you okay?

MICHELLE   I'm smashing, pumpkin. Why do you ask?

RUNE   Well, because in spite of its variety, your diet lately would seem to lack balance.

MICHELLE   That kind of thinking is at least ten years out of date. Nobody eats anymore. Nobody fucking eats.

RUNE   And are you, apart from the self-medicating, taking the actual prescribed stuff on a regular basis?

MICHELLE   Oh, sure. More or less. But the regimen is a little unrealistic. I mean, take one when you get up in the morning, take one when you go to bed, who has that rigid a schedule?

RUNE   Yes.

MICHELLE   For a while I tried to tie it into my peeing schedule, but then I found myself taking nine or ten a day. So far, I haven't been able to find anything I do consistently twice daily that I can use to remember to take the friggin' pills.

RUNE   What about fucking strange men?

MICHELLE   Hmm. You may have something there. So, you expect him later? The boy?

RUNE   I don't know. I have no idea what's in his head. I'm amazed I care at all.

MICHELLE   Well don't worry. It won't last. *(rising)* You want a beer?

RUNE   No. I'm gonna go for a swim before the perv with the telescope gets up.

MICHELLE   Oh yes, him. I've been meaning to introduce myself.

RUNE   Have you seen my shoes?

MICHELLE   No. Use mine.

> MICHELLE *goes indoors.* RUNE *picks up a pair of rotting running shoes nearby. She then goes around the side of the cottage, takes a towel off the line, and heads for the dock. After a beat,* FRANCES *emerges, still in what she wore to bed, with a plate of toast. She sits. A splash is heard.*

FRANCES   *(to the swimming RUNE)* Are you out there by yourself? Do you
            have your shoes on? Eh? Which one of you is that?!

MICHELLE   *(from within)* It's her. Stop shouting, for God's sake.

FRANCES   It's her. I see. She's out there by herself, you know.

            A pause.

            You children exhibited a thorough contempt for the buddy sys-
            tem from the moment we bought this place. It's as though you
            wanted to drown and leave me to explain it to the authorities.

            A pause. She eats.

            As though your existence revolved around getting me into
            trouble. Have I ever told you about how we came to own this
            cottage?

MICHELLE   *(still within)* I forget. Tell me the one about the car crash instead.

FRANCES   The car crash?

MICHELLE   The New Year's Eve car crash.

FRANCES   Oh. Oh, yes! Good Lord, how did you know about that?

MICHELLE   I forget how I found out about that incident. You were in a
            car crash?

FRANCES   New Year's Eve, your father a young man, our latest new car,
            a company car. There was a new one every two years.

MICHELLE   Yes.

FRANCES   It rained while we were at the party.

MICHELLE   It was hardly a party.

FRANCES   Well, it was hardly a party. It would be cruel to call it a party.
            It was a function. It was dry and efficient and bloodless, and

we agreed that "function" was the perfect way to describe it. Your father, in a thin tie, putting his hands on the women's asses; and me, wearing something ghastly and forcing my tongue down the throat of a martini glass to get at the olive. You girls, toddlers I suppose, or less, at home in bed.

And it rained. And then it froze. And we departed after midnight, and your father, attempting to hold me up as we slid downhill, slid further and further away from the car we were trying to get into and start up so as to be safe; your father fell down and cracked his pelvis. He didn't know it then. Cracked his pelvis in two places.

Tom enters. He stands, embarrassed, as she speaks.

And even then, he wouldn't let me drive his precious car. And so it was his inability to sit down properly in the driver's seat or even to use the pedals properly, owing to the severely broken pelvis, that made us sitting ducks, as it were, for the truck that slid through the intersection, coming straight for us. Well. Turning, lazily, like a curling rock, but still, straight for us.

TOM   Frances?

FRANCES   Oh. Tom.

TOM   Were you talking to someone?

FRANCES   You were here.

TOM   Yes, and—

FRANCES   And now you're back.

TOM   Yes.

FRANCES   Thank God. I thought I might have just imagined that you were here before. I was asleep, and then you were here.

TOM   I had the part on the truck.

FRANCES   You did.

A beat.

So you brought it.

TOM   That's right.

FRANCES   I see. Well. Hello. Tom.

A pause.

TOM   Listen, I—

MICHELLE walks out, drinking a beer and eating a carrot.

FRANCES   Oh, dear.

MICHELLE   Hey, Mr. Ilesic. Didn't you leave?

FRANCES   He did. And then he came back. He had the part, you see, on the truck.

MICHELLE   Right on.

FRANCES   And now he'll leave, and return in the morning to install it.

FRANCES smiles at TOM.

TOM   I guess so.

FRANCES   The mildly incompetent Tom Junior will be waiting.

TOM   Right. See you tomorrow morning.

FRANCES   Yes you will.

TOM leaves.

Excellent timing, as usual, dear. And do you know what I lost as a consequence of that car accident?

MICHELLE   No. Yes. Instincts. The way a person hit on the head loses their sense of smell.

FRANCES A whole raft of instincts. Instincts for useful life skills. I lost the ability to dress myself and, critically, others, in clothes that weren't filthy. I lost the ability to provide, I lost the ability to be careful. I lost the idea of moderation. I lost the idea that in spite of everything, you have to try. That you have to want to try.

I had no instincts left that might make me a person among people, and yet I forced myself to remain among people. I forced myself to assume a shape, as if assuming might make it real.

A pause.

MICHELLE And did it?

FRANCES Hmm? Oh, no dear. Not as such. I mean, ask your fucking father.

A pause.

You seem to have a problem, dear.

MICHELLE Have I?

FRANCES Well, haven't you?

MICHELLE No.

FRANCES Oh. Well. There you go. No instincts. I rest my handbag.

MICHELLE I am fucking pregnant.

FRANCES Oh, well.

MICHELLE Don't tell anybody.

FRANCES I can't imagine why I would, dear. Or who. But this is awful.

MICHELLE Well.

FRANCES You're woefully unqualified. If I may.

MICHELLE laughs.

The sort of thing I'd expect out of your sister. She's the amateur. Is this why you arranged to have us all up here? To tell us?

MICHELLE   You arranged for us all to be up here. You begged us for months.

FRANCES   I did not. I could not care in the least if you and your sister ever set foot on this property again.

MICHELLE   You said if we didn't come out here with you, you'd initiate legal proceedings.

FRANCES   No.

MICHELLE   You did.

FRANCES   No.

A pause.

Did I ever tell you about the time I was sued by Procter and Gamble?

MICHELLE   Do you have to?

They look each other in the eye.

FRANCES   You know I do. I will unpack my heart. I will divest myself of all this filth, and you can listen or not listen.

MICHELLE   Okay.

FRANCES   Your sister does not understand.

MICHELLE   Okay.

MICHELLE looks away and FRANCES resumes her normal tone.

FRANCES   One day, there was a knock at the door, and a man handed me papers outlining Procter and Gamble's lawsuit against me. This came completely out of the blue. To be sued by a large corporation: we all know it could happen—most of us believe it's only a matter of time—but I was absolutely shocked.

MICHELLE   Yes.

MICHELLE rises and goes inside.

FRANCES   I had to engage a lawyer, without your father's knowledge. Your father has a disgust for the legal profession that is now only rivalled by mine for him. Do you know, he drew up his will by hand? Literally? He found out that a handwritten will is perfectly legal, and this man who I used to have to hog-tie and beat senseless before he'd write a birthday card sat down and wrote out his entire will only so as to thwart our family lawyer.

Procter and Gamble had letters, they alleged. Letters from me. Threatening letters. From me! It was absurd!

MICHELLE re-enters with a fresh beer and a box of salt.

They produced one of these letters, gave it to my lawyer. Several closely typed pages, promising violence and accusing Procter and Gamble of a vast conspiracy. Rambling, lunatic verbiage. And then, there it was: my signature at the bottom.

RUNE enters, wrapped in a towel, her night clothes in her hand. She kicks off the running shoes. She sits and MICHELLE gives her the box of salt. During the following, RUNE pours salt on a good-sized leech that's attached to her calf.

I was aware, of course, of the horrifying things Procter and Gamble was doing. Good God, we all were. I mean, turn on the television. It was common knowledge: the animals they used, the gross financial abuses. The stunted babies. But to say that I was somehow motivated to sit down and write— *(of the leech)* Isn't that awful, dear.

RUNE pours more salt on the leech.

RUNE   No, not really.

They watch the leech for a few beats. She then pulls it off.

FRANCES   Where was I?

MICHELLE	You were—
RUNE	We don't know. Weren't you listening either?
FRANCES	I— No, I guess not. *(rising, to RUNE)* Your sister has some news. I forget what.

FRANCES goes inside.

MICHELLE	*(after a beat)* You have news? Can I guess?
RUNE	I don't.
MICHELLE	I bet I can guess.
RUNE	She said you have news.
MICHELLE	Is it about the job?
RUNE	No, I haven't decided about that. And she was talking about you.
MICHELLE	*(rising unsteadily)* You want a beer?
RUNE	No.
MICHELLE	Sure you do. You have to canoe later.

MICHELLE goes inside. RUNE pours more salt on the dying leech, now curling up on the step beside her. She empties the contents of the box on the leech. MATTHEW appears. He carries a travel coffee mug.

MATTHEW	Hi.
RUNE	Right.

A pause. Nobody moves.

MATTHEW	I hit the hole you have in the driveway.
RUNE	Road.

MATTHEW   I sort of left the car in there.

RUNE   Uh huh.

MATTHEW   I'm not sure it'll come out. I'm pretty sure I broke the floor. Pretty sure I cut my forehead on the steering wheel.

RUNE   Well, nice to see you.

MATTHEW   Nice to see you.

> *A pause. RUNE gets up, walks around the side of the cottage, takes off the towel, and puts on some clothes hanging on the line.*

So, anyway, this is it, huh? Man, I'm tired. I drove like all night it felt like.

> *A pause.*

RUNE   Take a swim.

MATTHEW   Yeah.

> *A pause.*

You know what?

RUNE   What.

MATTHEW   I think you should get married.

> *A pause.*

RUNE   What?

MATTHEW   *(simultaneous with above line)* Shit. I think we should get married. I think we should get married. We.

RUNE   Oh.

MATTHEW   Fuck. Ha ha. Nice. How long's the drive up here? Like four hours?

RUNE   Two and a bit.

MATTHEW   It's more like four if you get lost. Four hours practising that. Then I tell you to get married.

                RUNE, dressed, comes around the side of the cottage.

RUNE   Why.

MATTHEW   Yes. Well, it seems the right thing to do.

RUNE   How so.

MATTHEW   Well, I mean, have you ever felt like this before?

RUNE   Felt like what?

MATTHEW   Like this. You haven't. You haven't felt like this before.

RUNE   How do you know. Oh. I told you.

MATTHEW   You told me.

RUNE   Yes I did.

MATTHEW   Yes.

RUNE   But.

MATTHEW   Yes?

RUNE   But that doesn't mean anything.

MATTHEW   No?

RUNE   It's a thing to say. In that situation.

MATTHEW   It wasn't true?

RUNE   No, it was true. I didn't, I hadn't felt like that. That's true. But so what?

MATTHEW   But, so—

RUNE   Where were you yesterday?

MATTHEW   Yesterday?

RUNE   Fucking yes.

MATTHEW   In bed. Why?

RUNE   You were in bed yesterday?

MATTHEW   Yes. In it, or sitting, you know, on the edge, looking into my shoes. I also spent some time looking at the bed. From a distance. Why?

RUNE   You were supposed to be here yesterday.

MATTHEW   Yesterday?

RUNE   Yes. It's what we said.

MATTHEW   No.

RUNE   Yes.

MATTHEW   Well, not, no.

RUNE   Yes, you stupid— It was so embarrassing.

MATTHEW   What day is it?

RUNE   I waited all day. It was humiliating.

MATTHEW   You're lucky I didn't come up yesterday. I was a complete mess yesterday. I thought we were going to break up.

              A pause. She goes to him, kisses him. She then retreats to the other side of the stage again.

              It's nice out here.

RUNE   No it's not.

MATTHEW   No?

RUNE   But it's nice of you to say.

    A pause.

    I'm sorry. We should get married?

    She laughs. They laugh together.

MATTHEW I was thinking that, yes. It makes all kinds of sense. I mean, neither one of us seems to know what to want. I don't know what I'm doing in law school, you don't seem particularly passionate about whatever it is you're studying. I assume you still don't have a clue about whether or not to take this job?

RUNE   No.

MATTHEW No. You're completely ignorant about it. We share that. And into all this ignorance about what to want, about our futures, comes this. Prompting you to say things like "I've never felt this way before," which, okay, it's a thing to say, but also apparently true, and so, it has a great momentum behind it, that; and incidentally I was feeling that as you said it. By the way. I was feeling that too. You said it, and I thought: "Me too." Or, rather, "Me neither."

RUNE   You said, "That's sweet."

MATTHEW I know.

RUNE   "That's sweet."

MATTHEW I know.

RUNE   Me: "I've never felt this way before." You: "Oh, that's sweet."

MATTHEW I know. But I was thinking: "Me neither."

RUNE   You incredible jerk.

MATTHEW No, I know.

    A pause.

RUNE   So what if I don't know what I want to do with myself?

MATTHEW   Well, that's my point.

RUNE   Like, that's a reason? I tell people that when they ask why I
              got married?

MATTHEW   Of course not. You'll sound like an idiot.

RUNE   So—

MATTHEW   But you—

RUNE   Just because I don't know what I'm—

MATTHEW   Can I—?

RUNE   What?

MATTHEW   Can I? Because, look. Okay. I have, my parents, they stopped
              being a couple around 1979. '78 or '79. But before that, they
              were just... they had this thing about them, an awareness of
              each other, an understanding, a, a, a thing. And they were
              better as a team than they were as people. I didn't know that,
              I couldn't have told you that then, all I knew was they got
              each other's jokes. They had shorthand. They, worked. They
              worked. They made, as people, a more competent group than
              they did individuals. On their own, my father, driving all over
              the city, no sense of direction; my mother, yelling at the dry
              cleaner for something she'd later admit was probably her fault.
              Like separately, they weren't menaces or anything, that came
              later, but they were just better together.

              And I have this funny feeling that I will be too. And you seem,
              and there seems to be this, momentum, between us, and as
              far as I can tell, that qualifies us for what they had.

RUNE   Your parents can't stand each other now.

MATTHEW   Well, yes. Try not to focus on that part.

              A pause.

RUNE   What will we do?

MATTHEW   Well, you know.

              A pause.

RUNE   If I say yes, do you know why?

MATTHEW   Do I know why you'd say yes? 'Cause it's a helluvan idea, and—

RUNE   No, shut up. Because the morning after we, uh, met, we were
              sitting outside on a bench and I had to go to I don't know,
              Western Religions or friggin' Classical Survey or something,
              and I was talking about my sister, complaining about her, and
              I could tell you stopped listening. And I thought, fuckin' guy,
              gets what he wants, one night in bed, and he stops listening.
              And then you said: "You're very well lit."

              A pause.

MATTHEW   Well, you are.

RUNE   And I went: "Hey. Wait a minute."

              A pause.

              You seem so certain.

MATTHEW   I know.

RUNE   It's kinda fuckin' disgusting.

MATTHEW   Don't worry. It won't last.

              A pause.

RUNE   I feel like it, okay? And I, and you seem to be making very ex-
              cellent points. You've clearly had a lot of time to...

              And I feel like it. I feel it, too. I do. It's not just something to
              say. And so, I think, say yes, and I do in my head, and then I
              go: what's the problem?

MATTHEW   What are you, like scared?

RUNE   Well, sure. Of course. Jesus Christ, Matthew.

MATTHEW   But that's good, probably.

RUNE   But that's not it. That's not the problem. The problem, the problem is...

MATTHEW   You don't have to decide now.

RUNE   No, it's... I don't know who I'd be. I don't know who I'd be.

MATTHEW   You'd be...

RUNE   I mean, I'm nothing now.

MATTHEW   No. No, you're not nothing.

RUNE   Well, yes.

MATTHEW   What a thing to say.

RUNE   I don't mind. I mean, I assume I won't always be nothing. But that's why the idea of this seems—

MATTHEW   Seems.

RUNE   I'm just, I'm not qualified to be making any decisions right now.

MATTHEW   You don't have to decide now.

RUNE   I just did.

MATTHEW   No, you didn't.

RUNE   Yes I did. I love you so much.

MATTHEW   You what?

RUNE   I do. I love you so much.

MATTHEW   ...But.

RUNE   Yes.

                A pause.

MATTHEW   I don't understand. You love me so much.

RUNE   I don't, I just, I can't—

MATTHEW   No, I don't want to understand. Don't, like, stand there and explain it.

                A pause.

                Well. So. I'm gonna go sit on the... *(motions toward the dock)*

RUNE   The dock?

MATTHEW   The, yes.

RUNE   Okay. Did you bring a suit?

MATTHEW   I don't know. Did I bring a suit. Um. Against who?

RUNE   No, I mean—

MATTHEW   Oh. Right. Did I— No. Not really. So. But.

RUNE   Okay. You have to go that way *(indicates off right)* for the path. To get down there. *(indicates the water ahead of them)* Sorry.

                He wanders off. A pause. He charges back on again.

MATTHEW   My feeling is, if you are nothing, you don't wait to become something, and then do things as that person. You do things, and then you go: "I'm not nothing, I'm the person that did those things." Otherwise, you stand around for like a fuck of a long time doing nothing.

RUNE   I don't know.

                A pause.

MATTHEW   Are you sure?

RUNE   Of course I'm not sure. What kind of a question is that?

MATTHEW   Yes. Sorry.

RUNE   I mean, fuck.

MATTHEW   Yes.

RUNE   I mean—Matthew?

MATTHEW   Yes?

RUNE   Maybe we...

MATTHEW   Yes?

> *A longish pause. Finally, FRANCES enters, sees his mug.*

FRANCES   Is that coffee?!

RUNE   *(to MATTHEW)* No.

MATTHEW   No. Okay. *(to FRANCES)* Hi. No. I'm all out.

FRANCES   Weren't you supposed to be here yesterday?

MATTHEW   I'm gonna go down and sit on the... thing.

> *He wants to leave, is confused about which way to go.*

RUNE   *(indicating the path)* That way. Sorry.

> MATTHEW *leaves.*

FRANCES   What was his name again?

> *A pause.*

Did your sister tell you her news?

> *A pause.*

I think your sister could use someone to talk to.

RUNE	So talk to her.
FRANCES	Darling. I don't talk to people. Do you really think I was too abrupt with Tom Ilesic?
RUNE	I don't know. I don't know anything.
FRANCES	I know, but I was asking for some speculation. I was actually asking you to pull your head out of your twenty-year-old ass and give me a fucking opinion. I don't want you to tell me facts, I don't want you to carve out a plan of action regarding this man, I don't want anything concrete from you, I just want to talk about it. He came back, did you know that? He did. Why would he do that? I want to blather away about it, as is our way, and in the end I suppose I want to figure out, using the most loopy, roundabout methods available, why it is that even though I have no interest in this man, none at all, he suddenly became interesting to me when he showed some interest in me. I guess I want to run all over that a few times and see how flat I can get it, as it were. I also want, I suppose, to know how a man can seem interested in such an awful, exhausting old woman.

RUNE gets up, hugs her mother.

RUNE	Maybe he's going deaf.
FRANCES	You know, I don't know anything. I don't know anything. How did I get this way? How do you get to be this age and not know anything? Did I know things? Was I a person? How did I get along? Did I ever know how to see other people? Was it your father? Did I do something to your father? Did he do something to me?
RUNE	*(adding to her list of questions)* Do you want to have a nap?
FRANCES	Is there still no coffee?
RUNE	Do you smell any coffee?
FRANCES	There still not being coffee is a sign of contempt, you know. For your mother.

RUNE   That's exactly right, sweetie.

            FRANCES rises.

FRANCES   I'm going to lie down. Oh. Your sister's pregnant. Help her.

            FRANCES goes inside. As she does:

            Michelle! Get out here! Your sister has something to tell you.

            *RUNE takes several steps away from the cottage, looking toward
            the dock. MICHELLE plunges out the door, misjudging the step
            down to the porch. She's scrutinizing several pills in her hand.*

MICHELLE   The fuck is that one? Can you identify it?

            RUNE goes to her.

RUNE   Is that ecstasy?

MICHELLE   Fuck that.

            MICHELLE tosses the pill away. While it's still in the air:

            No!

            *MICHELLE follows the pill, which has landed in a bush. She
            begins to look for it.*

RUNE   Mother says you told her you're pregnant.

MICHELLE   Do you know why she told you that?

RUNE   No.

MICHELLE   Because she has a big, cavernous, needy fucking mouth.

RUNE   Yes.

MICHELLE   And she doesn't understand the notion of confidence. Of when
            she's being taken into a confidence. No idea how to be of any
            use at all, how to try to be of use to a person, and really no

idea at all *(She has turned and yells briefly at the cottage.)* HOW TO MAKE AN EFFORT.

A pause. MICHELLE *looks for the pill.*

RUNE   Is it true?

A pause. MICHELLE *finds the pill, regards it.*

MICHELLE   Yes.

MICHELLE swallows the ecstasy.

RUNE   What are you going to do?

MICHELLE   Well. I'm going to take everything I can get my hands on over the next few months, by way of introduction. And then, if it still wants to come out, I'll have a thing. A baby.

A pause.

Then I'll be the mother. Who the fuck is that?

RUNE   It's Matt. He showed up.

MICHELLE   It's Matt? The Matt?

RUNE   He proposed.

MICHELLE   To you?

RUNE   Yes.

MICHELLE   Well... what did you say?

RUNE   I don't know.

A pause. From the dock MATTHEW *cries "Aw, Jesus!"*

MICHELLE   He proposed marriage?

RUNE   Yes.

MICHELLE   Nobody proposes marriage. Huh. Nice move. Uh oh. Here he comes. Just act natural.

                MICHELLE rises, moves about aimlessly, settles. MATTHEW enters, pants rolled up, shoes off, with a leech attached to a leg. To RUNE:

MATTHEW   I didn't even go in. I didn't even touch the bottom. I was just sitting there, you know, dangling over the side, and it found me. Latched onto me. I... can you get it off? I'm, I can't look at it. I'm gonna puke.

                He sits.

RUNE   Okay. Just a sec. I'll get some salt.

                RUNE goes inside. MICHELLE moves into MATTHEW's view.

MATTHEW   Oh. Hi.

MICHELLE   I'm pregnant.

                A pause.

MATTHEW   Oh no.

                A pause.

MICHELLE   Really, any response you might have had would seem inadequate, but that one was really, don't you think?

MATTHEW   I'm sorry. I... what are you going to do?

MICHELLE   Nothing.

MATTHEW   Nothing?

MICHELLE   No. Nothing.

                A pause.

MATTHEW   What do you mean when you say "nothing," because I don't know if I—

MICHELLE   No. It's done. I wanted to tell you and see what you would have to say, but really, you can consider the whole thing over. Terminated.

MATTHEW   Terminated?

MICHELLE   Yes. Terminated. As far as you, Matthew Somethingsomething, are concerned. I terminated it.

MATTHEW   Oh. Michelle. Oh.

MICHELLE   Sorry to have brought it up. Thank you for being so clear. You proposed to her?

MATTHEW   Michelle.

MICHELLE   You proposed to my sister. It's sweet. You're the guy who's sweet.

MATTHEW   Michelle, listen—

MICHELLE   You have to shut up now.

                RUNE enters with a box of matches.

RUNE   We're out of salt. But we can burn it off. Hold still.

                RUNE strikes a match and MATTHEW offers his leg. He looks away. Unfortunately, MICHELLE is in his field of vision when he does so and they lock eyes. A pause. MATTHEW flinches, moves his leg, and is burned.

MATTHEW   Ah! Crap!

RUNE   Sorry, sorry!

FRANCES   *(from inside)* What's happening?

RUNE   Sorry!

FRANCES   *(from inside)* What's going on? I was still asleep!

RUNE   Hold still.

Matthew	Sorry. Sorry.
Michelle	You'd better hold still. You'd better not, you know, move, mister. She's got you now.

Rune strikes another match, slowly approaches Matthew's leg. Frances appears at the screen door.

Frances	what's going on?!
Rune	Nothing. Be quiet. Jesus.
Frances	i will not be quiet. don't you tell me to be quiet. i was asleep.
Michelle	Mother—
Frances	I don't know if you know just how startling it is to be asleep and then violently startled awake. You people shout constantly, you make noise above me just when you think I don't know who it will be. You do it on purpose. You do it on purpose! You—
Michelle	—do it on purpose. All right. It's clear, okay? You're being quite clear. You just woke up, okay? You're awake now. It's okay. You can go back to bed now. Go back to bed.
Frances	I can't sleep. What's going on here?

Frances comes outside.

Rune	*(to Matthew)* Hold still.
Frances	Who is this?
Matthew	Hello, Mrs. Arlidge.
Frances	I thought I said no visitors? I thought I said no people?
Matthew	Sorry, I just, um, ow!

The match burns Rune and she drops it.

Rune	Fuck.

FRANCES	All I wanted was to not have to worry about people. I wanted time for the three of us. I wanted the three of us to be together. I wanted—
MICHELLE	Mother.
FRANCES	I wanted to have you here. I wanted to have you, just us. I told you that.
MICHELLE	It's okay.
FRANCES	No, it's not okay. I told her what I wanted, I told you both. But she never sees it. She's so busy with her, her life that she makes no allowances for me or for us. You know it's true.
RUNE	*(removing the leech)* Got it.
MICHELLE	Mother.
FRANCES	She's an awful person. She used to be so loving, she used to be a sweet little kid, and now, she's become this thing nobody recognizes. *(wheels on RUNE)* It's true. You used to be so helpful and sweet and all the time we worried about her, we knew you'd never do anything as awful as her. You were the one. What happened? What happened to you? Answer me! I'm going to die, do you know that? Answer me!
RUNE	*(to MATTHEW)* You should go.
MATTHEW	Okay, yes.
FRANCES	Don't you see what you were? Don't you see what we wanted? How can you do that? How can you do that? Why can't you help anyone? It's, you're infuriating me! Why do you do that?
RUNE	I'm coming too.
MATTHEW	Okay.
FRANCES	You what? Oh, no you're not, young lady. You've got a fucking canoe to paddle.
RUNE	I'm ready now.

MATTHEW   Oh? Okay.

FRANCES   You have always been the most selfish, awful child. You're needed. Don't you see you're needed here? I'm going to die. Your sister needs you. Your sister.

MICHELLE   MOTHER.

MATTHEW   What about your stuff?

RUNE   I'm ready now.

FRANCES   Did you hear me? I'm going to—

RUNE   NO YOU'RE NOT.

> RUNE *rises and walks off.* MATTHEW *rises.*

FRANCES   Where does she think she's going?

MICHELLE   Get the fuck out of here.

MATTHEW   Michelle, let me—

MICHELLE   No! You have to leave me alone.

> MATTHEW *exits.*

FRANCES   That's right. You're not the only one with needs. I'm not the only one with needs. What about her? Hey? RUNE? HELP YOUR SISTER. RUNE: WHY DON'T YOU HELP YOUR SISTER?

> *A pause.*

What time is it? What's that smell? What got burned?

> *Blackout.*

ACT TWO

*The same, ten years later. The cottage has slid a foot to the
left. Paint has peeled, foliage has encroached. Mid-afternoon,
the height of summer. FRANCES sits in her seat on the porch,
in loose clothing. A series of strokes have left her nearly im-
mobile and without speech. She weeps freely throughout the
act and will grunt at points but never speak. The lights snap
up and we see HARVAR, thirty-eight, wearing only a Speedo.
He has the makings of a pot-belly, red hair, and is suntan
oily. He holds two hot dogs and is offering one to LILLIAN, ten.*

HARVAR   Want one?

LILLIAN   What are they?

HARVAR   What do you mean, what are they. It's a hot dog. Do you want
it or not?

LILLIAN   What will you do if I say no?

HARVAR   What do you mean what will I do. I'll eat it.

LILLIAN   No, the other one.

HARVAR   I'll eat it, too. Do you want it?

LILLIAN   You'll eat both?

HARVAR   Do you want one or not?

LILLIAN   No way. I want to see you eat both.

HARVAR   Okay. Suit yourself. Where was I?

LILLIAN   The guy with the beard?

HARVAR .   Oh yeah. So, I'm sitting there, and he's talking away, and
the bartender is bringing us drinks, without our asking for
them, they just come from like out of nowhere, and I'm like:
"Great," and then a couple of hours later, the guy's girlfriend
comes in. Dressed just like him. You know, vest, tattoos,

leather chaps and the whole bit. And she is hot. She's like stripper hot. And suddenly I go: "Holy shit. They aren't motorcycle enthusiasts. They're like bikers!" I been drinking for four hours with a biker! I threw a rock at a biker, and I picked a fight with a biker, and now I'm sitting drinking with a biker and his girlfriend.

LILLIAN   No way.

HARVAR   I shit you not.

LILLIAN   What's a biker?

HARVAR   What? How old are you.

LILLIAN   Nearly ten. I have a bike.

HARVAR   No no no. Bikers ride motorcycles and they control all the criminal activity in Quebec and also here. They sell drugs and push people around and that sort of thing. They like kill people.

LILLIAN   They kill people?

HARVAR   They totally kill people. They mostly try to kill other bikers, but sometimes the general public gets in the way and then they get killed, too.

LILLIAN   Okay.

HARVAR   So, I'm sitting there, right? And suddenly I'm going over the whole afternoon in my head, trying to figure out if there's anything I said that would make a biker mad. Like, I kind of told him some things, you know how you do, when you're sitting in a bar with a stranger and you get talking, not necessarily all the things that come out of your mouth are completely true?

LILLIAN   Right.

HARVAR   So, I'm talking away, and I'm drinking, and I'm thinking about what I've already said, and I'm trying to think if I'm getting myself into more trouble here, I mean, I already picked a fight with the guy, and I threw a rock at him, and so maybe he's just filling time drinking with me, you know, pretending to be nice, while actually he's going to kill me for throwing a rock at him. So my brain is suddenly working like really hard, I'm sweating and trying to talk away to the guy in a calm, friendly way, and all of a sudden, I feel something against my leg.

LILLIAN   What.

HARVAR   Exactly. That's what I'd like to know. It's rubbing up and down against my leg, under the table. And then a guy comes up to talk to the biker guy, and while he's distracted, the girlfriend winks at me.

LILLIAN   She winks at you?

HARVAR   The biker's girlfriend like totally winks at me. I shit you not.

LILLIAN   Like this?

          LILLIAN tries to wink.

HARVAR   Sort of. And I. Freak. Out.

LILLIAN   I bet.

HARVAR   Do you know how dead I'd be if the guy finds out his girl-friend has the hots for me? But, also, I'm a little drunk too, so I think: "Hey. Maybe this is something I can actually get away with. Maybe I can get it on with the biker chick and the boyfriend will never know." Like, that's how drunk I am. By the way, this is way before I met your aunt, okay?

LILLIAN   Okay.

HARVAR   We had not even met yet, okay?

LILLIAN   Okay.

HARVAR   Okay. So she's rubbing up against me and she's showing me her tattoos, and then the guy goes to the bathroom. And she leans toward me, real close, and I lean in too, and I notice she's got a lot of makeup on, right? And then I look at her throat, and I notice she's got like an adam's apple, except it's covered with lots of makeup, right? But I'm so drunk I don't really get what I'm seeing, right? So—

LILLIAN   Eat the other one.

HARVAR   What? Oh, no, I don't want it.

LILLIAN   You said you would.

HARVAR   No, five's my limit. Here.

LILLIAN   I can't eat it.

HARVAR   Go ahead. You must be starved. All you do is swim all day.

LILLIAN   Okay.

>   LILLIAN *takes the hot dog.*

HARVAR   So, where was I?

LILLIAN   I don't know.

HARVAR   Oh, yeah, so the girlfriend is rubbing all over me, looking at me, the whole bit, and suddenly—

MICHELLE   *(from inside the cottage)* Lillian!

>   MICHELLE *comes out onto the porch. She has white, creased pants on, and shoes inappropriate for a cottage. As she speaks, she rests a hand on* FRANCES's *shoulder.*

What is that?

LILLIAN   He gave it to me.

MICHELLE   You know you can't eat that. Good God, Harvar, she can't eat that.

HARVAR   No, it's okay. I'm full.

MICHELLE   Give me that.

LILLIAN gives MICHELLE the hot dog, which MICHELLE holds behind her back for the rest of her time on the porch.

Your lunch will be ready at one o'clock, young lady.

LILLIAN   Okay.

MICHELLE   Are you hungry now? Do you want a carrot?

LILLIAN   No.

MICHELLE   *(to HARVAR)* Is she bothering you?

HARVAR   No. Not really. Where's Rune?

MICHELLE   Don't bother the adults, darling. Don't you feel like swimming?

LILLIAN   No.

MICHELLE   Well, don't bother the adults. *(She leans over FRANCES.)* Mother? Do you want anything?

        FRANCES grimaces.

Where's your hat?

        FRANCES grunts with displeasure and MICHELLE finds the straw hat and puts it on her head.

There you go. I'll bring you something to eat in a minute.

HARVAR   Hey, Michelle?

MICHELLE   Yes?

HARVAR   Where's Rune?

MICHELLE   We're doing the family accounts.

HARVAR   So, what, she's inside?

MICHELLE   Yes.

HARVAR   Okay.

MICHELLE   Did you want her?

HARVAR   No, I just, I thought I lost her there for a second. Okay.

MICHELLE   *(to LILLIAN)* Come inside for a carrot.

LILLIAN   Okay.

HARVAR   Michelle, what are you going to do with that hot dog?

MICHELLE   Do you want it?

HARVAR   Do you want it?

> *A beat. She hands him the hot dog and goes inside. HARVAR takes a bite of the second hot dog and then puts it down.*

Hand me those sunglasses, okay?

> *LILLIAN gets the sunglasses. As she does so, she walks past FRANCES. She removes FRANCES's hat and throws it on the ground. She delivers the sunglasses.*

LILLIAN   These are cool.

HARVAR   Those are John Cusack's business manager's sunglasses. He left them in the back of my car.

LILLIAN   Cool.

> *A pause. HARVAR has reclined.*

So, what about the guy with the beard?

HARVAR   *(without sitting up)* Hmm? Oh, it was a real mess. It went on and on, for like thirty-six hours. Ended in a motel room in Hull. I'll tell you sometime.

MICHELLE   *(from the cottage)* Lillian!

LILLIAN   Coming!

Lillian rises immediately and exits toward the water instead. A pause. Frances watches Harvar closely. Rune comes out of the cottage. She is brittle and slightly nervous. She manages to ignore Frances utterly. She goes to Harvar, stands over him.

HARVAR Hey!

RUNE Hi. How are you?

HARVAR I'm fantastic. How are you?

Harvar gets up and kisses Rune.

RUNE Tremendous. Do you want a beer?

HARVAR Of course I want a beer. Did you bring me a beer?

RUNE No, but I can.

HARVAR Or, I can get it.

RUNE No, I'll get it. I should have brought one with me.

HARVAR Why? I've got two legs.

RUNE I know, but I brought it up.

HARVAR No, it's, really, it's okay. I'll get it. Sit down. How's it going in there?

RUNE It's wonderful fun. Bank accounts with six dollars each in them scattered around the city. That sort of thing.

HARVAR It's like that show.

RUNE What show.

HARVAR The one where the people go all over town to get things like, you know, six dollars out of a bank account. It's a race.

RUNE You're kidding.

HARVAR   You've seen it. It's hosted by that guy, what's his name, I had him in my car once...

RUNE   It's hosted by John Travolta?

HARVAR   No, not John Travolta. Never mind. Do you want a hot dog, sweetie?

RUNE   Hmm. No thanks.

HARVAR   You got to get a barbecue up here.

RUNE   It's true.

HARVAR   And a, like a hammock for between those two trees.

RUNE   Yes.

HARVAR   And a jet ski.

RUNE   Oh yeah. And a functioning toilet.

HARVAR   Oh, yeah. I was gonna fix that.

RUNE   No, it's okay. Someone's going to come later and do it.

HARVAR   But I said I would.

RUNE   I know. Nobody took you seriously. It's okay. Don't tell Lillian the biker story, okay?

HARVAR   I wasn't.

RUNE   Yeah, you were.

HARVAR   Well, she makes me nervous. She's a weird little kid.

RUNE   Yes.

HARVAR   I feel like I have to keep talking or she'll do something.

           A pause.

RUNE   I spoke to your mother yesterday. About the wedding.

HARVAR   Jesus Christ. I'm sorry.

RUNE   She either wants to invite seven more people, or seventeen. I couldn't figure it out due to the tick Norwegian ec-cent.

HARVAR   I don't believe this. I'm sorry. I'll get on the phone and bitchslap her.

RUNE   No, it's okay.

HARVAR   No, she's got to shut up about the wedding. Honest to God. Could she be any more Jewish? I'll call her, tell her to shut her piehole. Gawd.

RUNE   I actually like talking to your mother.

HARVAR   Yes. You're very polite to her. You're like the first one of my girlfriends she can stand for more than five minutes. I think she likes you more than she likes me. Lucky fucking you.

RUNE   Your mother is funny. She's not that bad.

HARVAR   Yeah, well, try telling her you're dropping out of high school to sell drugs full time, and then see how you like her. It doesn't matter that I only did that for a few years. And never got caught, I might add. As far as Elva's concerned, I'm a career Colombian drug lord for life. Good thing I found me a girl with a respectable job.

RUNE   It's actually not all that respectable.

HARVAR   Sure it is. Telling people what you think, week after week. This guy's great because he like built a shelter for the homeless, this guy's an asshole 'cause he's fucking up the environment; believe this, don't believe that. Newspapers are great. Even the little hippie ones, like yours.

RUNE   Not that you read them.

HARVAR   Fuck no. But still, it's like a total public service, telling people what to think.

RUNE   Not everyone considers it a public service. You know the mail I get.

HARVAR   You still getting the ones where people tell you and your commie friends to burn in the piss rivers of damnation? I love those.

RUNE   I had one from a guy who was so incensed about my views on same-sex marriage that he wanted to violate me anally.

HARVAR   Already? I just put that in the mail like Tuesday.

RUNE   I didn't know you wanted to violate me anally.

HARVAR   Well, I don't know. I probably do. What exactly does violate mean again?

RUNE   What did you do with that dictionary I gave you?

HARVAR   I sold it. That was a dictionary?

RUNE   Oh my God.

HARVAR   Oh my God. Rune Arlidge.

     A pause.

RUNE   Listen, Harvar...

HARVAR   Oh, fuck. Yes?

RUNE   Can we talk about your bachelor party?

HARVAR   What. We're not going to do anything.

     MICHELLE *comes outside with a carrot.*

MICHELLE   Lillian! Lillian! Do you think I peeled this for my health? *(to* RUNE *and* HARVAR*)* Honest to God.

LILLIAN   *(from off)* Okay.

HARVAR   What's that you're playing with there, Michelle? Made a new friend?

MICHELLE   Look, stop telling my daughter biker stories, okay?

HARVAR   She started it.

MICHELLE   Did she.

HARVAR   Yeah. She said, "Mommy loves the part where you cold-cock the biker chick with the bag of frozen peas."

MICHELLE   I do not.

HARVAR   You love it. You know you do. *(rises)* I'm getting a beer. Anyone else?

MICHELLE   No thank you.

RUNE   No.

HARVAR   *(yelling)* Lilly! You want a beer?

LILLIAN   *(from off)* What?

HARVAR   Do! You! Want!—

MICHELLE   Never mind!

HARVAR goes indoors.

RUNE   You could be nicer to him.

MICHELLE   No, I could not.

MICHELLE puts FRANCES's hat back on.

Are you okay? Do you want to go inside?

FRANCES grunts in the negative.

Do you want to go to sleep?

FRANCES grunts.

Don't tell me to fuck myself. I'm the only one in this family who pays any attention to you.

Frances grunts.

Oh, yes it is. It's absolutely true. You know it's true. Do you want to have a nap or not?

Frances grunts again, struggles to rise. Michelle helps her. When Michelle is close enough, Frances grabs her hair and pulls. Michelle screams. Frances won't let go. Rune ignores the event. Harvar runs outside.

HARVAR   Jesus! Leave the old lady alone!

MICHELLE   She pulled my hair!

HARVAR   I was talking to your mother.

Frances! Come inside. Here we go. I have some delicious crystal meth I want you to try. That's it. Right this way. Just ignore those horrible daughters of yours. What the hell did you do to deserve children like these, anyway? You kill somebody?

Frances and Harvar go inside.

MICHELLE   God. I don't know why I—I swear to God, that's it. I can't handle her anymore. I never could handle her.

RUNE   No.

MICHELLE   She was never the least bit appreciative, and now she's becoming violent.

RUNE   Yes.

MICHELLE   What the hell are we going to do about her?

Rune will not respond. There is a pause.

Can I ask you something? It's gonna sound weird.

RUNE   Is it about her?

MICHELLE	No.

RUNE	Okay.

MICHELLE   It's a feeling I have. You know how Lilly has been a sort of awful child since birth?

RUNE   No.

MICHELLE   Yes you do. She has. She doesn't listen, and she's willful, and it's just on and on with her. You don't know. You never see it. That's what I want to talk to you about. She's that way, all the time, except when anyone else is around. She's awful. She is. Unless somebody other than me is there to see it. We can scream and scream at each other for hours, and as soon as the door opens and someone walks in, she's sweet as can be.

RUNE   Yes, you've told me this.

MICHELLE   I know. I know you don't believe me. But listen, and just tell me if this sounds paranoid—

RUNE   Yes, it does.

MICHELLE   Just listen. I think it's not that she remembers how to be a decent human being when other people show up, I think she does it on purpose. I think she might be doing it on purpose. And if that's true, then do you know what that means?

RUNE   What does it mean.

MICHELLE   It means she's worse than a bad kid. It means she's actually, like, evil. She has evil intent against me. I know how that sounds.

RUNE   You don't know how that sounds or you wouldn't say it.

MICHELLE   I know. I know. And yet, I can't shake the feeling that she's actually doing something here, something long-term and, well, evil. And I'm the only one who sees it.

RUNE   Michelle.

MICHELLE   Okay, okay. Fine. Forget it. Forget I said anything. I'm just the crazy lady with the totally sweet daughter.

RUNE   Do you want her to come and stay with me for a while?

MICHELLE   Look, it's bad enough I don't have anyone to talk to in this family, you don't need to compound things by taking my daughter away.

RUNE   No one's trying to—

MICHELLE   Thanks very much. I mean, fuck. I try and try and I get no help with any of it. I couldn't be more alone. You know? I could not be more alone. Never mind.

> *MICHELLE rises. LILLIAN enters, wet from swimming and wrapped in a towel. She's also wearing old, beat-up running shoes that are soaking wet.*

(hands her the carrot) Here.

LILLIAN   Thanks for the carrot.

RUNE   *(rising)* Lilly, just stay put, okay? Eat the carrot and just stay there.

LILLIAN   What's wrong?

RUNE   It's okay. There's a leech on your leg. Wait here.

MICHELLE   Oh my God!

> *MICHELLE grabs LILLIAN's head and holds it to her to keep her from looking down. LILLIAN eats the carrot. RUNE goes inside.*

It's okay. It's okay, Lilly.

LILLIAN   I know.

MICHELLE   Don't look down.

LILLIAN   Can I ask you something?

MICHELLE   What is it, Lilly?

LILLIAN   You aren't going to try for Harvar, are you?

> *A beat. MICHELLE is stunned by this. After a moment, the door busts open, HARVAR and RUNE come out, RUNE with salt.*

HARVAR   Let me see. Oh crap! That is like the most disgusting thing I've ever seen. Lilly, it looks like a big, black tit is sucking all the blood out of your system. That's exactly what it looks like, a huge black blobby tit that's getting fatter and fatter on the blood of a little girl. Has she passed out yet?

LILLIAN   Yes!

HARVAR   I am seriously going to be sick. That's disgusting. Oh my God. How much blood loss can a girl sustain before she dies, I wonder? How much do you weigh?

LILLIAN   I weigh eighty-eight pounds.

HARVAR   Not anymore you don't. This reminds me of a girl I knew, growing up in Oslo, and she—

RUNE   You grew up in Scarborough.

HARVAR   And this girl, Priscilla her name was, she went swimming in a fjord and she had just gotten her period for the first time and the leeches were just—

> *LILLIAN screams, RUNE and MICHELLE yell "Shut up!"*

I know! Gross, eh? Oh, well. It was nice knowing you, sweetie.

> *HARVAR returns inside.*

MICHELLE   Honest to God.

RUNE   I know. Very matoor.

HARVAR   *(from inside)* I heard that! Whatever it means.

RUNE   Here we go.

                The leech falls off. MICHELLE wipes away a bit of blood remaining. LILLIAN removes the sneakers.

MICHELLE   Go get changed now. I'll make your lunch.

                LILLIAN goes indoors.

                Look, forget I said anything, okay? I didn't mean it.

RUNE   Okay. I'm sorry. Nobody thinks you're nuts.

MICHELLE   Yeah, right. Will you come in and deal with mother while I get lunch?

RUNE   Michelle, I have to—

MICHELLE   Please.

                MICHELLE goes inside. RUNE hesitates, then sits down. HARVAR comes out, wearing a T-shirt and drinking a beer.

HARVAR   Hey.

RUNE   Hey.

                HARVAR sits beside RUNE, kisses her.

HARVAR   Oh, crap. You want a beer?

RUNE   No.

HARVAR   Here. Take this one. I'll get another.

RUNE   No, it's okay, I don't want one.

HARVAR   Sorry. Sometimes I'm a pig.

                A pause.

                I got burnt.

RUNE	You did?

HARVAR lifts his shirt.

HARVAR	Look at this. You've got to tell me, you know. You've got to make sure I don't spend too long in the sun. It's a wife's job, you know.
RUNE	Is it.
HARVAR	Absolutely.
RUNE	Well, I'm not your wife yet, mister.
HARVAR	And my job is to tell you that you don't look fat in your new pants.
RUNE	I see.

A pause.

HARVAR	Everything okay?
RUNE	Hmm? Yes.
HARVAR	Is it the bachelor party? I swear to God, it's just going to be beer and poker. And dancers. That's all. No hookers. Some hookers might come, okay, because they're my clients, but just as guests. I swear to God. And I won't let Andy or PJ or Bishy or any of those guys get outta hand, okay? No matter how drunk we get, I won't let them talk me into anything stupid, okay? Okay?
RUNE	It's okay.
HARVAR	No it's not. It bothers you. I thought I'd finally found someone that wouldn't be bothered by this kind of shit, but it looks like not. Ah well, what the fuck. Why should I be the first guy in history?
RUNE	Really, I don't mind. I'd prefer it didn't happen the night before the rehearsal, that's all.

HARVAR But, there's nothing I can do about that.

RUNE I know, I know.

HARVAR Look, either you trust me or you don't.

RUNE That's the stupidest thing you've said in a while.

HARVAR What?

RUNE Nothing.

HARVAR Did you just call me stupid?

RUNE No. No. I just said that that was a stupid thing to say. Trust comes and goes, it's there or not there, you know, it's untrustworthy. It's an idea. It's not a fact.

 HARVAR has risen; he's suddenly upset.

HARVAR *(He drops his voice.)* Look, okay? I want to say—I know who I am in this, okay? I know that I'm the stupid one in this relationship. I know that. But you can't use stupid on me like that.

RUNE What's wrong?

HARVAR I just, I have the feeling that the way we work is if neither of us notices that there's this huge difference between us. I mean, if I was like a fat fucking pig, and you were just normal-sized, you could never, ever call me fat, you know? So...

RUNE Okay.

HARVAR Do you know what I mean?

RUNE Sort of. Okay. I'm sorry.

HARVAR Okay.

 He sits down again.

 You can call me fucking fatty as much as you want, by the way.

RUNE   Great.

HARVAR   Unless I get fat.

RUNE   Right.

            A pause.

HARVAR   Um. Hey. Do you know who Don McKellar is?

RUNE   Sort of.

HARVAR   Did I ever tell you about the time Don McKellar held me up at gunpoint?

RUNE   I don't think so.

HARVAR   Film festival, three or four years ago. I'm working eighteen, twenty hours a day for like three weeks. Last night of the festival, I'm so tired I can't even see straight, I mean, I've been eating bennies for days but still, and I'm parked in front of like Roy Thomson Hall, and Don McKellar gets into my car and starts screaming at me, right? "Drive! Drive, motherfucker, drive!" And, like, it's not his car, right? I'm there waiting for whatshisname, the guy from TV, the chunky guy, the bald guy?

RUNE   Uh huh.

HARVAR   You know who I mean?

RUNE   Sure.

HARVAR   So I say: "Look, man, I'm sorry, but I'm not your ride, okay dude?" And Don McKellar starts to cry. Honest to God starts to cry in the back of my car. So I go: "Hey, it's okay there, little buddy, just sit there, take as long as you like, get your shit together." And he sits there, and gets himself together, and he's about to go, and then he starts crying again. So then—

RUNE   Harvar.

HARVAR   Yes?

RUNE	You don't have to entertain me, you know.
HARVAR	No, I know. Okay. Thanks. So then he's like: "Okay, sorry, whatever," and he gets out of the car. But then he jumps into the front seat and pulls out a gun, and I have to drive him to like Burlington. And he's all—
RUNE	Harvar?
HARVAR	Rune Arlidge?
RUNE	Why do you want this?

A pause.

HARVAR	Well, um, shit. I don't know. I guess because you're fantastic. And you love me. And I'm like thirty-eight.
RUNE	Okay.
HARVAR	Okay?
RUNE	Okay.

A pause.

HARVAR	Should I ask you that?
RUNE	No. It's okay.
HARVAR	No, but really. I suddenly feel like I should ask you that. Suddenly, I'm going: "What the fuck is she doing with me?" You know? Like, it's a little fuckin' late, but that never even occurred to me before. You always seemed just to be there, and to be, you know, there. If you know what I mean. Since we met.
RUNE	Yes.
HARVAR	So?
RUNE	So?
HARVAR	So what are you doing with me?

RUNE   What am I doing with you?

HARVAR   Yeah.

                A pause. RUNE goes to him.

RUNE   Whatever I want.

                She kisses him.

HARVAR   Right on.

                From in the house:

MICHELLE   You are not done your lunch, young lady!

HARVAR   So, when's the toilet guy coming? I'm pushing cotton here.

RUNE   He should have been here by now.

HARVAR   Damn.

MICHELLE   Come back here!

LILLIAN   *(also inside)* No way.

RUNE   There's always the woods.

MICHELLE   You are not excused. Don't be so awful, come back here.

LILLIAN   No way.

HARVAR   No fuckin' way.

MICHELLE   You're driving me out of my mind! Sit down!

LILLIAN   If you didn't want me, why did you have me?

MICHELLE   Who knew that it would be you?

                LILLIAN bursts outdoors.

HARVAR   How was lunch?

LILLIAN	Lunch was very nice, thank you.
HARVAR	I bet. What'd you have?
LILLIAN	Chickpea and lentil patty.
HARVAR	You're shitting me.
RUNE	Harvar.
HARVAR	No, I'm serious, that's totally child abuse. It's the summer, for God's sake.
RUNE	It's what she and Michelle eat.
LILLIAN	It's what we eat.
HARVAR	No, but I know, but look: it leads to a warped view of your like life, and then you get out in the world, and you look around, and you freak out. It's like, well, it's like— Okay, look. One day my father comes home and there's this girl at the house, she's I guess about seventeen, I forget her name, and she's supposed to be there every night because my mother has a job, right? She's there to make dinner, okay?
RUNE	You had servants?
HARVAR	No, she was like, she made dinner.
LILLIAN	*(to RUNE)* She was a cook.
HARVAR	No, she just— And so, anyway, I'm like I don't know, eleven or something.
MICHELLE	*(from inside)* Rune!
HARVAR	And I wind up upstairs with her, fooling around, and my dad comes home and fires the girl and says to me: "That's it. No sex for you until you're sixteen." Which is ridiculous, right?
RUNE	Is this story appropriate?

HARVAR	It's totally about what I'm talking about. So when I finally hit sixteen, I just freak out, like, if you know what I mean, and my grades go bad, and everything. In fact, that's when the whole thing started. All the shit that took all these years to straighten out.
MICHELLE	Ow! Jesus! Rune!

RUNE gets up.

HARVAR	One day after you leave home, you're gonna walk into a Taco Bell and you won't come out for like two years. Is all I'm saying.

RUNE goes inside. A pause.

Sorry about that story. It might not have been appropriate.

LILLIAN	No, it was good. I wish we had a cook.

A pause.

Why's it called a honeymoon, do you know?

HARVAR	No idea. Honey. Moon. No idea. Your mom might know.
LILLIAN	No, she doesn't. Where are you guys going again?
HARVAR	I don't know. Like Europe. Your aunt pretty much picked it.
LILLIAN	Don't you care?
HARVAR	Sure. But it's kind of her thing, you know? It's all sort of her thing.
LILLIAN	Getting married?
HARVAR	Generally speaking, it's the girl's thing.
LILLIAN	Or the woman's.
HARVAR	Exactly.

LILLIAN   But you proposed.

HARVAR   Well, no, not really.

LILLIAN   She proposed?

HARVAR   Well, we were talking, and it sort of came up. We both agreed, though.

LILLIAN   That's good.

              A pause. LILLIAN puts the sneakers on.

              My mother says she can't believe you'd get married.

HARVAR   She said that?

LILLIAN   Yes.

HARVAR   And what did she mean by that, do you think?

LILLIAN   I don't know. She said you still had stuff in you. Do you want to go for a swim?

HARVAR   Not right now. I'm fighting with those hot dogs.

              LILLIAN goes to the dock. A pause. MICHELLE comes out to the porch. She sits.

              Lentil patties? Are you nuts?

              MICHELLE begins to cry.

MICHELLE   Probably. It's good food, though, it's good for—

HARVAR   What?

MICHELLE   Fuck.

              She turns away.

HARVAR   You okay?

MICHELLE	I'm just—
HARVAR	Um, what's wrong?
MICHELLE	What's wrong is my fucking mother hates my guts.
HARVAR	No, she doesn't. She's just, she's fucking pissed off at having to sit there like that all day.
MICHELLE	I hate it. I hate it. She needs me and she hates it. I hate that people like you are so fucking understanding of her. Of her terrible situation.
HARVAR	Well, yours kind of blows, too. Anybody can see that.
MICHELLE	Really?
HARVAR	Of course. It's just that nobody gives a shit about you.
MICHELLE	That's right.
HARVAR	You know, where I come from, we put the old people into the leakiest, shittiest boats in the village and push them out into the sea.
MICHELLE	Really.
HARVAR	We get them drunk, give 'em a handjob, and then off they go. Sometimes it's really sick, right, because sometimes the tide pushes them back to the shore, so we have to go down the beach, push them out again, over and over, like maybe ten times.
MICHELLE	Really.
HARVAR	And they're like crying and begging and everything: "Please, don pus me beck to da sea!" It's fuckin' awful.
MICHELLE	Sounds like it.
HARVAR	But really quite beautiful, in its way.
MICHELLE	Who the fuck are you?

HARVAR   Yeah, I know.

              A pause.

              You're gonna be okay.

MICHELLE   I don't know.

HARVAR   Yeah, you are.

              He goes to her, awkwardly. There's an intimate moment be-
              tween them, which expires in a pause.

MICHELLE   You've very good with Lilly.

HARVAR   No I'm not.

MICHELLE   Yes you are.

HARVAR   Your daughter scares the shit out of me, actually.

MICHELLE   You have trouble taking compliments, don't you?

HARVAR   I don't know. I guess so. I've always been a self-defecating
              kind of guy.

              MICHELLE laughs. HARVAR seems confused by her laughter.
              The sound of a truck pulling up.

              Is this the toilet guy?

MICHELLE   Yes.

HARVAR   Thank God.

MICHELLE   What's the matter with the woods?

HARVAR   No fuckin' way. What is it with you people? Your whole fam-
              ily wants me to do that.

              TOM Ilesic enters with tools.

MICHELLE   Hello, Mr. Ilesic. Thanks for coming.

Tom	Hello, Michelle. You must be Rune's fella.
Harvar	I must be. Harvar Blumis.
Tom	Tom Ilesic. Toilet trouble?
Michelle	Yes—
Harvar	Looks like it. I think it's the ballcock? I had a look, but I didn't bring my tools, so...
Tom	I'll get after it.
Harvar	I wish you would. I'm really looking forward to dropping the kids off at the pool, if you know what I mean.

Tom goes inside. A pause.

Michelle	So, do you have to work on Monday?
Harvar	Hmm? Oh, yes. Or no. I forget. What's on Monday?
Michelle	I don't know. Are you guys going back on Monday?
Harvar	I think we... I forget. Are you?
Michelle	No. My first client is on Wednesday.
Harvar	Oh. That's good.

Rune comes out of the cottage.

Rune	She's asleep.
Michelle	No, she's not.
Rune	Yes, she is.
Michelle	No, she does this thing where she lets you think she's asleep, and then when you leave, she throws herself onto the floor beside the bed.
Rune	No, I think she's actually asleep.

MICHELLE   Well, we'll see. If you actually managed to get her to sleep after all the times I tried, I'll fuckin' kill myself.

RUNE   Maybe you should get a nap, too. We'll keep an eye on Lilly.

MICHELLE   Okay. Mr. Ilesic's here.

RUNE   I saw.

MICHELLE   I'll never get to sleep with him banging around, but okay.

RUNE   Okay.

         MICHELLE goes indoors. RUNE moves away from HARVAR.

HARVAR   Sweetie?

RUNE   Uh huh.

HARVAR   Everything okay?

RUNE   *(She's crying.)* Sure.

         HARVAR goes to her.

    That fucking awful woman.

HARVAR   Which one?

RUNE   God. What must this be like for you? I'm so sorry.

HARVAR   I'm okay.

RUNE   Are you sorry you came?

HARVAR   No.

RUNE   Really?

HARVAR   Look, of course I am, okay? But I'm not gonna say so, so stop asking, okay?

RUNE   Okay. I'm sorry.

HARVAR   I mean, fuck.

RUNE   Sorry.

HARVAR   Sorry.

            A pause.

            Where are we going, again? On the thing? Your niece asked
            me and I couldn't tell her. Made me feel like a fucking jerk.

RUNE   Italy. Tuscany.

HARVAR   Don't you think we'd better choose, one or the other? Time's
            running out.

RUNE   Can we talk about the bachelor party again?

HARVAR   I, fuck, no.

RUNE   Not the content. The timing.

HARVAR   I told you, there's nothing I can do about it. They decided, and
            they had to figure out everyone's schedule, you know? And,
            like, we invited your father, and nobody thought he'd come,
            and then he said yes, but he was out of town and so most of
            it had to do with fitting in your father.

RUNE   I know.

HARVAR   So, like, talk to your father.

RUNE   I'm actually talking about the timing of the whole thing.

HARVAR   The whole thing?

RUNE   Yes. I don't know, okay? I don't know what I'm saying here.
            I don't have a thing here I'm trying to talk you into, okay?

HARVAR   Okay.

RUNE   But it just seems that we picked badly. We picked days badly,
            and times, and everything.

HARVAR	For like, what. The whole thing?
RUNE	Who gets married on a Friday morning?
HARVAR	It was the only time they had.
RUNE	I know, but—
HARVAR	And you needed it to be that week.
RUNE	I know, it's my fault, but—
HARVAR	And I got all those limos lined up for the Friday.
RUNE	I know, I know, but— It seems like we made one bad decision early on, and it's forced us to make bad decisions all down the line.
HARVAR	Well, I didn't make them.
RUNE	That's not fair. You have been kept a part of the whole process. All you did was beg to be left out of the decisions, and I wouldn't let you.
HARVAR	Yes, okay.
RUNE	So don't say now that this is all happening without your consent.
HARVAR	Okay, okay.

A pause.

So what are you saying.

RUNE	I'm saying... I don't know.
HARVAR	That we should change everything?
RUNE	I just, I wonder if it would all work better if it got pushed off a couple of weeks. Could we do that? Do you think?
HARVAR	A couple of weeks?

RUNE	We might lose the deposit on the place and everything, but I'm sure my father wouldn't mind.
HARVAR	We'd have to call everybody.
RUNE	Yes. I could do that.
HARVAR	I'd have to see how many cars would be available.
RUNE	Would you mind doing that? That way we could hopefully do it at a better time. It just seems too weird, the way we've been sort of forced into doing it.
HARVAR	Yes.
RUNE	Do you mind doing that?
HARVAR	No.
RUNE	Okay. Good. So...
HARVAR	So, okay.

A pause.

What are we talking about here?

RUNE	Two weeks. Maybe the Saturday the nineteenth or something.
HARVAR	We're talking about two weeks.
RUNE	Yes. If they can do it.
HARVAR	Are we talking about two weeks?
RUNE	Yes. Of course. Yes. Okay?
HARVAR	Okay.
RUNE	Okay.

A pause.

	What.
Harvar	No. Nothing. I'll do it.
Rune	Thank you. We'll do all that stuff once we get back to town on Monday, okay?
Harvar	I don't have to be in on Monday.
Rune	You don't?
Harvar	No.
Rune	Well, I do.
Harvar	Oh.
Rune	Okay?
Harvar	Sure.
Rune	What, are you dying to stay out here? Just say so.
Harvar	No, no. We'll go back Monday.
Rune	Thank you.
Harvar	But what's Michelle going to do with your mother?
Rune	She'll figure it out. Mother is her responsibility.
Harvar	Okay.
Rune	I have to be back to go to work.
Harvar	But you work from home. You keep saying you could do your job from anywhere.
Rune	I have an editorial meeting. What is this? I thought you'd be thrilled to get away from my family.
Harvar	Yeah, okay.

RUNE   What's going on?

HARVAR   Did your shrink tell you to put the wedding off?

              A pause.

RUNE   No. And I'm not putting anything off. We're just adjusting it,
              okay? Okay?

HARVAR   Okay.

RUNE   Kiss me. I'm sorry. Kiss me.

              They kiss. He looks at her.

HARVAR   It's okay to be scared. You should be scared. I mean, fuck,
              look at me. But be scared with me, okay? Not by yourself.

RUNE   I'm not.

HARVAR   You sure?

RUNE   I'm not scared.

HARVAR   If you're not scared, that makes you the stupid one. Ha ha.

RUNE   I'm going to clean up the kitchen. Do you want anything?

HARVAR   No.

RUNE   Do you want a beer?

HARVAR   Maybe later. I'll get it.

RUNE   Okay.

              *RUNE goes inside. HARVAR takes his shirt off, puts on his sun-
              glasses, and lies down. LILLIAN comes in, dripping wet. She
              stands over HARVAR, dripping on him. She has a wriggling
              sunfish in her hands.*

HARVAR   That better be water coming off you.

LILLIAN	It is. Look.

HARVAR sits up.

HARVAR	What is that, like a fish?
LILLIAN	No, it's a dump truck, stupid.
HARVAR	Where did you get that?
LILLIAN	I caught it with my hands.
HARVAR	You caught that? Bare-handed?

A pause while they look at the fish.

LILLIAN	Do you know my mother won't tell me who my father is?
HARVAR	Really.
LILLIAN	She says it's none of my business.
HARVAR	Well, she's probably got a point there.

A pause. The fish stops wriggling. LILLIAN holds it by the tail.

LILLIAN	Want it?
HARVAR	Um, no thanks.

LILLIAN throws the fish into the bushes.

No, Lilly.

LILLIAN	What.
HARVAR	You can't throw that there.
LILLIAN	Are you telling me what to do? Uncle Harvar?
HARVAR	I, fuck, no. But you leave that there, it'll start stinking. You gotta throw it back in the water or into the woods or something.

LILLIAN   Why.

HARVAR   Because it'll stink. You caught it, you killed it, now it's your
              responsibility, okay? You got to take responsibility for the stuff
              you do.

LILLIAN   Okay.

              LILLIAN goes to the bushes, starts searching. HARVAR lies down.

              You just gonna lie there all day?

HARVAR   Sweetie, I'm not going to do anything physical until I can get
              into the bathroom and flash out a loaf.

LILLIAN   Until what?

HARVAR   Nothing. I have to poo.

LILLIAN   You have to poo?

HARVAR   I have to poo.

              A pause.

LILLIAN   You could poo in the woods.

HARVAR   I'm not pooing in the woods.

LILLIAN   Why not? I did twice yesterday.

HARVAR   Because you may not know this, but when you poo in the
              woods there's a very strong chance of some *thing* crawling up
              your ass.

LILLIAN   That's not true.

HARVAR   Yes it is.

LILLIAN   Don't be ridiculous.

HARVAR   I'm not.

LILLIAN   Yes, you are. Just like Aunt Rune said. She said you were ridiculous.

HARVAR sits up.

HARVAR   She did? When did she say this?

LILLIAN   I don't know. She said you were ridiculous, but that there was nothing she could do. She was taking a huge chance getting married to you.

HARVAR   I see. Okay.

LILLIAN   You were the best that she could hope for.

HARVAR   Uh huh.

LILLIAN   And immatoor.

HARVAR   Uh huh.

LILLIAN   Does she mean immature?

HARVAR   I guess.

LILLIAN   I get that all the time. Come swimming.

HARVAR   No thanks. I'm gonna... I'm gonna go for a walk.

LILLIAN   Chickenshit.

HARVAR   That's right.

LILLIAN   Ridiculous.

HARVAR   Right. See you later.

HARVAR goes. LILLIAN finds the fish, and as she does so, the door bangs open and FRANCES makes her way onto the porch. FRANCES sits. She is breathing hard. She and LILLIAN lock eyes for a moment, then LILLIAN walks toward the cottage. LILLIAN pulls back the lattice that covers the crawl space, and throws the fish under the cottage. Then she walks off toward the water.

Frances touches her blouse, smoothing it with her hand. She repeats this gesture until it becomes frantic. She tears open her blouse and sits back, her hand fluttering over her eyes. Tom exits the cottage, sees Frances, and sits beside her.

Tom   *(He's fixing her clothing and eventually takes her hand.)* Here you are. I wondered where you were.

Toilet's fixed for now. The seal's going to go on it soon. When that happens, I might as well replace the whole thing. Toilets are so cheap these days.

Were you having a rest? Did you eat yet? Michelle make you something?

Did I tell you I got down to Toronto a few weeks ago? Maybe I did. Took myself to a few movies, that kind of thing. I called you, I think I told you. Did Michelle tell you I called? She couldn't manage to work out a time for me to come and see you, but I hope she told you I called while I was in town.

Oh. I sold the business to Tom Junior last week. Did I tell you? Signed everything last week. It's all his. And now I work part-time for him. Isn't that hilarious? He'll be fine, I think. There's lots lined up for the fall, two or three houses, and he said he wanted to hire a full-time bookkeeper, and that sort of thing. So he's got plans. I guess if he can keep his head out of his ass and his ass out of the drunk tank he'll be okay. I guess. I hope. But what the hell. It sure was odd, sitting in the lawyer's office, my son already had a couple of beers in him, I'm sure, listening to the guy, our lawyer, just calmly take my business and hand it over, like a, a, I don't know. Like it was nothing. Like it wasn't in fact forty-eight years of my life. Thomas Junior didn't even take his sunglasses off.

I made a flan last week, do you know what that is? I didn't. It's pretty much a flat pie with no, you know, lid. I had all these strawberries, I'll sometimes go to Hutchison's and pick them, and I'll sort of forget myself and look up and I've picked way more than I need. You ever do that?

So I found the recipe in a cookbook Shelagh left behind, and it took forever to do, but I figured it would take as long as it takes, just like when you build anything, you know? And it pretty much did. Crust took me three tries.

I don't know how long that cookbook had been sitting there. First time I noticed it since she moved out. She moved to her sister's in Peterborough. You know, I know I wanted to be alone, but I sure as hell can't remember why anymore.

I should have brought you some. I ate almost all of it, though. Watching God knows what. That program with the black people yelling at each other. Have you ever seen that? I was watching it, and eating this thing, and I laughed once or twice at it, and then I felt embarrassed for laughing? All alone, sitting there, feeling ashamed because I laughed at this program.

You cold? You feel a bit cold. No?

Damn, I should have brought it. I had a letter published in the local paper. Some guy, some nitwit got permission to build this car wash, you know, where you go into the stalls and wash the car yourself? Put money in the thing and the hose squirts water for five minutes, you know? That kind of thing? You ever seen these places? They look just awful.

The lights begin to fade.

And he gets permission to build it right downtown. Right beside the cenotaph, in between it and the fountain, right there where the old city hall was, right on that site. Stupidest goddamned thing you ever saw. I should have brought the letter I wrote.

Frances, I tell you, you have just about the worst view from here of what is just about the prettiest lake. I don't know.

I guess he's gonna have to change the lettering on the trucks, and get new business cards printed up—

Blackout.

ACT THREE

The same, fifteen years later. The cottage has slid another foot and a half to the left, trees now hang low over the roof. The paint has continued to degrade and now weeds push up between the floorboards of the porch. Early morning. MICHELLE and TOM JR. are seated on the porch in the same configuration as their parents at the end of the previous act. MICHELLE is in pyjamas. TOM JR. has a beer between his knees and is looking at some pills in his hand. Through the following he will choose one of the pills, swallow it with some beer, and put the remaining pills in a shirt pocket.

MICHELLE   ...and the stoplight is coming up, and we're just going faster and faster, and now, the kids in the back seat are screaming, and this girl, and I know this girl, right? She has a reputation already, this girl, sixteen years old, and the other ones talk about her like she's filth. So I have a soft spot for this girl, more or less, I mean, I know where she is at that moment, that moment in her life, boys and her parents and all the judgment and hatred at school; I mean, how does anyone get anything done at all between the ages of thirteen and eighteen?

TOM JR.   I know.

MICHELLE   Honestly. So there we are, screaming towards the red light, accelerating, I'm standing on my brakes, even though I know they're disconnected, temporarily disconnected, but still, at that moment of course it matters little how temporarily, and I grow calmer and calmer as the noise in the car grows and grows. Calmer and calmer. I think whole, complete sentences, I plan for a few different scenarios, post-crash scenarios, I have time to do this. And then—

TOM JR.   And then you sail through the intersection.

MICHELLE   That's right.

TOM JR.   Everyone was okay.

MICHELLE   That's right.

TOM JR.	Except when the girl finally pulled over, she side-swiped a parked car.
MICHELLE	I've told you this?
TOM JR.	Let's go into the woods.

A pause. Of the view:

MICHELLE	Isn't it awful here.
TOM JR.	You know, the rest of the lake's not bad. This is just like, an ugly spot.
MICHELLE	Did you ever swim here? Before?
TOM JR.	Sure. You and I swam a bunch of times.
MICHELLE	It was awful.
TOM JR.	Back when you let me come over to swim and et cetera.
MICHELLE	We used to have to wear old shoes to go swimming, to keep the leeches off, and also because the stones were so sharp.
TOM JR.	That's right.
MICHELLE	Until finally Rune got sick of it and hired someone to dredge out the whole bay.
TOM JR.	Yeah, Michelle. That was me.
MICHELLE	Was it? And then she had all that sand trucked in. She tried to make a little beach. And it didn't work. The next spring, we came back and the sand was gone, the rocks were back, and now there were weeds so thick that you couldn't see the bottom. And, also, part of our shoreline fell off and disappeared.
TOM JR.	That'll happen.
MICHELLE	And then Rune gave up. What was that?
TOM JR.	What was what?

MICHELLE   What was that you just took?

TOM JR.   Oh. Not sure. I think it was like a muscle relaxant, from when Tammy hurt her back. Want one?

MICHELLE   No thank you. I'm always curious to see what people are taking. Your father built this porch.

TOM JR.   I helped him.

MICHELLE   Oh, no. You couldn't have. It was years ago.

TOM JR.   I was little.

MICHELLE   Oh, no. You couldn't have.

TOM JR.   I did.

MICHELLE   No you didn't. My mother could never figure out why he stopped. She asked him to build a screened-in porch. He built the porch, but never screened it in. My mother was too embarrassed to ask him to finish.

TOM JR.   Well, my father, and this won't come as a big surprise, spent most of his time screwing the townies on their renovations. He'd start a job, start the next one before finishing the last one, never get around to doing any of them all the way. People always paid. Jesus, people loved him. The more he'd screw them, the more people loved him.

MICHELLE   People were at his mercy. And he always pretended they weren't. That's why people liked your father.

TOM JR.   I deal honestly with people, you know, for the most part, and they hate me. All they want to talk about is what a guy my father was.

MICHELLE   Can you see Lilly? I can't see Lilly.

TOM JR.   I have four guys working under me. I have a girl that does the books. I actually pay taxes, for fuck's sake. He till the day he died told me I'd ruin the business. His business.

MICHELLE   You pay taxes?

TOM JR.   ·Yes.

MICHELLE   I've never paid taxes on my business.

TOM JR.   Well, see, there you go.

MICHELLE   As far as they're concerned, I've never made a dime. Do you see Lilly?

TOM JR.   No. Let's go into the woods.

MICHELLE   No. I... I don't do that anymore.

TOM JR.   You don't do that anymore?

MICHELLE   No.

TOM JR.   Since yesterday?

MICHELLE   Oh. Was that you?

TOM JR.   What do you mean, was that me?

MICHELLE   Damn it. Okay then. Soon.

TOM JR.   Who else do you take into the woods?

            A pause.

            Michelle?

MICHELLE   Nobody.

TOM JR.   Are you sure?

MICHELLE   I... yes. I just thought that maybe I just thought I was in the woods having sex with someone, yesterday.

TOM JR.   No. That was a real event. That's why I'm back.

MICHELLE   Okay. I did wonder, why, if it happened only in my head, was the sex so bad. If it was a real event, that explains it. Okay. We'll go, soon, but you have to promise the sex will be better.

TOM JR.   I can do that. Well, I can promise that.

MICHELLE   Okay. When did she leave, do you remember?

TOM JR.   Who.

MICHELLE   Lilly. She went for a swim across the lake.

TOM JR.   Lilly's here?

MICHELLE   No, that's what I'm saying, she's in the lake.

TOM JR.   I didn't know Lilly was up.

MICHELLE   Of course she is.

TOM JR.   I didn't see her yesterday.

MICHELLE   Of course she's here. I told her she had to come with me.

TOM JR.   Doesn't she live in like England, or something?

MICHELLE   She did.

TOM JR.   But not anymore?

MICHELLE   That's right. I asked her to come home.

TOM JR.   Uh huh.

MICHELLE   I don't trust her. At that distance.

TOM JR.   So, Lilly's here.

MICHELLE   She's in the lake. She likes to swim the lake. You had sex with her, did you not?

TOM JR.   What? No. I didn't even know she was here.

MICHELLE   When she was still in high school.

TOM JR.   Of course not.

MICHELLE   I'm sure it was her fault.

TOM JR.   Look, I don't know what she told you, but we never had sex.
            I never had sex with your daughter.

MICHELLE   I'm sure she did it. You're just lucky she didn't swallow you
            whole.

TOM JR.   I, look, I—

MICHELLE   Junior. It's okay. She did it, not you. We'll go into the woods
            soon. When she gets back. Do you want another beer?

TOM JR.   No. Not yet.

MICHELLE   Okay then.

            A pause.

            I'm just, I'm stalling, right?

TOM JR.   Sure.

            A pause.

            What's your sister's problem?

MICHELLE   Rune? Rune has no problems. What do you mean? She's fine.
            She's a difficult person, but...

TOM JR.   She treats me like I'm snot or something.

MICHELLE   Oh, well, yes, she detests you. But I don't think she considers
            that a problem.

TOM JR.   Why? What did I do?

MICHELLE   Well, she's pretty hard on people in general. And, well, you're
            from the country.

TOM JR.   That's nice.

MICHELLE   And also, she's very protective of me. I'm all she has, more or less.

TOM JR.   Still, it's no reason to be such a bitch.

MICHELLE   It's actually a pretty good one, Junior.

TOM JR.   Please don't call me that.

MICHELLE   I know. Still stalling.

    A pause.

How's your wife? What's her name?

TOM JR.   I don't want to talk about her. I told you that.

MICHELLE   But what's her name?

TOM JR.   Tammy.

MICHELLE   That's right. It's not really appropriate for a middle-aged woman, is it? Tammy? Do you suppose her parents assumed she'd never reach middle age?

TOM JR.   You said that before.

MICHELLE   I'm allowed to repeat myself. I'm allowed to repeat myself. I'm allowed to repeat myself.

TOM JR.   Okay.

MICHELLE   I'm allowed to repeat myself.

    A pause.

Did I ever tell you the story of how my parents found this place?

TOM JR.   Yes.

MICHELLE   Did I?

Tom Jr.	Yes.
Michelle	Ah.

A pause.

They were in a canoe, from that place across the way—

Tom Jr. stands.

Tom Jr.	I'm gonna go.
Michelle	Don't go, Junior. You don't have to listen.
Tom Jr.	Yeah. But. You don't seem... into this whole idea, like you were yesterday.
Michelle	I'm just, I'm nervous, okay? Lilly came back.
Tom Jr.	Maybe you just need some time to yourself.
Michelle	I'd, God, I'd love some time to myself. Between Rune and this one, Lillian, and everything, I can't get a minute to myself.
Tom Jr.	Michelle.
Michelle	Junior?
Tom Jr.	Lilly's not here.
Michelle	Yes she is.
Tom Jr.	No. Michelle. Lilly's not here.
Michelle	She's swimming.
Tom Jr.	No, she's not. God.
Michelle	She's not?
Tom Jr.	See ya later, Michelle.
Michelle	Wait! Did you fix the thing?

TOM JR.   I told you. I need a part. I'll be back on Monday. See ya.

MICHELLE   Of course.

               TOM JR. exits. A pause. MICHELLE stands, peering out into the lake.

               HEY! HEY!

RUNE   *(from inside; startled awake)* What? What is it?

MICHELLE   GET BACK HERE!

RUNE   What is it? Michelle? What time is it?

MICHELLE   HEY!

               RUNE comes outside. She's wearing pyjamas.

RUNE   Stop shouting. What are you yelling for?

MICHELLE   Lillian's got away again.

RUNE   What?

MICHELLE   She's too far out.

RUNE   Michelle. Goddamn it.

MICHELLE   I can't see her.

RUNE   Lillian's not here.

MICHELLE   Yes she is.

RUNE   Michelle.

MICHELLE   Yes she is. She came last night. She came in the middle of
               the night.

RUNE   Lillian moved away, remember?

MICHELLE   I know that. Jesus. I know that. Never mind. I'm going out in
               the canoe.

RUNE   Let me come with you. Something will happen.

MICHELLE   I'm just going out in the canoe. You stay here.

RUNE   Michelle. Something always happens.

MICHELLE   No.

RUNE   Are you sure?

MICHELLE   Yes. Of course. I would do this anyway, even if you weren't here.

RUNE   Don't go far.

MICHELLE   No. I know what you must think of me.

RUNE   Oh, Jesus. I do not.

> MICHELLE *exits toward the water.* RUNE *watches her go. She turns to go inside and stops to examine the face of the cottage. She picks at the paint, absently pulls up a weed or two. She turns to watch* MICHELLE *again. She goes inside. A pause.* MATTHEW, *now forty-eight, walks on, looks around, and eventually sits.* RUNE *comes out of the cottage with toast and a spatula.*

MATTHEW   Hey. Hi.

> RUNE *stops.*

RUNE   Hi. Hello.

MATTHEW   Hello.

RUNE   Well... shit. Hi.

MATTHEW   Nice to see you, Rune. I'm not... it's not too early, is it?

RUNE   Nice to see you. What are you doing here? I mean, holy shit.

> *They hug.*

MATTHEW   I was at a friend's cottage, and we drove past here on the way up. I thought of you. I wondered if you still had this place.

RUNE	I know. I can't believe it either. We all hate it so much. Bloodsuckers get bigger every year.
MATTHEW	It's nice here.
RUNE	It really isn't. So. You're here. Are you here? In Toronto?
MATTHEW	Yes. I moved back in April.
RUNE	From?
MATTHEW	Calgary.
RUNE	That's right. I don't blame you for returning.

A pause.

I'm sorry. I'm a terrible snob.

MATTHEW	Yes. But I knew that already, from the newspaper.

A beat.

No, you're right. Calgary's the kind of place you wind up if you're not paying attention.

RUNE	You're in produce, is that right? Is that what I heard?
MATTHEW	Well, yes. More or less. I was a lawyer for an egg company for a bunch of years. Then I was a lawyer for the wheat board. Then I took some time off. Now, I work with the federal government for some potato people. I'm a potato lobbyist.
RUNE	Wow. All things I can no longer eat.
MATTHEW	And you're doing well. I read you all the time.
RUNE	Thanks.
MATTHEW	Sometimes I even agree with you.
RUNE	Well, thanks.

MATTHEW   Actually, I'm just being polite. I never agree with you.

RUNE   Thank God. I have no respect for people that have any respect for what I write.

MATTHEW   But you're entertaining.

RUNE   That's exactly right. You got married, no?

MATTHEW   I did. I was married for about ten years.

RUNE   I'm amazed and thrilled you had the courage to ask someone else after I turned you down so brutally.

MATTHEW   Well. I found somebody who made it pretty clear she wouldn't say no. And you?

RUNE   No, I never did.

MATTHEW   Really.

RUNE   No. I just shot them down, one after another. You were the first in a long string of brutalized suitors. The beaches were strewn with the lifeless corpses of the men whose hopes and dreams I enflamed and then destroyed.

MATTHEW   Really.

RUNE   No. I'm just being... a complete asshole. It's nice to see you. Do you want some coffee or anything?

MATTHEW   Oh, no thanks. I'm off coffee.

RUNE   You?

MATTHEW   Yeah, well, it gave me colon cancer a few years back, so...

RUNE   Oh. Well, for fuck's sake.

MATTHEW   Yeah. That's what I said.

RUNE   And how are you now? You look well.

MATTHEW   Oh, I am. I beat it, to everyone's surprise. I'd love a glass of water.

RUNE   Of course. Just a sec. Will you hold these?

> RUNE *hands him the toast and the spatula and goes into the cottage.* MATTHEW *looks down toward the lake.* RUNE *returns with water and they exchange props.*

MATTHEW   Thanks.

RUNE   Sure. Listen. I have to confess something.

MATTHEW   Okay.

RUNE   I can't remember your name.

MATTHEW   Really.

RUNE   I know exactly who you are, but I just, I'm so fuckin' awful with names. It's a curse. I'm so sorry.

MATTHEW   Well, Rune, that's a bit of a blow.

RUNE   It's the kind of thing that, if we manage to have an entire conversation without you finding out I don't know, then you leave, I remember your name the second you're out of sight.

MATTHEW   Really.

RUNE   Yes. Except now, instead of putting myself through the agony of all of that, I just admit it and get it over with.

MATTHEW   I see. That sounds much healthier.

RUNE   So...

MATTHEW   Much more grown up.

> *A pause.*

RUNE   Are you going to tell me?

MATTHEW   Well, Rune, I don't know.

RUNE   Look, you bastard, I said I'm sorry, just remind me what—

MATTHEW   Matthew Grant.

RUNE   (almost simultaneous with the above line) Matthew fuckin' Grant. Sorry. Sorry.

MATTHEW   I was the guy, '94, I proposed—

RUNE   Yes, yes, I know—

MATTHEW   Offered to take you away from all this—

RUNE   No, I know.

MATTHEW   You described me at the time as the love of your life—

RUNE   I know who you are. And I never called you that.

MATTHEW   Well, it was something like that.

RUNE   Was it?

MATTHEW   Something like that. I recall it quite clearly.

RUNE   Well, what was I, eighteen or something?

MATTHEW   You were nearly twenty-one.

RUNE   So.

               A pause.

MATTHEW   Don't remember much about the actual proposal. I do remember driving back to the city the next day, with you, and that was fun. Very long drive; very, very uncomfortable.

RUNE   Yes. I can remember... seeing the road rush by between my feet. It was an old car.

MATTHEW   That's right.

RUNE   Whole chunks of it were missing.

MATTHEW   That's right. And I think you got out before the car had actually stopped.

            A pause.

            How's your mom?

RUNE   She died.

            A pause.

MATTHEW   It was the smart thing to do, turning me down.

RUNE   I was just standing here wondering if that was the wrong thing to do.

MATTHEW   Oh, no, absolutely. It was, I was... I had no idea what I was doing.

RUNE   Yes.

MATTHEW   Plus, you would have wound up in Calgary.

RUNE   That's right. Oh, God.

MATTHEW   But it's funny. I feel in a lot of ways like it was the last deliberate thing I ever did. I agonized, I decided, I did it, it didn't work out, and in a funny way, it's like everything since then has been sort of accidental.

            A pause.

            Or maybe I'm just romanticizing it. Maybe I've never done anything deliberate.

RUNE   Maybe.

MATTHEW   Maybe I've gotten through all this time without a single deliberate act. I feel as though I was born without any guiding principles, any instincts. Of any kind.

RUNE   Yes. My mother used to complain of having no instincts.

MATTHEW   Well, she was right to complain. It would be great, don't you think, to actually have strong, ingrained feelings about the things you're confronted with, day after day? To have some sort of system down deep, organizing you and making you do things spontaneously, with certainty, and in the knowledge that right or wrong at least you're acting with some sort of integrity.

RUNE   You've given this some thought.

MATTHEW   So have you. I can read it in your column.

A pause.

Or maybe I'm reading that into it.

RUNE   No. I don't think so.

MATTHEW   Anyway. Sorry. Hi.

RUNE   Yes. Hi. Don't apologize. You're absolutely right. Instincts would be useful.

A pause.

MATTHEW   So, apart from the column, what have you been up to?

RUNE   Oh, you know, this and that.

A pause.

Nothing.

A pause.

MATTHEW   What's the spatula for?

RUNE   Hmm? Oh. I had just this minute decided I was going to scrape off the old paint.

MATTHEW   I see.

RUNE   And then probably repaint. That was the idea. My mother would be mortified by the state of the place. I suddenly thought.

MATTHEW   Right.

RUNE   I was asleep, I woke up, I thought of my mother. And then you appeared.

            A pause.

MATTHEW   You look well. I should have said that before.

RUNE   Thanks. It's okay.

MATTHEW   How's the perimenopause working out?

RUNE   You can see it, can you? It's that obvious?

MATTHEW   You wrote a column about it.

RUNE   Oh, fuck, yes. That's right. I'm so desperate for ideas from one week to the next that—

MATTHEW   I liked that column. I don't know who wrote it, but it was not written by the person that usually writes your column.

RUNE   I know, I tried to get it back after I submitted it. I felt ridiculous afterward.

MATTHEW   It was good. It was a nice break from all the...

RUNE   Yes?

MATTHEW   Well, bile, I was going to say.

RUNE   Yes.

            A beat.

            I figured out something early. If you're going to write about society, you'll seem much more interesting if you do one thing: blame the wrong person. If there's a victim, blame the victim. If someone is at a disadvantage, if someone is misinformed, if someone you know to be virtuous shows bad judgment, attack them.

MATTHEW   I see.

RUNE   I mean, newspapers are crammed with writers sticking up
             for these people.

MATTHEW   Yes.

RUNE   So I provide balance by appealing to everyone's worst feelings.
             It's my one true talent.

MATTHEW   I find that hard to believe.

RUNE   Oh, yes it is. I'm an awful person. It's second nature now.

             A pause.

             Anyway. Can you, do you want to stay for lunch?

MATTHEW   Listen, do you want to get married?

             A pause.

             During the half a year when I seriously thought I was dying,
             all I thought about was you.

             A pause.

             How's Michelle?

RUNE   She's fine. She sort of took over up here when Mother died.
             She wouldn't let me sell it.

MATTHEW   Does she still work in restaurants?

RUNE   Michelle never worked in restaurants.

MATTHEW   She didn't? Wasn't she a chef somewhere? Or training to be
             a chef?

RUNE   No.

MATTHEW   That's funny. I always thought she was a chef.

RUNE   No. She has a small business she runs when she feels like it.

MATTHEW Ah. Doing what?

RUNE   Teaching kids to drive.

MATTHEW Really.

RUNE   I know.

A pause.

MATTHEW Listen. I'm a very stupid man. I've drifted through much of my life, barely attached to things, to people, without really participating in anything. And I don't expect that to change. I'm forty-eight. I'm, this is it. I don't know anything. I mean that. I don't know what happened to me, I don't know where all my time went, I don't know why I didn't die, I don't know why I'm here. I'm incapable of understanding my own motives. And I think I can safely say at this point in my life that those are things that aren't going to change. So there you go: I'm offering you very little, and I have no real understanding of why I'm doing it. And I'm under no illusions about suddenly becoming a person who believes in things, does things, or understands why he does them.

RUNE   Well when you put it like that, how could a girl resist.

A pause.

You know, I actually do understand my motives. I spent years working at it, figuring it out. With a variety of professionals. I know why I do the things I do. But Mark?

MATTHEW Matthew?

RUNE   Fuck. Matthew? The thing I've found out is that knowing why you do things doesn't change a motherfucking thing. It doesn't help.

MATTHEW Well, that's good to know—

RUNE   It's fun, right? It's a great distraction, uncovering the mysteries of your own behaviour. It kills time while you continue to do exactly the same things you've done over and over, all your life. It can even provide the illusion of change, for a while. But eventually, you return to the person you always were, held back by the things that always did, making the same bad decisions you always made. So, what I'm saying is, don't bother. Don't bother trying to figure out why you are the ridiculous way you are, because it doesn't help.

MATTHEW   That sounds pretty... hopeless.

RUNE   I suppose. And yet, I'm not.

MATTHEW   Hopeless?

RUNE   Yes. I'm not.

MATTHEW   Well, so, that's good.

RUNE   Yes. I'm really not, I don't think. No.

        A pause.

MATTHEW   So, about the other thing...

RUNE   Yes. Oh. Oh. I really don't think it's a good idea.

MATTHEW   Yes, but—

RUNE   You see

MATTHEW   I didn't ask what you thought of it as an idea. I asked if you wanted to do it.

        A pause.

RUNE   Yes.

MATTHEW   Really.

        RUNE nods.

Really?

RUNE   Sure.

MATTHEW   Well, holy crap. All right. Thanks.

RUNE   Sure.

MATTHEW   Way to go.

RUNE   Way to go.

      A pause.

I want you to know, I'm terrible at this.

MATTHEW   Yeah. Well. Look who you're talking to.

RUNE   And I really thought I was done with this stuff.

MATTHEW   Yes.

RUNE   So, please.

MATTHEW   Please what.

RUNE   Just, please. I'm going to be terrible at... I'm, I don't know how to...

MATTHEW   That's funny.

RUNE   What.

MATTHEW   I seem to remember you behaving more or less this way when you were turning me down.

RUNE   Really?

MATTHEW   Pretty much.

      A pause. From the water MICHELLE *yells: "Rune!"*

RUNE   Oh, shit. Sorry. That's Michelle. *(to the lake)* WHAT! STOP YELLING!

MATTHEW   Is that Michelle?

MICHELLE   I can't paddle anymore!

MATTHEW   Oh.

RUNE   WHY NOT!

MICHELLE   I just can't! Come out here and get me!

RUNE   YOU MUST BE KIDDING!

MICHELLE   I dropped the paddle!

RUNE   YOU WHAT?!

MICHELLE   You heard me! Get out here!

> RUNE *pulls off her pyjamas. She's wearing a bathing suit underneath.*

RUNE   Sorry about this. You remember Michelle. I'm afraid she's about the same as the last time you saw her.

MATTHEW   Really.

RUNE   More or less. Anyway. I wanted a swim this morning. I'll be back in a couple of minutes. Hand me those shoes?

> MATTHEW *hands her the beat-up sneakers at his feet.*

Honest to God. I could kill her. I could always kill her. I'll be right back. Make yourself at home. Eat that toast.

MATTHEW   Okay. Listen, can I, I have to tell you some—

RUNE   You'll be here when I get back?

MATTHEW   Yes. Yes I will.

RUNE   Well, good.

> RUNE *goes. She returns and kisses* MATTHEW.

MATTHEW   Hi, Rune.

RUNE   Yes. Hi.

MATTHEW   Matthew.

RUNE   That's right. I...

MATTHEW   Yes?

RUNE   I was thinking about the paint, and my mother, and there you were. I have a hard time believing this... just happened.

MATTHEW   Me too.

RUNE   But it did, right?

MATTHEW   Yes.

RUNE   Yes. It was a real event. Hang on, okay?

MATTHEW   Yes.

RUNE   Okay.

            She leaves again. MATTHEW watches her. He looks away. RUNE re-enters, stops, and looks at him a long time. Finally he turns around and sees her. Then she exits again.

            There is a splash. MATTHEW eats toast. He finishes the water. He goes inside the cottage. A pause. LILLIAN, twenty-five, walks on in a bathing suit. She goes around the cottage, removes the bathing suit, and wraps herself in a towel. MATTHEW comes out onto the porch, drinking a second glass of water. LILLIAN comes around the corner.

MATTHEW   Oh! Hi!

LILLIAN   Hello.

MATTHEW   Matthew Grant. I didn't realize anyone else was...

LILLIAN   I got here last night. Lillian.

MATTHEW   Hi.

LILLIAN   Hi.

MATTHEW   I'm a friend of Rune's.

LILLIAN   Rune has friends?

MATTHEW   Oh. Uh, I don't know, actually. But I, uh, I guess I'm an old friend of hers.

        A pause.

        Sorry. Don't let me monopolize you. You must want to, uh...

        MATTHEW *moves away from the cottage door.*

LILLIAN   What.

MATTHEW   Well, get dressed.

LILLIAN   *(She doesn't move.)* I'm okay. I was swimming. I got tired, so I got out of the lake and walked back. Most people don't know enough to get out when they're tired.

MATTHEW   No.

LILLIAN   You knew Rune back in the old days.

MATTHEW   I guess so. University.

LILLIAN   Old boyfriend.

MATTHEW   I guess so, yes.

LILLIAN   I see. Did you bring a suit?

        A beat.

MATTHEW   Oh, no. I didn't really know I was coming.

LILLIAN   You got here by accident?

MATTHEW	Well...
LILLIAN	That's a helluvan accident.
MATTHEW	Ha ha.

A pause.

How's the water?

LILLIAN	Are you staying for lunch?
MATTHEW	I am, I think.
LILLIAN	Fantastic.
MATTHEW	Yes it is.
LILLIAN	It's great for Rune to have company. Even company from the past.
MATTHEW	Is it?
LILLIAN	It really, really is. She's unspeakably lonely.
MATTHEW	Well, so, good then.
LILLIAN	Rune's a difficult... person.

A pause.

What do you do, Matthew? Mind if I guess?

MATTHEW	No. Although I don't think—
LILLIAN	Quiet.

LILLIAN *takes a couple of steps toward him, looks at him very intently.*

Do you, in the course of your daily routine, do you deal at all with paper?

MATTHEW   With, sorry?

LILLIAN   With... papers?

MATTHEW   Well, yes.

LILLIAN   Hmm. Let me see your hands.

> MATTHEW *holds out his hands. She takes them and feels the palms.*

They feel like... are you in shoes?

MATTHEW   Shoes?

LILLIAN   Are you in shoes of any kind?

MATTHEW   No. Potatoes.

LILLIAN   Really? A shoe buyer? A shoe salesman? Can you size me?

> *She offers her foot, losing her balance a little. He grabs her foot to steady her.*

MATTHEW   Oops.

LILLIAN   Oops.

MATTHEW   Uh...

LILLIAN   What size is that?

MATTHEW   Uh... Oh Jesus.

> *He drops her foot.*

LILLIAN   What is it?

MATTHEW   I think you've got a...

LILLIAN   *(feeling the underside of her foot)* A leech? Ah, yes. There she is. Tucked up in my extraordinarily high arch.

MATTHEW	Yes. Is there any…

He sees a box of salt. Handing it to her:

Here you go.

LILLIAN	Can you get it? Here. Sit down.

He sits. She sits on the ground and puts her foot in his lap. He pours the salt on the leech. LILLIAN's towel falls open, and were she to open her legs even slightly, he would see everything, as it were.

MATTHEW	Hold still.
LILLIAN	Yes.

They're frozen as the salt does its stuff.

MATTHEW	I'll just. Put some more on.
LILLIAN	Yes.

Some spills on her leg. She wipes it away.

MATTHEW	Sorry.

A pause.

LILLIAN	Can you pull it off?
MATTHEW	No. I can't.

She removes her foot from his lap, crosses it over the other leg. She removes the leech. She stands before him.

LILLIAN	Thank you.

She opens the towel and, facing him, sits on his lap.

Thank you.

MATTHEW	No, listen—

LILLIAN   No.

     She kisses him. MICHELLE enters.

MICHELLE   Lillian!

LILLIAN   Go away, Mother.

     RUNE enters.

MICHELLE   Junior?

MATTHEW   No.

RUNE   What's happening?

MATTHEW   Please.

MICHELLE   Get off him!

     MICHELLE pulls LILLIAN off of MATTHEW.

MATTHEW   Michelle.

MICHELLE   You're not Junior.

MATTHEW   No.

RUNE   Matthew?

MATTHEW   I didn't—

MICHELLE   Who the fuck are you? What are you doing to her?

MATTHEW   Matthew—

RUNE   It's Matthew Grant. *(to LILLIAN)* What did you do?

LILLIAN   It was a bloodsucker.

RUNE   *(to LILLIAN)* What are you doing here?

MICHELLE   It's who? Who are you?

LILLIAN	I got in last night.
MATTHEW	It's Matthew Grant, Michelle. Hello. Sorry. Rune.
RUNE	What.
MICHELLE	Matthew Grant? Matthew Grant?
RUNE	Michelle. Go indoors.
MICHELLE	Matthew Grant. I had sex with Matthew Grant.
RUNE	You what?
MICHELLE	I had sex with you. Didn't I? Were you my lover?
LILLIAN	Oh yes?
MATTHEW	No, I, yes. We—
MICHELLE	When was this?
RUNE	When was this?
MATTHEW	A long time ago.
RUNE	When? Matthew?
LILLIAN	When was this?
MICHELLE	*(to LILLIAN)* Oh, fuck, oh no. Go indoors!
LILLIAN	I'm not a child.
MICHELLE	Go! Now! Go! Now! Go!
LILLIAN	Stop shouting.
RUNE	When was this?
MATTHEW	It didn't mean anything.
MICHELLE	It didn't mean anything? What you did to me?

MATTHEW   No, Michelle, it didn't. You know that.

MICHELLE   Tell her that!

               Meaning LILLIAN. *A pause.*

LILLIAN   Oh. Oh yes. I see. That's... funny.

               LILLIAN *approaches* MATTHEW.

               Well. Daddy. Hello. That was close.

               LILLIAN *leans over and, holding his face, kisses him. She then goes inside.*

MATTHEW   *(to* RUNE*)* I... I'm sorry.

MICHELLE   What are you doing here?

MATTHEW   I don't know. I just... it was an accident. I came to see Rune.

MICHELLE   Rune doesn't need that.

MATTHEW   I'm sorry.

MICHELLE   We can't have these problems. She can't do it. She's not set up to have things like this. Rune can't handle things like this. She doesn't need you. She's with me. You have to go.

MATTHEW   Rune?

RUNE   What.

               MATTHEW *can't find a thing to say to her.* MICHELLE *abruptly charges him. She hits him and clutches at him.*

MATTHEW   Michelle.

MICHELLE   You can't come here. You can't come here.

MATTHEW   I'm sorry.

               MATTHEW *has broken free.*

Okay.

MICHELLE   You—

MATTHEW   No, okay. Okay.

MATTHEW leaves.

MICHELLE   He can't do that. Not now. Rune? You don't want that.

RUNE   Michelle. It's okay.

MICHELLE   Why was he here? Why was he here?

RUNE   I don't know. It's okay, Michelle. You're okay.

MICHELLE   He left us. He can't do that. He can't do that. This is why we shouldn't invite people here.

RUNE   He... wasn't invited.

MICHELLE   That's right. Lillian! Oh God. Lillian!

MICHELLE goes inside.

Lillian! I'm sorry, Lilly. He's a friend of Rune's okay? He came here by himself, okay? And we didn't plan for any of it, for him to be here when you were here.

RUNE walks off. Music begins.

LILLIAN   *(crying)* Mother. Shut the fuck up.

MICHELLE   What did you say? What did you say to me?

LILLIAN   You deserve all of it. You deserve every awful thing that's ever happened to you.

MICHELLE   What? No I don't. You come back here! Lillian! You come back here!

The music rises and the arguing fades. A long pause with music. The lights change to dusk, then to dawn. It's now sometime in the future. Eventually RUNE *enters from the cottage, sits on the porch. She's in pyjamas. The music fades. To herself:*

RUNE   Pretty.

A pause.

I hired that man, I spent God knows how much, and they came with a load of sand for our little bay, to make it a more decent swim. I wanted... to be able to swim without fear, without having to worry. But. It just remains an embarrassment. When people come here, what must they think? Mother used to handle people. Their disappointment. Mother used to handle disappointment. She—what is that smell?

A pause.

There is so little comfort. So little comfort. That when it's offered, you can't... you mustn't hesitate to take it. Just because of where it comes from.

A pause.

I tried to make this a motherfucking project. I did try. *(over her shoulder)* Are you making toast?

A pause.

Darling? Are you making toast?

A pause.

That little criminal. Brought all that sand, took all the stones away. Took our money. A year later it was all gone, and the stones were back. His father never would have. His father would have done a proper job. He liked mother. He liked mother. *(over her shoulder)* Did you? Have a cottage? In Calgary? *(to herself)* Do they have cottages in Calgary? What would be the point? My parents found this place.

MICHELLE enters in pyjamas. She has toast.

MICHELLE   Did you say something?

Rune?

RUNE looks at MICHELLE, confused. She looks back at the cottage. She looks at MICHELLE.

Did you say something?

A pause.

RUNE   No. I didn't say anything. I was just talking.

MICHELLE   Toast? Rune?

Lights slowly fade to black.

Rune? Rune?

RUNE   I'm okay.

Blackout.

THE OPTIMISTS

MORWYN BREBNER

The Optimists premiered at the Theatre Junction in Calgary, Alberta, in February 2004 with the following company:

CHICK...Ryan Luhning
TEENIE ....Adrienne Smook
DOUG ....Doug McKeag
MARGIE .... Lindsay Burns

Directed by Eda Holmes
Set designed by Yannik Larivee
Costumes designed by Deneen McArthur
Lighting designed by Darrell Moore
Sound designed by Peter Moller
Stage managed by Kelly Reay
Assistant stage management by Michael Gesy
Fight instruction by Kevin McKendrick

It received its Toronto premiere at the Tarragon Theatre in September 2005 with the following company:

DOUG .... Michael Healey
CHICK.. Randy Hughson
TEENIE ....Holly Lewis
MARGIE .... Sarah Orenstein

Directed by Eda Holmes
Sets designed by Deeter Schurig
Costumes designed by Alex Gilbert
Lighting designed by Kevin Lamotte
Sound designed by E.C. Woodley
Stage managed by Maria Costa

Based in Toronto, Morwyn Brebner was born in Cardiff, Wales, and grew up in Ottawa. She is a graduate of the National Theatre School of Canada's playwriting program and since 2000 has been playwright-in-residence at the Tarragon Theatre, where most of her plays have premiered. Her first, *Music for Contortionists*, was co-produced by Tarragon Theatre and the Shaw Festival in 2000 and nominated for a Dora Mavor Moore Award and a Chalmers Canadian Play Award. Other plays at Tarragon include *Liquor Guns Karate* and *Little Mercy's First Murder* (co-produced with Shaw, with composers Jay Turvey and Paul Sportelli), which won six Dora Awards, including outstanding new musical. She was a finalist for the 2008 Siminovitch Prize in Theatre and her most recent play, *Heartbreaker*, premiered at Alberta Theatre Project's Enbridge playRites Festival in 2011. She has translated plays including *Strawberries in January*, *Bashir Lazhar*, and *Public Disorder*, all by Évelyne de la Chenelière, as well as *Motel Hélène* by Serge Boucher and *Mathilde* by Veronique Olmi. Morwyn is also the co-creator of the ABC/Global hit series *Rookie Blue*.

Although Morwyn Brebner's *The Optimists* received its world premiere at Calgary's Theatre Junction in 2004, it was conceived as a ten-minute playlet for the Tarragon's annual Spring Arts Fair a few years prior with the title *Coupe de Ville.*[1] That short piece featured actor Randy Hughson, whose performance left such a strong impression on Brebner that she developed the piece further. No wonder that when it opened at the Tarragon in September 2005, Hughson stood out as Chick, the car salesman, a role that Ryan Luhnig originated in Calgary (where I first saw and reviewed it) in an electrifying performance.[2]

You can call it an actor and playwright coming full circle but nothing about *The Optimists* fits into an easy shape or pattern. The only confining aspect of the play is its setting in a Las Vegas hotel room where Chick and his much younger girlfriend, Teenie, plan to get hitched and have invited the former's childhood friend, Doug, for the low-key celebration. Everything else in *The Optimists* flows—much like the booze the characters consume over the course of the evening—in different but compelling directions. Brebner—one of artistic director Urjo Kareda's discoveries and a writer-in-residence at the Tarragon to this day—believes in a vision of theatre as a debating society. She loves nothing more than to let her characters go at each other, defending and fighting for their thoughts, and their lives. The cabin-fever atmosphere of the hotel room only cranks up the heat on the ideas and on the passionate exchanges that almost lead to blows. In this instance, love and marriage take centre stage on the podium/stage. What's of particular interest, however, is what *The Optimists* brings to the table on the taboo subject of class.

Not only do we as Canadians like to believe that we live in a classless society, but our cultural expressions on the stage have by and large segregated the classes. Playwrights as different as Judith Thompson and George F. Walker have built their reputations on their fascination with characters and situations unfolding on the bottom rungs of the social ladder. Brebner, by comparison, brings together two Canadian couples, one from the working lower middle class (a car salesman and a receptionist at the dealership) and the other represents the "waspy hauteur" of two well-heeled doctors. The men have been friends since childhood through the mere fact that both

1   Michael Posner, "Things are all write in Brebner's world," *Globe and Mail*, September 20, 2005, R3.

2   Kamal Al-Solaylee, "Rolling the dice for love," *Globe and Mail*, February 13, 2004, R4.

attended the same public school, but their paths in life diverged dramatical-
ly. Each did what was expected of him: Chick floundered; Doug prospered,
materially at least. Neither lets the other forget his successes or failures. *The
Optimists* may be set ahead of a planned heterosexual wedding but it's the
two straight men who are bound together for eternity to fight the class war
and its attendant anxieties over and over.

And yet we must believe, even if the script doesn't entirely convince us,
that the two men share a unique kind of brotherly love. (Doug's mother certainly thought of Chick as one of her own, we're told.) It's here that Brebner
asks her audience to follow Chick's advice and show a little bit of optimism.
You leave this play hoping that her plan of action will pan out for all four
even though their creator has stacked the cards against them. Is it a lot to
ask? Many critics, in Toronto at least, thought so. The Calgary production was
more positively received, with Bob Clark in the *Calgary Herald* commending
Brebner on her skills in orchestrating the disintegrating relationship of her
four characters "with precision and sharp-pointed humour."[3] In Toronto, by
contrast, John Coulbourn found the characters to be particularly unappealing
and dismissed the play as a "dollar-store retelling of *Who's Afraid of Virginia
Woolf?* with four actors locked in competition for the role of Martha."[4] Even
the hipper *Eye Weekly* saw Brebner's creations as "petty caricatures."[5]

While the Toronto reviewers seem to revel in the same verbal play they
see as detrimental to *The Optimists*, they, more inexplicably, either sidestep
or ignore the theatricality of Brebner's writing. Not only does she love words
and ideas, but she knows how to extract the maximum dramatic impact out
of them. In one of their many heated exchanges, Chick criticizes Doug in a
phrase that captures his very essence: "Your idea of excess is very controlled."
This linguistic facility is one of Brebner's great assets and it's not a coincidence
that this anthology contains another example of it in the English translation
of *Motel Hélène*, which forms the basis of Judith Thompson's adaptation.

The French connection must not go unnoticed. In her relatively young
career as a playwright, Brebner has translated a number of plays from France
and Quebec, including Evelyne de la Chenelière's *Strawberries in January* and
Bashir Lazhar, the latter also seen at the Tarragon in the 2008–'09 season.
And it's no wonder she found a second home at the Shaw Festival, where
her adaptations of Russian and Eastern European plays for the lunchtime
series found a huge audience and a largely warmer critical reception. She
inhabits a world of debate and dialectics that Toronto theatre doesn't always
know how to receive. Is she too young to be intellectual or too old to be pre-
tentious? And does the fact that she's a woman play a role in this uncertainty,

---

3   Bob Clark, "Junction Scores with Optimists," *Calgary Herald*, February 7, 2004, D4.

4   John Coulbourn, "Pessimistic view of The Optimists," *Toronto Sun*, September 22, 2005, 94.

5   Paul Isaacs, "On Stage: The Optimists," *Eye Weekly*, September 29, 2005, 41.

particularly in Toronto where the critical establishment is almost exclusively male? After all, Jason Sherman, another Kareda disciple who started at a young age, never had to shrug off charges of intellectualism or pretention. He just wrote his plays.

I vote for Brebner the intellectual, but I also think that her dramatic choices leave her more vulnerable than the average playwright to the vagaries of productions. Give her words to the right director and cast and they shine onstage. When the cast, or even part of it, is not on the same page, as happened in the Calgary production of *The Optimists*, the gap shows more. Luckily most of her original work has been championed by the likes of Jackie Maxwell, Eda Holmes, and, as a translator of the risqué *Mathilde* by Veronique Olmi, Kelly Thornton. Is it a coincidence that all are women? Hardly. While I wouldn't describe Brebner as a feminist playwright, her work examines gender—male and female—with deep humanity and even deeper wit. Her place in Canadian drama is unique—even if she, like her plays, doesn't fit into an easy political or social box.

CHARACTERS

CHICK
TEENIE, younger
DOUG
MARGIE, pronounced with a hard "g"

SCENE 1

Suite in Las Vegas hotel. Doors to bedrooms leading off. Kitchenette. You could stay somewhere better for the same money. CHICK, TEENIE, and DOUG sit around the coffee table, toasting. DOUG looks middle-class, prosperous. CHICK's clothes look somehow less clean than DOUG's, although they're probably not; CHICK just has that kind of inherent loucheness that can't be shook. TEENIE is blond, cute. She has a bubbliness and sweetness that covers what has probably been a hard life.

TEENIE   *(laughing)* It was the first time I'd met you!

CHICK   It wasn't a very suave move, I know!

TEENIE   He grabbed my ass! On the stairs!

CHICK   I couldn't help it, I—!

TEENIE   You were showing off for the mechanics!

CHICK   I, I, all right I was! But your ass was just so... I couldn't help it. You have a fine, fine ass. To Teenie's ass!

DOUG   Should I drink to that?

TEENIE   Sure! To my ass! *(They drink.)* Anyway, *(to DOUG)* I got the job. So say what you want about the car business but I just say, thank God I'm employed! But we didn't get together for a while after that, eh Chick?

CHICK   We did not. And I don't think I saw your ass for like, another six months. She wore a cardboard box over her shoulders like a Halloween costume.

TEENIE   I did not!

CHICK	When she was on the floor she wore a big caftan, like Maude, so I couldn't even imagine her ass.
TEENIE	I never did! I, what do they say, I eyed him from afar. I watched him at his desk or talking to a customer and, I don't know, there was something about him. He was just different, sweeter. Kind.
CHICK	She's making this up.
TEENIE	He brought me coffee and a doughnut every day for a month.
CHICK	I felt guilty!
TEENIE	No, you liked me. Anyway. I guess it's not the most romantic story, he didn't sweep me away to Paris or anything, but... It's the one I'll tell our kids.
CHICK	Oh, "Dad touched my ass, that's why we're together." Lovely.
TEENIE	I'll word it differently. So Doug: how did you and your wife meet?
DOUG	Ah, in med school actually.
TEENIE	That's sweet, young doctors in love.
DOUG	She was afraid of needles so I used to do her IVs for her.
TEENIE	Oh I could never do that. Would you put my IVs in for me, Chick?
CHICK	*(making drinks)* Sure, sweetie. How is Margie, Doug?
DOUG	Good. Good. She says hi.
CHICK	Hi Margie.
TEENIE	It's so sad she couldn't come. Do you know where Chick and I went on our first date?

CHICK groans and covers his eyes with his hands.

(smiles) Well, he wanted to take me to a screening of *Behind the Green Door—*

CHICK *throws up his hands apologetically.*

But I knew what that was. So instead we went to Swiss Chalet.

DOUG   My God. And you're marrying him?

TEENIE   He didn't order any fries because he was trying to lose weight so he just ate all of mine. Can you believe I stuck with you after that date? Can you?

CHICK   *(moans)* Enough, enough. I changed my stripes, did I not?

TEENIE   And at Swiss Chalet, this was the highlight of our date, there was an old woman with I guess he was her retarded son, sitting next to us, and her false teeth kept sort of popping in and out of her mouth and Chick, Chick became fascinated by this and couldn't stop watching!

CHICK   It's true! It's all true!

TEENIE   So our first date was spent with me watching him watching those teeth. Click suck, click suck, click suck... *(laughs)* Can you believe that!

CHICK   I wasn't in my program yet.

TEENIE   Oh God. It was so awful, but then, first, you walked me home, which was the right thing to do, and, when we got there, he didn't make a cheesy move or anything like that. He just took my hand and kissed my fingers and said, "I'm sorry." Then he turned and ran down the street with his raincoat flapping out behind him. Like an elf.

CHICK   Oh God!

TEENIE   That was how we met! *(She claps her hands a little.)* Oh!

CHICK   Three things: *Behind the Green Door* was a joke. Besides which, some people think it's an arty thing to do, right Doug?

DOUG   Sure.

CHICK   Second, we only went to Swiss Chalet because it's around the corner from the dealership, and I had an up come in at the last moment and it was too late to start going anywhere, and third, I never looked like an elf.

TEENIE   You did!

DOUG   I can see you looking elf-like, Chick. Elfin.

CHICK   Anyway. And the false-teeth woman, that was truly fascinating.

TEENIE   It was, kind of. Do you know what I think is the most horrible thing in the world?

CHICK   Cover your ears, Doug.

TEENIE   There was a documentary on TV, about the, oh, Allegheny, Appalachian? mountains and it said that unscrupulous dentists used to go around these mountains, and the people were poor, Doug, like we can't imagine today, uneducated and, and starving, and these dentists, because there was like a Medicare or something, would go to these poor people and convince them to have all their teeth pulled and replaced by false teeth. So the dentist could make money. Can you imagine? Being so poor and then not even having your teeth? I think your teeth are one of the most important things you have.

CHICK   Honey, maybe you should drink some water.

TEENIE   No, I'm fine. I'm a little tipsy, that's all. So on the documentary they showed a picture, and it was of a young couple getting married. They were probably only in their teens, although they looked older because they were starving, and they were smiling for the camera, and in most of the pictures nobody was smiling, and she had some flowers in her hand and the whole thing would have been perfect, except *(TEENIE begins to weep a little.)* she had false teeth! They didn't fit right and you could tell, oh!

CHICK   Teenie, ah...

DOUG   Shh, it's all right, it's all right...

TEENIE   *(catching hold of herself)* I'm so sorry! I hoped, Doug, I hoped your wife would come so I would have a girlfriend here, because I have nerves! I'm so nervous! *(laughs nervously)*

              I can't help it! Chick's been married before, but I never have and... well it's nerve-racking!

              DOUG takes out his wallet, opens it, pulls out a little photo.

DOUG   *(showing the photo to TEENIE)* This is Margie, my wife.

TEENIE   Oh, she's so pretty. And she's a doctor?

DOUG   Mm-hm.

CHICK   A psychiatrist.

DOUG   All her own teeth too.

TEENIE   *(laughs)* You must have a good bedside manner.

DOUG   With patients.

TEENIE   Okay, I feel better! Doug, tell me about Chick when he was little. He won't tell me anything, but I'm sure he had a childhood, so spill the beans.

DOUG   Well... *(drinks from his drink)* He was blond.

TEENIE   Really!

DOUG   Mm-hm. His hair turned dark as a punishment for all the bad things he did.

TEENIE   No!

DOUG   Yes. He could charm the fruit from the vines, as my mother used to say. He was good at everything.

TEENIE   Really?

DOUG   Everything. Chick was a marvel, Teenie. An only child almost, to misquote, a motherless child, good-looking, elfin if you will, he made the mothers swoon and the rest of us do bad things for which, amazingly, Chick himself never got caught.

CHICK   He's making me out to be much more interesting than I was.

DOUG   He usually wore a stripey shirt, like a cartoon character, and, after he turned twelve, he always had dope.

CHICK   That's true.

DOUG   He was sent home from school once for blasphemy.

TEENIE   You went to a Catholic school?

DOUG   No. And the girls were all in love with him.

TEENIE   Wow.

DOUG   That's Chick.

TEENIE   Now your turn. What was Doug like?

CHICK   Doug was my best friend.

                Beat.

DOUG   That's all? That's all the introduction I get after the one I gave you?

CHICK   Doug always had dark hair, so I guess he must have been born bad.

DOUG   Too true.

CHICK   He never had dope. He was a mooch.

DOUG   A lie!

CHICK   His mother is a saint. She saved me from malnutrition. And his father is a hard-driving bastard. You should worry about getting his gut, eh Doug? He's one of those men who looks like he's pregnant with a Volkswagen.

TEENIE Chick, you're not saying anything about Doug!

Beat.

DOUG So have you kids booked a chapel?

TEENIE We thought it would be more fun to be spontaneous.

CHICK We're just going to wander through.

TEENIE We thought we'd do it before breakfast then go to Denny's to celebrate. We could have pancakes.

CHICK What do you think?

DOUG Well, if you wanted to do it later, we could have dinner...

TEENIE We'll get married, have breakfast, and spend the afternoon in the TV room watching the first round. They have hundreds of TVs, Doug. With everything happening at once. I'll bet. And Chick will hold my hand.

DOUG What'll I do?

CHICK Bring me drinks! Speaking of which...

CHICK goes to the kitchenette to make new drinks.

DOUG So, ah, what are you going to wear?

TEENIE *(beaming)* I bought a dress!

DOUG Let's see it.

TEENIE Chick can't. It's bad luck.

DOUG He'll close his eyes.

TEENIE He'll peek.

CHICK   It's true. I will.

            Teenie impulsively takes Doug's hand.

TEENIE   Come and I'll show you.

            They run away into the bedroom.

CHICK   *(after them)* Don't do anything I wouldn't.

            Chick brings drinks to the coffee table, sits, pours himself one. He listens, sips, idly peruses some flyers on the table. The following is heard from off.

DOUG   Very nice.

TEENIE   You really think?

DOUG   It's very nice.

TEENIE   You don't think it's too revealing?

DOUG   No, no.

TEENIE   Because it's not meant to be a wedding dress.

DOUG   You'd never know.

TEENIE   I bought it on layaway.

DOUG   Oh yeah?

TEENIE   Can you believe they still do that some places?

DOUG   I hadn't really thought about it.

TEENIE   I made them add the tulle underneath. You don't think it's silly?

DOUG   No.

TEENIE   I feel like a bride.

DOUG   You look like a bride.

CHICK	Hey, Doug!
DOUG	What?
CHICK	You following baseball?
DOUG	Sure, a little.
CHICK	Who do you like?
DOUG	Oh I don't know. It's too early to tell.
TEENIE	Do you really think so?
DOUG	Yeah, it's great on you. *(to CHICK)* I thought you weren't supposed to follow sports.
CHICK	Huh? *(He half picks up the phone, realizes what he's doing, puts it down.)* All right, enough in there! I don't want Doug picking up my conjugal duties for me!
TEENIE	Yeah, we're doing it right now!

DOUG emerges from the bedroom.

DOUG	It's a very pretty dress.
CHICK	*(quietly)* I know.
DOUG	You've seen it?
CHICK	Sure. What?
DOUG	You're not supposed to.
CHICK	I was curious. Hey, check this out. *(shows him a brochure)* Ladies. They were stacked underneath the *TV Guide*.
DOUG	Put them away.
CHICK	Margie's not here.
DOUG	Put them away!

Teenie comes in in her regular clothes.

CHICK   Honey, there's brochures for whores!

TEENIE   Does that mean you're not going to make me a drink?

CHICK   *(winks at Doug)* I'm marrying her for her witty repartee.

TEENIE   Do you want to know what I was like as a girl, Doug?

DOUG   *(He's caught off guard.)* Uh?

CHICK   *(hands her a drink)* Teenie.

DOUG   *(suddenly)* Is that your real name?

TEENIE   What?

DOUG   Teenie?

TEENIE   Well no, Christine, but...

DOUG   Because, I... I wonder where those names come from sometimes. Cindy. Well I guess that's a real name. Candy, Candy or... Mindy.

TEENIE   They're just names.

CHICK   Are you implying something?

DOUG   No, I'm—

CHICK   Doug's used to women with names like "Ashley" and "Chase Manhattan."

DOUG   Chick.

CHICK   It confuses him to be down with the people.

TEENIE   Oh my God! Chick! Do you remember that thing I said!

CHICK   What?

TEENIE	The first day I worked at the dealership? I was having a hard time remembering all the names, the mechanics and the salesmen, you know, to match them to the extensions, because there's no time to look at the list, you have to memorize them, and Chick said, he was flirting with me—
CHICK	I was.
TEENIE	He said, are you having a hard time? And I said, yes, with the names, they're all such *Welcome Back, Kotter* names! Can you believe that! Like I'd never met an Italian guy in my life. I was so insensitive!
CHICK	It was cute.
TEENIE	I grew up very sheltered. *(She drinks.)* Well not sheltered, but isolated. I was in foster homes.
DOUG	Oh.
CHICK	But not all the time.
TEENIE	No. Oh no.
CHICK	It was like when I lived with your family, but with strangers.
TEENIE	Yeah. *(She takes out a gold chain from inside her blouse, displays a little cross.)* I believe in God. That's what got me through.
DOUG	Uh. *(visibly uncomfortable)* I believe in dinner! I believe in the all-you-can-eat buffet! What do you say? You guys feeling lucky?
CHICK	Always!
DOUG	Well, just, um, let me call Margie, then let's go.
CHICK	Sounds dynamite.
DOUG	Teenie?
TEENIE	Uh huh.

Doug	Okay then.

> Doug *takes his cellphone from a bag, disappears into the other room.* Chick *and* Teenie *are left alone.*

Chick	How do you feel, honey?
Teenie	Oh, good. Really good. *(She does not seem "good.")*
Chick	Are you sure?
Teenie	Would I lie? Doug said my dress was pretty.
Chick	I'm sure it is.
Teenie	Just let me go put on my face.

> *She goes into the bedroom, leaving* Chick *alone with his drink.*

> *Blackout.*

SCENE 2

> Chick *sits on the couch trying to look "Ocean's Eleven." He's leafing through flyers for call-girl services.* Doug *enters from one of the bedrooms.* Doug *wipes his fingers off on a hand towel.*

Doug	So she's stopped vomiting.
Chick	Thank God.
Doug	I laid her on her side.
Chick	Thank you. I just, I couldn't...
Doug	*(looks for somewhere to put the hand towel, goes behind the kitchenette)* Do you know, she was wearing children's underwear.
Chick	What?

DOUG   *Hello Kitty.* You know? Japanimation, what's it called now?
        Anime. On the back, the ass, there's a drawing of two kittens,
        hugging. Underneath, it says "Sisters."

CHICK   *(still perusing his flyer)* How do you know they're children's?

DOUG   Margie buys them for Faith.

CHICK   Uh.

DOUG   You don't find it disconcerting that your bride-to-be wears the
        same underwear as my eight-year-old daughter?

CHICK   What I find disconcerting is that you looked at her underwear.

DOUG   I'm a doctor.

CHICK   You're not a gynecologist.

DOUG   It's nothing I haven't seen before.

CHICK   *(looking up)* You looked at "it"?

DOUG   *(a grinding noise, it stops)* Hey, they got a garburator. *(He tries
        to garburate the corner of the towel, the noise changes ominously.)*
        Did you know she wore those panties?

CHICK   Underwear. Panties is a demeaning word.

DOUG   Is it a kinky thing you two have?

CHICK   You left them on, right?

DOUG   What do you think, I'm an animal? She was all curled up.
        Curling and puking. Her dress got hitched up. Would you
        rather I'd yanked it down and actually touched her ass?

CHICK   It's a nice ass, eh?

DOUG   Fine. *(He gives up on the towel, throws it in the sink.)* So what
        are we gonna do?

CHICK   Wait, I mean, I guess if she's on her side it's... Unless you think we should call someone...

DOUG   Tonight. I mean tonight.

CHICK   Oh.

> CHICK *looks toward the bedroom door.*

DOUG   Poker? Blackjack? Slots? A little three-card monte?

CHICK   Doug, don't...

DOUG   Peep peep peep, Chick Chick Chick-ee!

CHICK   Doug...

DOUG   What kind of bachelor party is this?

CHICK   It's not a bachelor party—

DOUG   But it could be. I mean, she's on her side...

CHICK   Doug!

DOUG   *(smiles wickedly)* Let's have a little fun.

CHICK   I don't have fun anymore.

> *Beat.*

What kind of fun?

DOUG   Wholesome fun.

CHICK   Wholesome gambling fun?

> DOUG *tilts his head to one side, cocks an eyebrow.*

DOUG   That sounds about right. Wait, I'm getting a communication from the aliens. They are saying, "We have only one night to live." One night, Chick, that's it. One night and it's all over. The aliens are saying, "Go have some fun." What do you say?

CHICK	Make yourself a tinfoil hat while you're in there. Ah I don't know, Doug. I dunno.
DOUG	I'm a doctor and I'm telling you it's fine. She'll be fine. You want a drink?
CHICK	Sure. Have you seen these? Legal prostitution!
DOUG	Decriminalized.
CHICK	*(whacks at a photo of a lady with his index finger)* Now that's hello kitty.
DOUG	Meow. You know, we could get a couple.
CHICK	*(genuinely shocked)* What?
DOUG	I'm joking! Not that Cindy-Candy-Mindy-Mandy—
CHICK	Don't call her that!
DOUG	—would notice. But of course we wouldn't want Chick to get eaten by a pussy.
CHICK	What's wrong with you!
DOUG	Nothing, ah... I'm just, ah, you know, away... The job, you know, I'm used to the stress and the hours but the book... It's waiting for the reviews, it's waiting to see if it sells. I spent the advance. I don't know how. Do you ever wonder where the money goes?
CHICK	Oh I pretty much know.
DOUG	You know you can buy a kind of flooring now that cleans itself?
CHICK	What?
DOUG	It's coated.
CHICK	With what?
DOUG	I have no idea.

CHICK   They all have boob jobs. Even the men. You think I should get one?

Doug laughs despite himself.

DOUG   Big soda, small soda?

CHICK   Medium soda.

Doug brings him a drink.

DOUG   Third time's the charm.

They drink.

CHICK   How do you guys stay together?

DOUG   Waspy hauteur. I work all the time. Margie works all the time. Even Faith works all the time. We keep a bottle of vodka in the freezer. At about eleven at night, if we're both home, we knock back a couple of stiff ones and... *(laughs)*

CHICK   Why's that funny?

DOUG   It's the balance. Before the first drink, we feel close to each other, like, ah, brother and sister if that's not too sick. Two drinks, she starts to look alluring, you know, if she's wearing a tight shirt. Three drinks and she's enough of a stranger. We usually end up having sex. But if I slide too quickly over drink three and move onto drink four... It's gone. It's completely, totally gone. It's just, she's just, an extension of me. I can't feel any... whatever you feel. We joke sometimes, "Our sex life has a three-drink minimum."

CHICK   Do you screw around?

DOUG   Nah. Who wants to get some disease.

Beat.

CHICK   Dammit I still feel sick from the buffet.

DOUG   It was the chicken feet.

CHICK   I have to try everything.

DOUG   Why is that?

CHICK   I always think, no matter what I'm eating, I mean back in my animal mind, here, I'm like, maybe this is it. Maybe this is all the food, and there will be no more. You know how I got so thin?

DOUG   I'm afraid to ask.

CHICK   The wife *(He laughs.)* nah, you know *(gestures to the bedroom)* started buying one-size servings of things. She goes to Costco, I kid you not, buys like a vanload of Lean Cuisine, individual pudding cups, boil-in-bag rice, and she puts it all in this giant freezer she's got in her back room, and each day, she brings me over my rations. I don't know what the hell I'm gonna do when we live together. You remember how I was.

DOUG   You looked great.

CHICK   I was a pig. No more. Doug, it's a complete reformation. You can't even imagine it.

DOUG   *(uncomfortable)* What. Have you found God?

CHICK   If I could, I would. She's my God. In there. Can you imagine? The state she found me in. Can you imagine? That she would love me? That she would kiss me? Did you ever see me in the morning, back in those—? You wouldn't have. But I would, I would come into work, not hungover, not still drunk, but halfway drunk, halfway to getting as drunk as I needed to. The time I had off from leaving work at seven at night to coming into work at seven in the morning that's—

DOUG   Twelve hours.

CHICK   —twelve hours, I know, was not enough time for me to get as drunk as I needed to. I was smoking eighty cigarettes a day. I don't even know. I was calling phone-sex lines... The home shopping network. I had a crush on Ivana Trump. On the back of her hand. She'd spread the cream around a little... So imagine, you know... This nice girl. And at the dealership, they treat the girls like shit. So that she would...

DOUG   Hey...

CHICK   I get sentimental. And after Nancy...

DOUG   That, you gotta admit, you had coming.

CHICK   No lie there.

DOUG   It's good to see you. I was touched to be invited.

CHICK   *(nods)* You're my buddy, man. So your mom's good?

DOUG   Mom's good. She asks after you. Often.

CHICK   What do you tell her?

DOUG   I tell her you're good.

CHICK   Thanks. I am good.

         Beat.

DOUG   So did the guys at the dealership give you a send-off?

CHICK   Nah, I asked them not to. I feel like for a while there every third week we were having my bachelor party. Besides, I don't drink anymore. Well I have a drink. But I don't drink.

DOUG   Nobody drinks anymore. It's all water and yoga in our circles. Margie bought some face cream with caviar in it.

CHICK   No shit?

DOUG   Hundred dollars for a jar the size of a, like a tin of Carmex.

CHICK   Can you see a difference?

DOUG   No! It's snake oil. I tell her that, I mean, nothing she puts on her face is going to fundamentally alter her genetic propensities towards aging, or—

CHICK   Can you eat it?

DOUG   We should. Make some canapés and have some people over.
            We could sip our water and watch each other get younger.

CHICK   So what's the book about?

DOUG   Oh... sort of a popular history of oncology. For the layman,
            you know?

CHICK   Ah.

DOUG   Dry stuff, I know, but after the articles they approached me
            and I thought, why not? I mean who wouldn't like to see a
            book with their name on it? You should write a book.

CHICK   Doug—

DOUG   No, I'm sure you could. A personal history or... I'm sure you
            have some thoughts.

CHICK   I don't want to write a book.

DOUG   Hey, ah, Mom found some stuff of yours in the basement,
            mixed up with ours, a ah, what was it? A sculpture you did?
            Oh my God, it won a fucking prize. What was it? *The Three
            Faces of Eve?* Was that—

CHICK   *The Man of Three Faces.*

DOUG   Jesus.

CHICK   I was the pumice master.

            They laugh.

DOUG   Hey, let's have some fun here. Who comes to Vegas to sit in
            a hotel room and talk about elementary school? Maybe in a
            bit we can check on her and go see a show.

CHICK   No strippers.

DOUG   The ladies with their tops on.

CHICK   Oncology for the layman, eh? What was your advance?

Doug	Well, it's not...
Chick	Come on.
Doug	Twenty-five thousand.
Chick	Jesus.
Doug	American publisher.
Chick	What did you do to celebrate?
Doug	Hm?
Chick	Dinner, I mean, did you... buy a suit.
Doug	I guess we... *(laughs)* It didn't seem like that much of an event.
Chick	If twenty-five grand fell in my lap, I would celebrate.
Doug	Maybe we should go downstairs and test that theory.
Chick	*(cocks a finger at him)* Don't tempt me, boyo. No celebration at all?
Doug	Nah.
Chick	What is it, that's a, a Honda Civic. I guess it's not that much money.
Doug	Are you trying to sell me a car?
Chick	Hey, I'm not, but what do you drive?
Doug	Ah, a big ol' suv.
Chick	*(shakes his head)* You don't want something sportier?
Doug	What, am I balding?
Chick	A guy came in the other week, he said, "I'm looking for a car like *Starsky and Hutch.*"

DOUG   What did you say?

CHICK   I said what the fuck are you doing in a Toyota dealership?

DOUG   Faith's practically old enough to drive.

CHICK   What does she want to do when she grows up?

DOUG   I think she's evenly divided between scientist and supermodel.

CHICK   If I had a daughter I'd send her to a, what's it called? all-girl, *unisex* school.

DOUG   Really?

CHICK   You know what boys are like.

DOUG   It seems a little drastic.

CHICK   A unisex school like run by Rapunzel. I would want her educated. Too educated to fuck up her life.

DOUG   We trust our daughter, Chick.

CHICK   Who's the first girl you fucked?

DOUG   Oh, Jesus...

CHICK   That's not a question that needs a pause. You're just embarrassed. Was it Whatsherface? The one whose mom had the smokes?

DOUG   *(half smile)* Could have been.

CHICK   If I had a kid I'd want it to be a daughter.

DOUG   Some days I wish for a son.

CHICK   Little boys are shits. As soon as they stop being eunuch-y, they become shits.

DOUG   Not all women are saints, Chick.

CHICK   I guess. You remember Peanuthead? Guy from my work? Are
          you having another drink?

DOUG   Sure.

CHICK   *(going behind the kitchenette)* So Peanuthead tells me he
          wants to get married. Teenie, sweet Teenie, works with an-
          other receptionist, Teenie's full-time, seven-to-six, this girl's
          noon-to-nine. And this other girl is married. To a gangster.
          A freaking organized-crime gangster. She loves animals, this
          girl—dogs, cats, you name it. She dyes her hair twice a week.
          Every dress she buys, she has the skirt shortened. You know
          the type, right? In peril of his own life, Peanuthead is fuck-
          ing this girl. Oh, it's sad. Well, but they're in love. So we're
          taking up a collection, at work, so she can get a divorce.

DOUG   Really?

CHICK   Mm-hm. I think it's more likely we'll use it for whatever plas-
          tic surgery Peanuthead needs when the gangster finds out,
          but... What can you do, it's love.

DOUG   How do they know?

CHICK   What?

DOUG   Sometimes people are deluded about love.

CHICK   Oh they are.

DOUG   Sure. What looks like love is sometimes just desperation
          and lust. I think, and a lot of people I know seem to be get-
          ting divorced so I have lots of time to reflect on this, that
          love, adultery, whatever you want to call it, is just a desire
          for escape.

CHICK   For escape.

DOUG   It's like the suicide fantasy of a depressed person. That person
          doesn't want to die. He wants somebody to look after him.
          The adulterer—

CHICK   "Adulterer."

DOUG	The person having the adulterous relationship, if you will, doesn't want love, he just wants change. His old love doesn't feel like love anymore, and he wants change. Or excitement. But it's not love. It's the simulacrum of love you feel when you're sixteen. It's just lust plus excitement. It feels good, but it's not real emotion. You might as well snort some cocaine and jerk off.
CHICK	Is that something you've done.
DOUG	I went to university.
CHICK	I don't think of you as a man who does bad things.
DOUG	You're the one who won't let us get strippers!
CHICK	I'm in a program!
DOUG	What program lets you drink!
CHICK	I'm not drinking! I'm having a drink!
DOUG	Your program distinguishes?
CHICK	Sure!
DOUG	It's not that "moderation" bullshit I read about in *Time*?
CHICK	No! And drinking's not my real problem. It's a symptom of my real problem.
DOUG	Which is?
CHICK	Nobody ever loved me. *(Beat. He laughs.)* Gambling! Gambling, you idiot!
DOUG	So this is you trying the Gandhi cure?
CHICK	He had a gambling problem?
DOUG	No. To test his celibacy, he would sleep with young nubiles. Not sleep with, just, they would lie in bed with him. He would test himself that way.

CHICK   Nah, I'm over it, I'm over it. Teenie always wanted to come here for the Final Four, that's all. So I said, I'll take you.

DOUG   Is she going to bet?

CHICK   Sure. Why not?

DOUG   It just seems like putting yourself in harm's way, that's all.

CHICK   Nah. You know, she played high-school basketball.

DOUG   Yeah?

CHICK   Helluva guard, apparently. And cute too. She showed me a yearbook picture.

DOUG   But not university?

CHICK   She didn't go to university. She's the receptionist at a car dealership, Doug.

DOUG   Oh, sorry.

CHICK   It's not a defect.

DOUG   I'm not saying it is.

CHICK   But secretly you think it is.

DOUG   I just think, if you can, why not?

CHICK   Because not everybody wants to.

DOUG   Just because you didn't like it—

CHICK   I don't need confirmation of my intelligence.

DOUG   That's not the only reason a person gets an education.

CHICK   I don't need a piece of paper that confers upon me legitimacy and the—

DOUG   Please, I didn't mean to—

CHICK —make more than twenty K a year.

DOUG I'm only saying, you could have been a lawyer.

CHICK But not a doctor.

DOUG Sure.

CHICK And you could have sold cars. Anyone can do anything. Up to a certain point.

DOUG That's the received liberal wisdom.

CHICK You don't think I could have done what you did?

DOUG What's "could"? I could pull a knife out of that drawer and saw my leg off.

CHICK Do it.

DOUG Ah...

CHICK Nancy brought me home the LSAT booklet once.

DOUG Oh yeah?

CHICK Her nephew and I used half the front page, in little incremental rips, to make filters for our joints. It was like a mouse was slowly eating it.

DOUG All right. What are we gonna do for fun! I've got two days off, the most I've had in what, a dog's age? An elephant's age! I'm not spending it deliberating philosophy. I'm going to go check on her and then I say we go out.

> DOUG *goes off into the bedroom.* CHICK *sips his drink. He traces the outline of a breast on one of the call-girl flyers. He sings to himself. He laughs.*

(enters) Still on her side, still breathing. As they say on the west coast, it's all good.

CHICK Is that what they say?

DOUG   So I hear. Shall we? We can see if you still have the magic.

CHICK   What magic?

DOUG   With the ladies.

CHICK   Ah I never had magic.

DOUG   No?

CHICK   It was voodoo.

DOUG   It looked like magic.

CHICK   You didn't do so bad.

DOUG   I wasn't saying I did.

CHICK   Neither was I.

DOUG   You know oncology, full of hotties.

CHICK   Really?

DOUG   Sure. Smart young things. Liberated. Sexual. A slim woman
          in scrubs is very sexy.

CHICK   You sleep with them?

DOUG   It would be an abuse of my position.

CHICK   Any man who doesn't use whatever power he has to get laid
          is an idiot.

DOUG   Deferred gratification. It's why I don't spend all my money
          on a fancy car. I invest.

CHICK   I had a guy come into the showroom once. He claimed we'd
          made his cousin spend all his money on a truck.

DOUG   Did you?

CHICK   You can't make a man spend his money. A man wants to spend his money.

DOUG   Well, that's a salesman's perspective.

CHICK   What should my perspective be?

DOUG   Why do you keep acting as though I'm attacking you? Can I not have my own opinion?

CHICK   What's your opinion?

DOUG   Huh?

CHICK   On money. What's your opinion? You must spend it since you don't know where it goes.

DOUG   I have a house, I have a kid, I...

CHICK   Suits, food...

DOUG   Sure. What, are you angry I never bought a car from you?

CHICK   I'm just trying to make a point.

DOUG   What point?

CHICK   Deferred gratification? What is it, Margie? Is she your deferred gratification? I only ask because if you won't spend all the money you earn, your fat advance, your... I'm saying, what is the point.

DOUG   Of living?

CHICK   Hey, I understand, I'm getting married, I'm just saying, before you defer the gratification, maybe you should have some to remember.

DOUG   So I should sleep with an intern?

CHICK   So you shouldn't judge the man who would spend your advance on a convertible. That's all.

DOUG   So you're that man, and I'm the other man. The dull man. Mutual-fund man.

CHICK   Doug, you're not any man.

DOUG   Thanks.

CHICK   You're a specific man. I'm a specific man.

DOUG   I'd like to have some excesses right now, but you're in a program!

CHICK   Let's go downstairs and I'll watch you gamble the entire twenty-five Gs.

DOUG   Fuck you!

CHICK   Your idea of excess is very controlled. It's because of your mother.

DOUG   Tell me, Freud.

CHICK   The way she dished out the portions at dinner. It was like watching *Wok with Yan* measure a tablespoon by eye.

DOUG   You ate it.

CHICK   And I was a thin young man. Another drink?

DOUG   No.

CHICK   Yes. *(making some)* You can say mean things about my mother. I don't mind.

DOUG   She had a legitimate problem.

CHICK   She was a woman you had to turn on her side. She was a sloppy, excessive woman. She would make breakfast for me once a month. Sometimes it was all bacon. Sometimes it was all eggs. Never both. At your house, I got two eggs, three bacons, two toasts, one orange juice, water even, if I wanted it. Which was better?

DOUG   I think you should be grateful for what my family—

CHICK	All the bacon in the world every so often, or a regular, carefully rationed—
DOUG	Your bizarre reverence for your mother makes no sense!
CHICK	I don't revere her! I just like bacon!
DOUG	You know what it symbolizes!
CHICK	There's no symbolism in real life!
DOUG	The car! The bacon! It's too much, Chick!
CHICK	Oh, dole it out to me, Doug. Dole it out!
DOUG	Do you even have an RRSP?
CHICK	No, but I own four cars! And each of them is beautiful!
DOUG	Well I own one car and it gets me where I need to go!
CHICK	You don't go anywhere!
DOUG	I'm here!

Beat.

CHICK	Well are we going out?
DOUG	We are not going out. It would be irresponsible for you to leave your adored intended Cindy-Candy-Mindy-Mandy in her state.
CHICK	Do you call her that because she's young or because you think she's stupid.
DOUG	I call her that because I like to say all four names nicely in a row.
CHICK	Well don't.
DOUG	Or what?
CHICK	Just or.

Doug	What?
Chick	I'll fucking beat the shit out of you. Drink?
Doug	Is this you manifesting pre-wedding jitters?
Chick	No, this is just me.
Doug	It's not just you. It's like, you-plus.
Chick	Do you know, when you're free of your addictions you have extra energy.
Doug	Really.
Chick	When I quit smoking, I woke up every day, after the phlegm cleared, thinking I could run a marathon. Now, with the gambling gone, I feel every minute like my mind is so crammed with facts, with information occupying the space that used to worry about gambling, horses, cards, football, the shelf is clear and filling up with all kinds of useful stuff. I feel so smart I could write a book an hour.
Doug	Why don't you.
Chick	Because I don't want to.
Doug	But you could.
Chick	Sure.
Doug	A book about oncology?
Chick	Give me a month or so to learn the stuff... So. Do you cheat on Margie?
Doug	I already told you I don't.
Chick	I'm not going to cheat on Teenie.
Doug	Well, that's good.

CHICK   You know what the problem with infidelity is? I mean, there are many, but... It's like, you go to a restaurant, and you want to eat everything. Or, you order one thing and later you look over at the person you're with, and wish you'd ordered what they did. Why can't you just enjoy what's on your plate? I mean, unless it's really bad. Why can't you? What the fuck is so wrong with what you got?

DOUG   I think it's a cost-benefit analysis.

CHICK   Huh?

DOUG   Adultery. Is what I have now better than what I could have if I chose X. If I fucked X. Would it be worth it to give up what I have, Y, to temporarily have X. Because the exciting new thing always becomes the routine old thing. That's just how life is. So if X becomes Y, I just need a new X. Is that worth it?

CHICK   But say Y, fuck I can't work this way, let's call her Susie, say you and Susie get along, it's what you said, not the most exciting relationship in the world, but it's good, you have some things in common and you go fuck X, Xaviera, and Susie—

DOUG   Y.

CHICK   Yolanda, whatever, never finds out. Is it still adultery?

DOUG   That's a moot point.

CHICK   If she doesn't know, is anything really diminished?

DOUG   Of course it's diminished. It's diminished imperceptibly. A lie always diminishes you. A liar is de facto living in a reduced state.

               Beat.

               You know what, I hope you don't cheat on Cindy-Candy-whatsherhead because, well I just hope it.

CHICK   You know, it's not inherently wrong to just live a little.

DOUG   I live a lot.

CHICK   Anyway, I'm a changed man.

> *Beat.*

You gonna bet on the basketball?

DOUG   Sure, I guess. A little.

CHICK   Who do you like?

DOUG   I'm more of a hockey fan, I—

CHICK   Teenie likes North Carolina.

DOUG   The Tar Heels, right?

CHICK   *(shakes his head)* I'm going to bet on the Rhode Island Blue Hens.

DOUG   Are they good?

CHICK   No. They're terrible. I feel sorry for them, and… Since they will definitely lose, it's not really gambling.

DOUG   Your program allows this?

CHICK   Do Christians follow exactly the teachings of Christ?

DOUG   So you can bet if you know you'll lose?

CHICK   It's beautiful, isn't it?

> *Doug rolls his neck as though suddenly feeling a cramp. Chick is laughing silently to himself.*

DOUG   Ah Chick, you know you should have finished school.

> *Beat.*

Sorry. I didn't mean that. Not the way it sounded. There's nothing wrong with what you… Ah, fuck. I'm not, ah…

Beat.

*CHICK picks up a sex pamphlet off the coffee table. Begins idly
leafing through it—idly in the way where pretend casualness
covers a simmering, inchoate anger—as DOUG talks.*

When I told Mom I was coming to see you, she said, how is
Chick? What is he doing? He always had such promise. He
was the brightest boy we ever knew. And I'll tell you, Chick,
she never said that about me! No! Or Evan or... She kept
your sculpture and your drawings and... I guess she likes to
mythologize it. Like you were some kind of Horatio Alger
story, from rags to... well, the middle class. I didn't tell her
what you were doing because—

CHICK   There's nothing wrong with what I do.

DOUG   No, there isn't but... For the sake of argument, let's say I got
a job, I don't know, selling aluminum siding—

CHICK   You have a trade.

DOUG   *(laughs)* Sure, well... But say I didn't.

CHICK   But you do.

DOUG   But if I didn't, okay... Wouldn't you say, uh, that I was...

CHICK   Living beneath myself.

DOUG   I wouldn't put it so harshly. I'm just saying, people are like,
well, like beakers. Some are a hundred millilitres, some
are two hundred millilitres—well, if you're a five hundred
millilitre beaker, why are you only carrying a hundred millilitres of liquid? You see what I'm saying? *(beat)* You see
my point?

CHICK   *(still reading)* You think I'm a large beaker with very little liquid in it?

DOUG   No! Oh... I'm just... Fuck it. Forget it. I don't want to butt in,
I... It's a happy occasion.

CHICK   *(reading)* "Nice Canadian girl likes everything." What do you think of that?

DOUG   Excuse me?

CHICK   "Nice Canadian girl likes everything." That's perfect on so many levels.

He reaches for the phone.

DOUG   What are you doing?

CHICK   I'm going to call her.

DOUG   Your fiancée's in the—

A knock at the door.

CHICK   Maybe she read my mind.

DOUG   Did you call when I was in the—?

CHICK   When? *(dialing)* You better get that.

DOUG   *(going to the door)* Don't be an asshole, Chick! *(opening the door)* Yes?

It's a chic and frighteningly present woman holding a stuffed-animal moose. She raises an eyebrow at DOUG.

(frantic, to CHICK) Cancel that order! Cancel it now!

Blackout.

SCENE 3

Las Vegas hotel room, same as before. The moose is on the table. CHICK makes drinks for DOUG and MARGIE.

MARGIE   I felt like it was the first time I was really seeing an airport. I was in the gift shop—buying you a gift, Chick. I don't want you to get bored by a story that's not about you. It's partially about you. Anyway, there's nothing good in gift stores. Ever. There's nothing you would ever want to give as a gift. If you weren't in an airport, in a sort of forcible confinement with all this terrible crap, you would never even consider these alleged "gifts." Anyhow, as I was there, amongst the merchandise, I started to notice the people. I think of myself as a people person. *(to DOUG)* Why is that funny? I like people. *(She smiles in a way that suggests DOUG is not "people.")* The people, Chick. Oh, the people... They just looked lost. Even the couples. They looked plucked from their natural habitats. The only people who had any vitality were the teenage girls. That's what I noticed. They looked fresh. They looked dewy. Like *Lolita*. The book? You see the point of that book. I don't see it in Faith—I don't let her dress like that. She's marginally too young, I guess. Anyhow, the teenage girls, I felt an, I won't say hatred, but... a kind of stupefying envy, for these girls. I imagined myself in various contests, pitted against them. In every contest, I lost. I couldn't think of a single instance where I would be better at something than a teenage girl. Except getting a job. *(a beat)* You would have liked it, Doug. You both would have liked it. The only thing men are sexually attracted to is youth. I don't even know if the young thing has to be human. *(to DOUG)* I'm surprised I don't come home sometimes and find you screwing the dog. He's so bouncy and perky. *(to CHICK)* So, that's how my flight was. Thank you for asking.

> *She accepts a drink, tastes it.*

Well, Chick, this is it. Matrimony number three.

CHICK	You sound like you disapprove.
MARGIE	Why would I? It's not my job to save the women of the world from your devious machinating.
CHICK	Some women don't want to be saved.
MARGIE	No doubt. *(looking around)* Am I horning in on your bachelor party action?
DOUG	Not at all.

CHICK   *(handing her a drink)* Did you come to save Doug from himself?

MARGIE   From you you mean? No. Faith had a sleepover and my seminar was cancelled, so I thought...

DOUG   Why not hop a flight?

MARGIE   Why not? So where's the bride, Chick? Unless it's all a sham and you're just gambling again.

CHICK   She's in the bedroom.

MARGIE   Waiting?

CHICK   Sleeping.

MARGIE   Well I can't wait to meet her.

DOUG   She's lovely. Absolutely lovely.

              MARGIE nods, sips her drink.

MARGIE   Bride of Chick... Well, congratulations. I wish you every happiness.

CHICK   Oh you do.

MARGIE   I do. Of course I do. I don't dislike you, Chick. Despite what you may think.

DOUG   Margie...

MARGIE   In fact, I'm extremely fond of you. *(holds the moose out to him)* Mazel tov.

              Beat.

DOUG   Chick's fiancée, Teenie...

MARGIE   *(practically a spit-take)* Teenie?

DOUG   —Was hoping you'd come. For support.

MARGIE   Excellent.

                *She closes her eyes and sips her drink, making little kitten
                noises.*

CHICK   Well...

                *Long beat. Without announcement, CHICK goes into the bed-
                room. MARGIE opens her eyes. She regards DOUG from under
                heavy lids. They do not speak. From the bedroom, they can
                hear CHICK and TEENIE.*

                Baby... Baby... Teenie...

TEENIE   Chick? Chick, I...

CHICK   It's okay, honey. How do you feel?

TEENIE   Oh better. Much better. But I...

CHICK   Your hair's all rumpled.

TEENIE   Oh! *(She laughs.)* Does my face look like a squished-up loaf
                of bread?

CHICK   You look gorgeous.

TEENIE   You're lying! Oh...

CHICK   What's wrong?

TEENIE   I dunno, I just... I was having the most horrible dream.

CHICK   I came in to tell you—

TEENIE   No, I'll forget... I was, I was... Well, it was awful really. *(She
                laughs.)* I was being chased, I guess, pursued, by this brass man.
                Like, a man made out of brass, the metal? He said to me, you
                have a thirty second head start. And then he started counting
                down, you know, twenty-nine, twenty-eight... And I realized
                I had to go so I started running and he was chasing me. And
                he caught me—I realized he'd been chasing me *forever*, like,

a long time—and he caught me and he threw me off the roof! *(She laughs.)* Of a skyscraper! And I landed! They say you're supposed to wake up before you do, but I landed! And I got up, and I could feel that my insides—all my guts and bones and everything—were all crushed up. Like a bag of potato chips where the chips are like... But sloshier. And I got up and I started walking. And I realized that on the outside I looked all right. I was walking down the street and nobody could tell that anything was wrong. I went into a store and bought an orange Popsicle. And I tried to tell the guy who sold me the Popsicle what had happened, that I was all crushed up, but he didn't understand me. So I just paid for my Popsicle and left.

> MARGIE *raises an eyebrow at* DOUG. *He shakes his head curtly and looks away.*

CHICK   It's okay now...

TEENIE   Oh I know.

CHICK   Margie's here.

TEENIE   Who?

CHICK   Doug's wife.

TEENIE   Oh! Oh that's great!

CHICK   Do you want to come out?

TEENIE   Oh of course I do! Of course!

CHICK   Great, okay. Well...

TEENIE   You go out and wait. I'm just going to get... Presentable.

> CHICK *emerges from the bedroom.* MARGIE *has closed her eyes again.*

CHICK   She's gonna come out.

DOUG   Great.

MARGIE nods, her eyes still closed.

MARGIE   So what's the plan, Chick?

CHICK   For tonight or for the wedding?

MARGIE   Either-or.

CHICK   Well, tonight this is it. And tomorrow we'll get married in the morning and then go out for breakfast.

MARGIE nods again.

DOUG   Open your eyes.

MARGIE   *(not doing it)* What?

DOUG   For God's sake, open your eyes!

She does, very angry.

CHICK   Hey, I don't mind.

DOUG   I'm sorry. I just...

MARGIE   You don't have to yell at me.

DOUG   I'm sorry. Again. It's just that, that *affectation* you've picked up.

MARGIE   It's not an affectation. I'm resting my eyes.

DOUG   You're a doctor! You know perfectly well that people don't need to "rest" their eyes!

MARGIE   *(opens her eyes, looks very slowly at CHICK)* He's writing a book, you know. *(looks at DOUG)* I need to rest my eyes from the constant *looking*, if you must know. It's very exhausting to take everything in. My psychiatrist...

DOUG   Oh for... *(He rolls his eyes and wiggles exaggeratedly in his chair.)*

MARGIE   *(to* CHICK, *pointedly ignoring* DOUG*)* My psychiatrist suggested
          that constant perception was exhausting me.

CHICK   *(sincerely)* Margie, that's the most fucking ridiculous thing
          I've ever heard.

          *TEENIE emerges from the bedroom. She is presentable, but
          somehow unfinished-looking.*

TEENIE   Well, it's me!

          Blackout.

SCENE 4

          *Las Vegas hotel room, same as before. Everyone is laughing.
          TEENIE is blushing a little.*

MARGIE   Your ass! That's brilliant! Absolutely brilliant!

TEENIE   So how did you... How did you?...

MARGIE   I met Doug and Chick at the same time. Actually.

TEENIE   Really?

MARGIE   They've known each other for a long time, you know.

TEENIE   I know.

MARGIE   I met them both in a bar.

TEENIE   You did?

MARGIE   Oh my God I did.

CHICK   Don't tell this story!

TEENIE   You say that about everything! Tell me! Tell me!

MARGIE   Well. We were undergraduates. Doug and I were undergraduates. And Doug asked me on a date, our first date, and we went out and we had pizza, I believe.

DOUG   We had two kinds of pizza. A white pizza and a vegetarian pizza.

MARGIE   Doug always interrupts me at this point in the story. He wants you to know he wasn't cheap. We also had a bottle of wine. Then, at about ten, Doug told me he had to go meet a friend, which I thought meant he was trying to extricate himself from the evening. But he insisted he wasn't—

DOUG   I was pretty sure she'd sleep with me.

MARGIE   He also always intervenes there. He wants you to know he didn't like me *that* much, he's a *guy*. So we go to a bar. And Chick is there.

CHICK   I am.

MARGIE   Chick is there sitting at the bar, drinking a quart of beer out of the bottle. He's wearing a pair of black sweatpants, a formerly white Pierre Cardin dress shirt, and shoes with no laces. No socks either. Can you imagine?

TEENIE   Oh my goodness.

MARGIE   Yes. Doug is, of course, mortified. And I have a great, urgent desire to leave. But. Chick gets up from his bar stool, opens his arms, and embraces Doug. He says, (DOUG *and* CHICK *repeat with her.)* "My friend, my friend, my only friend." And so we stayed. I got loaded. I got shit-faced for the first time in my life. Oh my God. We drank until closing. Then Chick took us both to a strip club he knew that would serve you after hours. We watched the pole dancers and drank more and then at some point Chick disappeared and it was Doug and me in this... strip club. You know, those blue lights make everyone's skin look really good.

TEENIE   Gee.

MARGIE	You're a louche motherfucker, Chick.

She raises her glass to him.

DOUG	You know, I find it really... compelling that the memory you have of our first date is mostly about Chick. I find that fascinating.
MARGIE	I'm telling it to Teenie, who is marrying Chick.
DOUG	No, you always tell it that way. I wonder, and this is purely theoretical, what would have happened if Chick hadn't disappeared.
MARGIE	*(extraordinarily cold)* What do you mean?
CHICK	Doug, you're taking it too seriously. Like everything.
TEENIE	*(to MARGIE)* Will you be my maid of honour? Matron? Maid?
MARGIE	Well, uh... Um, I'd be delighted. Of course.
TEENIE	That's great.
DOUG	*(his eyes closed)* How would you feel if my memory of our first date was of one of the strippers?
MARGIE	The subject has moved on.
DOUG	And, for that matter, how do you know it's not?
CHICK	Enough, Doug.
MARGIE	I don't know. I don't know and I don't care. Perception is a complex issue, Doug. I'm sure you noticed the strippers. And I'm sure you noticed me. And I'm sure I noticed the strippers. And I'm sure on some level I noticed Chick. But the fact is that I slept with you and you slept with me and we got married and neither of us slept with Chick or with the strippers so how exactly is this germane?
CHICK	Moving on!
DOUG	We can't move on because this is exactly the core, the *core* of what is wrong.

MARGIE	*(laconic)* Nothing's *wrong.*
DOUG	No, what's wrong, this is the core of it. Perception is a complex issue, and I'll tell you something, Teenie, Chick, as a word to the wise: beware perception. Just beware it.
CHICK	*(half laughing)* What?
DOUG	It'll be your undoing. She thinks one thing, you think another thing. Nobody's right.
CHICK	*(to DOUG)* Teenie and I aren't planning on having that complex a marriage.
DOUG	You can't avoid it.
CHICK	Yes you can. Not everyone is so...
MARGIE	Mired in self-reflexive perversity?
CHICK	Yes. Some people are simple, Doug. I'm simple, Teenie's simple, our whole marriage is just going to be about life. Right, Teenie?
TEENIE	Right. Except, but well I can see what Doug is saying. That people are complex.
CHICK	Doug's not saying that people are complex. He's saying that he's complex, which is a whole other thing.
MARGIE	Doug's complex, you're complex, I'm complex... Moving on...
TEENIE	I'm complex too.
MARGIE	Yes, you are. We are all complex beings made of cells and atoms and metabolic processes. Don't you agree, Doug?
DOUG	How can I not agree? You thwart me, Margie!
MARGIE	I do nothing of the sort.

Beat.

TEENIE   What kind of house did you grow up in, Margie?

MARGIE   *(a little taken aback, but not rude)* I don't know. It had walls and a roof. Windows. How about you?

TEENIE   Oh, I grew up in a lot of houses.

MARGIE   We actually lived in the same house the entire time I was growing up. My parents moved when I went away to university but until then... *(smiles)* It was quite a nice house, actually. The window trim was painted yellow. At least that's what I remember.

TEENIE   I have dreams about houses.

MARGIE   Do you? Have you and Chick chosen one, I mean, are you going to live in a house?

CHICK   What does that mean?

MARGIE   Nothing, it doesn't mean anything. Maybe you'll be living in an apartment, I don't know. It's not an insult, it's a question.

TEENIE   We're going to live in my apartment.

MARGIE   *(to CHICK)* Don't you still own your house?

TEENIE   He does, but we're going to live in my apartment. To start fresh.

MARGIE   But that seems perverse. If Chick owns a house...

CHICK   It's a fucking horrible house, okay Margie?

MARGIE   *(to TEENIE)* Have you seen it?

TEENIE   Yes.

MARGIE   And is it? Fucking horrible?

TEENIE   No.

MARGIE   Well then why not live there?

CHICK   For lots of reasons!

MARGIE   Like what?

CHICK   What do you mean?! What does this have to do with you?

MARGIE   I just don't understand your logic!

CHICK   I lived there with Nancy!

            Beat.

MARGIE   Oh.

CHICK   Yeah. You know, when you're in... the program I'm in, they tell you: break your habits. By which they mean not just your "habit," but also your associations with that habit. If you drink, don't go to bars. If you gamble, don't hang around the track. It you smoke crack, don't go to the crack den.

MARGIE   Are you saying Nancy was your problem?

TEENIE   *(to MARGIE)* Did you know her?

CHICK   *(ignoring TEENIE)* Nancy wasn't my problem, she was just *before*. Now it's after and I don't really want to live in the house of before. You get my drift?

MARGIE   So why don't you just renovate?

DOUG   She's unbelievable, isn't she?

CHICK   Don't you have regret, Margie? Don't you ever want to be far from your regret?

MARGIE   I regret the things I haven't done.

CHICK   Well kudos to you. I'm selling the house and Teenie and I are starting again.

MARGIE   As a wedding present, let us give you the down payment on a house.

DOUG   What?

MARGIE   As a gift.

CHICK   Fuck you.

MARGIE   Excuse me?

CHICK   You heard me.

MARGIE   Well excuse me for being generous.

CHICK   Your generosity is shit!

MARGIE   It's an honest offer!

CHICK   Your generosity is contempt!

TEENIE   Chick!

> TEENIE *chases after* CHICK *into the bedroom, closing the door behind them.*

DOUG   Why did you say that?

MARGIE   I don't know. It was an impulse. We can afford it.

DOUG   No "we" can't.

MARGIE   Well I guess I knew he'd say no then.

DOUG   Why did you come?

MARGIE   I told you.

> *Beat.*

DOUG   How's our daughter?

MARGIE   Good. Good.

DOUG   Does she miss me?

MARGIE   Sure. *(She looks away.)*

DOUG   I hope you got another room. You can't stay with me.

MARGIE   I know. Although I miss you... At times, Doug, I miss you.

DOUG   *(looks away)* You can't have it both ways.

MARGIE   I know. I'm not trying to. I'm just saying...

DOUG   I'm *just saying.* You can't stay with me.

MARGIE   Did you find a couch?

> DOUG *looks at her as though she's an insane person who has also said something incredibly inane.*

Because an apartment without a couch is not a home.

DOUG   An apartment is not a home, as I believe you just finished explaining.

MARGIE   I'm not going to say anything. To them, I mean.

DOUG   I don't give a fuck at this point. I don't give a goddamn.

MARGIE   You cheated on me.

DOUG   I never did.

MARGIE   And you lied and you lied and you lied.

DOUG   You cheated on me. And you didn't lie. And I'd like to ask you which is worse.

> TEENIE *emerges from the bedroom.*

TEENIE   He'll be out in a second. I told him to take a quick shower. He has jitters.

DOUG   Sure.

TEENIE   Can I freshen either of your drinks?

MARGIE   No, I think we're fine.

TEENIE   Oh. *(beat)* Well, I'll just go back... into the bedroom then.

         She leaves.

DOUG   That was slick.

MARGIE   I didn't think we were finished talking.

DOUG   Why did you come here?

         MARGIE says nothing.

         Why did you come here, Margie? Why?

         MARGIE closes her eyes. Fade to black.

SCENE 5

         Las Vegas hotel room, same as before. CHICK has changed out of his pants and is wearing a pair of tight black sweatpants. He poses, re-poses, looks at MARGIE.

CHICK   Whattaya think?

MARGIE   They're not the same ones. Surely.

CHICK   I'm through being presentable for you, Margie. Honey, what do you think.

TEENIE   I wish you wouldn't wear those, Chick.

CHICK   I wear them at home. My home. The house I'm leaving and you suggest I keep, Margie. This is what I wear around. Is it penance? Is it comfort? I don't know.

DOUG   You've proved your point, Chick. Go change.

CHICK   I will not. *Fini* the *politesse.*

TEENIE	What?
CHICK	*(to MARGIE and DOUG)* The bizarre politeness that shellacs you and keeps your hair so neat. I'm just sick of it. It's my wedding and I want to wear my fucking sweatpants.
MARGIE	Maybe Teenie would like you to wear real pants.
CHICK	Teenie?
TEENIE	I guess it's okay.
MARGIE	It's not okay.
CHICK	Why not! It's fine, its fine. *(to MARGIE)* Go put on your sweatpants, I don't give a fuck. Go put on a nightie or a catsuit or... armour. Whatever it is you like to wear around the house. *(to DOUG)* What do you wear around the house?
DOUG	Me?
CHICK	Yes Doug, you. Is this too pointed a question?
DOUG	I wear clothes.
CHICK	Clothes.
DOUG	Chinos and a sweater, clothes. I don't know. What season is it? Is it night? Is it first thing in the morning? I wear clothes!
CHICK	And you, Margie my dear?
MARGIE	What do you think I wear, Chick?
CHICK	I imagine you in a sort of Joan of Arc getup. Would that be accurate?
MARGIE	You know what I wear around the house?
CHICK	Tell me.
MARGIE	I wear a cheerleader outfit.

CHICK   Oh yeah? Is that right.

MARGIE   And I dust in it. I stand on a ladder in my short skirt and I
               dust the lintels.

CHICK   Do you.

MARGIE   Uh huh. And when that's done, I bend down and I scrub the
               floors.

CHICK   On your hands and knees?

MARGIE   That would be the way to get them clean.

               Beat.

TEENIE   I wear sweatpants around the house sometimes. Or jeans.
               But I don't think it's the most interesting topic in the world.
               Maybe I'm wrong.

DOUG   No, you're right. Teenie, why don't you show Margie your dress.

TEENIE   Sure, if she'd like to—

MARGIE   In a moment. Now tell me, Chick. Do you wear your sweat-
               pants with anything else?

CHICK   Are there any other components of my outfit, you're asking?

MARGIE   Well I was very frank with you.

CHICK   Nope. There's nothing else. Just me and my sweats. Nothing
               comes between me and my sweats.

MARGIE   *(smiling)* That's revolting.

CHICK   You know what I remember about you, Margie? The time we
               all met?

MARGIE   No.

CHICK   How willing you were to go to the strip club. How willing you
               were to just throw yourself into the sleaziest, vilest of situations.

How it didn't seem to phase you. How despite the fact that you were so, well, fuckin' well-coiffed, you did not seem to be afraid of mixing it up. I can't believe you're a shrink.

MARGIE   No?

CHICK   You know what you remind me of?

MARGIE   I'm afraid to ask.

CHICK   I read a book on Japan once. It's true, Doug, I read a book. And in it, there was an interview with a pornographer and he talked about how he chose his girls. He said he never looked for the prettiest girl. What he looked for was the less pretty girl with the inferiority complex. Because she was the one who would be wild in bed.

MARGIE   I don't have an inferiority complex, Chick.

CHICK   Maybe not now. But you're Capricorn, aren't you? Yeah. Capricorns age in reverse. So you're becoming younger. When you were young you were old and worried and now you're younger.

MARGIE   *(shaking her head)* I think you mistake me.

CHICK   That could be. I'm not infallible, fuck.

CHICK and MARGIE smile at each other.

TEENIE   Let's talk about something serious.

CHICK   Huh?

TEENIE   I'd like to talk about something serious. I feel like people spend so much time talking and we never talk about anything serious. *(at MARGIE and DOUG)* Maybe you do... Maybe you have... discussion groups or... but we don't, the people I know don't... *(She looks to CHICK for help.)*

CHICK   It's true. It's true. Okay... Teenie?

TEENIE   Well... I've had some thoughts on global warming.

CHICK   Yes?

TEENIE   Well it worries me!

DOUG   It should!

TEENIE   *(encouraged)* And I think, if there's a hole, that hole, with its
               ragged edges, just hovering there, above the Arctic just, just
               (She moves her hands around the perimeter of the imaginary hole.)
               growing, how is it that it will ever stop growing? How is it?
               And, and, if it doesn't, and the ozone all goes... Then what?
               Then what will we do?

MARGIE   I think it's extremely unlikely that the...

DOUG   *(cutting her off)* Why?

MARGIE   Excuse me—

DOUG   Why is it unlikely?

MARGIE   You didn't let me finish.

DOUG   I think Teenie has a valid point. What'll happen?

CHICK   Jesus, Doug, nobody knows.

MARGIE   If you'd let me finish, I think it's unlikely that such a thing
               will actually come to pass.

DOUG   Why? Because you find it untenable, is that it?

MARGIE   No, because—

DOUG   Because you can't imagine it?

MARGIE   Let me—!

DOUG   I'll tell you why you think it's unlikely. You think it's unlike-
               ly because it would be horrible. It would be just too fucking
               horrible to imagine. Living in a world where every day was
               something out of Bangladesh, where instead of driving Faith
               to school you'd wade through a, a river of waist-high sewage

to your oxen you'd take to the, the market where you'd, you'd sell yourself as a whore!

Margie cracks up.

MARGIE   Doug!

DOUG   Well it's true! What other skill would you have in a post-apocalyptic world? Finding edible mushrooms? Siphoning gas? I don't think so!

Teenie giggles.

TEENIE   I have a skill.

She glances coyly sideways. A beat.

DOUG   Well what?

TEENIE   I can charm snakes.

DOUG   Can you?

TEENIE   I can. *(She looks at CHICK.)* You didn't know this.

CHICK   No...

TEENIE   I went to a snake church once and I charmed a snake.

MARGIE   You mean you can *handle* snakes.

TEENIE   No.

DOUG   What did you do?

TEENIE   Well I, I... *(She giggles again.)* I was in a trance, a sort of trance and I just... reached out and picked up a snake and I charmed him. He was a rattlesnake.

CHICK   Where the hell was this church!

MARGIE   *(over him)* That's called *handling* snakes! Charming snakes is something out of... *Aladdin*, or—

TEENIE   In Mississauga there's just a little storefront church. They don't always but there was a man there up from the States and he brought a bag of snakes.

DOUG   *(laughing almost but not unkindly)* A *bag* of snakes?

TEENIE   Yeah. Just a bag, with some rattlers. And we prayed and some people spoke in tongues and I... I charmed a snake. *(She holds out the palm of her hand, face up, as though there's a snake swaying on it.)* Mm-hm.

DOUG   Jesus!

TEENIE   I know.

CHICK *looks acutely uncomfortable.*

MARGIE   What faith are you exactly, Teenie?

TEENIE *just looks at her.*

TEENIE   Christian.

MARGIE   Yes, but...

TEENIE   Oh, I... I just like to go. I just like to be comforted. By the Word.

MARGIE   But aren't you, I don't know, Pentecostal or?...

TEENIE   No. I just like to go. I don't really worry about it too much, Margie.

MARGIE *narrows her eyes.* CHICK *can't bear it.*

CHICK   I don't want to talk about this! I've had enough of this!

MARGIE   Wait. So, Teenie, if you're not doctrinaire, if you don't have a specific Christian slant, then what do you believe in?

TEENIE   What do you mean?

MARGIE   *(patiently)* Well, if you were Catholic you'd believe in the Eucharist, you know, eating the body of Christ, and you'd be anti-abortion—

TEENIE	I'm not—
MARGIE	And if you were evangelical and belonged to a snake-charming church, you'd believe the rest of us were going to hell unless we converted. Is that right?
TEENIE	No.
MARGIE	Well then what do you believe in?
TEENIE	I just... I don't understand the point of this question.
MARGIE	I'm only asking, what do you believe in?
TEENIE	God. I believe in God.
MARGIE	And I'm saying, if your God has no discernable characteristics, you don't really believe in anything. Your God is just, what, a big sweater in the sky?
TEENIE	Uh...
MARGIE	Making you warm when you feel sad.
DOUG	People want to be religious, Margie! They want to believe in something!
MARGIE	Not everyone! I don't think Chick really wants to believe in something! Am I wrong here, Chick?
CHICK	I'm not particularly religious, if that's what you're asking.
MARGIE	In fact, you seem extremely uncomfortable with Teenie's zealous Christianity. Is that a fact?
TEENIE	I'm not zealous!
CHICK	And I'm not having fun!
MARGIE	Fine! But I think it's right to point out inconsistencies in this kind of thing. I think that just because people profess some kind of "faith"—and don't mention my daughter's name, I realize it was a mistake!—they shouldn't be allowed to slide

by! This kind of false comfort that you crave, Teenie, is just that, false.

TEENIE   *(in a small, determined voice)* All comfort is false, but I'd like to at least be allowed some.

MARGIE   Well that's your choice. But it's the same thing as having a drug habit.

CHICK   You know, what... Have you been reading Nietzsche, Marg?

MARGIE   Fuck off.

CHICK   Because you sound like a teenage boy with something to prove.

MARGIE   Fuck off double.

CHICK   Fuck off triple.

> *They smile at each other.*

TEENIE   *(speaking as though to nobody in particular)* Chick didn't want to be married in a church. I wanted to be married in a church but he said no, so I had always wanted to see the Final Four, *(to MARGIE)* that's American college basketball. Not that we can *see* it, but on TV, so we...

DOUG   *(gently)* Chick said you're going to bet?

TEENIE   Yeah, I like the Tar Heels. Who do you like?

DOUG   I don't really follow it, but...

TEENIE   Bet on Duke. You can't go wrong if you bet on Duke.

DOUG   Duke. Where is that?

TEENIE   Oh. I don't know. It's a university in... I don't know.

DOUG   *(to MARGIE)* Do you know where Duke University is?

MARGIE   Huh?

DOUG   Duke. University. Where is it?

MARGIE   Oh, uh, Raleigh? Salem? It's in North Carolina somewhere.

                 A beat. CHICK hasn't really moved. He has been thinking.
                 He stands suddenly.

CHICK   *(to TEENIE)* Show them your cross.

DOUG   What?

TEENIE   I don't want to.

CHICK   Show them. Show them.

TEENIE   No.

MARGIE   What's going on?

CHICK   Teenie had an incident at work.

TEENIE   It wasn't an incident, I...

CHICK   Just show them.

                 TEENIE glares at him then disappears into the bedroom.

                 Just don't... *(He looks up and around, then back at DOUG and*
                 MARGIE. He shakes his head, almost laughs, doesn't, shakes his
                 head again.) It's not, I mean... I guess everything seems nor-
                 mal after a while. You do things, they seem normal. You do
                 other things. They seem normal too. After a while, how do
                 you know?

MARGIE   What's going on, Chick?

CHICK   I don't know. Nothing probably.

                 TEENIE comes back in. Around her neck she wears a huge
                 wooden cross. It dangles from a short length of rope that func-
                 tions as a chain. A beat.

MARGIE   Well. That's really something.

TEENIE   *(to* CHICK*)* There. I did it. Now you all know... May I take it off, Chick?

CHICK   Is it normal?

TEENIE   Why do you have to make me feel bad about this!

CHICK   Is it?

DOUG   Teenie, take it off. Okay, sweetheart?

TEENIE   There's nothing wrong with it! There's nothing wrong!

MARGIE   Did you make it yourself?

DOUG   Margie!

TEENIE   As a matter of fact I did! I made this cross last week. And I wore it to work and they said they'd fire me if I wore it again. Mr. Young said that! But so what! Aren't I entitled to freedom of religion? Who is it offending? Nobody! Don't tell me it's ridiculous! So what! So what and who cares! I was at home, Chick, you had just phoned to ask me to marry you—he didn't even come over!—and I got off the phone and I felt, just, depressed, and a voice in me said, "Make yourself a cross." Not a crazy voice, just... So what! I did it. I did it, I put it on, and I felt better. So why can't I wear it! Why not! So what! What's so wrong with...

> TEENIE *puts her arms out in front of her body. She holds them out, shoulder-height, like Frankenstein's monster or a blind person. She closes her eyes and takes a few steps in front of her, swaying slightly. She is humming something barely audible to herself.* CHICK *puts his hands over his eyes, he takes them off, he looks away.*

DOUG   Uh?...

MARGIE   Teenie? Teenie?

CHICK   Stop it! Just stop it!

> TEENIE *does stop. She looks calmer than before. She is defiant.*

TEENIE   That's what I do. Can you fire somebody for that? It comforts
         me.

         A beat. TEENIE turns sharply and goes into the bedroom.

MARGIE   Jesus.

DOUG   Shut up...

         *CHICK laughs. TEENIE re-emerges, this time without the cross.
         She seems pretty normal, really.*

TEENIE   I'm going to have another drink. Would anybody like another
         drink?

         MARGIE shoots her hand up.

CHICK   Yeah, uh... *(to MARGIE)* I have to tell you, I... *(looks at DOUG,
         but includes MARGIE too)* You feel like you're slumming here,
         I know... But this is, this is... *(He passes his hand over his eyes
         again.)* This is... Things get low, things get... Teenie?

TEENIE   *(blithely)* What?

CHICK   Things get... *(He squints, thinks.)* You know what it's come to?
         (He laughs a little.) This is what it's come to. The other day,
         I'm sitting in my living room and I realize I've been there, sit-
         ting in my underwear, watching TV, drinking cans of Molson
         Golden Peanuthead gave me for finding his wallet, I've been
         here for three days, drinking these cans, drinking a bottle of
         Jack Daniel's, watching TV, smoking cigarettes, having the oc-
         casional nap, in my underwear, wifebeater and underwear,
         pulling up the blanket around me when I'm cold, sleeping,
         waking up to a channel, no channel, snow... an infomercial,
         and I realize suddenly, it's sunny outside. It's a beautiful sun-
         ny day. So I go, I realize we got a... in the garage, so I go to the
         bedroom and look around for my clothes and the only thing
         I can find clean is a pair of adidas shorts Nancy left and I put
         them on. I go out to the garage where we got a banana-seat
         bike left over from the time Nancy's pothead nephew stayed
         with us. I get on the bike, and I start riding. It's truly a beauti-
         ful day. Sunny. Blue. Neighbours hosing their lawns. Things
         just getting green. You know, you never do forget how to ride

a bike. Wind in my hair. I feel like I'm fuckin' twelve years old. The grass on the lawns looks like shavings off a four-leaf clover... Beautiful. Totally fuckin' beautiful. And then, a kid throws a rock at my head. A kid, on the sidewalk, in some fuckin' stripey sweater, chucks a rock at my head. And it hits me, and I start to bleed down my face and suddenly I see myself from the outside. Here I am, a fat weirdo in a pair of women's shorts riding a kid's bike. *(to Doug)* You ever wink at a young girl? Like a really young girl? You forget for a moment who you are, you feel inside like you're young so you wink? Then you realize? *(beat)* So I get off the bike. I pick up the bloody rock. I go over to the kid and I say, "Is this your rock?" He's like, I don't know what, ten? And he starts to cry. Cry! His hairy Portuguese father comes down off the porch, I'm waving a bloody rock, wearing women's shorts, screaming *"Is this your rock!"* The father clocks me. One punch. I go down like a sack of shit. And he says, "Fuck off, you pervert." Then I have to walk home because the angry Portuguese father tears my bike apart with his bare hands. By the time I get home it's dark. I left the door open and a breeze is blowing through the empty house. And I felt like... One time, early in our relationship, Nancy offered to buy me dinner. But she brought the wrong purse and when she went to pay, there was nothing inside it but a dime and a tampon. That's how I felt. *(to Teenie)* So I called you and I asked you to marry me.

TEENIE   *(handing Margie a drink)* That's when I made my cross. So you can see.

MARGIE   Yeah, uh... *(She sips.)* Doug and I are...

DOUG   Not offended by your story. There's nothing so wrong... People are just who they are. They do things. Like you said, Chick. We do things and they seem normal. *(He looks at Margie.)* We've all done things that seemed normal at the time.

MARGIE   I haven't done anything.

DOUG   That's not true.

MARGIE   Yes. It is.

DOUG   No. It's not.

MARGIE   It is, Doug. It is.

DOUG   But...

MARGIE   No. I only said it because you wouldn't say it. I hope it made
             you feel bad.

DOUG   It did.

MARGIE   Well.

             A beat.

CHICK   That was cryptic.

DOUG   It's nothing.

MARGIE   *(sudden and full of longing)* Chick, did the rock give you a scar?

CHICK   Huh?

MARGIE   *(pushing his hair back off his forehead)* Did it? Shh, let me look.
             There is a little something. Right there. Can you see that? Can
             you feel it when I?...

             MARGIE runs her thumb gently over a tiny scar. It's an em-
             barrassingly intimate gesture.

CHICK   I don't have a scar.

MARGIE   Yes, you do. You do.

TEENIE   Stop that! Stop it!

             MARGIE is sitting on CHICK's lap. He doesn't stop her. She
             kisses the scar gently.

MARGIE   Does that make it feel better?

TEENIE   Stop it! Stop her! Chick why won't you stop her!

             TEENIE runs into the bedroom. MARGIE stands and takes
             CHICK's hand. She nods to the other bedroom.

Margie	Is that your room, Doug?

She takes his silence as confirmation.

(to Chick*)* There's something I need to show you.

She leads Chick *into the other bedroom and closes the door.* Teenie *enters wearing her cross.*

Teenie	Where did they go?

Doug *shakes his head a little.* Teenie *looks frantic. Then she sticks her arms out and begins to do her little humming-walking dance. She comes out of it, no less frantic.*

Where did they go!

Doug	Nothing. It's nothing.
Teenie	Where did they go! Where did they go!

Doug *bundles a struggling* Teenie *into his arms.*

Doug	It's okay. It's okay. It's okay.
Teenie	I don't understand where they went!
Doug	It's okay. It's okay.
Teenie	Oh Doug, he's such a cruel man!
Doug	It's okay. I know...

He kisses her and pats her.

Blackout.

SCENE 6

Las Vegas hotel room. Teenie *emerges from the bedroom. Her hair is all messy and she wears an odd combination of clothes. She opens the curtains—it's morning. She looks around then goes to the little fridge. She opens it, roots around, extracts a beer. She can't find the opener. It won't twist off so she whacks it against the edge of the counter. When it still won't open she throws it in the garbage. She goes to the couch, finds the remote, and turns on the game. She turns the sound lower.*

CHICK emerges from the other bedroom. He wears his sweatpants and has a bath towel wrapped around his shoulders for warmth. He pads tentatively into the room. TEENIE hears him but doesn't turn. He gets a beer out of the little fridge. He twists the top off, takes a sip.

CHICK   You know what a hangover is?

She gives him nothing.

Physical remorse. That the Tar Heels game?

TEENIE   I had a dream where my hand was exceedingly narrow and long. My wrist was long? And I reached into the corner of your eye—where the tear comes out?—and I gripped your brain with my hand and I pulled it out. It was like a sponge.

Beat.

CHICK   What did you do with it?

TEENIE   I just held it for a while. In my hand. I didn't know what to do with it.

CHICK   Well.

TEENIE   Yeah. I should have ripped it into little pieces and checked for signs of mad cow disease. Or fried it up in a pan. That's what I should have done.

CHICK   I'm glad you didn't.

TEENIE   Sure. Could you not... stand there.

CHICK shuffles a few steps.

Further. Go further. Go further away from me. Jump out the window then land on the sidewalk then fall into the sewer then drift out into the ocean then get eaten by a shark and die.

CHICK   I'm sorry.

TEENIE   I hate you. I hate you so much I can't even explain it. I used to like all your... things. How you were so dependent and hopeless. With your eating problem and your drinking problem and your gambling problem. Now I think of you and you're like a Jell-O mould with cabbage in it. One of those salads? You make me sick.

CHICK   Teenie—

TEENIE   I hope you die. I hope you die and no one finds you and you bloat up with gas and when they find you they stick you with a pin and the smell is so horrifying they won't even bury you. They just leave you there. They just leave you there. In some horrible room, they just...

         CHICK sighs heavily. TEENIE shakes her head.

         I'm not a piece of dirt. I have my problems. But I'm not a piece of dirt.

         CHICK buries his face in his free hand.

CHICK   I don't think you are.

TEENIE   Sure you do. You think I'm lucky to have you.

CHICK   I think *I'm* lucky to have—

TEENIE   *(over him)* Well I'm not!

CHICK   Teenie—

TEENIE   "Teenie, Teenie, Teenie..." "All the salesmen have slept with Teenie! Just take her out and get her drunk! She's an idiot!" *(quietly)* I used to like hotels. I used to like going to hotels with men. But they're cold, sterile places and I hate them now.

Margie sticks her head out the door. This is not a good moment to try to escape. She disappears again.

CHICK   I made a mistake.

Teenie is about to say something then stops herself.

TEENIE   Just don't apologize to me. You apologize like you're selling a car.

CHICK   I love you.

TEENIE   And I love chocolate. So what. So the fuck what! Birds love to sing and grass loves to grow AND SO THE FUCK WHAT!

Margie, very bold, steps out into the room.

MARGIE   Well. I'll be going.

Doug slinks out from Teenie's room.

DOUG   I'll be going too.

CHICK   What the *fuck!*

DOUG   It's a hard situation. Let's not make it worse.

CHICK   How would that be possible?

DOUG   Just can it, Chick.

Margie starts marching across the room. Doug follows, keeping his eyes on her like he's negotiating a minefield.

CHICK   You motherfucker! You duplicitous sack of shit! You bastard piece of bastard shit!

He throws himself on Doug, taking him down.

DOUG   Fuck off! Get the fuck off me! I can't fight! Ugh!

CHICK   You can't fight! *(pounding him)* You can't do *anything!*

I'll beat the shit out of you! I'll beat the shit out of you and I'll fuck your wife and I'll take your job! I'll write your fucking book for you! I'll steal your friends and I'll live in your house!

DOUG   Nothing happened!

TEENIE   It's true!

MARGIE   Get off him, you stupid asshole!

CHICK   *(getting off)* I'll wear your goddamn suit. I'll take your daughter to school. Fuck you.

MARGIE   You're both idiots.

TEENIE   I hate you.

MARGIE   Oh, shut *up. (to DOUG)* Get up. *(to CHICK)* "I'm gonna fuck your wife." *(to TEENIE)* "I hate you." What are we, children? "I'm gonna fuck your wife." Please! It's the day now. Everything's different in the day.

TEENIE   How?

MARGIE   Because it's light out. And this is when things are real. You can't have a snit forever. It's simply not tenable. No matter how drunk you get the night before, no matter what you do, you still have to get up the next day and go about the business of living. That's just the truth.

DOUG   You're saying that because you *started* everything!

MARGIE   How! How did I start everything!

DOUG   With the... Kissy-kissy scar-scar...

MARGIE   No, you started everything by sleeping with that resident then denying it!

CHICK   You did, I knew you did!

DOUG   So what! Everybody's done something bad!

TEENIE   I can't stand this! We're not ladies, we're not gentlemen, our lives are impossible!

CHICK   Ah, fuck it. Just fuck it. Teenie, put your fuckin' dress on and let's go get married. Come on. What's the other option? We split up? You rip the gauze off the bottom of your dress and try and take it back?

TEENIE   You looked at my dress?

CHICK   I have a very hard time resisting temptation.

TEENIE   How can I trust you?

CHICK   Well, the evidence shows that you probably can't.

Beat.

TEENIE   Fine.

TEENIE stomps off into the bedroom.

CHICK   *(to DOUG)* Gimme your shirt.

DOUG   No!

CHICK   Ah, just do it! Come on! It's the least you can do. Ass-grabber!

DOUG takes off his shirt. CHICK puts it on. TEENIE emerges from the bedroom wearing her wedding dress. It is not, in fact, a wedding dress, but it is white; tulle pokes out from underneath the skirt.

TEENIE   How do I look?

CHICK   You look very beautiful.

He takes some flowers from a vase by the door. They drip water as he hands them to her.

Here. There. You look... Well you look like a beautiful, beautiful bride. You look like the most beautiful woman in the world.

TEENIE   No, I look stupid. In my layaway dress with these wilty flowers.

CHICK   Six of one... Half full. Half full, that's how we have to see it.

He takes the flowers back from her. As he talks, he takes them into the kitchenette and whacks the bottom off them.

An up comes into the showroom... That's the person you sell a car to, an "up" like, "You're up"... So the up comes in, and it's probably not anyone who wants to buy a car. It's probably a mental patient from the hospital down the street. It's probably just a bullshit nothing up. And you have to recognize this, so you don't waste your time, but you also have to remain optimistic. Optimism is the only possible course of action when you're selling a car. Peanuthead is not an optimistic man and right now he's paying more for his desk than he's making in commissions. He's paying to work. Why? Because he's a pessimist and he assumes he's never going to sell a car so he never does sell a car. I know, Doug, you're unimpressed with the hackneyed rhetoric of sales. But you're an optimist. An oncologist is an optimist. A doctor is an optimist. If you weren't, you'd be a funeral director.

He hands TEENIE the shorter bouquet.

So they don't drip on your dress. *(to MARGIE)* You're an optimist in that you named your daughter Faith. It's true! Aside from the head-doctoring, which I probably am discounting in your case because you're a woman and I don't take your career seriously. And Teenie, Teenie, my love, you're an optimist because you're with me.

TEENIE   I think that is very selfish of you to say.

CHICK   Then you're an optimist because you love basketball and you're alive at all.

TEENIE   Maybe I'm not an optimist. Maybe I think we'll get divorced.

CHICK   But you think we'll get married first, and that's an optimist. We're all optimists. This morning, in this hotel room, we're optimists. We're in Las Vegas, the city of optimism, in America, the land of optimism, and although we're Canadian, let's be optimistic, for just a day. Let's imagine things will work out. Let's imagine a future better than the past. Let's wish for happiness. Let's believe in Teenie's God, let's, let's... Let's be optimists, let's be optimists. Let's believe the Rhode Island Blue Hens will win the championship. Let's believe this despite the fact that it can't happen. Let's be optimists. Let's believe in luck. Let's believe, let's believe... That when I took you to that strip club that night I wasn't trying to fuck Margie. Let's believe our resentments have faded into nothing. Let's believe that the half of our life not yet lived is the good half. Let's believe that all the bad we do adds up to nothing, and that all the good we do adds up to a lot. Let's be optimists. Let's believe that all eight of Teenie's foster homes meant well. Let's believe Teenie can charm snakes. Let's believe Doug can charm women. Let's believe in love! Let's believe that Margie and Doug are in love. Let's believe we're in love. Let's put on our dresses. Let's be optimists. Let's open our curtains in the morning, let's shut them in the evening, let's lock our fridge and just take out what we need, let's stick to the program, let's write our book, let's raise our children, let's spend our money and cream our faces with caviar, with winning, with money and hope. Let's get breast implants and clean floors. Let's be optimists, even though we're not. Let's ignore the hole in the sky and be optimists. Let's... Let's... *(He runs his hand over his face.)* Ah fuck it.

TEENIE   No, let's.

CHICK   I suspect I'm an opportunist, Teenie.

TEENIE   No. Even if we're not, let's try. I'll try. Even if I'm the only one. Chick's right.

She heads into the bedroom.

MARGIE   Where are you going?

TEENIE   *(off)* I'm getting a sweater. *(emerging)* They keep the air conditioning so high. *(to* CHICK*)* I'll meet you in the lobby. I'm just going to go. And see. If you don't come I'll marry somebody else.

She leaves. A beat. CHICK *shrugs.*

CHICK   I better go too.

He leaves.

MARGIE   You know, I thought about sleeping with Chick, that night, at the strip club. But I chose you. *(a beat)* I came for revenge, Doug.

DOUG   *(nods)* Margie, let's go get breakfast. *(He holds out his hand.)* That's the plan. They're getting married then we're all going out for breakfast.

MARGIE   *(She takes his hand.)* Okay.

Suddenly, unexpectedly, she yawns very big. She covers up her mouth.

Oh my God! Excuse me.

Blackout.

The end.

I, CLAUDIA

KRISTEN THOMSON

For my mother, Lucinda Williams (nee Wiley).

I, Claudia premiered at the Tarragon Theatre in March 2001 with the following company:

DRACHMAN, CLAUDIA, DOUGLAS, AND LESLIE .... Kristen Thomson

Directed by Chris Abraham
Sets and costumes designed by Julie Fox
Lighting designed by Rebecca Picherack
Sound designed by John Gzowski
Stage managed by Shauna Janssen

Portions of *I, Claudia* were introduced in Theatre Columbus's Mayhem showcase and then subsequently expanded through Tarragon Spring Arts Fair in 1999 and 2000. The play then moved to several developmental workshops at the Tarragon.

Kristen Thomson is an actress and playwright. She has performed in theatres across Canada and is known for her one-woman play *I, Claudia*, which was adapted to film in 2004, directed by Chris Abraham. In the play and film, Kristen plays all of the roles, using masks to change character. Kristen's second play, *The Patient Hour*, premiered at the Tarragon in the 2008–'09 season and received its French premiere with Montreal's Theatre de la Manufacture in 2011 with the title *Attends Moi*. Her film credits include *Away From Her, Flower and Garnet*, and *I Shout Love*. She has received Gemini, Genie, ACTRA, Leo, and Canadian Comedy Awards for her film performances. She has also won three Dora Mavor Moore Awards for her stage work. She lives in Toronto with her husband and three children.

I, Claudia, Kristen Thomson's sensational and award-winning debut as a playwright, became the runaway hit of the 2000–'01 season, not just for the Tarragon but for Toronto theatre. It scooped two Dora Mavor Moore Awards in 2001, one for Thomson as an actress and another as a playwright, beating out *Zadie's Shoes* by Adam Pettle, the odds-on favourite in the outstanding new play category. Separating the two may have been a procedural decision for the Dora Awards committee but it's nearly impossible to do the same in examining the play. Thomson the playwright and Thomson the performer embrace each other so tightly it's hard to tell where one begins and the other ends.

But there's another side to this intimate relationship between playwright and performer: the physical space that showcased both. The Tarragon's Extra Space has been one of Urjo Kareda's many lasting legacies, a space in which the theatre can experiment with and give new life to different kinds of performances. Over the years, the one-person show—and more specifically, such one-woman shows as Carole Fréchette's *Elisa's Skin* and Morwyn Brebner's *Music for Contortionist*—became the trademark of the Extra Space. *I, Claudia* happens to be representative of that space and counts as one of the Tarragon's most successful original productions in many years. It's often talked about in the same breath as *Two Pianos, Four Hands* as the small show that grew and grew.

It certainly started small and in a roundabout way.[1] While its roots go back to Thomson's years in the National Theatre School's mask classes, *I, Claudia*'s more defined entrance came through two smaller events, a fundraiser for NTS and a sketch for Theatre Columbus's Mayhem Festival, "an event that let audiences in on the creative process by displaying embryonic work."[2] Andy McKim, then the Tarragon's associate artistic director, saw it there and invited Thomson to present a more developed version at the Spring Arts Fair. Kareda caught it there and immediately commissioned the full-length play for the Tarragon, where in 1990 a young Thomson first saw Judith Thompson's *Lion in the Streets* on its stage and made a life-altering decision to study theatre.[3] (Incidentally, *The Crackwalker*, Thompson's 1980 breakthrough play, also originated as an exercise in writing with masks.)

---

1   The most comprehensive account of the play's origins appears in Kate Taylor, "Character that's bred in the bone," *Globe and Mail*, April 16, 2001, R3.

2   Ibid.

3   Taylor, "Twenty seasons at the Tarragon," *Globe and Mail*, September 15, 2001, R12.

Of the twenty-six masks that Thomson was exposed to as a student, she picked four and created corresponding characters: the titular Claudia, the self-confessed precocious teen; Drachman, the eastern European school janitor who in effect stage manages Claudia's secret performances in the boiler room; Leslie, Claudia's future stepmother; and Douglas, her grandfather. The play's defining moment comes when Claudia, who's already in mourning over her parents' separation, realizes that her father is about to marry his new love, whom he may have started seeing while still married to her mother.

As such, *I, Claudia*—which Thomson admits is in some parts autobiographical—emerges as a story of multiple betrayals and heartaches. But Thomson hides her own characters' pain in a comedy that relieves the dramatic tensions and makes it easy to identify with the different vulnerabilities of each one of her characters. Thomson built her reputation as stage actress up to that point through a series of performances where comedy and tragedy intersect: Shelagh Stephenson's *Memory of Water* and George F. Walker's *Problem Child*, for example. While sympathizing with Claudia is expected, the sophistication of this piece of theatre—in text and in performance—lies in its empathy for Leslie, a creation who could have easily slipped into the realm of the evil stepmother or, to use a more contemporary reference, *The Real Housewives of Wherever*.

It comes as a surprise to realize that most of the opening-night critics, who uniformly loved the play and its creator–performer, took issues with the supporting characters. In the *Toronto Star*, Richard Ouzounian noted that they are "less successful and stick out as unassimilated pieces of artifice."[4] Rachel Giese in *Eye Weekly* dismissed them as "oddly superfluous."[5] Robert Cushman was at once the most critical and forgiving. The "lapses" in the play's structure and cast of characters were reasonable in a debut play. Still, the two male creations, he adds, "offer very little in the way of perspective."[6]

I agree with the general view on the grandfather character, particularly as he exists on the page, but, on closer examination of the text, Drachman stands out as a co-lead in this drama. For one thing, he shares the physical space where Claudia seeks refuge from the outside world. For another, he creates that space for her. The act of giving birth to a performance extends to him. Thomson begat Claudia and Drachman made her performance possible, as a midwife or stage director. (By that logic he also passes as director Chris Abraham's stand-in, as the work morphed from rehearsals to performance to film, to which it was adapted in 2004.) Once a renowned theatre director in his home country of "Bulgonia," Drachman understands not just

---

4   Richard Ouzounian, "Claudia is masked for success," *Toronto Star*, April 5, 2001, np.

5   Rachel Giese, "Thomson's Claudia needs no distractions," *Eye Weekly*, April 5, 2001, np.

6   Robert Cushman, "She, Claudia, has a few thoughts on the subject," *National Post*, April 5, 2001, B8.

the nature of theatre but its magic as well. "I was finding after such a long years on the theatre that if you are simple putting red curtain, all sort of crazy thing have the possibility to happen."

I don't want to turn *I, Claudia* into just a celebration of the power of theatre, despite its very nature as a performance (and therapeutic) piece. Doing so undermines the many social issues that Thomson subtly and successfully uses to create a real-world context for Claudia's heartaches. I suspect that this social sensitivity and not the experiment with masks made the play a popular hit with its first audience at the Tarragon. Somehow the experiences of divorce, wily children on the cusp of puberty, and aging grandparents seem a natural fit for the middle-aged, middle-class demographic of Canadian theatre and the Tarragon in particular. The same audience can probably recognize Drachman's distinctly Canadian immigrant experience. (I, myself an immigrant, lived in a building in downtown Toronto where two back-to-back cleaners enjoyed past lives as classical musicians in their home countries of Uruguay and the Philippines.) These nuances give the text of *I, Claudia* heft that belies its mere twenty-two pages. A decade later, it remains Kristen Thomson's most recognizable and lauded achievement as a playwright.

CHARACTERS

Drachman
Claudia
Douglas
Leslie

A red curtain hangs across the space. Drachman enters, pulls back the curtain, revealing the boiler room of an elementary school and, in a magical way, reveals a series of placards: "Drachman Presents;" "I, Claudia;" "Starring Claudia;" "And Others." Then Drachman pretends to look for a fifth placard, which he can't find, swears in his native language, and addresses the audience.

DRACHMAN   Frescia!

Lady and gentlemen, please to apologize. I was finding a missing placard—and that was a real disgrace because that was my favourite placard to say welcome to each person that was coming here. So now I must to say on behalf of that placard such a welcome to each person really from my heart, such a welcome. Welcome to each person.

As he goes to leave, Drachman pretends to be surprised to find a top hat.

What the hell is this?

He examines it. There is a flash of fire and Drachman magically produces a butterfly from the top hat. The performer then changes into Claudia, using some reflective surface, perhaps a mirror, and looks at herself for a while.

CLAUDIA   Ever stare at yourself so hard that your eyes practically start bleeding? I do.

I invited some girls over to my house to work on our science fair topic. Ya, well, most of them didn't want to come. I don't know. I don't live in the same neighbourhood as them anymore so they said it was too far on the subway to get to my house. But I don't think that's true 'cause it only takes me twenty minutes to get home. So I think they might be lying. I don't know maybe their parents are stunned and don't let them go on the subway, right, so maybe that's possible. Some parents are very overprotective of their children. And then others, then some others educate their children to be street smart. And I'm street smart. Yeah. I went to a workshop one weekend with my mother. Well she thought it would be a good idea because now I have to take the subway from my house *and* from my house at my dad's. Some people would say that downtown Toronto is not very safe. But I would not say that at all, right. I would not say that at all. What I think is if you are someplace where there's nobody there then that's not safe right because there's nobody else to kind of protect you or to see, or to see if you might be in trouble. So that's what I say is not safe. If nobody is there to watch you. Right? So, safety is a very big concern for me. Yeah. Yes, it's a very big concern for me for very sickening reasons because you know, there are vulnerable people in this society, and I am one of them. Like if I lived on a farm, if I was like a farm girl, then maybe it wouldn't be so scary just to be alive. Except I might be afraid of getting my hand severed off by a machine. But I live in a very major urban centre and women and children... which is not to say that, not to say, I mean, I know that there are also racist crimes and there are kinds of crimes against people because of their sexuality and there are also crimes against people like if they are poor. Terrible things happen to poor people. I already know that. I already know that. And I know, I know that I am not poor. Like financially, I'm not very poor at all. Except I'm an only child so I am sibling poor. So, I don't have enough siblings. But I have goldfish. Romeo and Juliet. Two fish, they're really nice and they... I think Romeo might be pregnant. Yeah! Because I got them mixed up. I think that Romeo is a girl and Juliet is a boy! Yeah! I know! But it's hi-larious but it's true. Life is like that sometimes, isn't it? Life is sometimes... sometimes life is so true it's hi-larious! Don't you find that? So anyway, I think they might be having children, like guppies. Um, is that what you call baby fish? Guppies? And I tell you, that's very satisfying for me. Yeah. And also I want a hamster for my room at my dad's. So cute. Well because in science class we're dissecting frogs, right, so, I don't want a frog because I've already seen one dead. But, but anyways I want a hamster and some ger-bils. Something just like, I don't know, just to like enrich my life so I have like a wilderness in both my bedrooms. Like wildlife. Like an ecosystem of two apartments and I would be like the migrating bird with two nests, but not like north and south. More like messy and clean. Yeah! My room at my mom's, which is my house, is the messy room. Well, it was the messy room. But my mom said I had to clean it 'cause it was a pigsty with my clothes for carpeting, plus, she said she was going to go through everything with a fine-tooth comb because—now I'm totally embarrassed.

Because I'm going through puberty. Oh my God, I don't even want to talk about it, it's disgusting! Yeah, like oh, oh, "You're going through puberty" and everybody thinks they can say things like about if you need a bra or something. It's so embarrassing! It's so disgustingly embarrassing! And you can't even say anything, you can't even say, you can't even say, "STOP IT! STOP IT! STOP IT! STOP TEASING ME!" Right? 'Cause everybody thinks it's so funny and everybody, all the grown-ups, think because they went through it they can just torment you! But they can't. It's totally disgusting and unfair!

> *As she talks,* CLAUDIA *gets a snack from her lunch box. She takes out a single man's sock with something in it. She takes a juice box from the sock, sips as she continues to speak, and just tosses the box away carelessly whenever she's finished with it.* CLAUDIA *should drink as many juice boxes as she wishes throughout the show.*

So anyway, because I'm growing, she said she wanted to take a bunch of my stuff that doesn't fit me anymore to the Goodwill and so she said—I had to go through all my stuff, get rid of everything I didn't want anymore, and then she said she was gonna go through it all with a fine-tooth comb. My own *Private*! My own *Private* Sanctuary or Domain! She was gonna go through it with a *Fine-Tooth Comb*, that's what she said, you know, exact words, *Fine-Tooth Comb*!

Well, I had some very private objects in my room that isn't stuff I want to give away and isn't stuff that my mom is allowed to comb through. Like, there were things hidden underneath my bed. Like evidence and secret objects, and personal musings. Like, essentially the whole stock of my private emotional life, which I so can't let my mom see and I so can't put it at my dad's because a lot of it is stuff that I... well, um... I kind of... took... or—as the police would say, stole from his apartment.

So I can't really put it there 'cause I only get to see him once a week, so he can't think that I'm, like, his criminal daughter who steals from him.

So I brought it all to the school, down here in the basement, in the boiler room, where nobody goes, except me. Weird and mysterious, eh? Oh, and except the janitor, but he doesn't even wreck it for me, he just leaves me alone. So now this is where I hide my stuff. Men's socks go in here.

She jams the sock into an electric box that is already crammed with socks, and from various hiding spots she produces other objects.

DIARY. Sex book. This very terrible coffee mug. Baggy full of hair. Bunch of other stuff. And, on Tuesday mornings, which is the worst day of my entire life, I even come down here to hide my face.

CLAUDIA changes into DRACHMAN. She may begin speaking before the change is fully complete.

DRACHMAN   I am finding that girl down here every Tuesday morning. She is very, I'm going to tell you, she is *mitchka* is what we say. She is too young to think on it but hiding this sock in the electric box could cause a very danger. So I am watch always to keep a safety...

He opens the electric box to show how he has sectioned off the interior.

So, you see, I was make this barrier here. And so the sock is separated from the electrical wire, and so. But still, I am watching for her... because she is *mitchka*. Ya? *Mitchka* mean boiling, kind of... *mitchka*... kind of a privacy boiling. Simmer? Is that a privacy boiling? Simmer? But *mitchka* mean that she boil. What a great consequence, yeah? She is *mitchka* in the boiler room. I am tickle to myself on that.

Ah, you see, I am knowing your language! Before I come to Canada, I was translator. Ya? So, I am knowing your language, very details of your language. Example, think on this. In English the word *desire* is passive word. It's important word, ya? You want, you need, you love—but, you do nothing. Is something else that move you. But, in Bulgonian, that's my language, *udipine* is translate desire. *Udipine*: to lunge, to lurch, to seize upon, to fall like a bleeding monkey on all the bananas! *Udipine* is desire that have the will to possess. When your heart is full of *udipine* you are doing all sort of crazy thing. And that is the Bulgonian way and so, of course, I miss my country, ya? Bulgonia. "Mistress of the Black Sea. He caresses her shores, just above the knee." This is from our national poet, Ungar Bienheim. It is not possible to think on Bulgonia without thinking on Ungar Bienheim. He was carving that nation with his pen. He say: "We are white bears feeding. We are black bears hunting. Great deer loping. Eagles swooping. Every jagged cliff is my home!"

I am not such an eagle in Canada, yeah? Except this bald head of mine. This hair of mine, I lost it when I was twenty-two. That was my first shit luck. I was actor at this time. It was like, it was like a signal from the theatre god—Drachman, don't act. Nobody want to see a bald leading man. Nobody wants to see bald twenty-two-year-old. Everybody want him off the stage immediately. So, I went from stagecraft acting to kind of translator, yeah? And then became dramaturge. Then, I was... ya...

He catches his reflection and points at it.

...Finally that guy right there, he was Artistic Director National Theatre of Bulgonia. It's a comic. I was speaking in images to a mutilated nation and now I am, uh, sweeping your dust bunnies. But, that was my luck. That was my shit luck. And life is like that sometimes, isn't it? Life is sometimes... sometimes life is such a shit luck, it's hilarious. Don't you find that? And, as the famous Bulgonian axiom say: *Ich bat boekin ja wahlieh peitenieh*. The man who is always the same is a stranger to himself. It's a comic. I am used to work in the very best theatre, ya? Very highly trained performers, very physical performers, very precise physical work. So what, what I'm doing here? Uh? What I'm doing here? Uh? I'm custodian, ya? Kind of caretaker here at Greenfield Senior Elementary. So, now, ya, I am sweeping the floor, I'm polishing your knob, I am picking this vulgar juice box. But still, I have image and language for my blood and I have my red curtain. Practical the only thing what I was bringing with me from Bulgonia... because I was finding something so magical. I was finding after such a long years on the theatre that if you are simple putting red curtain, all sort of crazy thing have the possibility to happen. All sort of crazy thing... Like this.

> DRACHMAN *turns on some teenage pop music and changes into* CLAUDIA, *who is rocking out.*

CLAUDIA   Some kids are mad when they're teenagers, right? Like in movies and at school lots of kids hate their dads. For different reasons at different times. Some kids hate their dad 'cause they want to shoot speed into their arms! Dads don't let them. Dads try to stop them. They say, "Fuck off, Dad. Fuck off! I'm shooting speed into my arm and you can't stop me!" And that's 'cause they're into speed.

But I would *never* do that 'cause I don't hate my dad. My dad is my best friend and I get to see him every week! It starts Monday after school at 3:45. I wait for him in the park across the street from the school and he is never late like other kids' parents and we do something totally bohemian together like go bowling or for pizza. And I have to say, it is the best moment of my entire life because there's so much to talk about and we're both hi-larious. Like every time I say, "I'm thirsty," he says, "I'm Friday," which is just something between us, like father-daughter. And then we go to his apartment which is a downtown condo where I have my own room with a name-plate on the door that says "Albert" for a joke, and so I say to him, I say, "al-BERT"—and I have lots of posters, no pets, and I do homework and we just hang out and then I go to sleep. And when I wake up on Tuesday morning it is the worst day of my entire life because it's the beginning of the whole next week of not seeing him. So I come down here on Tuesday morning before class to get control of myself.

But Tuesday is also sophisticated because my dad leaves for work before me so I get about twenty minutes in the apartment all by myself, which is a very special time for me which I think of as my teen time. Like, I drink juice but I drink it out of a coffee mug. I look out over the vast cityscape and listen to the top music of my time and, um, okay. Mostly, I do my thing that I do. I take one of my dad's socks from a pair and pack a snack in it, like a juice box, pudding cup, whatever. I just do it for a joke-game to see if he notices that something is missing... And then I put hair from my mother's brush under my dad's pillow to help them get along. I learned that in voodoo class. And then I... um... well... kind of, um... sneak around to find out information. And there is a lot of information. Look what I found for example six months ago! These! *(high heels)* I went to my dad next time like, "Look what I found by accident. What's? Like whose are these?" And he goes, like, fake normal, "Oh those belong to Leslie."

I'm like, "WHO?"

"Leslie is a special friend of mine."

Now, I don't want to sound precocious, but I know a euphemism when I hear one. And then, when I finally saw her I KNEW from her boobs how special she was. They were like two flying saucers from another planet that came down and landed on her chest! She came walking into my dad's apartment on a MONDAY night all globbed over in nail polish and lipstick and perfume AND wearing a mink coat with no care for the animals and high heels six feet off the ground! Which are bondage! They are bondage for women! You can get very, you can get very good supportive shoes. My grandmother died from osteoporosis and the bones in her feet like crumbled, they fell apart, and they had big knobs on them so she couldn't even hardly walk and she told me that it was from wearing high heels. So, I'm only twelve and three-quarters and I already know that. And so Leslie is not very... um... not very... Leslie is... like... stupid... She says, "Kiddo." She says, "Let's you and me be such good friends, and just do girl stuff together, stuff your dad can't do 'cause he's a guy, and we can be such good girlfriends and you can tell me all your problems..."

And I'm like, "Think about it, Leslie."

Like, that's just one example of her brain.

I find all my information from sneaking—all the important information about my own life, I find it from sneaking around. Like, I already knew my parents were getting separated from hearing my neighbours through the fence even though they didn't do it until my grandma died. And I already know that my grandpa's giving me my grandma's cameo for my thirteenth birthday. And... I know something else, bonecrushingly agonizing.

Okay. Here's what happened. Stacey and Tracey stopped talking to me again. We were doing our science fair project on rust—just pouring bleach on steel wool and observing it. But then they started ignoring me and passing notes. I was making the pie chart but now they can just shove it. So, then, I wanted to be partners with my best friend, Jojo. She is making a dinosaur out of chicken bones. Her father is an alcoholic on weekends, so she stays with her grandparents on Saturday night. They save the chicken bones and dry them out for her. But Jojo is in a different class, so I wasn't allowed to be partners with her.

And by the way, speaking of alcohol...

She produces a small flask of alcohol that DRACHMAN *has sipped from earlier.*

Booze. I'm not going to say anything but he could get so fired for that!

So, anyways, you know I have two goldfish, right?

She brings out her goldfish.

Romeo and Juliet and Romeo is pregnant! So, I thought I would have an experiment of observing the new family since I heard that goldfish eat their babies. I didn't even know if that was true, so I went to my mom's office to use the computer but she was on the phone so I eavesdropped. Is that the right word? I listened. I heard her say like "blah blah blah... David's getting married and moving to Brantford. Blah blah blah..."

I'm like WHAT? I didn't even know if that was true. So this morning, at my dad's, I'm just sitting there eating Froot Loops, which I am too old to eat, and when he's just about to go I go, "Congratulations!" He has a cardiac attack. Says he wanted to tell me himself. So I felt really bad about that. Said

Leslie wants me for the flower girl. Said Leslie is honoured for me to be the flower girl.

(to goldfish) I bet you never saw a flower girl before. Flower girls never get to say anything. They just have to stand there. They are usually five, which is probably old in fish life but it is young in human life. They don't get a statue on the cake. They dress you up like they don't want you to look cool. They *want* you to look like a loser.

You're not supposed to tap on the fish bowl 'cause it causes a sonic boom for the fish. I was going to take the fish up to class like, "Yeah, you have rust, well, I have fish," but then I thought Stacey and Tracey might pour bleach in the water so now I'm keeping them down here where it's safe. So now my topic is like to observe "The Effects of Darkness and Greasiness on Goldfish."

Observation one. Spoke to the fish, no response. Conclusion. They don't speak English. Observation two. Fish grazed the side of the bowl. Conclusion. Swimming in circles.

You know what? If I was a real scientist, I would, I would slap the side of the bowl to discover what the sonic boom really does.

> CLAUDIA *changes into* DOUGLAS *in silhouette behind the red curtain. He emerges as if looking out the window of his home in the early morning.*

DOUGLAS

I can hear those few wee birds just behind the traffic. Lovely. They've been keeping me sane since I moved up here. Big change to move up here. Very big change. I haven't lived alone since my wife passed, Eileen, so I moved up here about a week ago, maybe a few weeks. Yeah. That's right, I moved up here three months ago to be near my son—that's what I was thinking I wanted to say. That's why I moved. To be closer to my son David, my granddaughter Claudia, and his beautiful wife Cynthia. She's a custom-made lady! When those two met, they were so young, it was just like Romeo and Juliet— and now it's all gone to hell. That's right, and now he's mixed up with this new girl, this so-and-so. What's her name? Aw, Jesus Christ, what in the hell is her name? Now, I share my birthday with Jesus Christ's, so I figure that gives me a pretty good reputation. So for his sake and mine I wish to hell I could remember the name of that girl. Audrey?

He begins the long process of unwrapping a candy, speaking throughout.

Got a weakness for suck candies. Always have. Sweet tooth. That's me. Sweet tooth, sweet toes, sweet heart. My wife, Eileen, always said a different part of my body. "Douglas, you've got sweet knuckles." That's from knuckling around in the candy dish, my darling. I have never seen a wrapper so in love with a lozenge. Come loose, you devil. Eureka! We have contact.

So, my son David's coming over with Claudia and that new girl, whatsername? I'm meeting her parents. More in-laws. Told Claudia I'd be her date to the wedding. Meanwhile there's a nice lady down the hall, I was hoping to take her. In any case, I'm going with old Hickory Dickory—that's Claudia. Old Hickory Dickory Dock! That's what I call her. She did the cutest little tap routine when she was... let's see now... five or six years old. There was barely a tap in it. Hickory Dickory Dock, tap, tap—that was it. The mouse ran up the... you know, and then she'd spin around like she was running up the clock. She puts up a fuss, but she'll still do it if I razz her. In any case, they're coming to pick me up at six o'clock. That's about eleven hours away. Got to get an early start. Arthritis. Pain. That's what I say now when people ask, I say, "Don't mind me, I'm just one big pain!" I think Eileen would agree with that, wouldn't you, dear?

"Douglas!" That's what she'd holler at me. Endlessly. "Douglas!" But, when she was in hospital, she started calling me Tom. She watched out the window of her room and said she saw fish swimming out there in the parking lot. "Did you feed the fishies, Tommy?" That was her baby brother. Very confused. Very confused. But then right at the end there, she did, she looked right in my eyes, said: "Douglas, who was that pretty girl, Audrey?" Just like it was yesterday. But I never would have remembered that girl's name, not in a million years. Jesus Christ. All those years ago Eileen just showed up at the office. She just came walking into the office with the baby—and I was, I was, I was—mixed up with that girl. But she never said anything about it. She never. Not in all those years… until it was just near the end. I was touching her hair. She didn't have much left. Like a nest of feathers. She looked at me right in the eyes and said, "Douglas, who was that pretty girl, Audrey?" I don't know who she was. I don't know. It's better to forget that… that…

That's what I wanted to say. They say that the first sign of going crazy is talking to yourself. Well, not in my case. In my case, it's about the fourth or fifth sign in my case. You hear those stories once you get to a certain age that you accept it and you want to move on? Well, nevertheless, I don't especially want to. I'd like to uh, I'd like to take another spin around the block. I really would. Which puts a nasty thought in my head. You hear that scandal in the papers about the nursing homes where the older people are living? They don't have enough staff, of course, goddamn places never do, and when they're getting too busy they're tying the old people up in the beds. Well, I thought, myself, I wouldn't mind being tied up by a few nurses. That doesn't sound half bad to me. Heavens. I say nonsense like that. You stop me. You stop me before I get started! Because that's the kind of nonsense, I'll say it though. I will. I'll say it.

> DRACHMAN *appears from behind the curtains and re-opens them. Takes the suck candy from his mouth: "I'm not so crazy on that suck candy;" picks up a juice box from the floor: "More mitchka;" approaches his music source and before pressing play on some dance music says "This is going to be fun." Changes into* LESLIE *using the high heels that* CLAUDIA *showed us.*

LESLIE

Come on! Come ON! Pick it up! Pick it up! What's that name tag say? David? Leslie! Come on, you can do better than that, David! Hustle, baby, hustle! You are dancing with the creator of the regional supply network! I don't want to brag but did you come to my seminar? I'm kidding. I'm kidding. I just want to party! I just want to have a helluva good time! That's why they hate me. That's why Michael's over there staring into his dink… I mean his drink!

When I started with the company Michael was my boss. He taught me everything about the company. He put in a lot of extra time with me *and* it's possible that there was a certain amount of... attraction on his part. I can hardly deny that. But, I'll tell you, he's a Christian and so I never thought it would end up in anything. I mean, I went over to his place for dinner a lot with his wife, Peggy, they've got three, Patty, they've got three lovely kids. They were very, you could tell that they'd been to church, please and thank you everything. After dinner, Michael would take me through every detail of the company's acquisition and distribution systems, which is where the RSN was born, really. RSN? Regional supply network. That's the system I developed! Come on, David, get with the program. Anyway, some nights we'd just sit in the kitchen and I'd spend the whole time just chatting with Peggy... I mean Patty. I was always calling Patty Peggy. I thought she was just going to take my head off.

What? What? Here I am going on about myself. Enough about me, what do you think of me, David? I'm kidding.

Meanwhile, I am dating every conceivable version of Mr. Wrong. I was dating this one guy, so good-looking, and he was pretty nice, treated me quite well. And uh, and then he just started acting like a maniac. He drove this big gold Jeep. He used to come and park it out front of my building, all night long. Finally I did, I had to call the police—who did nothing. Until I spray-painted "*Stalker*" on his Jeep. Told him if I ever saw his effing Jeep again anywhere, I would do the same.

ALL OF WHICH, you see, brought out this overprotective thing in Michael because that's when he started dropping by my apartment. Then the gifts and the notes started. I told him, you know, Michael, well, just look at him over there—I said to him, "Michael, you're fantastic, you're the best, you have been so good to me, but you're more like a father or an uncle to me than a"... yeah. Then he went away. Yeah. After I told him that. I mean he went to Florida. And do you know what I think? I think he went down there and had a few affairs because that's when Peggy-Patty left him. And he blames me for that. Oh yeah! He blames me for her leaving and she blames me for him having the affair! Oh yeah! Welcome to my world, David. That's par for the course. I'm used to it. Everybody! Got a problem? No, I'm serious. Any problems? Blame Leslie! Go for it! Do you have gas? It's probably my fault. Tell me, David, do you ever feel inadequate? 'Cause if you do, you can call me names till you feel better.

I don't know why I just said that. I'm kidding. I'm kidding. That doesn't actually happen. But seriously, seriously, it is, it is, it is challenging to be the only woman manager in that office—which is why I am so thrilled, don't tell anybody, I mean, who would you tell, but don't tell anybody. I've been offered a head office posting! Yeah. Brantford. Brampton? Did I say Brantford or Brampton? I always get those two mixed up. It's either Brantford or Brampton. It's Brampton. No, no, it's... where the hell is Brantford, anyway? Do you want to dance?

Leslie dances into Claudia, leaving her high heels in the space.

CLAUDIA   I'm growing my hair out for my school photos. You know those school photo packages? I'm getting the one with me. Two blow-ups, one for my mom and one for my dad, and then two smaller ones and then six wallet-size photos. One for my mom, one for my dad, one for Jojo, one for Grandpa, one for Leslie, can you believe it? My dad said I have to give her my wallet-size photo and I have to put on the back of it like, "LOVE Claudia." Anyway, it's going in my eyes so I've been getting eye infections. Yeah. Like, the grease on the end of my hair goes in my eyes and it makes my eyes get infected. But, right now they're fine. I can see you perfect. Yeah. I think my hair looks pretty good.

Some girls aren't even wearing their uniforms for their picture. Stacey told everybody that she's wearing hot pants and makeup. I might wear bell bottoms and platforms, but not hot pants. I think that they're just too short and my legs would just stick out of them, so probably I wouldn't want my legs sticking out like that. Probably not. Especially for the homeroom photo where it's not just your face but your whole body plus the whole class plus the homeroom teacher, Mrs. Pritchard.

I like Mrs. Pritchard. She's hi-larious. She's so fat, she's sooo funny! She just is laughing all the time. Yeah. She teaches English. She gave us an assignment last week. So hard for the imagination. She said, "Use a metaphor to express something about yourself." Like, that's pretty hard, right? Use a metaphor! That's just, like, for one thing. I do feel a bit shy about using metaphors and also, when you're an official pre-teen like I am, it's considered totally, like, pathetic to express anything about yourself. You're just supposed to act like, duh. Attitude, right? Like, what's an example? Okay. If an old-fashioned type of adult is trying to make friends with you they go, "Oh, what do you want to be when you grow up?" Right? And you should go, you go like this. "I don't know," just shrugging your shoulders, and like all over your face is like, duh. Right? But really the whole time underneath I know I wanna be a DJ or a VJ, 'cause that would rock! That would so rock my universe! Except it might be considered a bit pathetic. Because, like if I said it people might say, like, "How can you be a VJ? You're too ugly." Yeah. That's what people might say to me. But like if I said it I would have to be really cool to be able to say it. So I was just pretending when I said I wanted to be a VJ.

So anyway, I tried to write a poem for my assignment, 'cause I like to write poetry. My dad said it's 'cause I'm sensitive. He said it's 'cause I'm sensitive and my mom said it's 'cause I'm emotional. But I couldn't finish it. I wanted to write about butterflies for my own personal reasons and how they start off as basically maggots and then go in a cocoon and then become a miracle but I could only write the first line, like:

You glide, you are throttled through
the black tunnel coming as
a shadow amongst shadows
with urges for light.

But, uh, I got writer's block for the rest of that poem. So then I remembered an old dream poem that I wrote before I got my fish, dreaming that I had a sister. Yeah, an older sister. Like a sister who was like a rainbow with many different colours and many different moods and like arching over me to protect me. Just from anything. Just from grey skies. Yeah. But I lost it. Too bad, 'cause that was a very favourite poem of mine. So I had to hand in something, so I handed in one that doesn't make any sense that was very um, unfortunately, that was very uh, that was very ugly, that's a very ugly nightmarish image called "Black Serpent" with the black serpent that lived in my stomach. And that sometimes got caught in my throat. And I would choke on it and in my poem I would choke on the black serpent but I could never get it out and I would be choking on the black serpent trying to push it out of my stomach, but it would always scoot back down in and lie there just coiled and ready to pounce at the bottom of my stomach. So, I got an A+, higher than Stacey or Tracey. Tracey compared herself to a horse for running cross-country. Duh. But I never showed that poem to my mom and dad even though I got the top grade. No. 'Cause if I showed them, sometimes if I told them that I'm upset or that I am um nightmarish or that I'm choking or that I just feel like sometimes if I said like, "Uh, I'M NOT SO HAPPY AS I PRETEND TO BE!" I think that they would be pretty upset by that. If I just, "IT'S A BIG CHARADE," I think that would really upset them. If I said, "YOU SHOULDN'T'VE GOT DIVORCED," I think that that would really upset them a lot. And I don't want to 'cause, like, I always pretend that my mom's just fine, but, I HEARD HER CRYING. And she's, she's you know we do stuff together but she's not... sometimes I just watch her through the crack in the door. Sometimes I go in and I say, "Oh are you okay? Do you want, um, some juice or like a foot massage or anything?" All the curtains are closed even if it's sunny outside. So, my mom is very sensitive. She is way more sensitive than me even though she's my mom. And my mom is way nicer than anybody else in the world. My mom is smart. My mom is brilliant. My mom is beautiful. And she is way better than anybody else, you know.

So, Leslie is not better than my mom. She is like, she is like the crap on the bottom of my mother's shoes. Now, I have to say something nice about her, I know I do. Just a second. What do I like about her?

CLAUDIA puts on her high heels and checks out her reflection.

Um... uh... I guess I feel kind of sorry for her in a way because I hate her so much because... I was looking through my dad's wallet and there was just one picture of Leslie in there. Like, the other picture was me and my mom so he couldn't keep that but... I still think he should have my picture in his wallet. But, I can't... "YOU SHOULD HAVE MY PICTURE IN YOUR WALLET." Like I could find another way to say it. A nice way to say it. Plus it's not a good time for causing problems. So, so, I just... I just one day, I just... I just said, "Oh that's a nice picture. Do you have any other ones?" So that's a different way of saying it—plus I'm getting my pictures done.

CLAUDIA becomes LESLIE in a bridal shop. LESLIE should wear a bridal veil at some point.

LESLIE   Hello? Hello? Anyone? How much longer is this going to be? What am I, some kind of second-class citizen? Well, I'm not. And what bothers me, and I don't think I'm acting out of turn here, what bothers me is that I told them I have to get back to work. The dressmaker just turned around and stared at me with a mouthful of pins. He was working on some other girl who arrived at exactly the same time as me. I don't know why they double-booked our fittings, but she has got, I saw her dress, and I don't like it. It has got those big puffy, I don't even know what you call them, those big puffy...

(cellphone) Hello... don't worry, the dressmaker's not here yet. What's up? It'll be gorgeous. Did David call? Oh. Michael? Oban? What did he want? Did you tell him I was out of the office? Oh, he can't, can he. What's urgent? He's known about that for two months. At you? What's his number—nine, eight? Five, eight? Thanks.

Admiring her new wedding shoes.

Aren't they sweet?

(cellphone) Michael Oban, please. Michael, don't yell at my secretary... don't yell at my sec... Don't. No, I'm not talking to you until you agree not to bully my... Yeah, bully. Bully, yeah... well, keep in mind that yelling is just a LOUDER VOICE and I can—not until you agree... all right. Oh Michael, you see that's not your department anymore, that's my department... He doesn't have the trucks or the staff to handle the contra... yeah, 'cause he's your buddy... It's not my job to keep him in business... That's not bottom-line thinking... as far as I can tell it's you who can't stop thinking about bottoms, just ask Pegpatty! ...Look, you've known about this for months... I already signed Flatfoot... You know I mean Fleetfoot... Well, you also probably think I shouldn't hang up on you right now but apparently I'm such a thoughtless bitch, I think I will... and anyway I'm at a fitting for my wedding dress right now. *(hangs up)*

They think they can just whip it together. Well, it's my wedding dress. It's not, uh, it's my wedding dress, it's not, it's not like uh some small thing. But nothing special can ever happen to Leslie... That other girl arrived with her mother.

My mother, the only thing she's really focused on is that she wants an organ to play "The Wedding March." But I don't want a traditional wedding in the sense of a traditional wedding. But, that's what she wants. She wants a great whining organ groaning out "The Wedding March." So, I said to David, I said, "Well, David, you know, maybe it's not such a bad idea, 'cause you know what they say is even more romantic than roses on a piano? Tulips on an organ!" He had to agree with me there!

I love this pearly detail. It's so... just sweet.

Anyway, David doesn't really mind. It's not such a huge thing on David's side. Not that he doesn't care, but with the divorce... so it'll just be Claudia, his father, and a couple of friends on his side. But on my side it will be a huge wedding because, well, it's my first marriage and, oh God, well, I have a bit of a reputation and it probably sounds stupid but I want, I want, I just want everyone I know to see me walk down the aisle with the man I love. That's what I want. And I really want my parents to see that. I want it to be a perfect day and I want to walk down the aisle right past them and give them a little, you know, "Fuck you." Like, you didn't think I could do it, well, I did it. Kinda where I'm coming from. I know it was the great joy of your lives to make me feel like an idiot, make Leslie feel like an idiot, the greatest joy of your lives... Pretty grim, eh?

She puts on her wedding veil.

But somewhere along the line, maybe watching my parents, I don't know, something snapped in my head and went, "I'm not going to be miserable." I'm not going to be that miserable. I don't wanna be. I just can't be that miserable. And when I met him David was. He was. That's just a sad fact. He just was a totally different guy. He was stiff, arrogant, he had a terrible haircut... I still tease him about it. We were at this conference and I was cutting loose on the dance floor, I was kinda hammered, and I saw him standing there behind his name tag, handsome... but kind of incarcerated in his suit. You know? Not at ease. So I just—innocently—grabbed his hand and pulled him onto the dance floor and he started just kind of tilting from side to side, you should have seen him. Pathetic. Truly pathetic. But by the end of the night he was covered in sweat, he had his suit jacket tied around his neck like a cape, I kept calling him Zorro, and his face was just beaming. So what are you gonna do? I met him at a time when he was feeling pretty depressed about his life, and I know that feeling. I know that feeling very well. I had to take a little trip to the hospital once 'cause of that feeling. So... we just grabbed each other while the grabbing was good. And the grabbing was good. And I see him with Claudia and I think, I want you to be the father of my children too, 'cause I am nuts about her dad. Kookoo. What's the word I'm looking for? Bonkers? I'm kidding. I love him. 'Cause he's just washing all the pain away... just the regular pain. And when he looks at me, he sees someone worth loving. Now that's... that's a miracle.

> LESLIE *is wearing the veil and looking at her reflection. She enters into a fantasy about her wedding. She dances with* DRACHMAN'S *magic top hat as if with David, finally placing her veil and the top hat in a kind of wedding portrait. This image lingers as she changes into* CLAUDIA.

CLAUDIA   Romeo and Juliet are dead. Juliet developed a big slimy growth, like infection on his eye. It was all long and white and trailing off his eye. And flowing around in the water. He looked like Leslie in her white wedding veil just trailing off her head like an infection, 'cause they got married on Saturday. It wasn't even magical. And on Sunday the fish died. Juliet didn't even seem to notice the infection even though in such a small, cloudy fish bowl you think you would go mentally insane with such a big, long infection.

Too much fungus. That's what my mom said—from over-feeding. But feeding fish is practically the only thing you can do with them—especially to observe them scientifically. Otherwise they are just swimming. And what's swimming? It's not science! So, I kept sprinkling and sprinkling and sprinkling and sprinkling and sprinkling food in the water—until I became a murderess. And then guess what I found out fish food is made of? Crushed butterflies. Each little flake is a dried, crushed butterfly wing. So I'm writing one eulogy for everybody before flushing:

Fish to water, Wings to air.
Farewell to all that's gold and rare.

And when I'm finished I guess I'll just flush them... And then yesterday, my science fair project was due. My class was supposed to set up our display tables in the gym but I just went home. I didn't even go to my dad's even though it was Monday 'cause he left on Sunday for his honeymoon in Italy. And today, it's Tuesday, so I wonder what's special about to-day? Armageddon? Just joking. I know what's special. It's a very special day.

Remember I said my grandpa was giving me my grandma's cameo for my thirteenth birthday? Well, what do you call this? That's my grandma when she was young. And who is wearing new platform shoes, even though my grandma wouldn't like it, and even though my mom always swore no way, no way, no way, she would never buy me high shoes, high shoes are bad for growing feet, but then she still bought me my dream shoes!

The shoes looks like a child's version of Leslie's shoes.

Rock! My dad gave me a million dollars to buy whatever I want. Just joking. He gave me two hundred dollars, though—one hundred for graduating and one hundred for my birthday! And... the guy who's the janitor, he has the wizard face. He doesn't even have a very nice face. Some kids think he's scary, but I don't. I saw him through a crack in the door. He pointed over there, said like, "Ja, Jaaa," and closed the door behind him so quiet like a total librarian. Too bad he doesn't even speak very much English, we don't even speak the same lan-guage, except this note which I found: "Miss. A minor token for your commencement. Sincere Regards, Drachman, The Caretaker." And there was this.

The top hat. She looks inside and reads.

Made in Bulgonia. Weird, eh. I guess when you're a teenager, everybody can tell. When you're thirteen, even if you don't graduate into high school, still, you are, you are commenc-ing on getting much needed guts and a subversive attitude towards the status quo.

Example. Science fair is going in the gym right now and I'm skipping 'cause I already know I'm going to fail. I already know that. So why should I pretend I learned something? And anyway that would be lying because I didn't learn anything. I just made a bunch of fake diagrams. Like this thing. This I did one day to show the swimming pattern of the fish in the bowl. What does it mean? I have no idea!

She tears the diagram.

So. Screw the science fair. So? Screw the wedding. Yup.

Stupid sucks, sucks so bad, that wedding sucked so bad. 'Cause I went to that wedding with my grandfather. I was just wearing sweatpants, I was just wearing crap pants to go and pick up my grandfather, 'cause I was supposed to get into my you-know-what dress. I had to go over to Leslie's with her and all the bridesmaids and I had to spend time with her and not with my dad even though it was more a special day of his and also it was practically my birthday-eve. I hated that day so bad. And that's why it makes me so mad and that's why I'm not going to talk anymore. And I already told them that. I was mad like a teenager gets mad. On any movies that I like now there's always a teenager that gets really mad and goes into rebellion fits, and I was like a total rebellion fit. So you know what I did? Um, I had a public rebellion fit. Because I was putting this dress—if you could have seen this thing— on the back it had a big bow almost as big as my whole bum, the whole bow. They even took a picture of me in it. And then there was also, like, uh, a carousel flower circling around my head. I took one look at myself—

And that's when I started screaming. I was! I was screaming like a maniac.

"STOP THE PROCEEDINGS! I DEFY YOU, STARS! NOBODY ASKED MY PERMISSION!"

Can you imagine such pureness in front of everybody? Staring at the congregation, shaking in my boots, knowing I wrecked everything. Wrecked it! Wrecked it! Wrecked it! Wrecked it! Wrecked it! Wrecked it! Wrecked it! Wrecked it! Wrecked it! Wrecked it!

Standing there with a needle in my hand, "WHO'S GONNA BE THE WISE GUY WHO ASKS MY PERMISSION, OR I'M GONNA SHOOT SPEED INTO MY ARM AND THEN I'M GONNA SNORT," like what do you do with crack cocaine? "DO SOMETHING WITH CRACK COCAINE TO MAKE ME ADDICTED FOR LIFE, AAAAND IF I'M SO ADDICTED I MIGHT END UP, I might end up killing myself."

The groom comes under a cardiac attack. Very serious. Drags me back to the vespers, like the quiet church place, whispering but screaming: "Why you little brat. How could you ruin this day?"

And then I go like, "Ooooh yea, well, how come you ruined my life? Now you only want to see me one Monday and now you want to move even further in a different city."

He's like, "Blah, blah, blah... Leslie lives in Brantford, Leslie is my wife, I love Leslie, Leslie, Leslie, Leslie, blah, blah, blah..."

"Oh, you precious, you are in love and now you get to do whatever only you want and I am the garbage kid that you can throw away in the garbage can of life!"

He says I'm old enough to understand. "YES! I am old enough to understand. So why don't I? Whose fault is that? Maybe yours 'cause of what I found out."

Don't tell my mom.

That this conference coffee mug that I stole from my dad's apartment actually belongs to Leslie. I thought it was my dad's because it's from a conference he goes to every year. But Leslie told me that it was hers. She said she went to the same conference as my dad. The date on this coffee mug is 1997. But my mom and dad didn't separate until Grandma died in 1999. "So you didn't split up because you were unhappy but because you were a little too happy with other people at a conference in 1997 when we were still a family."

Silence. Silence on the vespers. Okay.

He says that life is very complicated and that sometimes people don't mean to but sometimes people fail each other.

I said, "Yeah, you did fail. So I need some time to figure things out, so I need to wear my own outfits for a while and not be the flower girl."

And he said, he said, "You're right. You are not going to be the flower girl, you are going to be the best man. I have a tuxedo rented for you in the back. Go put it on and we'll walk down the aisle together, pal. My darling, my love."

I said: "Really? Do you really mean it?"

He said: "Yeah, I really, really mean it."

And I said: "Is there a top hat?"

And he said: "Yeah, there's a top hat."

And so I went and put on my tuxedo and my top hat and even though I can't dance I did a soft-shoe routine at the reception. And everybody laughed. And even my mom was there, she was, laughing and totally amazed 'cause everybody thought I was just gonna do Hickory Dickory Dock, but I did Fred Astaire. *Singin' in the Rain.*

That really happened, you know. In my mind, I didn't wear that dress. In my mind...

Like, it's not even so much, like sometimes, I don't even know why I think it's my fault. I don't even know why. Like, sometimes the only thing I could think of is that my dad thought I was just too ugly. Maybe that's why he left... but that... but maybe I'm a butterfly. Maybe I'm just in my cocoon right now. Maybe nobody thought of that but maybe I am. And maybe I will get better so that they, so that my mom and dad think that if I was good enough they better stick together to be my parents, right, 'cause I'm a really good kid. Has to have their parents, right? There's, there's, there's...

Unable to continue speaking, CLAUDIA becomes DRACHMAN.

DRACHMAN mops the floor as he talks. At the end the floor should be like a glimmering pool, reflecting the set, the lights of the theatre, etc.

DRACHMAN   To conclude, I would like to tell to you famous Bulgonian fable, very short story, that my mother was telling to me when I was crying, and so I was telling to my son, and so of course this story I am loving it very much. Yeah, I have a son, twenty-two, he is live in United State—but we are not talking on that.

Once upon a time, in a land as close as your thoughts, a naughty little spragnome was climbing through the window of a tiny straw hut and peek into the cradle of a newborn baby and whisper to her sleeping parents this promise. "Weave this child a basket to contain all what her heart desires and when it is full, I will return to make her wise." Now, I must stop to tell you that in Bulgonia we know this spragnome very well. He is very tiny, like my thumb, particular type of gnome which seem to do one thing, but always he is doing something else. So, to continue. Next morning, the farmer is cutting the straw and his wife is weaving that basket and for many years that child, she take her basket and she go in her life gathering, gathering, gathering everything that her little heart want. Until her basket is so full. And when it's so full she have to put it down. Now, it's too heavy. Even so much pleasure, ya, it's not possible to carry on like that endlessly. You know. So she put her basket and so she go and she have a little sleep, something, and when she wake up she come back to find that her basket was complete empty! How did this happen? Well, on this moment, after such a long years, that naughty little spragnome is appear to her. She point on that crazy midget yelling, "Thief!" And she begin to search on him and searching on every place for her stolen possessions until she see that she cannot find not one thing, not one hope remaining. All is gone. And so, she collapse on her basket and begin weeping, "Now I have nothing left but my sadness." And so she cry and she keep to cry until practical flood of tears was filling her basket. And when her basket is complete full of tears that spragnome point. He say: "Now, you see, your basket is no longer empty. Now it have very much inside. *Lugaldya.* Look." And when she look she saw that her basket was become a deep pool... brimming with her experience and dancing on the surface of her tears... yes, very clearly she perceived it. Reflected on the surface of her grief she saw herself.

     DRACHMAN *closes the red curtain.*

     The end.

MOTEL HÉLÈNE

SERGE BOUCHER

ADAPTED BY JUDITH THOMPSON
FROM A TRANSLATION BY
MORWYN BREBNER

Motel Hélène premiered at Espace Go in Montreal, Quebec, in March 1997 with the following company:

JOHANNE .... Maude Guérin
MARIO .... François Papineau
FRANÇOIS .... Stéphane Gagnon

Directed by René-Richard Cyr
Assistant direction by Lou Arteau
Set designed by Réal Benoît
Props by Normand Blais
Costume designed by Lyse Bédard
Hair and makeup by Angelo Barsetti
Lighting designed by Michel Beaulieu
Music by Michel Smith
Technical direction by Francis Laporte

The English-language version of *Motel Hélène* premiered at the Tarragon Theatre in April 2000 with the following company:

JOHANNE .... Jane Spidell
MARIO .... Tony Nappo
FRANÇOIS .... Brandon McGibbon

Directed by Jackie Maxwell
Set and costumes designed by Eo Sharp
Lighting designed by Andrea Lundy
Sound designed by John Gzowski
Stage managed by Kathryn Davies

Serge Boucher is one of Quebec's most popular and respected playwrights. In 1993 his first play, *Natures mortes* (*Still Lives*), was directed by Michel Tremblay. Since then, all his plays—*Excuse-moi, Là, Les bonbons qui sauvent la vie* (*Life Savers*), *Avec Norm, 24 poses (portraits)* (*24 Exposures*) and *Motel Hélène*—have been directed by René Richard Cyr. *Motel Hélène* and *24 Exposures* were both adapted for television and produced in English. Serge Boucher won a Gemeaux Award for his hit TV series *Aveux* and just completed a second TV series entitled *Apparences*, soon to air on Radio-Canada.

Judith Thompson is the author of *The Crackwalker, White Biting Dog, I Am Yours, Lion in the Streets, Sled, Perfect Pie, Habitat, Capture Me,* and *Enoch Ardenin the Hope of Shelter.* She has written two feature films, *Lost and Delirious* and *Perfect Pie,* as well as television movies and radio drama. Judith has won the Governor General's Literary Award for two of her books, *White Biting Dog* and *The Other Side of the Dark.* In 2006 she was invested as an Officer in the Order of Canada and in 2007 was awarded the prestigious Walter Carsen Prize for Excellence in the Performing Arts. Her recent plays include *Palace of the End* and *Such Creatures.* She's also the creator of the documentary dramas *Body & Soul* and *The Grace Project: Sick,* the latter premiered in 2011 at the NEXT Stage Festival in Toronto and nominated for two Dora Awards. *Palace of the End* won a Dora Mavor Moore Award for outstanding new play plus an Amnesty International Freedom of Expression Award and the Susan Smith Blackburn Award for best writing by a female playwright in English. It has been produced in many languages all around the world. She is a professor of drama at the University of Guelph and currently lives with her husband and five children in Toronto.

Based in Toronto, Morwyn Brebner was born in Cardiff, Wales, and grew up in Ottawa. She is a graduate of the National Theatre School of Canada's playwriting program and since 2000 has been playwright-in-residence at the Tarragon Theatre, where most of her plays have premiered. Her first, *Music for Contortionists,* was co-produced by Tarragon Theatre and the Shaw Festival in 2000 and nominated for a Dora Award and a Chalmers Canadian Play Award. Other plays at Tarragon include *Liquor Guns Karate* and *Little Mercy's First Murder* (co-produced with Shaw, with composers Jay Turvey and Paul Sportelli). It won six Dora Mavor Moore Awards, including outstanding new musical. She was a finalist for the 2008 Siminovitch Prize in Theatre and her most recent play, *Heartbreaker,* premiered at Alberta Theatre Project's Enbridge playRites Festival in 2011. She's also an experienced and prolific translator of French plays. Her credits as a translator include *Strawberries in January, Bashir Lazhar,* and *Public Disorder,* all by Evelyne de la Chenelière, and *Mathilde,* by Veronique Olmi. Morwyn is the co-creator of the ABC/Global hit series *Rookie Blue.*

As far as Toronto is concerned, Serge Boucher, one of Quebec's more prominent theatrical names, has been missing in inaction. Calgary premiered the English translation of *24 Exposures,* his follow-up play to *Motel Hélène,* in 2001 and, in 2009, Vancouver's innovative Ruby Slippers Theatre took first stab at the English version of *Life Savers.* His one major foray into Toronto theatres remains *Motel Hélène* in 2000 as part of the then-mighty World Stage Festival. But even in his one Hogtown outing, Boucher was eclipsed by two other and more high-profile Quebec theatre artists: Robert Lepage and Michel Tremblay, whose *The Far Side of the Moon* and *For the Pleasure of Seeing Her Again,* respectively, stole the media limelight at that year's festival. Nothing illustrates this invisibility even in his shining hour more than a Tarragon ad in *NOW Magazine,* which pastes a critic's blurb over, of all places, his name. The *Toronto Sun* review mentions everyone involved in the Tarragon production but Boucher.[1] The surprisingly ungracious treatment of Boucher in Toronto has only strengthened my resolve to give his superb play a new home in this anthology. (The only edition of the English translation you're about to read can be found in a Playwrights Guild of Canada copyscript.)

More than a decade since I reviewed the Tarragon production, my admiration for the play has strengthened and my recollection of that night at the theatre remains vivid. At the risk of descending into reviewese, it's one of those magic nights where, as a critic, you feel grateful to the job—for placing you in the opening-night crowd and giving you the platform to write about theatre. Jackie Maxwell's production elicited performances from the trio of actors—Jane Spidell, Tony Nappo, and Brandon McGibbon—that, in my opinion, remain career-defining. In fact, it's my contention that Spidell's next great performance came at the same stage in another play in this anthology, Michael Healey's *Rune Arlidge,* for whom (along with Ari Cohen) it was written.

Spidell plays Johanne, the working-class Québécois mother whose tragedy, we find out in the course of the play, is that her child seems to have been abducted, or the very least has gone missing. Her on-again, off-again lover (and father of the missing child) comes for regular visits (booty calls is more fitting in this context) to her home above the local store in a small town two hours from Montreal. François, the store owner's son, acts as both a narrator and agent of change in Johanne's small but tragic life. The title

---

1   John Coulbourn, "Just a few reservations," *Toronto Sun,* April 19, 2000: http://jam.canoe.ca/Theatre/Reviews/M/Motel_Helene/2000/04/19/742250.html

refers to a motel that we never see but hear accounts of from Johanne—accounts that may or may not be true.

If there's a recurrent theme to Boucher's play (and its Toronto critical reception), it seems to be physical and social voyeurism. Boucher structured *Motel Hélène* as a series of thirty short and giddy scenes that Maxwell described as "Polaroid snapshots."[2] François himself is a peeping Tom who watches the sexual encounters—and there's no shortage of them on and offstage—from his vantage point at the store. While Boucher emphasizes Mario's sexual appetite (literally so, given his penchant for whipped cream during sex), he casts Johanne in a similar horny light. When (the gay) François confesses that it's been more than a year and a half since he's had sex, Johanne is shocked: "Sacrement François how can you stand it? If I go a few days without it I go out of my mind." It's easy to conclude that Johanne and Mario fill in the gap left by their missing (and presumed dead) child with sex and food, but their stories suggest a deeper need for connection than the psychological. They belong together, whether that means they nourish or devour each other. Their sexual drive spares enough for the inactive François to get his own rocks off. Kate Taylor's review of *Motel Hélène* highlights the sexual voyeurism in both the text and production. Headlined "Playing with voyeurism may cause queasiness," the review explores the risks of presenting sexually explicit material onstage as opposed to film: "[S]how nudity and sex on stage with those naked bodies physically present in the room and the most lofty artistic project can start to make theatregoers feel they have wandered into a peepshow."[3] While Taylor commends Maxwell on her intelligent and sensitive treatment of the explicit context, she concludes the review by suggesting that Boucher's elevation of Johanne to a tragic figure toward the closing scenes may absolve Boucher of smuttiness but leaves the audience "twitching on the line."[4]

But there's another kind of voyeurism here that the Tarragon itself got sucked into in the reviews. To Coulbourn in the *Toronto Sun*, the play's lack of subtext, or what he calls "occasional glimpses behind the curtains of the soul," and its slavishly realistic set, suggest it is "simply a visit to a human zoo, undertaken by the middle-class for the express purpose of examining a sub-species of humanity."[5] At *NOW Magazine*, but in a more positive review, Glenn Sumi hints at a similar criticism by comparing Johanne to an older and looser version of Erin Brockovich, the working-class activist

---

2   Quoted in Sharon Younger, "Working-class poetry accents drama," *National Post*, April 15, 2000, np.

3   Kate Taylor, "Playing with voyeurism may cause queasiness," *Globe and Mail*, April 19, 2000, R3.

4   Ibid.

5   Coulbourn, "Just a few."

mother immortalized that year in a film starring Julia Roberts. Sumi then notes that the adaptation of *Motel Hélène* is by Judith Thompson, "the queen of working-class chic."[6]

He has a point there. But a more relevant one is the fusing of three recognizable strands of the Tarragon theatre in this orphan production of Boucher's play. For one thing, it continues the long-standing Tarragon tradition of premiering English translations of Quebec theatre. It's a tradition that started with Tremblay in the early seventies and continues to this date with both Carole Fréchette and Wajdi Mouawad. Without the Tarragon, our access to the French theatrical repertoire in Quebec would be severely curtailed, if not cut off. As well, in *Motel Hélène*'s English translation we can trace the workings of two of the theatre's representative female playwrights: the established Judith Thompson and the then-emerging Morwyn Brebner. (The former adapted the text from the latter's translation.)

The translation was one of Brebner's early forays into bringing the best of French-Canadian theatre into Toronto and her affinity to the material showed particularly in her sensitive reading of the young, gay narrator François. In combining gritty realism and soaring lyricism, *Motel Hélène* fits Thompson like a glove. The world of *Motel Hélène* feels close to that of Thompson—who, incidentally, was born in Montreal—in its exploration of a woman from the urban underclass whose struggles with "the maternal subject" echo many of her previous female characters, most notably those in *I Am Yours*, *Tornado*, and *Habitat*.[7] The small town two hours away from Montreal where *Motel Hélène* is set bears some resemblance to Kingston, where Thompson's 1980 play *The Crackwalker* unfolds. Boucher writes in French what Thompson has been exploring in English for many years—the all-consuming and repressed desires, the suffering of children, the undercurrents of religious (Roman Catholic) ritual point to shared grounds between the two.

What a shame that we never got to see *Motel Hélène* or other works by Boucher at the Tarragon or Toronto again.

6   Glenn Sumi, "Spidell Smokin'," *NOW Magazine*, April 19, 2000, np.

7   Ric Knowles, "Reading Judith Thompson," introduction to *Judith Thompson: Late 20th Century Plays 1980–2000*, v.

CHARACTERS

JOHANNE
MARIO
FRANÇOIS

SCENE 1: THE DEPANNEUR

Lights up. It's night. JOHANNE sits on the balcony. She rocks, drinks a glass of beer, smokes. We hear the music of her favourite band, Corbeau (in French). The television projects its pictures. FRANÇOIS is in the hallway that separates the depanneur from JOHANNE's apartment. JOHANNE's apartment door is open: through this opening FRANÇOIS sees JOHANNE.

FRANÇOIS   I still ask myself why. Why her door was open. Was it open just that night when it should have been closed so that I... just some person, could see her life. The picture of her whole... life? I mean I often saw her on her balcony but never, never like that. From the back, without her knowing I was watching her, like a voyeur, a thief, no never. Looking at her like that, from where I was standing, I didn't know anything about the woman sitting on her balcony; if she was happy or unhappy, what she thought, what she felt. She could have been anybody. But everything around her spoke. It spoke for her. I think that's what I find so... sad.

We've known each other for about two years, Johanne and I. Since I came back... here... to live with my parents. We know each other well. She lives right here, in my father's building, and she comes into his depanneur, all the time. I mean, really, this is the story of a depanneur. I have been serving this woman almost every day for two years, I know her. But there is something... that is not right, you know? A kind of a distance. And me, I have distanced myself from the whole world, in a way, as well. Since I have come back to live with my parents I have kept a kind of journal: I write about everything, about nothing, I write about Johanne. I write at the depanneur all the time between customers; it is actually insane the number of black notebooks I have filled in these two years.

Suddenly the telephone rings. JOHANNE gets up, FRANÇOIS disappears. She answers the phone.

JOHANNE   Hellooo? I'm not too bad, how are you? No, no, I was in the next room, couldn't hear it over the sewing machine. You've been drinking, haven't you, my *maudit*?... Uh huh. Uh huh. Well okay come on over then, but I'm warning you, don't take like ten hours!

She hangs up. She bustles around, returns to the balcony, picks up her glass, her pack of cigarettes, her ashtray. FRANÇOIS goes by with three cases of empty beer bottles. JOHANNE leaves her apartment, crosses the little hallway, and disappears into the depanneur. We hear her voice.

Don't look so sad, François, the evening is almost over. Hey, it's been one of the first beautiful Saturdays of the summer, I thought it would last forever. The parking lot out front has been full all day, the street is jammed with people, too bad we didn't have this weather for Saint-Jean, eh? So can you mark me down for a six-pack?

JOHANNE re-enters the hallway with a six-pack of Labatt Bleue and a big bag of chips. She meets FRANÇOIS.

(startled shriek) Ahhh! Oh my God it's hot, eh? I wouldn't mind spending the night in the freezer! *(laughing)*

So François, can you mark this down for me just until Thursday?

FRANÇOIS   Well... I don't know.

JOHANNE   Please? Come on. Mario's coming over, and I—

FRANÇOIS   You still owe me for last week, Johanne. I can't...

JOHANNE   Listen, it's okay, I'll work it out with your dad, don't worry! Hey, I bet you didn't have much time for your reading and writing tonight, eh?

FRANÇOIS   Yeah, it was busy.

JOHANNE   That's a really big book you're reading. Is it good?

FRANÇOIS   Yuh. Yuh it is good. I like it.

JOHANNE   So uh, listen, I was kinda wondering if you might have a book I could read, like, I'm getting my vacation in two weeks, and I kinda thought, hey, with the number of books that guy reads, hey! Maybe he could lend me one, you know, a book I could read easy, not too thick, a good story that's a good easy read, what do you think?

FRANÇOIS   Sure. Why not? Let me think about what book.

JOHANNE   You are a such a sweetheart. An ANGEL, you know? And ah oh, gimme a pack of Matinee king size with that if there are any uh... just in case, would you?

> FRANÇOIS *disappears into the depanneur,* MARIO *enters, we don't see them.*

Sacrement, Mario, where were you? Next door with that sexy little student who lives there?

MARIO   What, what time is it?

FRANÇOIS   Hullo, I close in five minutes!

JOHANNE   You should start picking girlfriends who live further away, Mario.

MARIO   François, you got any cheese curds?

JOHANNE   NO! Come on, let's go, it's almost eleven o'clock, François wants to get out of here. Give him my pack of Matinee, François, would ya?

> *She exits to her apartment.*

MARIO   And a pack of Export A medium for me, chief. Yeah, just put it on Johanne's account.

> JOHANNE *sticks her head out into the hall.*

JOHANNE   *Mon hostie,* I heard you, you!

MARIO   Listen to that, she's spyin' on me.

JOHANNE He pays for all his stuff.

Mario laughs, Johanne returns to her apartment.

MARIO Hey, a guy's gotta try, right? Night, chief. Sleep tight, huh?

Mario exits the depanneur, François closes the door that connects the depanneur to the little hallway. Mario enters Johanne's place, closing the door behind him, heads toward Johanne, who takes a bowl, empties the chips into it, opens two beers.

Jeez that kid's got a smartass face.

JOHANNE Leave him alone.

MARIO He needs a punch.

Mario grabs Johanne from behind and caresses her breasts.

How are my beauties doing? Huh? Mario's big beauties?

He sits down at the table, two feet up on the edge, flips channels, eats his cheese curds.

Jeez it's hot, we're not gonna sleep tonight.

JOHANNE Oh. You're planning on spending the night here?

MARIO Goin' to the four-by-four races tomorrow afternoon. Ti-Guy's goin' with me.

JOHANNE Oh yeah! Gaston called.

MARIO Gaston? When?

JOHANNE Sometime last week.

MARIO What'd he say?

JOHANNE Not too much, he wanted to talk to you. I told him to call the garage, but he said he had already called there and... and...

JOHANNE stands at the door, watches FRANÇOIS. MARIO goes to her, runs a hand inside her dressing gown, strokes her crotch. JOHANNE twists around without being seen by FRANÇOIS, who she talks to.

You must be real disappointed the evening's over, eh?

FRANÇOIS   Oh yeah. Real disappointed.

JOHANNE   Soon as the weather's nice, everybody is outside, all those people, walkin' the streets, comin' into the dep. They're makin' up for Saint-Jean, when they all stayed inside. You working tomorrow?

FRANÇOIS   I'm opening.

JOHANNE   Your dad likes to laze around on the weekend, huh?

FRANÇOIS   He's at a fiftieth tonight.

JOHANNE   Oh yeah, I forgot. Hey, that doesn't give you much of a weekend.

FRANÇOIS   Not really. But, it's no big deal, doesn't happen often. See you tomorrow, Johanne.

JOHANNE   Have a good night.

She closes the door, lowers the blinds, lights a cigarette.

MARIO   Go play in the traffic, ya little shit. Ha. Ha.

MARIO stretches out on the floor. JOHANNE hushes him and straddles him.

JOHANNE   You coulda *crisse* told me you didn't go to work Thursday morning, you bum.

He slides a foot into JOHANNE's crotch.

MARIO   Hey. Did you wash your thing for Mario? Huh?

Blackout.

SCENE 2: THE BOOKS

Lights up. It's night, after the depanneur has closed. Noise.

JOHANNE The little *sacrements*, I could kill them. They kept me up half the night with their noise. It makes me crazy. I'd *crisse* throw them out if I were you, François, I mean no one is gonna rent an apartment here with those low-lites around.

FRANÇOIS They're better than they were.

JOHANNE Just saw them headin' out for a big night. If they wake me up when they come in tonight, I'm gonna call the cops on them, I'm telling you I am so sick of it. That skinny one, *tabarnak*, I'm gonna stick my high-heeled shoe up his butt.

FRANÇOIS Johanne, I've been meaning to tell you, I have your books.

JOHANNE Sorry?

FRANÇOIS Your books. You were mentioning the other day...

JOHANNE Books? Oh yeah. The book.

FRANÇOIS I've brought you three.

JOHANNE Three, are you out of your mind? I only have two weeks' vacation!

FRANÇOIS Well I didn't know exactly what you wanted, so I thought I had better bring you three very different—

JOHANNE It's got to be easy, right? Nothing too complicated.

FRANÇOIS I know. I know. Any of these would be perfect for you.

Silence.

JOHANNE I'm sorry, I didn't mean to freak out on you before. I don't know what came over me. Maybe it's the heat. Sorry. And thank you. Jeez. Have you... ah... actually read all the books you have?

FRANÇOIS	Every one.
JOHANNE	That's amazing. Do you, like, remember them afterwards?
FRANÇOIS	The books?
JOHANNE	I mean, do you remember what you just read. In a book.
FRANÇOIS	Well yeah!
JOHANNE	I have a terrible memory, it makes me mental. I don't know, I just hated it in school, you know? When they would make us read those *maudit* handouts? From books? And then we had to like answer questions about them? I hated that, I mean I would finish reading the book and then I wouldn't know at all what I had just read, same with TV, I'm serious, I watch these soap operas? And the next day, I'll be talking with my girlfriend about them, and I can't remember what happened! I hate that. I hate it.
FRANÇOIS	Well, the important thing isn't so much to remember every detail, it's that the book leaves you with an... impression... and then there's the... pleasure, the pure joy you feel in the moment while you are reading, or when you watch your soap operas; you know, when you read and you are... captivated. That's where the joy is. You know what I'm saying?
JOHANNE	It makes me laugh how much it bugs your father.
FRANÇOIS	What?
JOHANNE	Your books, your writing, he doesn't think you should do it here.
FRANÇOIS	He told you that?
JOHANNE	He said there are plenty of things you should be doing in the depanneur other than wasting your time reading and writing. That's what he said to me. But don't tell him. I said to him, I said we were always "very well served by you, you were very polite and efficient and nice," and that I didn't think your reading or writing hurt your work one bit.

FRANÇOIS   Thank you.

JOHANNE   But François, tell me something. Why? Why *do you* read all those books?

FRANÇOIS   I don't know... it helps... me... to live!

Blackout.

SCENE 3: DYED HAIR

Lights up. JOHANNE bursts out laughing. FRANÇOIS listens attentively.

JOHANNE   No, listen, I'm telling you, François, it's my real colour! I know everyone thinks I have bleached hair, I can tell the way they look at me, well it's not BLEACHED HAIR, it's me getting back to my real colour, my NATURAL colour, see I was a blond, I mean a REAL BLOND, well, a VERY light brunette anyway, and this, what you see, is well, awful, but I'm stuck with it, gotta wait for it to grow out, it's Mario who made me do it, and I wanted to do it too. I needed a change and I really really liked it at first, it's just a bit strange when you're not used to it, you're a blond one day and raven the next, it's like a punch in the stomach but I'll tell you, when people meet me for the first time they are like "whoaaaaa," it's a shock, I mean it's really thick hair, I've got a lion's mane here, François, and when the ends grow out? I'm gonna go to a real trained hairdresser, I'm really gonna do something with this head.

Blackout.

SCENE 4: THE TICKET

Lights up. It's noon. MARIO has stopped by to eat with JOHANNE. She's finished eating, he makes himself a ham sandwich.

JOHANNE   She called yesterday. *Calice,* I knew she was up to something from the moment I heard her voice. And of course, I was right, it's one more of her stupid unbelievable predicaments.

What pissed me off about it the most was that she called me, knowing that I can't help her, knowing it but telling me anyway, right? In this innocent way, you know? But RUBBING in feeling so sorry for herself, oh she "knows I can't help her, it's not important," she says it like me, I'm not a good daughter because a good daughter would want to help her mother, but that's okay, that's okay, dear, don't worry about me about poor little me, *HOSTIE*.

MARIO   So what did she want?

JOHANNE   Oh I don't know, I didn't really listen, some story about some *maudit* buffet she wants to pick up on Saturday way the hell out somewhere at the brother-in-law's of one of her stupid friends, it's free of course she'll take anything that's free, and this buffet, man, it's going to change her life, right? But she won't be able to move it into her place all by herself. What's she gonna do for Christ's sake, she doesn't have room for it, she's just gonna put it in the basement anyway, I started laughing right into the phone I thought it was hysterical, her cluttering up her life with some big piece of junk she doesn't even need.

MARIO   Does she have to do it Saturday?

JOHANNE   I don't know. I think the people are moving or something... You know her...

MARIO   Listen. Call her up and ask her if the buffet is really big and heavy, what's it made of, and if it's not too bad, *crisse*, I'll go with her myself Saturday morning, *hostie*, I'll borrow Gaston's trailer, and I'll get her buffet for her and make her a happy woman.

JOHANNE   What? You don't have to do that.

MARIO   Hey. She wants the buffet, it's free, well *tabarnak*, let's make the woman happy, it's not gonna kill us.

                 Silence.

                 Saturday, eh? *Calvaire*, that makes me think! What's today? Wednesday? Tabarnak. Did I tell you my story about the ticket?

Man, two weeks ago in town, you know that big light at the shopping centre, at the corner of Jutras and Bois-Francs, okay, there was a big truck in front of me, the light was green but it turned yellow when I was right in the middle of the road behind my truck, blocking everything up, then on the other side there was a cop, I see the cop, it turns red, things start moving again, I go, then he stops me, *crisse*, he had a real face like a beef, he goes, "The light was red for six seconds, sir." I go, "It was blocked, man." He goes: "Yes, but you drove out into the street after it turned yellow." *Ben tabarnak* that pissed me off, I start yellin' at him, "You lie, cop, it was green, it changed after I was already in the middle." I mean like as if I would go right through the light with a cop right there, right? Like I just love gettin' tickets, right? He gives me the ticket anyway, the fat pig, *hostie* you know what it cost me? One hundred and ten bucks *hostie*, I've got to pay it before Friday, and Ti-Poil owes me money *calice* and I can't get it off him, I mean where am I going to get it? It's always the same when you lend someone money, you have to go running after them, I can't take it no more, Johanne, I'm tellin' you I'm not lending money ever again, *c'est fini*.

Blackout.

SCENE 5: THE STORY OF THE HUNGRY CHILD

Lights up. FRANÇOIS investigates.

FRANÇOIS   Do you think of him much?

JOHANNE   Some days.

FRANÇOIS   Do you miss him?

JOHANNE   For a long while after I would talk to him, all the time, like he was right here beside me, you know, gettin' in my way, like he used to.

Silence.

The last time I saw him... he had just come home from school and he said, coming in he said, "I'm hungry," every kid coming home from school says that, they're all hungry after school and he was very... normal, you know? He wasn't even in the apartment and I hear, "Mama, I'm hungry." So I go, "Hello Tit-Bout, you want Mama to make you a nice slice of bread with peanut butter?" That made him real happy I made him a nice slice of bread and peanut butter with a little sprinkle of sugar and then I don't know, I said something like how I was busy sewing, something like that, and he went out on the balcony with his bread and peanut butter and a sprinkle of sugar and he sat down on the steps of the staircase, I said, "If you're gonna play outside don't go too far, Tit-Bout, make sure you're home when Mario gets here for supper," I don't think I said anything else, just that, so then I went back to my sewing machine, and he just sat very quiet and he ate his bread and peanut butter.

Silence.

FRANÇOIS   Do you think... he suffered?

JOHANNE   Of course you imagine the very worst—I have imagined—every horror... pretty well every day since it happened. Sometimes I think I am really... going insane.

Silence.

I made his room my sewing room. I had originally been doing my sewing in the bedroom, you see, because Mario didn't want the machine and everything in the living room and our bedroom here is so big, but after a while you know, I just couldn't stand the mess: the machine, the material, the customers coming in to get fitted, I would have to do my cutting in the kitchen, and then bring it all back into the bedroom, ah! Ah! So I took everything and I moved it all into the basement, I made myself a little sewing corner at the back, but it was really depressing, you know, working away in this unfinished basement, so once Tit-Bout was... gone, I moved back upstairs. Into his room. It was nice. I could spread out as much as I wanted, didn't have to clean up when I finished, you know, when I leave I just close the door, I just close the door, I mean nobody has any reason to go in there; I put his bed in the basement, your father said that was fine; yeah, like I said, that's why I always keep the door closed, to my sewing room, it's a mess, right, you know I think that Tit-Bout, that he, he walked and he walked right out of the city and into the woods and he got lost, he got lost in the woods and he lay down and he fell asleep when darkness fell and I imagine him dreaming, he was dreaming about like, a house made of white sugar, he just forgot like he forgot to wake up, you know?

Blackout.

SCENE 6: CHEF BOYARDEE

Lights up. Mario *throws the* Journal de Montréal *down on the table, opens a can of ravioli, and eats it cold.*

MARIO   Crisse! Crazy witch! Have you heard about this? The woman in Montreal who burned her baby? In the oven *hostie*, you would have to be completely insane, I mean lost your mind *hostie*. MAN there are crazy people on this earth. Oh when I think about the fact that they're just gonna lock her up for what, two-three years, give her some psy—you know, mental tests, I mean anybody knows you have to be out of your head to do something like that, to COOK your BABY, you know what I would do with her, I would tie her to a chair and burn her piece by piece, that's what she deserves, I mean look what she did, look what she did.

JOHANNE   I guess she coudn't take it no more.

MARIO   *Calvaire*, then she should have thrown herself off a bridge, you know what I mean? Put a bullet in your head *hostie*, hang yourself; you hurt *yourself*, not a little baby, I mean imagine, the poor little kid shut up in the oven, imagine? He must have screamed and screamed.

JOHANNE   I guess she was not—herself.

MARIO   Hey. What time is it? Already twelve-thirty? Crisse. I gotta get back to work.

Silence.

Oh yeah, so what about Josée's wedding?

JOHANNE   What about it?

MARIO   Are you coming?

JOHANNE   I haven't decided.

MARIO   Well make up your mind.

> *He goes to the bathroom. She takes the paper, reads. He returns.*

JOHANNE   Okay I'll go.

MARIO   Good, I'll tell her to expect the both of us. And the present? What'll we get them? If it was just me, I wouldn't bother, *crisse*...

JOHANNE   Mario, we have to get them a present.

MARIO   Okay, so you're takin' care of that, right? I'll try to stop by later this week, pick it up.

JOHANNE   Did you see this about the neighbours? They said they just couldn't believe it, they never woulda thought she could do something like that. Listen to this: "I spoke to her every day and she seemed like a normal person. Just like the rest of us." One of her neighbours said that. God. Unbelievable.

> *Blackout.*

SCENE 7: WOMAN WITH BIG BREASTS

> *Lights up. Daytime. JOHANNE stands in front of FRANÇOIS.*

JOHANNE   Okay listen. I'm gonna ask you something that may sound strange but I want you to be totally honest. Okay? Promise not to be shocked? Do you think I have big breasts?

FRANÇOIS   I haven't really thought about it.

JOHANNE   Well you can see me, can't you? I mean do you or don't you think of me as a big-breasted woman?

FRANÇOIS   Why are you asking me this?

JOHANNE   Just answer me.

FRANÇOIS   Well... I don't really...

JOHANNE   François. Are you gonna make me shake them in your face?

FRANÇOIS   Please. What do you want me to say? I don't really care...

JOHANNE   Come on, tell me, do you think of them as big, medium, or small?

FRANÇOIS   Well. They aren't... small.

JOHANNE   Then you think they're big?

FRANÇOIS   Mmmm maybe.

JOHANNE   Really really big? Like, huge?

FRANÇOIS   Well no.

JOHANNE   Not too big.

FRANÇOIS   It depends on what you call "too big."

JOHANNE   I don't know. But do you think they're, like, gross?

FRANÇOIS   No.

JOHANNE   Well did you like notice them as soon as you saw me?

FRANÇOIS   I don't really remember.

JOHANNE   I mean like do you think if some guy saw me, some guy who didn't even know me, do you think he would like say to himself, "Wow, she's got really big ones"?

FRANÇOIS   Ahhhhh no, I don't think so.

JOHANNE   So they're not too... You know, in your face?

FRANÇOIS   No!

JOHANNE   They were really something when I was in school, I mean God, when you're young and ya got these huge tits everyone like... right after I had Tit-Bout they were unbelievable, you shoulda seen them, they were rock-hard and the milk would like spray out of them, right across the room, I was overflowing.

FRANÇOIS   How... old are you, anyway?

JOHANNE   How old do you think?

FRANÇOIS   Oh... I don't know. It's hard to tell.

JOHANNE   Come on, guess.

FRANÇOIS   I don't know. Thirty-five, thirty-six.

JOHANNE   *Calice*, are you sick?

FRANÇOIS   What, you're not older than that, are you?

JOHANNE   Well I hope not, *sacrement*.

FRANÇOIS   Johanne, I don't like these games. How old are you?

JOHANNE   I'm twenty-five.

FRANÇOIS   You're not twenty-five.

JOHANNE   Yes!

FRANÇOIS   Hey, you're teasing me.

JOHANNE   No!

FRANÇOIS   Well. I have to say I am... surprised.

JOHANNE   It's because I had Tit-Bout when I was sixteen! That's what's throwing you off, François, that's all. That's all.

    Blackout.

SCENE 8: THE FLAMING BANANA

Lights up. MARIO *and* JOHANNE *sit in front of the* TV. MARIO *reads a passage from* Collected Erotic Letters. *He bursts out laughing.*

MARIO   Tabarnak. Listen to this, Jojo! This is great. Hostie. It's called "Enjoying a flaming banana." These people are totally insane. "In the culinary arts there are two things that count: the quality of the produce and the preparation. On the produce side, you must pick bananas that aren't too ripe and are very long. As far as preparation goes, I'll give you the recipe: Invite your favourite girlfriend over. Mine is Mari-Jo, but yours might be somebody else. She accepts and within the hour she's at your place. You give her a kiss and propose a little snack. She is very hungry. You show her the bananas. She understands right away. You pull down her panties. There you will find a pretty pink pussy. Now you pet and you stroke that pink pussy till it gets nice and warm and all wet and now you peel the banana, should be quite green, and then, please, insert said banana into your sweet Mari-Jo's pink pussy! But just halfway! Now, please, straddle your sweetie and insert the other half of the green banana where you know it should go. And now, surrender to the moment and it won't be long before you both find ecstacy on the fruit that unites you. THEN, remove it from the oven. And what do you have? You have a flaming banana! Pour on a little rum and it's absolutely delicious!" Oh *calvaire*, they eat it! They eat it! Listen to this: "You may find this humourous, but Mari-Jo and I have had many a wicked banana party!"

He laughs.

Tabarnak, they are totally totally CRACKED.

JOHANNE comes and sits astride MARIO.

JOHANNE   Actually you know I am feeling a bit... hungry... I think I would really like a nice... banana split right now? You?

MARIO   Okay, baby, just the way it says, one end of the banana inside your pussy and the other... inside of my... arsehole. Whoooo hoo.

They laugh hysterically. Blackout.

SCENE 9: THE BLACK NOTEBOOK

Lights up. JOHANNE *reads an extract from the black notebook.*

JOHANNE   Mario spent the night at Johanne's. He just left with a dozen eggs, a package of bacon, the *Allo* and *Photo-Police*, and a pack of Export A. He put it all on her account.

At the age of eighteen, we should all kill our parents.

The clearest memory I have of Johanne's boy Tit-Bout is the very same thing: every Sunday morning he would come over in his little pyjamas; he would buy the *Allo* and the *Photo-Police*, a dozen eggs, a pound of bacon, and cigarettes for his mother and father. Every Sunday, Johanne would make a big breakfast for her little family.

> *She closes the notebook, puts it back in* FRANÇOIS's *bag. She's nervous, gets herself a beer.* FRANÇOIS *returns. She sits.*

I am *dead.*

FRANÇOIS   What?

JOHANNE   You know, tired? Dragging my butt, exhausted, flaked out dead, you never heard that? For tired? For when you really cannot stand it anymore, you are at the complete END of your ROPE, *calice* I can't wait until Friday.

FRANÇOIS   Hey, when you get home on Friday? We should go out to celebrate the beginning of your vacation. How about I take you to dinner, and then we go dancing?

JOHANNE   Are you crazy?

FRANÇOIS   What?

JOHANNE   Are you feeling all right?

FRANÇOIS   Why?

JOHANNE   Well... where we gonna go?

FRANÇOIS   Everywhere!

JOHANNE   You and me?

FRANÇOIS   Why not? We'll have a big night.

JOHANNE   You're outta your mind.

                  Blackout.

SCENE 10: HIGH-HEELED SHOES

Lights up. JOHANNE rocks herself on the balcony. She tells FRANÇOIS about her purchase: a pair of black high-heeled shoes.

The TV projects its pictures. The shoes sit enthroned on the kitchen counter, resting on newspaper because JOHANNE has applied a sealant to them. The important thing is the light created to showcase the shoes. JOHANNE is practically background noise. Inside, the TV is on.

JOHANNE   I took a cab from the mall all the way downtown, too hot to walk, right? And on the way, I see this sidewalk sale at Chez Beauchesne, oh my God I was *so* lucky. I mean my first idea was to go to Chez Beauchesne but since the mall is closer, I thought I would start with the mall, you know, just in case. Well I should have gone to Chez Beauchesne right away, because there is *always* something I like like right off, I'll tell ya I had a real good laugh with my saleslady, she's like really huge, right? I mean enormously fat, you gotta picture her, and she goes, "The tiny heel is just not right for me; when I see Ginette Reno walking around with high heels then maybe I'll go crazy but until then I'm happy wearing my nice flat heels." HAH. Oh my God I tried on these incredibly beautiful red spike heels, they were *wicked* but—I said to myself, "Johanne, don't get carried away with the red, be practical, it's a wedding AND you know what they say about red shoes, and black, black goes with everything, very tasteful, so that's why I got the black. I'm gonna practise with them this week, a little every night, to break them in, right? Because if I don't, I won't be able to dance on Friday, and I want to dance dance dance. Why are you looking at me like that?

Blackout.

SCENE 11: PRACTICE

*Lights up. J*OHANNE *wears her new shoes. She vacuums. She's put on a Corbeau tape. She has cranked the music louder because she's vacuuming. She hears her favourite song, stops the vacuum, dances. Blackout.*

SCENE 12: THE RED DRESS

*Lights up. It's night. J*OHANNE *and F*RANÇOIS *are going out tonight. She's getting ready. M*ARIO *and F*RANÇOIS *chat.*

MARIO   So, you're taking my wife out, are ya?

FRANÇOIS   I think so.

            *We hear J*OHANNE'*s voice yelling.*

JOHANNE   I'm on vacation, boys!

MARIO   You gonna take your daddy's big Cadillac, little guy? Just kiddin'. But the old man really loves that car of his, eh? HEY! *(to* JOHANNE*)* You gonna spend the night in the can or what?

JOHANNE   Shut your big yap.

MARIO   Eh, come on out, we're waitin' for the show!

FRANÇOIS   Do you... get a vacation?

MARIO   Next week. They don't close the garage down though, it's always open.

> JOHANNE *enters. She wears a very sexy red dress that she made herself and her high-heeled shoes.*

Oh *calice*! Calice!

JOHANNE	What? I'm on holidays!

> *Whistling.*

MARIO	*Sacrament*, Mama, you're wearing high heels! Hey François, what's your secret? *Crisse* it's been a while since I seen you done up like that. Is that dress new?

JOHANNE	Everything is new!

MARIO	So where did we get all this money, eh?

JOHANNE	I saved it up, you be quiet.

MARIO	Hey. I have a good one. It's the story of two dykes in a bar. There's this guy lookin' at them, right? And he likes one of them. Well the girlfriend, she gets up and she goes over to him and she goes, "She's sexy, eh?" The guy goes, "Yeah." She says, "You wanna know how she tastes?" The guy goes, "Oh yeah, would I ever," the girl, she looks at him and she goes *(He blows in FRANÇOIS's face.)* There ya go. That's how she tastes. HAH. So where youse going?

JOHANNE	We don't know yet! Hey, I have a roll of film that isn't finished, Mario, before you go, take a picture of me and François.

> *She exits.*

MARIO	You know Johanne, you can take her to the strip club, she gets a big bang out of that.

> *He laughs.*

JOHANNE	Moron! *(returns with her Kodak) Crisse*, you're an arsehole. Here, it's ready, alls ya gotta do is press the button. C'mere, François. We'll start with me and François, then we can take one of just me, then, if there's any more, we'll take one of me and you, Mario, okay? Oh, there's one more, okay, another

one of me and François just in case the one we took before doesn't turn out. That's great, Mario, you're good. You're good with your hands, baby. Okay. So, you done with your beer?

MARIO

Will you relax? I'm leavin', okay?

JOHANNE

Okay, so get out of here, ya *hound* dog. Go on!

MARIO

Keep an eye on her, eh? Dressed like that. Whooo. Okay, okay, I'm leavin'. See ya tomorrow!

He exits.

JOHANNE

I knew he'd show up to check us out. God. I still can't believe I'm on vacation.

FRANÇOIS

Your dress is really nice.

JOHANNE

I made it myself, you know, took all week. Ooooh I'm excited. And I don't look thirty-five anymore, eh? Oh, I hope I have enough cigarettes.

FRANÇOIS

So you ready to go—or—

She finishes her glass of wine, rinses it, deposits it on the counter, checks her cigarettes, takes a pack of gum, bursts out laughing.

JOHANNE

You wanna piece? You know Mario, like, he's always gone on about my big tits, right? Ever since he's known me he's like, "Jojo's big bazungas," right? I didn't let it bother me, I thought, "Well, they're big and he loves them," men like big tits, right? Then one day he turns around and he tells me, "You're gettin' a breast reduction." So I start laughing, right? I think he's kidding. He goes, "I'm serious, Johanne, your breasts are too big, when people look at you they laugh, it's all they see; just go and find out how to get them reduced." I couldn't believe it, I told him, "No way, I can't afford that," but he doesn't care, he says, "Do it, Johanne, or else," so what do I do? I go and I spend an incredible amount of money I didn't have, he didn't pay a cent, and I get this awful and painful operation and ya know what happened? After three months they were even bigger. I'm serious. God we laughed over that we pissed ourselves.

Silence.

I guess the red shoes really would have been too much, eh?

Blackout.

SCENE 13: CHILD'S PLAY

Lights up. After the night out, JOHANNE listens. She's slightly drunk.

FRANÇOIS — I used to play teacher when I was little. All by myself, it was my escape. I would lock myself in this little room in our basement and play for hours. I pretended to be this teacher who never actually taught me but who I had always adored: Lorraine St. Laurent. She was the most beautiful woman at the school, tall, thin, and... elegant. And her shoes: I always noticed her shoes. Isn't that strange? She had at least fifty pairs of shoes, I'm serious. The other teachers, it seemed to me they NEVER changed their dirty old shoes. So there I would be, in my basement, hiding from the world and dressing up as Lorraine St. Laurent, with this old yellowed curtain I found in a box, and old hairpieces my mother didn't wear anymore, some jewellery I would have borrowed from my mother, and of course, shoes, my mother's hideous shoes, but when I played the game they became beautiful, just as stylish as Lorraine St. Laurent's shoes, I was magnificent. So then I would teach, we had a board, and some chalk, and I would teach all these imaginary children. I was brilliant. I posed, I scolded, I praised, awarded stars, gave homework, all in the silky voice of Madamoiselle St. Laurent. I would play for hours and hours...

JOHANNE — I want to show you something special. *(She heads for her sewing room.)* You know, you would be fantastic with kids. I think that kids really need people like you.

FRANÇOIS — Yeah?

JOHANNE — Because you are strong and you're gentle. You're calm, you think. You... you want more... You are not trapped in your skin the way I am, you you write, you read, you are... free... some-how... *(She enters with a Barbie in her hands.)* Hey. I would like to present to you my Barbie: JoJo. *(Silence, FRANÇOIS doesn't know how to react.)* Isn't she just beautiful?

FRANÇOIS   She's... dressed... like you.

JOHANNE   Not bad, eh? It's a thing with me, everything I make for my-self? I make for her too, in miniature. She's my little princess, aren't you, JoJo? You know I've always wanted to do that, for a living, right? Design the Barbie clothes? I know I would do it very well. I mean look. Not everybody could do this, right? It is not easy at all, I'm telling you, it takes a very special tal-ent making tiny clothes, I mean like these buttons, right? Just try and find tiny buttons, it's incredibly hard, and the acces-sories? Oh my God I just love the challenge of figuring out where I'm gonna find these tiny accessories. I love getting it, you know, so it looks exactly, precisely like me.

    Silence.

How do you like the red shoes? Aren't they wild? Don't tell anybody but I STOLE them, I'm sorry but, princess, you know how much money Mama spends on you but this time I mean, there I am in the toy department of Hart's, and I see this per-fect little pair of red shoes with this perfect little red purse, I mean I had her in the red dress I made in time for our date, right? And I HAD to have the purse and the shoes but I was NOT gonna pay twenty-five bucks for a whole new Barbie so I just looked around and then I tore open the package and took out the purse and the shoes and put them in my pocket. See her little earrings? I made them myself with you know what? With the little coloured balls you put on cake icing! Isn't that brilliant?

You know, I'm sure that one day guys like you are gonna be able to get pregnant.

FRANÇOIS   I would rather kill myself.

    Blackout.

SCENE 14: GREEN BANANA

Lights up. It's night. FRANÇOIS is gone. All the blinds are drawn. JOHANNE unbuttons her blouse, caresses her breasts, sighs.

Picks up a banana from the bowl of fruit.

Blackout.

SCENE 15: THE WOUND

Lights up. It's day. JOHANNE investigates.

JOHANNE   One time your dad says to me: "I don't know what the hell he does there, there's nothing at all to do in Montreal, and according to the papers, it's a very, very dangerous place."

FRANÇOIS   You wanna know what I do? I pick up my welfare cheque.

JOHANNE   What?

FRANÇOIS   Yeah. I pick up my welfare cheque.

JOHANNE   Are you serious?

FRANÇOIS   Hey. I have to pay for my apartment there somehow.

JOHANNE   But your dad is loaded. How could you be on welfare?

FRANÇOIS   He doesn't give me a cent.

JOHANNE   So what did you do for two days in Montreal?

FRANÇOIS   I walked, I went to the movies, I browsed in bookstores, got my books for the month, I walked some more...

JOHANNE   Nice life.

FRANÇOIS   Also, I was... trying to decide whether or not I could live there again.

JOHANNE	Live there?
FRANÇOIS	I don't know. Whether I'm strong enough. I was kind of... hoping for a sign.
JOHANNE	Well... what would you do if you went back?
FRANÇOIS	I don't know.
JOHANNE	Write a book, maybe?

He laughs.

Well you write here, don't you?

FRANÇOIS	No.
JOHANNE	But I see you, in the depanneur, I come in and you drop your pencil, I see you.
FRANÇOIS	Well it's not... writing.
JOHANNE	Then what is it?
FRANÇOIS	Just... scribbling. It's nothing.
JOHANNE	Well if it's nothing then why do you do it?

Laughter.

It must be good money, writing books, eh?

FRANÇOIS	All I really want is to... you know, just be a good everyday citizen.
JOHANNE	Before you came back here, what did you do?
FRANÇOIS	Well. Before I came back here, I was having a nervous breakdown.
JOHANNE	Seriously, François. What did you do? Go to school? Work?
FRANÇOIS	I was in love.

JOHANNE   Mange la merde. You're laughing at me, aren't you? François, you just say anything that comes into your head, you think you are so smart you just made up that story about getting welfare, didn't you? I mean, what I am asking you is why are you here? You are all grown up now, what are you doing here?

FRANÇOIS   I am... healing.

JOHANNE   What, you're sick?

FRANÇOIS   Yeah. I have a crushed heart. You know. Haven't you ever had a crushed heart?

JOHANNE   Hah. Who has the time for that shit? I had just started goin' out with Mario when I got pregnant with Tit-Bout. He was my first boyfriend. That was that. C'est fini.

FRANÇOIS   I made the mistake of falling in love with my best friend. I mean it wasn't really love, it was infatuation, I needed, you know, my passion for him to fill up the... void, I think. I needed to love completely so I wouldn't see everything that was wrong with my life, so I wouldn't know how lost I was, you know? I became completely obsessed. I mean he was EVERY-THING. And then, when I accepted that he had never felt that way, and I found myself alone... again. I had to look at the disaster I had made of my life. I had been totally lost in my feelings, you see, but what I realize now is that the world of feelings is nothing but a mirage, you're still in the desert, but you are running towards this... illusion and then when it all disappears and you have a mouthful of sand you realize you are nothing. You are dull and small and utterly insignificant like a worm in all this sand. I loved stupidly, you know what I mean? Just stupidly and badly. And I don't ever ever want to fall into that again.

Blackout.

SCENE 16: TIT-BOUT'S BIRTHDAY

Lights up. It's night. MARIO knocks on the door. He's drunk. JOHANNE opens up.

MARIO   *(singing)* Bonne fête, Tit-Bout, bonne fête, Tit-Bout...

JOHANNE   *Sacrement*, Mario, do you know what time it is?

MARIO   Bonne fête, cher Tit-Bout, bonne fête a toi.

> *JOHANNE lights a cigarette. MARIO moves toward her, gropes her.*

How old would he be today? Huh? Is it eight, or is it nine? Johanne!

JOHANNE   Nine. He would be nine years old today.

MARIO   I never know people's ages. I don't even know your age. *(JOHANNE extricates herself, MARIO opens the fridge, eats ham.)* So... what grade is that?

JOHANNE   Grade four, he would be in grade four.

MARIO   Do you think... do you think he was gonna be tall... for his age, or...

> *Silence.*

He still woulda had that funny little face. No matter how tall he got. So, Johanne, what do you think we woulda got him for a present? Huh?

JOHANNE   I don't know, Mario.

> *He moves toward her, takes off her T-shirt, makes JOHANNE suck his salty fingers.*

MARIO   I know. A couple bright red trucks, to play in the dirt, *hostie*. A new two-wheeled bike. *(He caresses JOHANNE's breasts.)* Yeah, yeah, I would show him how to ride a two-wheeled bike. Tomorrow morning, I would go out with him, and we would go to the park and I would show him how to ride a two-wheeled bike, *hostie hostie*, Johanne, they look bigger every time I look at them. Hey. Lie down on the table.

> *JOHANNE stretches out on the table, he gets the whipped cream, puts some on her chest, licks, eats, spreads it everywhere.*

Oh sweet Jesus, it's good. You taste so good, my little pig, my little love pig, my most favourite piggy, there is no other woman in the world for me.

He coats Johanne's *sex with whipped cream.*

Tell me my Tit-Bout's coming back.

Silence.

Please? Just tell me he's gonna come back!

Silence.

Just tell me what happened is a terrible joke!

Silence.

Tell me Tit-Bout is NOT DEAD, Johanne. He is sleeping in his room, right now, sleeping right over there, and tomorrow we will wake him up early in the morning, and celebrate!

Silence.

Hostie, come on, Johanne, tell me, tell me he is in his room!

Johanne	Mario, please, not so loud.
Mario	Why not?
Johanne	Because. I don't want Tit-Bout to hear us.
Mario	Come on, *crisse*, he's sleeping, he's not gonna hear us.
Johanne	Let's continue this in our room.
Mario	NO! Here.
Johanne	Mario. I don't want Tit-Bout to catch us!
Mario	I'm telling you, Tit-Bout is sleeping, he is not gonna wake up.
Johanne	Lemme just go check on him.

JOHANNE extricates herself violently from MARIO, heads toward the bedroom, opens the door, peeks in, returns.

Shhhh. Let's keep it down.

MARIO   You know what, Johanne? You're out of your mind.

He pulls down his pants, sprays whipped cream on his penis.

Come and eat, Maman, my beautiful little piggy, come and eat your Mario's beautiful big banana...

Blackout.

SCENE 17: THE SEWING MACHINE

Lights up. It's afternoon. Everything is closed. JOHANNE's apartment is dark. The radio is on. JOHANNE is shut away in the sewing room. We hear the humming of the sewing machine. Blackout.

SCENE 18: THE UTENSILS

Lights up. JOHANNE reads an excerpt from the black notebook...

JOHANNE   "I was just masturbating while thinking about Mario. Sometimes when I'm at Johanne's and it's late, I kind of hope that Mario will show up and that maybe they will have sex with me watching.

I have such a dirty mind.

I have such... dirty eyes."

JOHANNE puts the notebook back in FRANÇOIS's bag. She returns to the counter and finishes drying the dishes. FRANÇOIS returns. JOHANNE turns her back to him.

FRANÇOIS   So listen, how'd it go?

JOHANNE   The way it always does. Some of it was good, some of it was bad. I'm glad you told me about yourself, François. But I'm curious, have you ever had a woman?

FRANÇOIS   No.

JOHANNE   Never once?

FRANÇOIS   No!

JOHANNE   You always knew...

FRANÇOIS   Always.

JOHANNE   You've never been attracted...

FRANÇOIS   Nope.

           She laughs.

JOHANNE   Ain't life strange.

FRANÇOIS   So did he stay the whole night?

JOHANNE   Are you kidding? When he got what he wanted he was gone.

           Silence.

           Yuh, it's quite amazing. He sweeps my chimney and he's out the door. HAH. I'm sorry.

           Laughs.

           He knows there is no one else in my life. When there is...

FRANÇOIS   He hasn't been around much lately at all, eh?

JOHANNE   Yeah. I guess he wanted a break from his dirty sluts or something. You know, the thing I hate most about doing the dishes is the drying; the drying of the forks and the knives and the spoons, especially: the things we eat food with. I don't know. I get out the tea towel and I start to dry and I get this little pain in my chest, like this little pinch, and it happens every time I dry, what do you call them, utensils. Yeah, utensils. It's like it's only when I'm drying utensils I really really realize, "My God, this is what it is gonna be for the rest, the rest of my life. It is going to be this."

FRANÇOIS   I like washing better than drying.

JOHANNE   Washing the utensils doesn't do ANYTHING to me, it's so weird. It's only the drying, the drying always does it to me.

JOHANNE joins FRANÇOIS at the table.

I can't believe you don't have a boyfriend.

FRANÇOIS   Well, I'm not planning on staying here forever, right?

JOHANNE   So when you are lonely, you go to Montreal for...

FRANÇOIS   Sex? You want to know if I have sex?

JOHANNE laughs.

Actually I can't remember the last time.

JOHANNE   Really? How long's it been?

FRANÇOIS   I don't know, take a guess.

JOHANNE   Five months.

FRANÇOIS   Longer.

JOHANNE   Eight months.

FRANÇOIS   Longer.

JOHANNE   Not a year?

FRANÇOIS   LONGER.

JOHANNE   Oh my God, more than a year?

FRANÇOIS   More than a year.

JOHANNE   Not more than a year and a half.

FRANÇOIS   Oh yes.

JOHANNE   *Sacrement*, François, how can you stand it? If I go a few days without it I go out of my mind. Since Mario moved out there are some weeks where it's like nothing, you know? And I HATE it. Sex is so incredible... well how long's it been for you?

FRANÇOIS   I'm not telling you.

JOHANNE   Two years?

           FRANÇOIS makes a "higher" sign.

FRANÇOIS   There must be something about me—I don't know, I guess maybe I'm not very approachable.

           Silence.

JOHANNE   I knew Mario would turn up last night. It was Tit-Bout's birthday.

FRANÇOIS   How old would he have been?

JOHANNE   Nine. Nine years old.

FRANÇOIS   It's been two years and six months exactly.

           Blackout.

SCENE 19: TWENTY BUCKS

           Lights up. It's almost eleven p.m. The scene takes place in the hallway that separates the depanneur from JOHANNE's place.

MARIO   You know where she went?

FRANÇOIS   No.

MARIO   She didn't tell you? Jesus it must be top secret.

Silence.

Uh, listen, François, I was wondering if you could cash a cheque for twenty bucks.

FRANÇOIS   We don't cash cheques anymore.

MARIO   Come on *hostie,* your father cashes them all the time for me.

FRANÇOIS   What can I say, he told me not to cash any more cheques.

MARIO   If he was here, he would cash it for me.

FRANÇOIS   I don't think so, Mario. I don't think he would.

MARIO   TWENTY BUCKS, *CALICE.*

FRANÇOIS   I'm sorry, Mario, I can't cash any cheques.

MARIO   Okay, then lend me twenty bucks, I'll give it to ya tomorrow.

FRANÇOIS   I can't.

MARIO   Johanne will show up sometime tonight, she'll give it back to you.

FRANÇOIS   It's eleven o'clock, I gotta close up now.

MARIO   She should be back any minute. Come on, can't you wait? What's the hurry?

FRANÇOIS   Mario.

MARIO   Okay okay, then just mark me down for a big one. I'll drink it on the balcony and wait for her to show up. Okay?

Blackout.

SCENE 20: MOTEL HÉLÈNE

Lights up. It's daytime. JOHANNE *looks radiant, like she's floating. She enters her place through the depanneur.*

FRANÇOIS   So where were you?

JOHANNE   At Motel Hélène. At Motel Hélène, in room number thirteen...
          (She hums a popular song.)

FRANÇOIS   Where's Motel Hélène? Never heard of it.

JOHANNE   You don't know Motel Hélène? Oh, I'll have to take you there
          one day.

FRANÇOIS   Why?

JOHANNE   It's at the edge of town on the way to Princeville.

FRANÇOIS   What were you doing there?

JOHANNE   What do you think?

FRANÇOIS   What, you and Mario?...

JOHANNE   *(burst of laughter)* Me and Mario? Oh no, no François, this was
          a man, a man I have never met before, a stranger. I still have
          his smell all over me, I don't want to wash it off, ever, oh yes,
          François, it was... divine divine, I never thought I would ever
          have a night like that again but I did, no, not with Mario.

          François, last night, last night I thought I would go mad with
          the heat in my place. I said to myself right out loud I said,
          "I'm not sittin' around here all night," so I take off to the
          mall, around 6:30, I walked over, and I'm like pouring sweat,
          I can't take this weather, François, I can't take it, so I sat, I
          sat on a bench in the mall and *crisse* I was fine, cooling out, I
          walked around Steinberg's, I wanted it to be colder and cold-
          er. I saw my boss, Mr. Plamondon's, wife, we said hello, I
          walked around, and when I went outside at around a quarter
          to nine, the air was so heavy I was suffocating, I mean I could
          not breathe. I said to myself, "I can't. I cannot go home and
          sit on my balcony all night, not sleeping." I went back inside,
          into the brasserie, I wasn't hungry not at all but I ate anyway,
          a small salad; there were lots and lots of people there, it was
          unbelievable, nobody could take the heat, the heat outside of
          the brasserie, there we all were so there I am, sitting all alone
          when he comes in, oh François, just talking about him I have

shivers all through me. He was from Drummondville, oh sweet Jesus, so different from Mario, big and tall and strong, his thighs, his THIGHS, François, we laughed, we sat and we drank and we laughed, he was very sweet and very funny, he liked comedy, Daniel Lemire, like me? And and that impressionist, you know, the one who does everybody, everybody, not just people from here...

FRANÇOIS   Uh, yeah, yeah... wait a minute, there's somebody there.

He disappears into the depanneur. JOHANNE collapses, her body bent in two, back to the audience. She stays in that position for a long time. It seems interminable. Nothing happens. She suffers in silence. FRANÇOIS returns. She recovers.

JOHANNE   All evening I was looking at his hands, I was thinking about what people say about a man's longest finger? And looking at his beautiful hands and when we left the brasserie he asked me if I wanted to go somewhere else, I said, "It will be impossible to sleep tonight with this heat," and he said, "Shall we sleep together?" I said, "Oh yes, yes, but we gotta have air conditioning, right?" And he said, "Okay, come on, I'll take you to a quiet little motel—it's no palace, but we can be together there." So when we got to the room he flicked on the air conditioning and he just... took off his clothes, I hadn't even put down my purse and he was all naked, François, and he goes, "I'm taking a shower, make yourself comfortable." So polite, and his cock was was like something out of one of those letters Mario reads. I started shaking, shaking, I don't know, I guess it was the heat and the air conditioning together and the fear, the fear. He came out of the shower naked, wet, I hadn't moved at all, he came to me, he took me in his arms, he had a hard-on already, he took my hand and put it on his cock, he undressed me, he put my dress on the little armchair in the corner, he took off my bra, my panties, he took me by the hand to the shower, he washed me, he soaped me all over, I could feel his penis against my side, he ran his fingers all over me, inside me, we landed wet, dripping wet on the bed, the room was getting nice and cool, he was heavy, but gentle, we did everything, everything, we didn't stop all night, I have his sweat, his sperm all over me, I smell like him, François, I smell like man.

FRANÇOIS   Hey! I got it! The name of that comedian!

Mario knocks on the door.

JOHANNE   Calice.

Mario knocks, François goes back to the depanneur, Johanne opens the door.

MARIO   Where have you been? Crisse?

JOHANNE   None of your business.

MARIO   Johanne. Where did you spend the night?

JOHANNE   I spent the night in my room, is that okay?

MARIO   You think I'm stupid, Johanne? I was lookin' all over for you, I was at your mother's, you're not there, I come back here every hour, I'm knockin' on your door...

                 Silence.

                 You want me to believe you stayed in your room in that heat?

                 Silence.

                 Tabarnak, I'm not stupid. You went somewhere to fuck someone, right? Right, Johanne?

                 She laughs. François watches the scene from the hallway.

                 You went to wet your pussy, right?

                 She laughs.

                 With that creep from the dep, you went to a motel, right? Right? Oh that is pathetic.

                 She laughs.

JOHANNE   François is a *tapette*, you stupid moron. A TAPETTE.

                 She laughs.

MARIO	Stop laughing, it makes you look even crazier than you are.
JOHANNE	Yeah, Mario, I fucked my brains out all night and it was awesome.
MARIO	Oh shut up.
JOHANNE	I haven't washed yet, either. I still have his smell all over me, like some kinda perfume.
MARIO	Stupid cow.
JOHANNE	I smell like sex, Mario.
MARIO	*Hostie*, SHUT IT.
JOHANNE	Hey. If you look close enough you can see him all over me. Look. Look.
MARIO	Yeah show me. SHOW me.

Silence.

You're so sad. You probably did stay in your room all night, just to piss me off. I know you didn't go with nobody last night, I went to all the bars, I didn't see you. You just shut yourself up in your little room and hid. God you really are crazy, aren't you.

JOHANNE	Go away, Mario, I can't stand the sight of you.
MARIO	It's just like the whole thing with Tit-Bout. The same thing. Crisse.
JOHANNE	Stop, Mario.
MARIO	Nothin' has been right around here since that day, Johanne. Tit-Bout disappears and you throw me out. It's bullshit.
JOHANNE	You know what? I don't feel like listening to this shit anymore. I had one night, one night when I felt alive, and and it lasted longer than fifteen minutes.

MARIO	I mean I just can't believe it, I can't believe that Tit-Bout was sittin' right on the balcony, right there, eating his bread with peanut butter, mindin' his own business, and that that some guy, some stranger comes up and starts talkin' to him, I can't...
JOHANNE	Leave.
MARIO	And then while you were in the kitchen playin' housewife, Tit-Bout follows this guy?
JOHANNE	OUT!

She throws him out, closes the door, locks it, lowers the blinds.

MARIO	Maybe he wanted to come inside but the door was locked, just like last night, like now, because his crazy mother was locked up in her room, just like last night, and and she heard him banging at the door but she didn't do nothing, you didn't do nothing, did you? Did you, Johanne?

SCENE 21: THE BLACK NOTEBOOK

Lights up. JOHANNE reads an excerpt from the black notebook. The door that leads to the hallway is open: FRANÇOIS watches JOHANNE. He doesn't move.

JOHANNE	I went out with Johanne last night. She got all dressed up. It was so sad, she looked like she was in some kind of costume, trying desperately to look young again. She wore a bright red dress that she made herself, and her body... her body looked almost deformed somehow... as if it had been deformed by life.

Blackout.

SCENE 22: THE PHOTOS

Lights up. JOHANNE smokes, seems a little distant, she drinks a beer. She and FRANÇOIS sit at the kitchen table.

FRANÇOIS   I mean gimme a break, you show up at a depanneur at five
            to five on a Saturday, with a bag full of empty bottles, the
            place is packed. I was furious but I didn't say a thing, I took
            the bottles out of the bag, one by one, I'm fuming inside,
            right? I felt like saying, "Listen, next time you clean out your
            basement, come on a Monday afternoon for Christ's sake,
            asshole." *Crisse* you never saw such a mess, Johanne, I mean
            I was too mad to say anything, you know? So I clench my
            teeth and I give him his money and he walks out and I'm
            standing there like, "duh."

            JOHANNE gets up brusquely.

JOHANNE   Oh! Before I forget!

            She heads toward the bedroom, returns with some photos.

            The pictures from last Friday night!

FRANÇOIS   Oh yes. *(Silence, FRANÇOIS looks at the pictures.)* Nice. These
            turned out well.

JOHANNE   I look so fat in them.

FRANÇOIS   Did you make doubles?

JOHANNE   No. Why?

FRANÇOIS   Well I'd like to have copies.

JOHANNE   What are you, mental? What for?

            We hear a car pull up.

            I bet you ten bucks it's Mario.

            FRANÇOIS moves to get up.

            François, you're not goin' anywhere. Sit down.

            MARIO knocks, enters.

MARIO   So what are youse doin' inside in this heat?

JOHANNE   It's no cooler outside.

MARIO   It's so dry out there, and it's not goin' to rain tonight, neither, the radio said. All the lawns are dying, man, over at my dad's? It's all burnt from the sun. This whole big lawn, yellow, like hay!

FRANÇOIS   And you can't water; the river's dry.

MARIO   That's what they were sayin' on the radio too, but I seen people with their sprinklers goin', their hoses, stupid assholes, I hope the cops catch 'em, give 'em a big fine and a boot in the face. Hey, got any pop?

JOHANNE   I think there's one Coke left. In the fridge.

MARIO   I'm thirsty, man. So what're you guys drinking?

JOHANNE   Nothing. Hey get me a beer, would ya? *Crisse*, I promised myself I wasn't gonna drink tonight. I been drinkin' every night of my vacation. OH WELL what the hell.

MARIO   Just Coke for me tonight. You, François?

JOHANNE   That means he has a hangover.

MARIO   *Calice*, she knows everything, right? Hey, François, what do you want?

FRANÇOIS   Nothing for me.

MARIO   She shuts herself up in the house, never goes out, doesn't even have a cat to talk to, but she knows everything. *(JOHANNE laughs, MARIO gets himself pop, her beer.)* Hey, did you hear about the crash this afternoon? The ambulances were like everywhere. Three fatalities, two critically injured, I'm serious, happened on the 116 goin' towards Princeville just after the turnoff leavin' town, you know there's the drive-in, right? The Colibri, then there's this other little motel...

JOHANNE   Motel Hélène.

           Laughs from FRANÇOIS and JOHANNE. MARIO looks at the photos.

MARIO	So looks like this *hostie* idiot was tryin' to pass at the turn-off and BANG, right? Head-on collision, three dead; DEAD; see these two kids were comin' into town to party, probably from Plessisville, comin' the other way, and the guy, the guy who did the passing, he's got a passenger, right? Passenger's dead now, dead as that doorknob, but the driver? Oh he's fine, right? Came through with a few scatches. Tabarnak. Typical, eh, the guy who causes three deaths comes out untouched; man the world is a rotten place, hey, those pictures are not bad, eh? The photographer musta been a real pro. HAH.
JOHANNE	So who was the guy?
MARIO	They're not releasin' the name yet. Oh and get this, the car that was passed? It was a couple in their fifties, they didn't have a chance, right? BANG. They're thrown into a ditch, and they die there. They lived so near, man, they were almost home, a couple more yards after the little bridge; can you imagine? You're a couple minutes away from home? And bang you're dead. You don't have a car, eh?
JOHANNE	Our François looks so serious in that one, eh?
MARIO	Oh! We gotta buy a couple a rolls of film for the wedding. Get 'em if you're at the drugstore, Johanne, film is cheaper there. HAH. I said to my brother-in-law, I go: "We're givin' you one hell of a stag, chief, watch out." He's scared shitless, man, my sister, she's yellin' at me: "Don't you get him all messed up right before the wedding, Mario." I love gettin' them goin'.
JOHANNE	That dress looks terrible on me. I'm gonna make myself another one for the wedding.

Blackout.

SCENE 23: THE BLACK NOTEBOOK (THE STORY OF THE HUNGRY CHILD, CONTINUED)

Lights up. It's night. FRANÇOIS sits with the black notebook on his knees. JOHANNE, sitting, not moving, has the impassive look of a condemned woman. FRANÇOIS has difficulty looking at her. He stares at his notebook.

FRANÇOIS   Tuesday, June 4th, '92. In the late afternoon, something hap-
             pened. When I went to take the empty beer cases to the shed,
             I heard the neighbour with her little boy. They live on the
             same floor as the depanneur, and I had to go through the
             hallway to get to the shed. So it was around 3:30, after school,
             and Joahnne was yelling at the little boy. I just froze. I hate
             it when people yell. She was raging, because he had come
             home too early or something. She said, "What the hell are you
             doing here? Get out, now!" He said he was hungry a couple
             of times. "I'm hungry." "How the hell did you get so filthy?
             Christ, didn't you see that the floor was clean?" "I'm hungry."
             "Well get over it, little boy. I can't believe this, I can't keep
             anything clean for more than five minutes in this place, *sacre-*
             ment, didn't you see the floor was still wet? You're like your
             father, you're goddamned blind, get out of my face, just go
             to hell." I think she grabbed his arm to get him out, again he
             said, "I'm hungry." "So starve! Get out on that balcony and
             stay there till I call you." Then a customer came, I didn't hear
             any more.

             When he went missing, it was chaos. Panic. Horror. Not real,
             somehow. Like a movie.

             Silence.

             It's not that well written. I don't think I made it up.

             She bursts out laughing. A terrible nervous laugh. She stops.

JOHANNE   I was in the bathroom when he came home. I had just put in
             a load of laundry and I was collapsed on the toilet, I remem-
             ber, I was holding my head in my hands, just exhausted, right?
             I didn't hear him come in, but it's strange I had said to my-
             self earlier: "Watch out for Tit-Bout, he's gonna come in and
             not notice the floor is still wet." Then when I went into the
             kitchen and saw him climbing his chair to get the sugar with
             his filthy running shoes, I don't know, when I saw my nice
             floor a mess, bread crumbs on the counter, on the floor, and
             the sugar all over the place, I went crazy, I pulled him off the
             chair, I just wanted to see my floor clean for five minutes,
             he howled at me that he was hungry, I didn't care, I was just
             thinking of my floor, of my future, of my linoleum, *tabarnak*,
             and I—I threw his bread and peanut butter in the garbage, he

yelled that he was hungry, so yeah, you're right, I did probably say "so starve." I don't know, I don't know what I said but I took him, I threw him outside. I think I said, "You're gonna stay there until your father gets home." And then I went back inside and I locked the door, I LOCKED THE DOOR so he would never come back inside. I SHUT MY CHILD OUTSIDE, I sealed the bread in its plastic bag, I put the jar of peanut butter in the cupboard, I wiped the counter, I got down on all fours to pick up the little bread crumbs off the floor...

> *She stops. She doesn't move. Her gaze is lost in the horror of her life. Silence. A long time passes, and then she goes on.*

HE'S DEAD, HE'S NEVER COMING BACK.

The night he disappeared, there were so many people here, it was so noisy; everybody coming, and going; I ended up there, at the counter, at one point, I was leaning right there and I don't know what happened, but like some kind of electrical blast I suddenly thought, "Don't come back, Tit-Bout! Mama doesn't want you to come back. Mama is too tired." And it's weird, but with all the crazy panic, I was okay for a few seconds, like I was soothed because because I knew what I really felt. And then when I came out of it, I played the game, right? I played along and since that time I have never felt okay or soothed again; I have been trying to erase what I thought for those few seconds, pretending for myself and everyone else that of course, of course I wanted Tit-Bout back, healthy and safe alive. Of course. I'm his mother.

> *Silence.*

FRANÇOIS   Forgive me.

JOHANNE   I tell myself Tit-Bout just got lost in the woods, right? And when it got dark, he just lay down and he went to sleep. He was dreaming a lovely dream about a little house made of white sugar and he dreamed and he dreamed and he forgot to wake up. That's all. He forgot to wake up.

> *Blackout.*

SCENE 24: THE GUY FROM DRUMMONDVILLE

Lights up. JOHANNE *stands in the door frame of the depanneur. She has just had her hair done.*

JOHANNE   It's wild, eh?

FRANÇOIS   It's a real change.

JOHANNE   I walked in to the hairdresser, I said: "I want a new look." Do you like it?

FRANÇOIS   Yeah, it suits you. I like it better.

JOHANNE   Apparently it's right in style. I said to her: "Please, whatever you do, make sure it's easy to look after." I mean don't even talk to me about these hairstyles that take like hours with the hair dryer or the mousse, or those cuts you have to come back for every couple of weeks, forget it. I can't wait to see his face.

FRANÇOIS   Mario's?

JOHANNE   Mario's? Are you mental? He wouldn't even notice.

FRANÇOIS   Who, then?

JOHANNE   My guy from Drummondville.

FRANÇOIS   No kidding?

JOHANNE   I wonder if he'll even recognize me. I'll feel really stupid if he doesn't recognize me.

FRANÇOIS   Wait a minute. He called you?

JOHANNE   Yes, didn't I tell you? This morning. I slid a pack of matches with my phone number on them into his jeans, right? I was sure he would never call, I was totally amazed when I realized it was him on the phone this morning. He said he would be at the brasserie tomorrow around ten. Can you believe it?

FRANÇOIS   Oh, I see. So that's why the new hairstyle.

Blackout.

SCENE 25: THE WEDDING PRESENT

Lights up. Daytime. We should feel that it is beautiful out-side. JOHANNE talks to her mother on the phone. She's also in the middle of dying her black shoes red.

JOHANNE   So anyways I called Josée and thank God she answered, I could have got her mother, who I will have more than enough of at the wedding, thank you very much, and so anyways she said to me, she said: "Johanne, the best present you could give me would be just to come to my wedding with Mario." So I told her we really insisted on getting her something like everyone else, I mean she should have something from us, right? Well typical Mario, he wants me to go to the wedding with him, he wants us to bring a nice present, but of course I'm the one stuck with getting it, even though it's his sister, I mean it's an important thing, a present makes you think about a person, like you know those oven mitts you brought me from Florida? Every time I put them on I think, "Oh these are what Mama brought me from Florida." I mean they're a wreck now, I should throw them in the garbage, but you know? I just can't bring myself to throw them out.

Blackout.

SCENE 26: LAST MEEETING

Lights up. It's night. MARIO enters with cheese curds, a can of barbecue sauce, and a bottle of Pepsi.

MARIO   I feel like poutine tonight. You?

JOHANNE   It's almost eleven!

MARIO   So what? I'm gonna get the fries at the snack bar. You want some?

JOHANNE   Why don't you just buy a whole poutine? Otherwise we have
             to dirty a pot for the sauce, a big plate...

MARIO   Because they don't put enough cheese and I don't like their sauce.
             I'm hungry and I'm gonna make my poutine the way I like it.

JOHANNE   Oh, all right. I'll pick off yours then. Oh, and bring me an all-
             dressed steamed hot dog while you're at it.

             He gets ready to leave.

             Mario, you feel like going out later?

MARIO   Tonight? Where we gonna go?

JOHANNE   I don't know, wherever you want. We could go to the strip club...

MARIO   *Crisse,* Johanne, what's got into you? You feelin' dirty?

JOHANNE   I don't know. My vacation is almost over. I want to go out.

MARIO   I don't know. We'll see.

             He goes to exit, comes back.

             I know. Tomorrow night I'll come by and pick you up, we
             can go to the house and bring Josée her *crisse* present, in case
             she wants it before the wedding, right? So we'll bring her the
             present and then we can go out if you still feel like it. Fridays
             are better, there's more people around. Okay? Tomorrow?

             Blackout.

SCENE 27: THE BLACK NOTEBOOK

             Lights up. FRANÇOIS *reads an excerpt from the black notebook.*

FRANÇOIS   "Mario came by the depanneur around ten forty-five; he
             went over to Johanne's with a pound of cheese curds, a

can of barbecue sauce, and a bottle of Pepsi. He told me he was hungry and that he was going to eat a whole poutine. I wonder— Are they going to eat poutine and then fuck? Or are they going to fuck and then eat their poutine after?

I am alone."

Blackout.

SCENE 28: THE STRIPPER

Lights up. It's night. MARIO exits, JOHANNE closes the apartment door. She wears a very short robe. She sees her high-heeled shoes lying around, puts them on. She starts dancing, she opens her robe, caresses her breasts, rolls her hips. She takes off her robe, stands nude in high heels. She wants to scream. Blackout.

SCENE 29: JOJO

Late Friday night. In the kitchen, all the chairs are on the table. There are rags hanging on the edge of a pail on the counter. We understand that JOHANNE has washed her floor. JOHANNE is wearing her red dress. She is sitting on the floor, beside the little table in the living room, holding her Barbie JoJo, who is wearing a wedding dress.

JOHANNE   Are you gonna come to my wedding? I'm getting married to my gentleman from Drummondville next week. I am so happy. I've never made love with a man, but my mother tells me it's wonderful. We're gonna have lots and lots of children, even though Mama has warned me about losing my figure, and I would really love it if you would be the godfather of my first baby; we'll choose the godmother from one of his friends, my gentleman from Drummondville. My wedding dress was very expensive, my poor mother went broke, she literally spent thousands on it but she said nothing was too good for her JoJo. She also calls me her princess, "My princess, can you come here; my princess, would you go to the depanneur and fetch me a pint of milk; oh princess, you are going to be the most beautiful bride anyone has ever seen." Most of the dress I made was from an old curtain that was lying around in a chest. I sewed three little rows of stars onto it that I cut out myself from the curtain then I painted them with silver Cutex to make them like diamonds. I did the same thing for her long veil; so when she bows it will be like a curtain call and there will be little glints when the sun hits it; the hardest thing was sticking the veil to her head, I really wanted to see her blond hair, I didn't want to hide her whole head. I will die in air conditioning; long blond hair is so beautiful, so in the end I made just a little hoop, I took a teeny teeny pin, you know garbage-bag ties? Well I took off the paper, then I made a little crown that held back her hair, so if there's a wind that day she won't have hair in her face. I made her a wedding ring with tinfoil just in case her gentleman from Drummondville forgets. You never can tell with men.

> *Long pause. She seems lost in thought. She stares at a particular spot on the floor, places the Barbie in the box, and crawls on all fours to the spot, picks up a crumb, heads for the pail, takes a rag, rinses it properly, goes back to the spot, and cleans it. She scrubs and scrubs and scrubs. She stands up and heads for the counter. She takes out the garbage bag, opens the fridge, empties it entirely. She looks on top of the fridge; throws out a bag of chips, the bananas, closes the bag tightly, and puts it in the entrance hall, for the garbage man. She walks to the kitchen table. She takes the chairs off the table onto the floor. She takes the pail of water out. She comes back to the living room and picks up the box with the Barbie, the photos and the letters and the red shoes. She puts it on the kitchen table and picks up the box cover, fits it on, and closes the box.*

SCENE 30: AIR CONDITIONING (FRANÇOIS IS IN THE HALLWAY)

FRANÇOIS   When she came to see me before going to the brasserie, it was about nine fifteen. She was dressed all in red. I thought at the time that it was a bit over the top. She never did get to the brasserie. I think she must have walked around the square and then came back and shut herself in her room. Anyway, she did come back here because the next morning when I opened, she had left me a note taped to her door that said,

"François, it's open, come on in, there is a present for you on the table." I was pleased, I thought she had got me something for my birthday, my first present of the day.

> FRANÇOIS *enters, sees the box and the red shoes on the table, the photos of the Friday date, and an envelope on the box. He takes the shoes, looks at the photos, opens the envelope. And reads the letter. Long pause. He reads.*

"I'm sorry for that ridiculous story about the guy from Drummondville. It's so tiring to lie about everything. But I want you to know that last week, when I was at Motel Hélène all alone, I cried. I cried my eyes out. You will never know how bad I felt inside, deep in my belly. Happy birthday, François! I know she's not much but take care of her. *(He opens the box and takes out the Barbie dressed in* JOHANNE*'s wedding dress.)* Whenever you see her in a drawer or the back of your closet or whatever, I hope you'll think of me. Hey. I am going to die in air conditioning. So, now do what I asked you, François. Motel Hélène, room thirteen."

> FRANÇOIS *cries. Blackout.*

> *The end.*

IT'S ALL TRUE

JASON SHERMAN

It's All True premiered at the Tarragon Theatre in January 1999 with the following company:

JOHN HOUSEMAN .... Richard Binsley
JEAN ROSENTHAL, VIRGINIA WELLES,
BEATRICE WELLES, AND OTHERS... Tamara Bernier
ORSON WELLES .... Victor Ertmanis
OLIVE STANTON, MOLL, EVA BLITZSTEIN, AND OTHERS .... Melody Johnson
HOWARD DA SILVA, LARRY FOREMAN,
BERTOLT BRECHT, AND OTHERS.. Martin Julien
MARC BLITZSTEIN.. Tom McCamus
Steve Smith plays the piano

Directed by Richard Rose
Set and costumes designed by Charlotte Dean
Lighting designed by Kevin Lamotte
Original music by Don Horsburgh
Stage managed by Susan Monis

A substantially revised version was produced by Necessary Angel at Buddies in Bad Times Theatre, Toronto, opening on October 14, 1999. Richard Binsley, Victor Ertmanis, Melody Johnson, and Martin Julien returned to the cast; Vicky Papavs and Joseph Ziegler joined it. Richard Rose directed. Garth Lambert was the pianist and Nancy Dryden was the stage manager.

Jason Sherman has written extensively for the stage, radio, and television. His other plays include *Remnants (A Fable)*, *Patience*, *Reading Hebron*, *The Retreat*, *The League of Nathans*, *An Acre of Time*, and *Three in the Back, Two in the Head*, which won the Governor General's Literary Award for Drama. An adaptation of *The Brothers Karamazov* was first seen at the Stratford Festival in 2005, and a contemporary version of *The Cherry Orchard*, called *After the Orchard*, had its premiere at the National Arts Centre the same year. He has written mainly for radio, TV, and film ever since. His CBC radio dramas have garnered several Canadian Screenwriting Awards, and include *National Affairs*, *Graf*, *A Stone's Throw*, and *Afghanada*, which he created and will have aired for over one hundred episodes by the end of its run. He writes a comic strip for the back page of *The Walrus* magazine, but he doesn't draw the pictures.

Looked at from a strictly pragmatic point of view, *Patience*—Jason Sherman's 1998 masterpiece—would be far more representative of the work of this playwright (among other titles he holds) at the Tarragon Theatre. Its retelling of the biblical story of Job in a contemporary setting captures both the secular and religious tensions of his creativity. After all, he would return to the Tarragon five years after *Patience* with *Remnants (A Fable)*, a modern take on another biblical tale, that of Joseph and his brothers. And let's not forget that two previous successes, *The League of Nathans* and *Reading Hebron*, saw the then-young and provocative writer diving into the turbulent waters of the Arab-Israeli conflicts and Jewish identity.

But while I saw, reviewed, and liked the revival of *Patience* at Canadian Stage in 2000, I'm still haunted by the first production at the Tarragon of *It's All True* in January 1999 and its even stronger revival at Buddies in Bad Times Theatre, which I reviewed, both in productions by Necessary Angel Theatre Company. In 1999 Sherman was at his prime, noted *Time* magazine, and rightly so.[1] Even if, with the possible exception of *An Acre of Time*, his subsequent work never matched the peaks of *Patience* and *It's All True* (and even if he seems to have deserted theatre altogether), this moment in his career needs to be celebrated. I still remember how hard I had to work as a theatregoer and critic to catch up with the wit and political sophistication of Sherman's reimagining of the real-life events surrounding the 1937 opening night of the agitprop musical *The Cradle Will Rock*. I'll admit that I knew nothing about this story and had to look up much of its background in the stacks at U of T's Robarts Library hours before the review was due to my editor at *Eye Weekly*.

While any research is good research, what matters most in *It's All True* is not the truth itself—however Sherman wishes to define it—but the many fictions that give it a theatrical outlet. "The paradox of theatre is that you have to lie in order to tell the truth," said Sherman in an interview before the play's opening at the Tarragon.[2] The craft of the playwright necessitates the creation of relationships, backgrounds, motivations for characters as diverse as the real-life ones that populate *It's All True*: composer Marc Blitzstein, director Orson Welles, producer John Houseman, and actor

1   Craig Offman, "Everything's relative," *Time*, February 1, 1999, 51. Offman was referring to Sherman's work on stage, radio, and television drama.

2   Quoted in Kevin Connolly, "Sherman's mark," *Eye Weekly*, January 7, 1999, 25.

Howard Da Silva. All live on the page and stage as full-fledged characters while also representing strong political and social views.

The struggle between fact and fiction is only one of many in *It's All True*. On a more literal level, there's the class struggle and political tensions within the unions representing actors and musicians on one hand and, on the other, their fight against the administration of President Roosevelt, whose public-arts project funded *The Cradle Will Rock* as part of its Depression economic relief. On a psychological level, Blitzstein battles the ghost of his wife Eva, who died prematurely of cancer, while simultaneously fighting off his homosexual desires, as Sherman makes clear in the revised text of the Buddies production.

While all these public and private battles strengthen the play's dramatic tensions, the struggle that animates it on a meta level concerns the battle between art and politics, between magic and reality. On the surface at least, Welles advocates for a version of *The Cradle Will Rock* that is much closer to the Broadway musicals playing in nearby theatres—except of course that his production is populated with steelworkers and prostitutes—while Da Silva and Blitzstein hold out for theatre that privileges the message over illusions. But while Sherman seems to root for the latter camp, his ending and the staging of *It's All True* align more with Welles's stance.

In both productions, director Richard Rose recreated the excitement of an opening night in New York circa 1937 within the context of his own opening night. As the performance of *The Cradle Will Rock* was forced to move from the stage to the aisles to overcome rigid union regulations, so does the final scene in *It's All True*. In a play where shifts in time and space explore 1930s American politics and the roots of hidden tensions among its characters, the lines between the old play and the one seen in 1999 were further fused. The Tarragon became Broadway and vice versa. Sherman made up for the difference in physical sizes between the venues in another, more significant way.

As Urjo Kareda noted,[3] the theatrical vitality of Sherman's plays starts from the "sheer size" of his characters' desires, imagination, and intelligence. The Welles of *It's All True* is therefore a distinctly Sherman creation. Kareda then adds that such characters elicit extraordinary performances from the actors playing them. *Globe and Mail* theatre critic Kate Taylor encapsulates actor Victor Ertmanis's lively performance as Welles in the second production at Buddies in Bad Times Theatre when she writes that he "has captured ego, humour, anger, intelligence and bombast and fills not only the stage but the whole room with them."[4] Is there any wonder that the final word in the play is "magic" and it's delivered by Ertmanis as

---

3   Urjo Kareda, "An Introduction" in *Jason Sherman: Six Plays*, ii.

4   Kate Taylor, "Truly, it's a night of magic," *Globe and Mail*, October 18, 1999, D5.

yet another reminder of the Tarragon's emphasis on the power of the right words and the right performance?

CHARACTERS

John Houseman
Jean Rosenthal
Virginia Welles
Beatrice Welles
Orson Welles
Olive Stanton
Moll
Eva Blitzstein
Howard Da Silva
Larry Foreman
Bertolt Brecht
Marc Blitzstein

NOTES

A note on sources: *It's All True* is not all true, but for the parts that are I am indebted to: John Houseman, *Run-Through* (for the most thorough and authoritative description of the events in the play); Orson Welles, *The Cradle Will Rock* (unproduced screenplay); Marc Blitzstein, *Marc Blitzstein Presents "The Cradle Will Rock"* (sound recording); Simon Callow, *The Road to Xanadu* (a Welles biography, which includes Welles's description of the death of his mother, quoted verbatim here); Eric Gordon, *Mark the Music* (a biography of Blitzstein); Lehman Engel, *This Bright Day*; Hallie Flanagan, *Arena*; and Lillian Hellman's *Unfinished Woman*, for Blitzstein's account of Spain.

A note on music: The original music for the songs of *It's All True* was written by Don Horsburgh, and is available through Playwrights Canada Press.

A note on piano playing: There are in fact seven cast members, the seventh being the pianist, who plays during rehearsals, as Olive's accompanist at her audition, and at the 21 Club. The actor playing Blitzstein plays the piano for the final scene.

ACT ONE
SCENE 1

June 15, 1937. The Maxine Elliott Theatre, New York City.
Marc BLITZSTEIN, the composer; John HOUSEMAN, the producer;
and Orson WELLES, the director, in the middle of an argument.

BLITZSTEIN   Why didn't you tell me?

WELLES   Marc.

BLITZSTEIN   Why didn't you say?

HOUSEMAN   It—

BLITZSTEIN   Yes?

HOUSEMAN   It wasn't.

BLITZSTEIN   Look.

WELLES   Marc, we didn't—

BLITZSTEIN   What?

WELLES   Didn't mean to—

BLITZSTEIN   Harm m— hurt me?

WELLES   No.

BLITZSTEIN   You did, you did.

WELLES   I—

BLITZSTEIN   All right?

WELLES	No, look.
HOUSEMAN	Be reasonable.
BLITZSTEIN	Be—?
HOUSEMAN	Yes.
BLITZSTEIN	Reasonable.
HOUSEMAN	Yes.
BLITZSTEIN	You...
WELLES	Look.
BLITZSTEIN	How long have you known?
HOUSEMAN	It's...
BLITZSTEIN	Answer the—
WELLES	Since...
BLITZSTEIN	How long?

Pause.

HOUSEMAN	For two days.
BLITZSTEIN	Two?
HOUSEMAN	Yes.
BLITZSTEIN	And you never...
WELLES	We couldn't.
BLITZSTEIN	Never said a word.
WELLES	We didn't want to— Marc...
BLITZSTEIN	Christ.

WELLES	Marc. We're on your, will you pl—we're on your side.
BLITZSTEIN	"My side."
WELLES	We are.
HOUSEMAN	Listen to him.
WELLES	Listen to me.
HOUSEMAN	That's why we—
WELLES	Let me.
HOUSEMAN	I—
WELLES	Will you let me talk?
HOUSEMAN	I was only—
WELLES	Let me talk.
BLITZSTEIN	Somebody.
WELLES	Marc.
BLITZSTEIN	Somebody talk to me.

Pause.

WELLES	We got the cable.
BLITZSTEIN	On Tuesday, yes.
HOUSEMAN	Yes, from the WPA.
WELLES	Yes, on, that's right, Tuesday.
HOUSEMAN	No. Well—I saw it Monday night.
WELLES	I didn't see it till Tuesday.
HOUSEMAN	I got it Monday.

BLITZSTEIN	You got it Monday.
WELLES	And I saw it Tuesday.
BLITZSTEIN	All right, all right. Will somebody tell me what, what—
HOUSEMAN	I'm trying to.
WELLES	Let him talk.
HOUSEMAN	They were rehearsing.
WELLES	It was a hell of a day too.
HOUSEMAN	I had to wait, you see.
WELLES	Couldn't get the wagons to work properly.
BLITZSTEIN	What?
WELLES	The wagons.
BLITZSTEIN	All right.
HOUSEMAN	Anyway, I was sent this, this, this...
BLITZSTEIN	Cable. From the WPA.
HOUSEMAN	Yes. Stating, quite clearly, that—
WELLES	That we're not to open.
HOUSEMAN	No. It said no shows—no shows were to open.
WELLES	Meaning ours.
HOUSEMAN	Including ours.
BLITZSTEIN	Have you got it?
HOUSEMAN & WELLES	What?

BLITZSTEIN   The cable.

HOUSEMAN   Matter of fact.

WELLES   He loves paper.

HOUSEMAN   The cable forbids...

BLITZSTEIN   You see? "Forbids."

HOUSEMAN   Just listen. "Because of impending cuts and reorganization any new play, musical performance, or art gallery to open before July 1st."

BLITZSTEIN   Bullshit. That's obviously aimed at us.

WELLES   No question.

HOUSEMAN   Where is it written?

BLITZSTEIN   Between the lines. We're being censored.

HOUSEMAN   I wouldn't...

BLITZSTEIN   Censored! The government is, Roosevelt is—

HOUSEMAN   Don't jump to any con—

BLITZSTEIN   "Jump to"!

HOUSEMAN   We can't—

BLITZSTEIN   Now look.

HOUSEMAN   We can't know for sure.

WELLES   That's true.

BLITZSTEIN   What is?

WELLES   That we can't...

HOUSEMAN   We can't know for certain that the cable was aimed at us.

WELLES   That's right.

BLITZSTEIN   *(to WELLES)* But you just said...

WELLES   Yes.

BLITZSTEIN   You just said it was.

WELLES   Well I... I may have... under the circumstances... Jack?

HOUSEMAN   The point is, we didn't think we ought to worry you with this.

WELLES   You were worried enough, Marc, about the show.

BLITZSTEIN   But—

WELLES   We just—

BLITZSTEIN   But now there is no show.

WELLES   Yes. We just didn't think you needed to know.

BLITZSTEIN   There are padlocks on the front doors of this theatre. I walk in here to—how could you keep this from me?

WELLES   We're sorry.

HOUSEMAN   Most truly.

WELLES   We were hoping it wouldn't come to, you know, to this.

HOUSEMAN   That's right.

WELLES   That's why I went to Washington, you see.

HOUSEMAN   You did?

WELLES   Yes. As soon as I saw the cable, I went to see Harry Hopkins.

BLITZSTEIN   And?

WELLES   Well, he assured me that, that—well, dammit he wouldn't see me.

BLITZSTEIN   Of course not, he was too busy dismantling the WPA.

WELLES   I spoke to his assistant, though.

HOUSEMAN   And?

WELLES   We reached an understanding, I thought.

HOUSEMAN   And what was that "understanding"?

WELLES   That we would be permitted to open *The Cradle Will Rock*.

BLITZSTEIN   His assistant said that?

WELLES   Yes. The problem is, he didn't say when. So I went after him, on this point. I pressed this point. I said, "Now, look," I said, "listen here," I said, "I'm a good friend of Harry Hopkins's, and further-more," I said, "I have campaigned for Mr. Roosevelt," and then: "if the Works Progress Administration chooses to, to—"

BLITZSTEIN   Censor.

WELLES   "To close the show, we would take it over."

HOUSEMAN   We would?

BLITZSTEIN   You said that?

WELLES   Yes—to both of you.

HOUSEMAN   Project 891?

WELLES   No. You and me. As independent producers.

BLITZSTEIN   And are you?

HOUSEMAN   I had *no* idea.

WELLES   Well, it's what we've been talking about, isn't it? Starting a company once all of this was over? Anyway, I thought they'd back down.

HOUSEMAN   To the great Orson Welles.

WELLES   Now, look—

HOUSEMAN   Wonder boy.

WELLES   I never—

HOUSEMAN   "Saviour of the New York theatre."

WELLES   At least I got on a plane.

HOUSEMAN   And straightened the whole thing out!

BLITZSTEIN   Christ, it's endless! The two of you! The two of you!

WELLES   Now look, Marc, I have to be honest with you.

BLITZSTEIN   That'd be refreshing.

WELLES   It was wrong not to tell you. But I couldn't know they'd do
               something so so so—

BLITZSTEIN   Fascistic.

WELLES   Now, Marc...

BLITZSTEIN   You tell me the difference between, between the federal
               government padlocking a theatre and and Joseph Goebbels
               burning books.

HOUSEMAN   I hardly think you can compare the situations.

BLITZSTEIN   This play is about a steel strike; and there are steel strikes go-
               ing on from one end of this country to the other. This play is
               about a union rally, and the murder of a union leader, and the
               complicity of the middle class in keeping the worker down,
               and if you don't think Washington wants to keep a lid on all
               of that, you're living some pretty little fantasy, Jack. And you
               thought I didn't need to know.

               Pause.

HOUSEMAN   We're sorry.

BLITZSTEIN	"Sorry." I don't accept sorry. I only accept "Well, then..." By which I mean, "Well, then, here we are, quite a pickle, what are we going to do?"
HOUSEMAN	"Do"?
BLITZSTEIN	Yes, "do."
WELLES	Well, if you mean "about the show"...
BLITZSTEIN	That is what I mean. What are we going to do about the show, now.
WELLES	"Now"?
HOUSEMAN	It's difficult, you see.
BLITZSTEIN	I don't.
HOUSEMAN	There are problems here.
WELLES	They've taken over the whole building, I...
BLITZSTEIN	I got in.
WELLES	Well.
HOUSEMAN	Naturally. It's not that they, that they want to...
WELLES	It's the public, Marc, that they want kept out of the...
HOUSEMAN	If they were to allow the public in...
BLITZSTEIN	Then let's find another building, goddammit!
HOUSEMAN	What?
BLITZSTEIN	Yes! Pack everything up and move it to another theatre, and if we can't find a theatre, do it in a park, a garage, a living room, I don't give a damn, but we are not giving in to these fascists, do you hear me?

Jeannie ROSENTHAL, *the stage manager, enters.*

ROSENTHAL	They took his wig!
BLITZSTEIN	(not hearing her) We are not giving in!
WELLES	(to ROSENTHAL) What?
ROSENTHAL	Howard's wig. They grabbed it off his—
WELLES	All right, this is...
ROSENTHAL	His head.
HOUSEMAN	They couldn't have just...
ROSENTHAL	I'm tellin' ya. These guards, they're all over the building, walkin' up and down outside the dressing rooms, making sure nobody takes nothin'.
HOUSEMAN	I hardly believe they could have just—

DA SILVA, an actor, enters.

DA SILVA	They took my fucking wig! Off my head! I walked out of my dressing room...
BLITZSTEIN	You see?
DA SILVA	...they...
BLITZSTEIN	You see what's happening?
DA SILVA	Listen, one of those guards, those Cossacks, took from my head, from my head my fucking wig.
WELLES	Okay, that's...
ROSENTHAL	They're fascists, you ask me.
BLITZSTEIN	Precisely.
ROSENTHAL	Fascists.
WELLES	Okay.

DA SILVA	We're under siege.
WELLES	All right.
DA SILVA	We gonna let 'em do this?
BLITZSTEIN	We are *not*.
WELLES	Hold on, everyone. Howard, what else have they got hold of?
DA SILVA	Everything!
ROSENTHAL	We can't get nothing!
DA SILVA	The sets, the props...
ROSENTHAL	His wig.

The phone rings.

HOUSEMAN	All right, here's what I think we should do.
WELLES	Here's what we're going to do. Uhh...
BLITZSTEIN	Maybe it's your good friend Harry.
WELLES	Maybe it is.
ROSENTHAL	*(in phone)* Project 891.
BLITZSTEIN	"It was all a mistake. We meant to shut down *You Can't Take It With You*."
ROSENTHAL	*(in phone)* Uh huh.
WELLES	*(to BLITZSTEIN)* You're not helping. Jeannie, where are the actors?
ROSENTHAL	*(in phone)* Hold on.
DA SILVA	Like you care about the actors.
WELLES	What's that, Howard?

ROSENTHAL   *(to WELLES)* What's that, Orson?

WELLES   Where are the actors?

ROSENTHAL   Downstairs. In their dressing rooms.

WELLES   Do they know what's—

ROSENTHAL   Of course.

HOUSEMAN   I told them myself.

BLITZSTEIN   The padlocks might have suggested something was amiss.

ROSENTHAL   *(in phone)* Sorry, hello?

BLITZSTEIN   "I don't remember rehearsing with these."

WELLES   Here's what we're going to do.

ROSENTHAL   *(in phone)* Sure, just hold on.

HOUSEMAN   Would everyone please be quiet?

ROSENTHAL   *(to HOUSEMAN)* Mr. Houseman?

WELLES   WHAT?

> ROSENTHAL *reacts to his yelling.*

Sorry, Jeannie, sorry, it's—

ROSENTHAL   It's all right. It's the Downtown Music Club.

WELLES   What do they want?

ROSENTHAL   They bought the house tonight, they want to know is there gonna be a show, or?...

BLITZSTEIN   How did they hear?

ROSENTHAL   He didn't...

HOUSEMAN   Give me the phone, Jeannie.

BLITZSTEIN   It's all over the goddamn city now.

WELLES   Is it?

DA SILVA   Don't worry, Blitz, we're gonna—

HOUSEMAN   Quiet. *(in phone)* Hello? John Houseman here.

                      Another phone rings.

                      Yes, Mr. Sanders... I see... Well that's not the case. No, I'm afraid it's— *(to the others)* Would someone answer the phone? *(in phone)* Sorry, I...

ROSENTHAL   *(picking up)* Project 891.

HOUSEMAN   Well, I don't know where you would have heard that.

ROSENTHAL   He's on the phone.

WELLES   Who is it?

HOUSEMAN   We have every intention of...

ROSENTHAL   I can give you Mr. Welles.

HOUSEMAN   Yes, of doing the preview.

WELLES   Who is it?

HOUSEMAN   We just don't know where.

ROSENTHAL   *(to WELLES) New York Times.*

DA SILVA   Hoo baby!

HOUSEMAN   Yes yes.

WELLES   I'll take it.

HOUSEMAN   Of course.

DA SILVA	Tell 'em about my wig.
WELLES	Will you be quiet about your wig?
DA SILVA	Hey, you don't do Faust without your ten pounds of makeup and putty nose, I don't do—
WELLES	*(taking phone from ROSENTHAL)* This is Orson Welles.
HOUSEMAN	The thing is—
WELLES	Yes.
HOUSEMAN	Yes.
WELLES	Yes yes.
HOUSEMAN	I don't know where you're getting your information.
WELLES	"Cossacks," we call 'em.
HOUSEMAN	Oh I see.
WELLES	About twelve I think.
DA SILVA	Fourteen, I counted.
HOUSEMAN	When did they call?
WELLES	Uh huh.
HOUSEMAN	Is that so.
WELLES	Hold on a second, will you?
HOUSEMAN	Well, Mr. Sanders.
WELLES	*(to HOUSEMAN)* Jack.
HOUSEMAN	Mr. Sanders, I...
WELLES	Jack.

HOUSEMAN   Just a moment, Mr. Sanders. *(to WELLES)* What?

WELLES   The *Times* got a call from the WPA.

HOUSEMAN   So did the Music Club.

BLITZSTEIN   Saying what?

HOUSEMAN   What do you think? That the show's been cancelled.

BLITZSTEIN   You see?

WELLES   What should we...

BLITZSTEIN   Burn our books!

WELLES   What do we tell 'em?

HOUSEMAN   What you told Harry's assistant. That you and I have taken over the show.

WELLES   I was bluffing.

BLITZSTEIN   Is that right?

WELLES   That's what it was.

BLITZSTEIN   Have you been bluffing all along?

WELLES   "All"...

BLITZSTEIN   You told me you loved this show.

WELLES   And...

BLITZSTEIN   Promised me you'd "make magic."

WELLES   Yes.

BLITZSTEIN   Here is your chance. Prove it. Prove to me you're for real.

Pause. Everyone looks to WELLES.

HOUSEMAN Orson?

WELLES The show's going on.

HOUSEMAN When?

WELLES I don't know.

HOUSEMAN Where?

WELLES I don't know.

HOUSEMAN Fine.

ROSENTHAL What do I tell the actors?

WELLES To hold onto their hats.

DA SILVA Now you tell us.

      WELLES and HOUSEMAN speak into phones.

HOUSEMAN Mr. Sanders?

WELLES Now here's the thing.

HOUSEMAN There will be a show tonight, Mr. Sanders.

WELLES There will be a performance tonight of *The Cradle Will Rock*.

HOUSEMAN We don't know.

WELLES We're not sure.

HOUSEMAN I can't tell you that either.

WELLES We're working on it.

HOUSEMAN Absolutely.

WELLES No question about it.

HOUSEMAN You just bring your people to the theatre here and we'll...

WELLES   Not at all.

HOUSEMAN   Well, I appreciate it.

WELLES   *(hanging up)* Morning.

HOUSEMAN   *(hanging up, simultaneously with* WELLES*)* Morning.

> *A pause.*

WELLES   Padlocks? On my theatre?

DA SILVA   Attaboy.

WELLES   No fucking padlocks on my theatre!

DA SILVA   Brother, what a day! This is what it's about, ain't it, Blitz? "The show will go on."

WELLES   And there is going to be a goddamn wig on your head before this evening is through.

DA SILVA
& WELLES   Yes, there is!

SCENE 2

> *Several months earlier.* WELLES, *on stage.* ROSENTHAL *and a stagehand, in the wings, provide the sound and light cues.*

WELLES   *(as Faustus)* Ah Faustus,
Now hast thou but one bare hour to live,
And then thou must be damned perpetually!

(to himself) Fake...

> *In the show, the clock strikes midnight.*

(as Faustus) O, it strikes, it strikes! Now, body, turn to air,
Or Lucifer will bear thee quick to hell.
(over thunder and lightning) O, soul, be changed into little water-drops,

And fall into the ocean—ne'er be found.
My God! my God! look not so fierce upon me!

Fake...

(as Faustus, speaking as the devils enter) Adders and serpents,
let me breathe awhile!
Ugly hell, gape not! come not, Lucifer!
I'll burn my books!—Ah Mephistophilis!

He disappears in a cloud of smoke.

SCENE 3

*WELLES, in his dressing room, after the performance. As he
removes his putty nose, enter BLITZSTEIN.*

BLITZSTEIN   Mr. Welles?

WELLES   Mm?

BLITZSTEIN   Marc Blitzstein.

WELLES   Blitzstein...

BLITZSTEIN   Yes, I... I hope you don't mind my coming backstage like this.

WELLES   No. Come in. Were you out there tonight?

BLITZSTEIN   I was. You're quite something, Mr. Welles.

WELLES   Orson.

BLITZSTEIN   You're quite something, Orson.

WELLES   It's quite a show. What did you think of the floating pig?

BLITZSTEIN   Well I... I have to admit I missed that.

WELLES   Fell asleep?

BLITZSTEIN   No, no. I did have my eyes closed, though. The better to hear you with.

WELLES   Don't tell me you believed a word of it.

BLITZSTEIN   Every word. I've read that play, a dozen times, and never, not till this night, did I *hear* it.

    Pause.

    Well look, I should let you get dressed.

WELLES   No, no, stay. I won't be shy if you won't be. Let me just scrape this face off. We need to talk.

BLITZSTEIN   Yes?

WELLES   About your opera. I read it. It's a wonder.

BLITZSTEIN   Thank you. Although "opera"...

WELLES   Yes?

BLITZSTEIN   Is a little grandiose for me. I prefer to think of it as a play with music.

WELLES   Fine, that's what we'll call it, just as long as you let me direct it.

BLITZSTEIN   You mean?...

WELLES   Yes?

BLITZSTEIN   You want to do it?

WELLES   I've already talked to Jack about it. He's all for it.

BLITZSTEIN   Jack?...

WELLES   Houseman. Runs the company with me. Or for me. Or—runs the company. I've got it all figured out. Hope you don't mind. Here, have a look at these.

    WELLES *digs up some sketches.*

BLITZSTEIN   What—?

WELLES   Just some doodles I did this morning.

BLITZSTEIN   What is this?

WELLES   It's your show, old boy. Here, is there enough light?

BLITZSTEIN   Yes. My God... is this?...

WELLES   Look, here. Here's the first scene. Alleyway. Very simple. We'll do it all with lighting. Maybe a lamppost, I'm not sure. Anyway, the prostitute, the moll, she, she's walking up and down, singing her song. "Are you the man I'm going to love, tonight?" Then our hero, Larry Foreman, wanders in. Very... simple. To start. Then—chaos. The cops arrest Foreman. They arrest the Liberty Committee. Everyone goes to jail. You see I—I want to do it so that we keep the action moving. With all those set changes and—

BLITZSTEIN   What are these?

WELLES   Wagons. You see, the idea is that the wagons contain all the sets and props, and the actors.

BLITZSTEIN   ...Yes...

WELLES   The actors push the wagons back and forth, you see, announcing the scenes and so on.

BLITZSTEIN   Lovely.

WELLES   Forty-member Negro chorus...

BLITZSTEIN   Good God.

WELLES   Thirty-piece orchestra, I'm still playing around with—everything all right?

BLITZSTEIN   You'll have to forgive me... I wasn't expecting... well I didn't think you'd be so far along with it.

WELLES   These are just the first ideas. You see what struck me about the play...

Pause.

BLITZSTEIN   Yes?

WELLES   Look, why don't we get out of here, go have a drink?

BLITZSTEIN   I'd like that.

WELLES   Fine. Hand me that cloth, will you? On the table? *(as* BLITZSTEIN *goes to the table)* You know I've never directed a musical. Thanks for thinking of me. Have you got that cloth?

BLITZSTEIN   Sorry. *(looking at a picture on* WELLES's *table)* This woman, she's beautiful.

WELLES   My mother. Beatrice.

BLITZSTEIN   Lovely.

WELLES   She was. Yes.

BLITZSTEIN   I'm sorry.

WELLES   It was a long time ago, Marc. Let's get that drink.

SCENE 4

The 21 Club.

WELLES   My ninth birthday. My mother lay on her deathbed. Her great shining eyes looked dark by the lights of the small candles. "That stupid birthday cake is just another cake," she said, "and you'll have all the cakes you want. But the candles are a fairy ring, and you will never again in your whole life have just that number to blow out. You must puff hard, and you must blow out every one of them. And you must make a wish." I puffed hard. Suddenly the room was dark and my mother had vanished forever. Sometimes in the dead watches of the night, it strikes me that of all my mistakes, the greatest was on that birthday, just before my mother died, when I forgot to make a wish.

Enter DA SILVA.

DA SILVA   Blitzstein! You gotta be Blitzstein!

BLITZSTEIN   Yes, I...

WELLES   Marc, I want you to meet Howard Da Silva.

BLITZSTEIN   Of course. Saw you in *Waiting for Lefty*.

DA SILVA   No kidding, you saw that?

BLITZSTEIN   Absolutely. It was brilliant. I loved it.

DA SILVA   Well, let me tell you something. *You* have written something even better. Hope you don't mind, Orson let me read it. He's offered me the part of Larry Foreman.

WELLES   Howard...

DA SILVA   Okay, okay, he's *thinking* about me for the part of Larry Foreman.

BLITZSTEIN   I think that's a terrific idea.

DA SILVA   There you go! I gotta do this part, Blitz. Look at these hands.

BLITZSTEIN   Yes?

DA SILVA   Two years in a steel mill did that. Slave fucking labour. And no union. That is why when I read your play, I flipped. I mean I absolutely flipped. And the score! Jumpin'! "Listen to that? What do you hear? Footsteps! A million footsteps marchin'!" You are a genius. You have written—a—a whole new kind of theatre, for a whole new kind of audience. It's exactly what we need today. No more exalted kings and queens and—all that bullshit. You have written for the voice of the average Joe—hookers and cops and—my God—workers. Nobody's written that.

BLITZSTEIN   Well, Odets...

DA SILVA   Ah, Odets, fuck him.

WELLES   Oh oh.

DA SILVA	What, is he here?
WELLES	No, no.
DA SILVA	Who cares if he is? Man's a sellout, and I'd say it right to his face. "Hollywood." One phone call, that's what it took. Say, mind if I have an oyster?
BLITZSTEIN	Go right ahead.
WELLES	Thank God we're pure, Howard.
DA SILVA	I ain't saying *that*. God knows... but in his case, how can a man write a play about the worker, spread the socialist gospel, and then go write that soulless crap—for money? You know what? *(eats the oyster, chases it down)* I always had a funny feeling about him.
WELLES	Funny how?
DA SILVA	Like did he really believe all what he was spouting, or was he just catching a wave? Well, now we know, and in fifty years when Clifford Odets is a footnote, the name Marc Blitzstein will still be making headlines.

BLITZSTEIN's wife, EVA, appears to him.

BLITZSTEIN	I'm not after immortality.
DA SILVA	Too bad, brother—it's yours! *You*, my friend, have created a masterpiece. You gotta let me be a part of it.
BLITZSTEIN	Well, if Orson says you're Larry Foreman, that's good enough for me.
DA SILVA	Ha ha! Let's drink to that! *(a toast)* To a new kind of theatre. To a new audience.
EVA	Moonlight.
BLITZSTEIN	To a new future.
DA SILVA	Hear! hear!

They drink. DA SILVA looks off.

George, how are ya? *(to the boys)* Kauffmann, another sellout.
Goddamn fraud artists everywhere you look. So, who else is
in this thing?

WELLES   I have a few ideas.

DA SILVA   Can I put in a word for the hooker? I saw this girl with the
                Brooklyn Unit? She's fantastic. A natural.

WELLES   Can she sing?

EVA disappears.

BLITZSTEIN   Doesn't matter. I don't want trained voices.

DA SILVA   Glad to hear it. Not just for myself, of course. We ain't doing
                no opera here. This is street theatre. No fancy sets, costumes,
                none of that rigmarole. All we need is one guy at a piano and
                the rest of us in our street clothes. Simple.

WELLES   You let me be the judge of that, Howard.

DA SILVA   Seems pretty obvious to me.

WELLES   All the more reason to doubt it.

DA SILVA   Come on, Orson, the power of this piece is the words and mu-
                sic, the connection to the audience. And the only way to get
                that connection is on a bare stage.

WELLES   Like *Waiting for Lefty*?

DA SILVA   No, not like—what was wrong with how we done *Waiting for
                Lefty*?

WELLES   Howard, the audience expects a little more than a bare stage.
                They expect magic.

DA SILVA   Magic. What do you call "magic," Orson. Flying pigs? I mean
                don't get me wrong, I loved *Faust*, I did. But let's just step out
                from behind the smoke and mirrors, okay? Let's admit the

truth for once, that we're all just a bunch of people, and we have come here tonight to figure out something about ourselves. Some of us are on stage, and some of us are not, but we are a group—that is something you get in the theatre and you can't get nowhere else.

BLITZSTEIN   I couldn't agree with you more. I'm all for simplicity.

DA SILVA   Glad to hear it.

WELLES   Well I'm all for another drink. Marc, why don't you get us another round?

BLITZSTEIN   Sure. Howard?

DA SILVA   Don't mind if I doodle. *(as BLITZSTEIN goes)* Orson, I got a terrific feeling about this show.

WELLES   So have I, if you'll learn to keep your station.

DA SILVA   My what?

WELLES   Your station. Your mouth—shut.

DA SILVA   What are you talking about?

WELLES   I'm talking about what's proper for you to say. And when.

DA SILVA   I don't get you.

WELLES   You let me direct and I'll let you act. Understand?

DA SILVA   I gotta do this play, Orson.

WELLES   Then stay out of my way.

                    BLITZSTEIN comes back.

BLITZSTEIN   The bartender will send over an "otra ronda." I picked that up in Spain. Howard, have you been to Spain?

DA SILVA   Hm?

BLITZSTEIN   Spain.

DA SILVA   Ah, no. No, I ain't. Don't like getting that close to dictators. Well, Marc, it's been a pleasure.

BLITZSTEIN   Leaving?

DA SILVA   Yeah. It seems I gotta rest my throat.

BLITZSTEIN   Well I hope to see you in rehearsals, then.

DA SILVA   Yeah. Likewise. Orson.

WELLES   Howard.

DA SILVA goes.

BLITZSTEIN   What was that about?

WELLES   Oh don't mind Howard. He's unpredictable. That's what makes him such an exciting actor.

Enter WAITRESS.

WAITRESS   Your drink, Mr. Welles.

WELLES   Thank you, darling.

WAITRESS   Didn't you order three?

WELLES   Yes, the third's for you.

WAITRESS   Aw, knock it off, I gotta work! *(stage whisper)* Till midnight. Get me?

WELLES   *(as she goes, to BLITZSTEIN)* Private tutoring... You just forget about all that bare stage nonsense. You want to give people truth? Fine. Just don't let them know you're giving it to them, it'll go down a lot better.

EVA appears again to BLITZSTEIN.

Think of the ending, when Larry Foreman tells the steel baron:

DA SILVA *appears as Larry* FOREMAN.

WELLES &
FOREMAN   You got it all wrong, Mr. Mister. It's your time's comin' to an end, not mine, brother.

WELLES   ...he hears the workers approaching... they're going to join him...

WELLES &
FOREMAN   Listen to that? What do you hear?

FOREMAN   Footsteps! *(continues under* WELLES*)* A million footsteps marching! Marching down the road to freedom!

The CHORUS *of workers appears.*

You better get in line, lady, 'cause these feet ain't stopping for nobody—that's right!

WELLES   And as he's singing, and the whole thing's gathering steam, the stage is filling with the chorus of workers, the stage starts to shake.

WELLES *and* CHORUS *end simultaneously.*

BLITZSTEIN   The stage.

WELLES   To...

BLITZSTEIN   Physically—?

WELLES &
FOREMAN   It rocks.

CHORUS   *(continues under* WELLE*'s speech)* Well now we're waking up,
the tree we're shaking up,
is the one that's nestling your cradle.
Now this is your warning, it's thund'ring, it's storming
and down is coming baby and all.
Yes down is coming baby and all.
So no more lies, the truth will win out,
the truth will always defeat the lies.

And down will come baby
Yes down will come baby
Now that we've opened up your eyes!
Yes, now that we've opened up your eyes!

WELLES   The stage is rocking, blinding lights shoot up from below, there's smoke and—fifes and drums! Yes, blaring from speakers all over the theatre, it's deafening now, and the stage is tilting and rocking, the whole damn theatre is rocking, the audience is knocked out of their seats, they're standing... and they, they've heard you, your message, only they don't realize they've been given a message, because they're so damned entertained by it all, and now, now they're ready to rush out there and tear down those fucking walls, baby, and there's your revolution, there is your revolution.

      The song ends.

What do you think?

SCENE 5

      Audition room. HOUSEMAN brings OLIVE Stanton to meet WELLES and BLITZSTEIN.

BLITZSTEIN   *(seeing something familiar in OLIVE)* Eva?

HOUSEMAN   This is Olive Stanton.

WELLES   Olive.

HOUSEMAN   Orson Welles.

OLIVE   Mr. Welles.

WELLES   Orson, please.

BLITZSTEIN   Marc Blitzstein.

OLIVE   Nice to meet you. It's a wonderful piece, Mr. Blitzsteen.

BLITZSTEIN	Stein, actually.
OLIVE	Oh. Okay. I'll try that then, ha ha.
WELLES	I understand you're with the Brooklyn Unit.
OLIVE	Uh huh, yeah.
BLITZSTEIN	Really. You staged the sit-down.
WELLES	Sit-down?
BLITZSTEIN	To protest the cuts.
WELLES	What cuts?
BLITZSTEIN	The cuts, Orson, we're going to lose the whole WPA.
WELLES	Rumours.
BLITZSTEIN	Yes. Washington rumours, which turn very quickly to fact. That's why what the Brooklyn Unit did was so beautiful. After the show, the actors got the audience to stay in their seats— they refused to leave the building until the press got there and they—well, you tell it, Olive.
OLIVE	Yeah. Uh, I can't.
BLITZSTEIN	Sure, you're among friends here, Olive.
OLIVE	Yeah but... I—I didn't stay.
HOUSEMAN	Let's move along.
BLITZSTEIN	Why not?
OLIVE	I couldn't. See, I, I'm on relief. I only make twenty-three six-ty-eight a week. I just can't afford to lose that money, and somebody was saying that, well the WPA would fire people if they, you know, did anything like that.
HOUSEMAN	All right. This isn't a cross-examination.

OLIVE   I'm sorry, Mr. Blitzsteen, I...

BLITZSTEIN   Stein.

OLIVE   I—yeah, sorry—you have to understand. My husband's outta work. I've got three kids.

BLITZSTEIN   That's... that's fine, Olive. Why don't you go ahead and sing for us?

OLIVE   Yeah. Okay.

HOUSEMAN   Olive's here for the role of Moll. Marc?

BLITZSTEIN   Hm? Yes. Fine.

WELLES   Whenever you're ready, Olive.

OLIVE   Yeah.

         She sings "Bei mir bist du schön," badly. Beat.

         I'm really not a singer.

WELLES   Good. *(more to MARC)* We really don't want singers. *(back to OLIVE)* Not trained singers, anyway. What did you do over there in uh—Brooklyn?

OLIVE   *Peter Pan.*

WELLES   Yes. All right. Thank you, Olive.

OLIVE   When do you think you'll know?

WELLES   I think we already do.

OLIVE   Sure. I understand. Thanks for seeing me. It really is wonderful. I mean that, and I hope you don't think any less of me for not—

HOUSEMAN   We would never judge you for what you do outside this room, Olive.

OLIVE   All right, then. Thanks again, Mr. Blitz... stein?

              She leaves; they watch her; when she's gone:

HOUSEMAN   That's the last of the lot.

WELLES   Yes. Well, she was the least worst. What do you say, old boy?

BLITZSTEIN   No.

HOUSEMAN   I rather liked her.

WELLES   Alas, the author did not. Let's discuss it over dinner.

HOUSEMAN   Orson, rehearsals begin in less than a week. We won't find anyone better, not from the relief list.

BLITZSTEIN   Then we'll find someone from outside the relief list.

HOUSEMAN   The government would prefer it if we used actors they're paying for.

BLITZSTEIN   What about Howard?

HOUSEMAN   We got an exemption for him.

BLITZSTEIN   Then we'll get another.

HOUSEMAN   We will not.

WELLES   You'll have to forgive Jack. Lost his millions in the crash—been counting his pennies ever since.

HOUSEMAN   *Our* pennies.

BLITZSTEIN   Look, I'm sorry—she's just not right.

HOUSEMAN   By which you mean "just not left."

BLITZSTEIN   Well?

HOUSEMAN   Only party members need apply, is that it?

BLITZSTEIN   Why do something if you don't believe in it?

HOUSEMAN   What she believes or not is—

BLITZSTEIN   She wants the job, that's all.

HOUSEMAN   Will that be a sin in the post-Blitzstein world?

BLITZSTEIN   No. But cowardice will be.

HOUSEMAN   Oh? Did you think it was cowardly of her to go on with the audition after the way you treated her?

BLITZSTEIN   The moll has the first song in the show, a song about a woman who's been exploited by men all her life. It sets the tone. If she doesn't believe what she's saying, doesn't understand it—

HOUSEMAN   Those are two different things. She may not "believe" it, but after two months' rehearsal with Orson, she will most definitely understand it.

A pause. EVA appears.

BLITZSTEIN   *(to WELLES)* Can we talk? Alone, I mean.

WELLES   Course.

HOUSEMAN   *(as they head out)* I'll need a decision by tomorrow.

They leave. HOUSEMAN stands there a moment.

SCENE 6

Central Park.

WELLES   Don't worry about Jack—just another mad Hungarian. Jacques Hausmann, that's his real name. Born in Budapest, grew up in London—hence the phony accent.

BLITZSTEIN   What about this "losing millions"?

WELLES Yes. Ran an international wheat concern. He was riding high, too, leading the glamorous life in a New York penthouse. Until a certain Friday in October of '29. As he walked out of the exchange, Jacques Hausmann, businessman, disappeared—John Houseman, artist, was born. Anyway, he found his way into the theatre. Actually directed me.

BLITZSTEIN Houseman?

WELLES Can you believe it! *Him.* He wasn't bad, mind you. But he's a better producer than director. Has some grand plans for us. Though sometimes I don't know if he's decided between riding my coattails or stepping on them. *(pause)* My God, look at that moon.

BLITZSTEIN Beautiful.

WELLES *(pause)* Two men in Central Park. I wonder what Hedda Hopper would say?

They laugh uncomfortably.

Come, we'll sit here awhile.

Puts down his jacket, takes out a flask.

BLITZSTEIN "Moonlight."

WELLES Mm?

BLITZSTEIN That's what we called it when we made love. "Moonlight."

WELLES Who?

BLITZSTEIN Eva. My wife.

WELLES Is she in New York with you?

BLITZSTEIN She died... last September.

WELLES Sorry, old boy.

BLITZSTEIN Or... no. It was the September before that. Doesn't seem...

WELLES	We both have ghosts, then.
BLITZSTEIN	We do. She was a tough little thing. Didn't let me get away with anything, you know. We met at a little artists' colony. She was sitting around with a bunch of wretched little swells when my cab pulled up. It was the first time she'd laid eyes on me.
EVA	Who's this fairy coming?
BLITZSTEIN	Marc Blitzstein. I'm a composer.
EVA	Eva Goldbeck. Novelist.
BLITZSTEIN	What do you write about?
EVA	Unhappy childhoods, hopelessness, fear of life, self-loathing, contempt for the happy, wish for death, fucked-up relationships. They're six-hundred pages long and either the most brilliant works since Proust or absolute shit destined, like me, for obscurity. Wanna read one?
BLITZSTEIN	Love to. Bring it by my room.
EVA	Knock knock.
BLITZSTEIN	Come in.
EVA	You're naked.
BLITZSTEIN	Embarrassed?
EVA	Yes, but only for you.
BLITZSTEIN	Did you bring the novel?
EVA	Sure.
BLITZSTEIN	Leave it on the desk. I'll have a look at it tonight.
WELLES	Did you really lie there naked?
BLITZSTEIN	I had nothing to hide. Anyway, I read it that night. It was dreadful. Really, an awful, bloated mess...

WELLES   I've had nights like that.

BLITZSTEIN   Haven't we all?

WELLES   You didn't tell her the truth?

BLITZSTEIN   Of course I did. She thanked me, closed the door, and took
               off *her* clothes. The door stayed closed for three days. We
               emerged in love. She received an official invite to Spain,
               and I tagged along. We travelled through the country, most-
               ly broke, read Marx and Engels and all the rest of it. The
               things we saw there, Orson. Ordinary people caught up in
               the fight—their hunger was the hardest thing to watch. And
               the bombing, the devastation. It was dreadful to see. Eva
               wanted to stay, but...

WELLES   Not your fight.

BLITZSTEIN   No. One day we were sunning ourselves on a Spanish beach.
               The papers were full of the auto strikes.

EVA   You're not happy here, Marc.

BLITZSTEIN   There's so much going on at home, Eva. I feel I should be
               there.

EVA   I've already packed.

BLITZSTEIN   We came home, got apartments in New York.

WELLES   You didn't live together?

BLITZSTEIN   Well... the thing is... We needed our own work spaces, you
               see.

WELLES   Of course.

BLITZSTEIN   Well one day I was fooling around, wrote a song for her. *(sings
               to her)* Are you the man I'm going to love tonight?

EVA   It's good, Marc.

BLITZSTEIN   You think so? Don't just say it.

EVA   Is that what you want? To write pretty-pretty songs? Live the life of a provincial artist, taking in the shekels and "believing" in yourself? Poor darling, grew up middle-class, wants to be so tough, a real worker. Wants to get dirty, but not down in the muck.

BLITZSTEIN   What can I do?

EVA   You've written a song about literal prostitution. Now try the figurative kind. We all sell out: the magistrate, the doctor, the professor. The artist.

BLITZSTEIN   After a while, she got sick. Doctors found a tumour in her breast. She lost weight. Wouldn't eat. Could barely go on. Obsessed with a vision she'd had years earlier, of her own death.

EVA   How about some moonlight?

BLITZSTEIN   No moonlight tonight.

EVA   Useless. No moonlight for a long time.

BLITZSTEIN   What will I do without you?

EVA   Work. That's all there is. That will get you through and you will write something wonderful one day, I know.

BLITZSTEIN   What do you weigh?

EVA   Why ninety-five pounds, my duck.

BLITZSTEIN   What can I do?

EVA   Do not weep for me. Sentiment is the enemy of progress. My second-rate life is coming to an end, as I knew it would on this very date: the date on the card: the card in the dream: you won't be alive, September 5th of '35.

BLITZSTEIN   And now?

EVA   Ninety-one.

BLITZSTEIN   Oh pretty quail...

EVA	Eighty-nine and dropping steady. *(laughs)* I won't need to die, just fade away, my arms like twigs to use for kindling. Yes, start a fire, burn my books, let the heat warm you, the flames lick you like you... *(in pain throughout)* Marc? Where are you, darling? Hold me, here, here, no! Give me a drink. Not water, what good is it to prolong the—ding dong! Who's there? Why it's a little fairy come to take me away! Light me a smoke. *Marc!*
BLITZSTEIN	Here I am, here I am, o dove.
EVA	Is there moonlight?
BLITZSTEIN	No moonlight tonight.

EVA dies.

She weighed seventy-five pounds when she died. I couldn't work for a year. Till I remembered her idea. I took that song, Orson, the one I'd sung for her. For five weeks, I worked, worked, just as she told me to. It came to me in a white heat, the entire play, I saw it before me. She put it there. I merely wrote it down, you see. It's her we have to stay true to. Now do you understand why I'm hesitant to use that simple-minded girl?

WELLES	I do understand. But wouldn't Eva want you to teach her?

A pause as BLITZSTEIN considers this. He takes a ring from his pocket.

BLITZSTEIN	Eva's Phi Beta Kappa ring. I take it with me everywhere. *(after a beat)* I really do hate sentiment, you know.
WELLES	Sentiment is the wish to return home, Marc. There's nothing wrong with that. Trust me, my friend. I will make magic.

SCENE 7

The Maxine Elliott Theatre, the present.

WELLES	...Even if I have to smash every one of those Cossacks to bits to do it.

HOUSEMAN   That I'd like to see.

WELLES   Meantime, I've got Jeannie begging for mercy. Or costumes, anyway. Jack, any word from—

HOUSEMAN   No.

WELLES   Let me finish.

HOUSEMAN   Beg pardon.

WELLES   Any word from Pratt about—

HOUSEMAN   No.

WELLES   Christ's sake, let me—

HOUSEMAN   Go ahead.

WELLES   Any word from Pratt about a house?

Pause.

HOUSEMAN   Done?

WELLES   Yes.

HOUSEMAN   No.

WELLES   Thank you.

BLITZSTEIN   Who's Pratt?

HOUSEMAN   Theatre—

WELLES   *(simultaneously)* Theatre broker.

HOUSEMAN   Excuse me, I think that was directed at me.

BLITZSTEIN   God's sake, why don't you two take this act on the road when this is all done? Who is Pratt?

HOUSEMAN   He's a tiny man in a bowler hat who's going to find us a theatre.

BLITZSTEIN	Has he found anything?
HOUSEMAN	I haven't spoken with him yet.
BLITZSTEIN	Well how was I supposed to know that?
HOUSEMAN	By listening to what I'm—
WELLES	All right, lads, let's be good. We might be here awhile. Christ, I'm starved, what about sending out for—
HOUSEMAN	No.
WELLES	For Christ's sake, will you let me finish.
BLITZSTEIN	Look, forget about food, what else is happening?
WELLES	What?
HOUSEMAN	I'll tell you what's happening. I have made a number of calls to—
WELLES	That I told you to make.
HOUSEMAN	To the musicians' union, the actors' union, the—
BLITZSTEIN	Why? Why call the unions?
HOUSEMAN	Because the rules of engagement have changed, and we'd better make damn sure we're going to be able to—

DA SILVA enters.

DA SILVA	Orson, I gotta tell the actors something.
HOUSEMAN	Sorry to interrupt.
WELLES	We were just talking about that, there's no news.
DA SILVA	Well that ain't good news.
HOUSEMAN	It's all we have.

DA SILVA   Well that's fine for you boys, but the ladies and gentlemen of the dressing rooms need to know if—

HOUSEMAN   I've called Equity for a ruling on—

DA SILVA   I ain't talking about Equity.

HOUSEMAN   Well what are you—

DA SILVA   I am talking about the WPA, which is from where we get our paycheques.

HOUSEMAN   Most of you.

DA SILVA   All right, most of us, and most of us want to know if we're gonna lose our jobs if we do this show.

BLITZSTEIN   Don't tell me the actors aren't going to—

DA SILVA   This is not against you, Blitz.

WELLES   Howard, there'll be no pink slips mailed to this cast.

ROSENTHAL enters.

DA SILVA   Yeah?

WELLES   You have my word.

Phone rings.

DA SILVA   You better be good for it.

WELLES   Jeannie?

HOUSEMAN   *(into phone)* 891.

ROSENTHAL   No dice on the costumes.

WELLES   Goddammit.

HOUSEMAN   This is John Houseman.

BLITZSTEIN   We're not gonna get anything.

WELLES   I'm working on it.

HOUSEMAN   Yes, Mr. Pratt, hello.

WELLES   Pratt.

HOUSEMAN   Yes, thank you for calling.

BLITZSTEIN   How shall we transport the wagons?

HOUSEMAN   Here's my situation.

BLITZSTEIN   Assuming we get them?

WELLES   I said I'm working on it.

HOUSEMAN   I'm producing a play...

WELLES   "He's producing a play."

HOUSEMAN   Yes, at the Maxine Elliott.

BLITZSTEIN   I mean this just doesn't make any sense.

WELLES   Stop worrying.

HOUSEMAN   Yes, that's right.

BLITZSTEIN   If we can't have the sets, the costumes...

WELLES   Marc, please.

HOUSEMAN   Well, we've been barred from the theatre, you see...

DA SILVA   Marc.

        DA SILVA takes BLITZSTEIN aside.

HOUSEMAN   What's that? Our re—requirements are... well, a building...
            with a stage...

WELLES   Proscenium.

HOUSEMAN   Proscenium if...

WELLES   Tell him to try the Norworth.

HOUSEMAN   What about the Norworth?

ROSENTHAL   Bigger.

HOUSEMAN   What about the Bigger?

ROSENTHAL   No, a bigger *theatre*.

HOUSEMAN   What? Sorry, Mr. Pratt.

ROSENTHAL   You seen what's doing outside? There's like this huge crowd, the Norworth'll never hold 'em.

HOUSEMAN   Just a second, Mr. Pratt.

                Phone rings.

WELLES   Tell him to try the Comedy.

HOUSEMAN   What about the Comedy?

WELLES   We need a balcony.

HOUSEMAN   *(snapping at ROSENTHAL to get phone)* Mm hm.

ROSENTHAL   And if the Comedy's no good, I think the Hippodrome's— *(into phone)* 891.

HOUSEMAN   Yes, well that's...

WELLES   Jack, tell him...

ROSENTHAL   Oh, hi.

HOUSEMAN   Just a second, Mr. Pratt. *(to WELLES)* What?

ROSENTHAL   Hold on.

WELLES	Tell him if the Comedy's no good to try the Hippodrome.
DA SILVA	Orson.
ROSENTHAL	Orson.
HOUSEMAN	Hippodrome.
DA SILVA	Orson, we been talking.
ROSENTHAL	*(to HOUSEMAN)* Or the Waldorf. *(to WELLES)* Orson?
WELLES	*(split between ROSENTHAL and DA SILVA)* What?
DA SILVA	It's about the wagons.
ROSENTHAL	It's the missus.
WELLES	*(to DA SILVA)* What about the wagons?
HOUSEMAN	*(into phone)* Mr. Pratt, we'll take whatever you can get.
DA SILVA	We think we should forget about 'em.
ROSENTHAL	Sorry, he says he's busy, honey.
HOUSEMAN	...and time is of the essence, thank you.

Hangs up. WELLES has approached DA SILVA and BLITZSTEIN.

ROSENTHAL	No, *I* said honey.
WELLES	Do we?
ROSENTHAL	Uh huh. 'Kay, so long. *(hangs up)* She says you oughta—
WELLES	Do we?
DA SILVA	Think about it. Let's even supposing we could get 'em out from underneath the Cossacks' noses, what then? How we gonna get 'em to this other theatre, I mean supposin' we even find one?
WELLES	We'll roll them.

DA SILVA   That's fine if the theatre's across the street, but what about—

WELLES   Look, I don't have all the answers, I just—

DA SILVA   Holy cow! Did I just hear what I just heard?

WELLES   Marc?

BLITZSTEIN Yes.

WELLES   You agree with Howard? About the wagons?

BLITZSTEIN It just seems that, under the circumstances...

WELLES   I see. Well, I'm not surprised.

BLITZSTEIN It's just that Howard...

WELLES   "It's just that Howard."

DA SILVA   Look, we gave your idea a chance.

WELLES   Bullshit! You fought me the whole way!

DA SILVA   That ain't true.

WELLES   No? Who wanted to do it on a bare stage? You did. And now, thanks to those Cossacks, that's just how we're going to do it—actors in street clothes, no sets, no props...

DA SILVA   Good.

WELLES   And no wigs.

DA SILVA   That's different! You took enough away from me on this show. And you know it—don't ya?

SCENE 8

Several weeks earlier. The Maxine Elliott Theatre, onstage rehearsal: OLIVE (playing MOLL); DA SILVA (playing LARRY); WELLES watching.

BLITZSTEIN *on piano.*

OLIVE   *(sings)* That's okay, honey
             just pretend you love me
             or at least you think I'm swell.
             Just be as real, real as you feel
             and I will too, baby, I will.

WELLES   Good.

             ROSENTHAL *signals two minutes.*

             Olive?

OLIVE   Yes?

WELLES   How you doing?

OLIVE   Okay.

WELLES   Olive?

OLIVE   Yes?

WELLES   Who's this fellow over here?

OLIVE   You mean Howard?

WELLES   No, I mean the character Howard's playing.

OLIVE   Oh. Larry Foreman.

WELLES   No, Olive. This is a stranger. You're a hooker. You don't know
             him at this point. What does he mean to you?

OLIVE   Five bucks.

WELLES   What else does he mean?

DA SILVA   I know it's not my place to—

WELLES   No it isn't, Howard, thank you. Olive... has anyone ever loved
             you?

OLIVE   Me?

WELLES   Your character, Olive.

OLIVE   Gee, I guess not.

WELLES   No. Do you want someone to love you?

OLIVE   I think so.

WELLES   Do you believe in love?

OLIVE   Well...

WELLES   You have sex with strangers. Strange *men* who pay you for the privilege of hiking up your dress in an alleyway. Do you believe in love?

OLIVE   I guess not.

WELLES   When you sing "Are you the man I'm going to love tonight," do you think you sing it with hope, or with bitterness?

ROSENTHAL   That's it, Orson.

WELLES   You used to believe in love, used to give it quite freely, but then you were hurt, and now you're afraid to show it. You're afraid that, if you give yourself to someone, for anything but money, that someone will disappear, vanish forever, no matter how much you wish she'd never left.

OLIVE   "She?"

WELLES   What?

ROSENTHAL   Orson?

WELLES   Yes.

ROSENTHAL   Time.

WELLES   All right. Thanks, everyone. See you tomorrow. We'll have to start at one, I've got to be at CBS all morning.

DA SILVA	*(under his breath)* La-de-da.
ROSENTHAL	Clear the deck, please. Gotta start settin' for *Faustus*.
DA SILVA	Olive?

HOUSEMAN emerges... DA SILVA leads OLIVE off.

BLITZSTEIN	Orson, I need to talk to you.
ROSENTHAL	Let's go, let's go.
BLITZSTEIN	We've been at it two weeks now, and Olive's no closer to getting it than when we started.
WELLES	She'll get it. She'll understand.
BLITZSTEIN	Do you think this is the right approach?
HOUSEMAN	Orson.
WELLES	What is it?
HOUSEMAN	I need a word. *(a nod to BLITZSTEIN)* Company business.
WELLES	All right. Marc, I'll meet you at 21 tonight, we'll talk then.
BLITZSTEIN	See you there. Night, Jack.
HOUSEMAN	Marc. *(as BLITZSTEIN leaves)* Did you have a chance to get some air? The weather's turning.

BLITZSTEIN has left. ROSENTHAL hovers.

WELLES	So's my stomach. Promise me you won't take up acting. What's on your mind?
HOUSEMAN	Harry Hopkins. He called me this morning. He had a call from a congressman, very interested in *The Cradle*. What was it about, exactly, and was there really a union rally in it? Harry's asked for a copy of the script.

WELLES   Good, send him one, with my compliments. Just be sure to mention it's a satire.

              Pause.

HOUSEMAN   Have you read a newspaper lately?

WELLES   Haven't got time.

HOUSEMAN   The steel strikes are worsening. Things are very tense. Those workers who were killed by the Chicago police—turns out they were shot in the back.

WELLES   What are you getting at?

HOUSEMAN   What if Harry doesn't appreciate satire?

WELLES   He's entitled to his opinion.

HOUSEMAN   Certainly. Just as he's entitled to cut our funding.

WELLES   You're being ridiculous. My God, you Hungarians have the most devilish sensibility, really, you do—that's what happens when you lose an empire, you assume someone's always lurking round the corner.

HOUSEMAN   "Ridiculous!" This *is* the government's money we're playing with.

WELLES   Of course, but this goes beyond all that, old man. Harry's a friend. He wouldn't do that to me.

HOUSEMAN   You're not that naive, are you, Orson?

WELLES   I have a great deal of faith in my friendships—most of them.

HOUSEMAN   Fine. I'll be wrong, as usual, and you can be right, as usual, and when the whole thing blows up, as usual, you can be the hero and put out the fire, as usual. In the meantime, I would be very careful about what you say in public.

WELLES   For God's sake...

HOUSEMAN	The WPA is under attack, Orson. Congress wants to get rid of it, and what better way to demonstrate the evils of welfare than to point to the arts programs. "Look, here," they will say, "why are we supporting such anti-American works as *The Cradle Will Rock?*"
WELLES	It's hardly...
HOUSEMAN	"Written by a known communist intellectual from New York..."
WELLES	Philadelphia, actually...
HOUSEMAN	"Who also happens to be a homosexual!"
	Pause.
WELLES	What if he is?
HOUSEMAN	Is he? I have heard rumours. Course you can understand him wanting to keep it a secret. The Party rather frowns on that sort of... activity... they consider it decadent.
WELLES	I take it they're not the only ones.
HOUSEMAN	I judge no one's private life—not even yours. I only raise it as an issue because, well, should it come to light, it might, well it might affect our ability to raise capital for...
WELLES	*(bursts out laughing)* You think I'm sleeping with him.
HOUSEMAN	Of course not. That's absurd. Even if you were—
WELLES	Oh, I am, though! He's quite good, too. I think you'd like him, Jack... Jack... Jack, you're turning beet red!
HOUSEMAN	Ridiculous!
WELLES	*(goes off laughing)* Decadent!
HOUSEMAN	Think of the future, Orson. The future!

SCENE 9

Outside stage door. DA SILVA and OLIVE after rehearsal.

DA SILVA   We're living in a hell of a time right now, Olive. The fight is on to see who's gonna live in comfort and who's gonna live in slavery. Now I don't know about you, Olive, but I don't plan on living in slavery. The place I'm living at? It's about the size of one of those wagons. There's a stench so bad out the window I keep it closed most the time. It's inhuman. Why should I be living like that when meanwhile there's a selfish few living off the fat of the land and fighting like hell to keep it that way. We're takin' sides now, and in twenty years, thirty, forty, when we all think back to this time, we're gonna have to ask ourselves, did I stand up and fight, or did I let it all happen without me? Listen, there's a march to city hall next Thursday. We're gonna show those bastards—sorry—that we're not gonna go down without a fight. You gonna come with?

OLIVE   Thursday? Gee, I think there's a rehearsal, Howard.

DA SILVA   Don't worry, I'm gonna talk to Orson and get us the afternoon off.

OLIVE   You think?

DA SILVA   Course. Besides, he's missed enough rehearsals, the least he can do is give us half a day off. Son of a— Runs off to do his famous radio plays.

OLIVE   "Who knows what evil lurks in the hearts of men."

DA SILVA   Oh please, he can't even do the laugh.

OLIVE   Really?

DA SILVA   Really! It's some other guy.

OLIVE   Sheesh. That ain't right.

DA SILVA   No it ain't, and it also ain't right that on account of him we end up staying till two in the morning some nights to make up for his missed rehearsals—is it?

Olive	Not really.
Da Silva	I mean how are we supposed to be productive at two in the morning after twelve hours of standing on our feet while the genius changes his mind for the hundredth time. "I have an idea." The four most dreaded words in all of New York theatre. And you, the way he rides you. I'd like to bust him in the chops just once.
Olive	Aw, that's real sweet.
Da Silva	I'm sorry I ever got you involved in this.
Olive	Whaddaya mean?
Da Silva	I'm the one who told Orson about you. Saw you there in Brooklyn.
Olive	You did?
Da Silva	Yeah. Anyway, for what it's worth, I think you're doing great.
Olive	Thanks, Howard.
Da Silva	In fact, I think you are great.
Olive	I think you're pretty swell, too, Howard.
Da Silva	Yeah? You know what? I think I'm kinda fallin' for you. Sorry. You're married. I shouldn't'a said that.
Olive	It's okay. It's real nice of you to think that.
Da Silva	Aw nuts. Nice's got nothin' to do with it. I'm dyin' to kiss you, Olive. Just once. I think if I don't kiss you, I think my head might just bust open.
Olive	Well. I don't know what to say.
Da Silva	Say "kiss me, Howard."

Blitzstein comes out of the theatre.

Heya, Blitz.

BLITZSTEIN   Howard. Olive.

OLIVE   Hello, Mr. Blitz... stein.

BLITZSTEIN   Got it that time.

OLIVE   I guess I'm not gettin' too much else right, though, am I?

BLITZSTEIN   You're doing fine, Olive, just fine. Nice night.

               Pause.

DA SILVA   Yeah.

               Another pause.

BLITZSTEIN   Well, I'll... let the two of you... Night.

DA SILVA
& OLIVE   So long.

               They look at each other, laugh.

DA SILVA   You gotta head home?

OLIVE   *(shakes her head)* Kids are at my sister's.

DA SILVA   Then uh... what do you say we go to my place?

OLIVE   You make it sound so attractive.

DA SILVA   It ain't that bad. Whaddaya say?

               They go off, hand in hand.

SCENE 10

At 21. BLITZSTEIN, alone. VIRGINIA goes to him.

VIRGINIA   Light me, would you?

BLITZSTEIN   I haven't got a match.

VIRGINIA   Perhaps if I hold it close to you, it'll catch fire all by itself. *(laughing)* Darling, you're the hottest thing in town. According to my husband.

BLITZSTEIN   Your husband?

VIRGINIA   Your director?

BLITZSTEIN   Well, isn't that!... I had no idea.

VIRGINIA   Why would you?

BLITZSTEIN   Well... look, Orson's on his way.

VIRGINIA   He certainly is. *(holding up a finger)* Ah, but where to?... Don't mind me. I just talk. Helps pass the time. That and cigarettes.

BLITZSTEIN   I'll get some matches.

VIRGINIA   Don't bother. Try this.

She hands him a lighter.

BLITZSTEIN   Nice.

VIRGINIA   Isn't it? Orson gave it to me. He gives me many things. Except what I need. Brought me here from Chicago, a promising actress—one of us is still promising. Did he tell you the one about his mother?... That's the thing about Orson. With that voice, he could have his hands around your throat while he tells you he loves you. And with your dying breath, you'd believe him. Oh dear. I've had two glasses of the local swill and I shouldn't, I shouldn't, I really shouldn't! *(pause)* "Blitzstein."

BLITZSTEIN   Yes.

VIRGINIA   Jewish.

BLITZSTEIN   Right again.

VIRGINIA   Awful lot of you boys compose music, why is that?

BLITZSTEIN   Well, a moneylender needs a hobby.

VIRGINIA   Cad. I didn't mean it that way. Are we going to be friends?

BLITZSTEIN   I'm all for that.

VIRGINIA   Are you? Your opera tells a different story.

BLITZSTEIN   Don't follow that.

VIRGINIA   Darling, I'm the enemy, according to you. Born rich, and with a little luck, I'll die that way, too.

BLITZSTEIN   I wouldn't say my play is an attack on the rich. That's too easy.

VIRGINIA   Are you making fun of me?

BLITZSTEIN   Not at all.

VIRGINIA   Why not? Because I'm sitting here? You certainly make fun of my kind in your play. Don't look at me like that, you know perfectly well what I'm talking about, that silly society woman, the one who loves to be surrounded by artists.

BLITZSTEIN   Yes, well, of course, that's a particular type. That's the point, you see, they're all just "types," cartoon characters almost, they're not meant to be real people.

VIRGINIA   Why not? Don't you know any real people?

BLITZSTEIN   I know a number of them. I'm just not interested in that old kind of theatre where the writer and the actor conspire to make you develop some sentimental attachment to a character. You laugh, you cry, you go home to sleep. Nothing changes. What's the use in that? We're surrounded by cheap sentiment. Keeps the population stupid. My theatre will wake people up, Virginia. It will help them understand the way the world works. How capital operates. How—

VIRGINIA   Maybe people don't want to be "woken up," as you say. Maybe people like things the way they are.

BLITZSTEIN   Bread lines, hungry children, people sleeping in the street?

VIRGINIA   Mr. Roosevelt says that's all changing, says the economy's turned the corner.

BLITZSTEIN   For whom, exactly?

VIRGINIA   Oh, for God's sake, we were talking about theatre.

BLITZSTEIN   I'm talking about life. Theatre's just a part of it, not the other way around.

VIRGINIA   *(sees ORSON enter)* Well, I have different ideas. I don't see anything wrong with developing sentimental attachments. In fact, I could use one right about now. How about you? *(to ORSON)* Hello, darling.

WELLES   Virginia. What brings you to town?

VIRGINIA   Being out of it. *(to BLITZSTEIN)* Never move to Connecticut. Unless you mean to raise a family.

WELLES   Have we ordered?

VIRGINIA   We're being ignored. Course now that you're here... *(to BLITZSTEIN)* By the way, do you?

BLITZSTEIN   Do I—?

VIRGINIA   Mean to raise a family?

BLITZSTEIN   Not just now. You?

Enter WAITRESS.

WAITRESS   Evening, Mr. Welles. Mrs. Welles.

VIRGINIA   Hello, darling.

WAITRESS   Say, Blitzface, how's that opera comin'?

BLITZSTEIN   Oh, just fine.

WAITRESS	How come you never cast me in it?
WELLES	You have to be on relief for this one, darling.
VIRGINIA	She is—comic relief. How about showing us how you fall flat on your face, cookie?
WAITRESS	What got up yer skirt?
VIRGINIA	Same thing that got up yours, I'm afraid.
WELLES	We'll have oysters. And Scotch. Two glasses.
VIRGINIA	*(to WELLES)* Aren't you drinking?
WAITRESS	Whatever you want, Mr. Welles.

WAITRESS goes.

VIRGINIA	"Whatever you want, Mr. Welles." Orson just loves plucking oysters from their shells.
WELLES	Aw, shucks.
VIRGINIA	Tell me, how's that little Pickle working out?
BLITZSTEIN	Pickle?
VIRGINIA	Or Olive or something.
BLITZSTEIN	We were just about to get to that. Orson promised to work a little magic, but so far it's more like a dumb show.
WELLES	Now now.
VIRGINIA	Perhaps she's just confused, dear.
BLITZSTEIN	Confused.
VIRGINIA	Imagine having to act like a red on the outside when you're all yellow on the inside. Lucky thing your director friend's a dedicated Marxist.

WELLES	I'll see you at home, Virginia.
VIRGINIA	Marc, set that to music, you'll make a fortune. *(sings)* "I'll see you at home, Virginia."
WELLES	Virginia.
VIRGINIA	"Virginia"! What do you think? Is there a place in your theatre for love songs? I guess not. There's no time for love when you're trying to change the world. All right, I'm going.

Pause. She finishes her drink. Stands up, none too steadily.

I think I'll go develop a sentimental attachment to a lamppost. At least it gives off a little warmth. So long, Blitzstein.

She goes, singing "I'll see you at home, Virginia..."

BLITZSTEIN	Will she be all right?
WELLES	Never mind her. You wanted to talk about Olive.
BLITZSTEIN	Yes. I was thinking, what if I worked with her?
WELLES	You?
BLITZSTEIN	Yes. During music rehearsals. She needn't know, I can steer her in the right direction. You're not opposed to that, are you?
WELLES	Look, friend, you came to me to direct this piece. Why don't you let me do my job?
BLITZSTEIN	Really, I only meant for the times you're not there.
WELLES	Are you questioning my commitment?
BLITZSTEIN	No, Orson, I'm merely—
WELLES	Don't tell me how to run my rehearsals! If you think— *(looking off)* Christ... Virginia! Look, Marc, I'd better get her home. I'll see you in rehearsal. *(goes, comes back)* Forget the harsh words, old boy. Been a long day.

> *WELLES goes. BLITZSTEIN leaves, walks along the street. EVA appears.*

EVA   Nice night... moonlight?

> *A man walks by, they make eye contact. BLITZSTEIN follows.*

SCENE 11

> *Rehearsals continue. Scene shifts among several settings: the theatre, an alleyway, ROSENTHAL's office, ORSON and VIRGINIA's home, HOWARD's apartment, and the WAITRESS's apartment. Through it all, we never leave the rehearsal. Scene begins with WELLES, OLIVE, DA SILVA, and ROSENTHAL at theatre, BLITZSTEIN in alley.*

BLITZSTEIN   Scene one. Alleyway.

WELLES   Whenever you're ready, Olive.

OLIVE   Are you the man I'm going to love tonight?

BLITZSTEIN   I want to submit.

OLIVE   Light me a smoke, honey.

BLITZSTEIN   To the working man.

OLIVE   But don't pay for that drink.

BLITZSTEIN   No pansy boys for me.

OLIVE   Don't want you thinking the worst.

BLITZSTEIN   No thanks, no dancers, chorus boys, artists, I want a man...

OLIVE   My father was a sailor.

BLITZSTEIN   A working man.

OLIVE   My mother was a gypsy.

BLITZSTEIN   I want muscles, stink, and danger.

OLIVE   The whole damn bunch of us are cursed.

BLITZSTEIN   Anonymous, in the dark, no faces, no soft touches, no love or kindness.

ROSENTHAL   Orson, we oughta break.

BLITZSTEIN   No moonlight.

WELLES   Back to the beginning, Olive.

ROSENTHAL   Orson?

WELLES   Whenever you're ready, Olive.

ROSENTHAL   Mr. Houseman says Equity's been getting complaints about overtime.

WELLES   Is that right? *(to DA SILVA)* From who?

              Silence.

              Olive.

OLIVE   Yes, Mr. Welles?

WELLES   Did you think about what we talked about the other night?

OLIVE   Well...

WELLES   Do you remember what we talked about the other night?

OLIVE   Yeah.

WELLES   Good. Let's see the result. Marc?... where the hell is Marc? Jeannie?

ROSENTHAL   What.

WELLES   Have you seen—

ROSENTHAL   No.

WELLES   Christ. All right, Olive.

OLIVE   Are you the man I'm going to—

WELLES   Hold it.

DA SILVA   Can I just say something?

WELLES   No you may not.

DA SILVA   It's about the scene.

WELLES   Yes?

DA SILVA   Well now that we're rehearsing with the wagons...

WELLES   Yes?

DA SILVA   I mean, I think it's just gonna take us some time to get readjusted.

WELLES   How much time do you think you'll require, Mr. Da Silva?

DA SILVA   It was just a thought.

WELLES   Stillborn, like the rest of them. Where's my fucking dinner? Jeannie?

ROSENTHAL   Yes.

WELLES   My goddamn dinner was supposed to be here an hour ago.

ROSENTHAL   It was. You ate it.

OLIVE laughs.

OLIVE   Sorry. I just thought a something funny.

DA SILVA's apartment. OLIVE and DA SILVA are laughing.

DA SILVA   You crack me up! Do that again!

OLIVE   *(imitating* WELLES*)* "All right, let's break for dinner." *(imitating* ROSENTHAL*)* "But Orson, we just did." *(*WELLES*)* "Oh, I thought that was an appetizer."

They laugh again.

DA SILVA   What a scream. Jeez, I'm nuts about you, you know that? Let's run away together, just you and me.

OLIVE breaks off.

What'd I say?

OLIVE   I don't like that kinda talk.

DA SILVA   Why not?

OLIVE   'Cause you don't mean it.

DA SILVA   Sure I do! I love you. And may I just remind you how many times I told you that—as opposed to how many times I've heard it from you.

Makes a zero with his finger and thumb.

OLIVE   Yeah, well, just 'cause I don't say it... *(pause)* Howard! I'm married. I got three kids. I can't just throw that away for some future which I don't know about.

DA SILVA   Olive, nobody knows what the future's *about*. All you can do is try to make it better. Or things can just go on like they are.

OLIVE   How'd we get talkin' about this anyway? You were supposed to help me with my character.

DA SILVA   I'm tryin', doll. All right. Now, here's the thing about the moll. She's down-at-the-heels, am I right?... Olive?

OLIVE   Huh? Yeah.

DA SILVA   Okay. Now in this song she sings, what is she doing? What is the action of what it is she's doing?

OLIVE	She's singing.
DA SILVA	Yeah. Okay, but what is she doing as she is singing? Is she begging?
OLIVE	Begging?
DA SILVA	Yeah. Good. Play that.
OLIVE	Okay. *(sings)* Are you the man I'm—
DA SILVA	Hold on. Not so fast. There's more to it than that.
OLIVE	'Kay.
DA SILVA	Now—what is it the moll is feeling as she is doing this action?
OLIVE	Um.
DA SILVA	Could it be that she is feeling lost?
OLIVE	Sure, yeah, lost.
DA SILVA	Okay. Now what I want you to do is, you gotta think about a time in your own life, in your own life, Olive, when you felt lost.

OLIVE thinks.

Well, think about, think about how you'd feel if, if you was to lose me.

OLIVE	Why would I do that?
DA SILVA	To give us an idea what this girl is feelin'. That's all.

Pause.

OLIVE	I don't think I like this, Howard.
DA SILVA	Well it's—
OLIVE	*(in tears)* Look at the time. I gotta be at rehearsal in half an hour. Toodle-oo.

Rehearsal.

WELLES   What is it, darling?

OLIVE   I'm a little...

WELLES   *(beat)* Teapot? Whenever you're ready.

OLIVE   Are you the man I'm going to love—

WELLES   Olive.

OLIVE   Yeah?

WELLES   Never mind.

BLITZSTEIN   Can I say something?

WELLES   Nice of you to drop by.

BLITZSTEIN   Just following the leader. Look, Olive. We don't want you to feel the emotion of the song.

OLIVE   You don't?

BLITZSTEIN   No. See, you're not playing a real person, Olive.

OLIVE   I'm not?

WELLES   Marc...

BLITZSTEIN   Look: when you're laughing, I want the audience to be crying, and when you're crying, I want them be laughing. Listen. Listen to the notes. It's all in the notes. *(plays and sings)* Are you the man I'm going to love... *(to OLIVE)* Now if you start walking towards me...

              ORSON and VIRGINIA's home.

WELLES   What a lot of shit.

VIRGINIA   Then why are you doing it?

WELLES   I like the opera.

VIRGINIA   Do you like what it says? What he says? You should have heard him going on about Roosevelt.

WELLES   What of it?

VIRGINIA   You campaigned for him! Now you're doing a play that attacks him!

WELLES   I'm not interested in that part of it.

VIRGINIA   No? Which part are you interested in?

Rehearsal.

WELLES   All right, Marc. Try it again, Olive.

OLIVE   From where?

WELLES   From the depths of your ignorance.

OLIVE   I don't remember that line. *(sings)* Are you the man I'm going to...

ORSON *and* VIRGINIA*'s.*

VIRGINIA   Where've you been?

WELLES   At the theatre.

VIRGINIA   I meant after that.

WELLES   There was no "after."

VIRGINIA   I won't live like this.

Rehearsal.

WELLES   Olive.

OLIVE   Yes?

ROSENTHAL	I think we ought to break.
WELLES	Noted.
ROSENTHAL	It's nearly midnight, Orson.
WELLES	Enter that in the minutes, someone.
ROSENTHAL	They're exhausted, Orson.
WELLES	We're all exhausted, but we are going to stay here until we get it right. Let's get something straight right now. There is one director in this room—one! If you can't do what I ask, it's either because you don't understand it, or you don't accept it. If you don't understand it, fine, we'll keep working till you do. If you don't accept it, get out. You think I have nothing better to do with my time than to babysit a bunch of fucking amateurs? I will not be undermined! Marc, have you heard the song yet?
BLITZSTEIN	Well...
WELLES	Yes or no?
BLITZSTEIN	No.
WELLES	There you have it. The composer has not yet heard his song. We are going to stay here until he does. Jeannie, do us a favour, love, run next door and get us a few sandwiches. Anyone hungry? No? Fine. And a tub of chocolate ice cream from the Chinaman.

WAITRESS's apartment.

WAITRESS	Can't you sleep over just one time?
WELLES	I don't sleep.
WAITRESS	Why not? Afwaid of all those widdle devils gonna dwag you down?
WELLES	Christ.

Rehearsal.

Olive.

OLIVE	Yes, Mr. Welles.
WELLES	Do you have any idea what this song is about?
OLIVE	I think so.
WELLES	Do you have any idea how important this song is to the show?
OLIVE	Well yeah.
WELLES	Then fucking show it to us.
DA SILVA	Look—
BLITZSTEIN	Orson.
WELLES	Whenever you're ready.
BLITZSTEIN	Orson.
OLIVE	Are you the man I'm going to love tonight?
WELLES	Goddamn it, look at us.
BLITZSTEIN	Okay.
WELLES	What now?
BLITZSTEIN	The wagons are getting in Olive's way.
WELLES	We've only had them two days.
BLITZSTEIN	There's too much going on. I can't—I don't know what the scene is about.
WELLES	Well I didn't write it!
BLITZSTEIN	*(after a beat)* Fine. I'm going for a smoke.

WELLES   Good! Choke on it! Olive!

OLIVE   Are you the man I'm—

HOUSEMAN's office.

HOUSEMAN   Can't do that, I'm afraid.

BLITZSTEIN   Why not? It's your theatre as much as his.

HOUSEMAN   The simple fact is that I'm barred from rehearsals.

BLITZSTEIN   That's a poor excuse to let this show go to hell.

HOUSEMAN   If it wants to go to hell, who am I to stop it?

BLITZSTEIN   Why won't you help me?

HOUSEMAN   Why did you cut me out of the decision to cast Olive?

The penny drops for BLITZSTEIN.

BLITZSTEIN   I see. So that's how it works.

HOUSEMAN   You're damn right. You can't have it both ways, my friend. If you want me to be part of this show, then you include me. If not, not. I've had it from Orson for many years now. As long as I'm selling tickets, or putting out his goddamn fires, I'm good old Jack, but the minute I try to have some say in what's going on on stage, then I'm cut out. I take that from him. I won't from you.

BLITZSTEIN   Well. It was a personal matter.

HOUSEMAN   So's this. Takes courage to stand up to Orson. Have you got it?

Rehearsal.

WELLES   Quiet back there. Olive.

OLIVE   Are you the man I'm...

WELLES   What is that noise?

DA SILVA   What noise?

WELLES   A noise, a noise, somebody's making an awful fucking racket and I am finding it difficult to...

DA SILVA   I don't hear any noise.

WAITRESS's apartment.

WAITRESS   So you admit it! You're sleeping with her! Why, you're probably still in love with her, aren't ya?

Rehearsal.

WELLES   Did I tell you to stop?

OLIVE   Are you the man I'm going to love...

WELLES   Goddamn it, do you have any idea what the word—

ORSON and VIRGINIA's.

VIRGINIA   —love might mean?

WELLES   For Christ's sake, be re—

VIRGINIA   Reasonable? The only time you're home is when I switch on the radio; otherwise you're out doing God know's what.

WELLES   I—

VIRGINIA   Or who. I want you home.

WELLES   Virginia.

VIRGINIA   Or I want out.

Rehearsals.

WELLES   Where the hell is Marc?

ROSENTHAL   How should I know?

WELLES   Keep going, Olive.

OLIVE   Light me a smoke, honey/but don't pay for that drink...

WELLES   Stop moving so goddamned much! I want you still, still, still.

OLIVE   Don't want you thinking the worst...

WELLES   Where's the fucking lamppost?

ROSENTHAL   Getting painted.

WELLES   Jesus.

> *Intercut:* ORSON *and* VIRGINIA'S, *rehearsals.*

VIRGINIA   Orson?

WELLES   Hello, darling. I missed you. I thought we'd go for a walk in the moonlight.

OLIVE   My father was a sailor...

WELLES   Rehearsals have been so damned awful these last few weeks, and— What was that?

VIRGINIA   What?

OLIVE   My mother was a gypsy...

WELLES   I heard a noise.

VIRGINIA   It's all right, Jimmy, come on out.

YOUNG MAN   *(emerging)* Evening, Mr. Welles.

WELLES   Well. Hello "Jimmy."

VIRGINIA   I got lonely.

OLIVE   The whole damn bunch of us are cursed.

WELLES   What the fuck are you doing?

OLIVE   Are cursed.

VIRGINIA   Orson.

WELLES   Bigger.

OLIVE   Are cursed.

VIRGINIA   Orson...

WELLES   Bigger, fill this place up.

OLIVE   The whole damn bunch of us—

WELLES   Bigger, bigger, for Christ's jesus cocksucking sake—bigger!

ROSENTHAL   Okay, that's it. Get out.

WELLES   What?

ROSENTHAL   You want to run yourself into the grave, you go ahead and do it. But I am not going to let you run these people down, you hear me? I don't care what names you call me. These people are going home. Go!

> *BLITZSTEIN observes as OLIVE and DA SILVA leave. Then:*

BLITZSTEIN   Why don't you go home?

WELLES   Not much of a home to go to right now.

BLITZSTEIN   She doesn't much like me, does she?

WELLES   Virginia? She likes you fine. Told me so herself. It's me she can't stand. And the more money I make, the less she can stand me.

BLITZSTEIN   Maybe she wants something more than money.

WELLES   I know that. I just can't give it to her. Poor me. Just another fucked-up artist who doesn't know how to love women.

BLITZSTEIN   So much the better for your art.

                BLITZSTEIN goes to the piano. Begins to play the tune for a new song.

WELLES   What's that?

BLITZSTEIN   Not sure yet.

WELLES   Are there words?

BLITZSTEIN   Perhaps.

WELLES   You do like to be mysterious, don't you—Mr. Blitzsteen?

                WELLES goes to the piano.

BLITZSTEIN   I've got a wicked idea.

WELLES   Have you?

BLITZSTEIN   Mm. About Olive.

WELLES   Ha! Peter Pan!

BLITZSTEIN   Don't mind, do you?

WELLES   I suppose you want to give her the hook?

BLITZSTEIN   No, no. You know about her and Howard, I suppose.

WELLES   Patently obvious. Couple of lovebirds.

BLITZSTEIN   Yes. Well... that's the problem. Because the moll doesn't feel love. Olive does.

                Pause.

WELLES   If I do this... wicked thing...

BLITZSTEIN   Yes?

WELLES   Howard's become quite a problem. And this will only add to it. You keep Howard off my back... and I'll keep Olive off hers.

Pause.

BLITZSTEIN   Nearly midnight.

> BLITZSTEIN *leaves. After a while,* DA SILVA *enters, looking for something on the stage. He doesn't see* WELLES. WELLES *watches for a moment.*

WELLES   Howard.

DA SILVA   *(jumping)* Christ. Don't do that!

WELLES   Lose something?

DA SILVA   Olive... dropped an earring. Asked me to... don't you ever leave?

WELLES   Thinking about a problem. Perhaps you can help me out with it.

DA SILVA   *(still searching)* Yeah?

WELLES   I'm worried about Olive.

DA SILVA   Oh yeah.

WELLES   I don't know what to do anymore.

DA SILVA   What is the nature of the problem?

WELLES   I think you know.

DA SILVA   She can't hit the notes, big deal.

WELLES   It's not about the notes, Howard.

DA SILVA   She just needs a bit more rehearsal is all.

WELLES   It's not about rehearsal. You see? It's... Well. I overheard a couple of the other actors talking about her.

DA SILVA   Yeah?

WELLES   Apparently she's having an affair.

DA SILVA   Really.

WELLES   With someone in the cast.

DA SILVA   Huh.

WELLES   These actors, they—

DA SILVA   Who were they, if you don't mind my saying.

WELLES   They were saying that Olive's been spending an awful lot of time with this person.

DA SILVA   Well. Let's supposin' that's true. I mean, what business is that of ours?

WELLES   It's our business if it's affecting her performance.

DA SILVA   I don't see it.

WELLES   Let's say she's in love with this fellow.

DA SILVA   That's a big assumption.

WELLES   Let's say she is.

DA SILVA   Okay, for argument's sake.

WELLES   Let's say then that she brings that feeling of love into the rehearsal room. You see what I'm getting at? She doesn't understand that the woman she's playing will never find what she's looking for. Right now, she thinks she has. You see?

DA SILVA   *(finding the earring)* Hm. Interesting theory.

WELLES   Yes. *(about the earring)* Is that it?

DA SILVA   Yeah.

WELLES   Well, here's what I'm wondering. Should I fire her now, which would give us enough time to find a replacement, or should I hope that this fellow she's seeing might end the affair and allow Olive to see through the—smoke and mirrors?

DA SILVA   You'd do that? Get rid of her?

WELLES   Yes, for the sake of the show.

DA SILVA   I do this—you're gonna owe me.

WELLES   It's the group, Howard, the group we need to think about.

> WELLES *goes;* DA SILVA *stays there, smoking.* OLIVE *enters.*

OLIVE   Howard?

DA SILVA   Yeah.

OLIVE   I waited at the apartment.

DA SILVA   Sorry. I got to thinkin'.

OLIVE   'Bout what?

DA SILVA   Quittin'.

OLIVE   The show?

DA SILVA   Nah. Forget it. Sometimes I say things don't mean nothin'.

OLIVE   "Kiss me, Howard." *(They kiss.)* You find it?

DA SILVA   Hm? Oh yeah. Yeah. *(handing it to her)* Rolled under the wagon.

OLIVE   Good. Now I got something for you. I was gonna give it to you at the apartment. Picked up some takeout from the Chinaman. Had a whole special thing planned.

DA SILVA   You did?

OLIVE   Yeah, dummy. It's our anniversary. One month! *(laughing)* See, I... I didn't lose the earring. I planted it!

DA SILVA   Well... you had me fooled all right.

OLIVE   *(handing him the present)* Go on, open it.

He unwraps it: a book.

DA SILVA   *Gone With the Wind.*

OLIVE   I hope you like it. I hear they're gonna make it a movie, and I figured, I figured maybe—

DA SILVA   I gotta stop seeing you.

OLIVE   —maybe there's a part— What'd you say, Howard?

DA SILVA   Said I...

OLIVE   Oh. You mean it, or is that one of them things you say that don't mean nothin'?

DA SILVA   I mean it.

OLIVE   Oh... What happened?

He shakes his head.

That's it? That's all I'm gonna get?

DA SILVA   I can't tell ya. I mean, I could lie, make something up, but that'd only be worse and...

OLIVE   You don't want to hurt me.

DA SILVA   No.

OLIVE   Well. That's awful swell a ya. Not to want to...

DA SILVA   I'm doin' it for you, Olive. You probably don't believe that...

OLIVE   Sure I do. I believe anything you tell me.

Beat.

You must think I'm made a cardboard or something... Just tell me one thing: when you were inside me, and tellin' me you loved me... did you mean it, Howard? Did you mean it?

Rehearsal.

(sings) That's okay, honey/just pretend you love me
or at least you think I'm swell.
Just be as real/real as you feel
and I will too baby/I will.

WELLES   Thank you, Olive. That's got it.

     Turns to BLITZSTEIN *for approval.*

BLITZSTEIN   Well done. Magician.

ACT TWO
SCENE 12

     The present, hours later. WELLES *doing a magic trick for* DA
     SILVA; HOUSEMAN *on the phone with Pratt.* BLITZSTEIN *tries*
     to pay attention to both.

WELLES   Now, replace the card in the deck.

HOUSEMAN   *(into phone)* Yes, Mr. Pratt. What about the Dillingham? *(to*
     WELLES*)* There's a picket line outside the Dillingham—is that
     a problem?

WELLES   Tell him to try the Comedy.

DA SILVA   Blitz, you watching this? I got five bucks says he can't do it.

     Enter ROSENTHAL.

ROSENTHAL   You guys really oughta have a look out there.

BLITZSTEIN   What's happening?

HOUSEMAN   Never mind then.

ROSENTHAL   There's gotta be a thousand people out there.

HOUSEMAN   What about the Comedy?

BLITZSTEIN	Is it the Music Club?
HOUSEMAN	The Comedy, Mr. Pratt.
ROSENTHAL	Some of 'em, yeah, but, it's like, they just been hearing about what's going on and...
HOUSEMAN	I see.
WELLES	I had our publicist make a few calls.
DA SILVA	Leave it to you.
HOUSEMAN	The owner of the Comedy is on vacation in Florida.
ROSENTHAL	Well whatever you did, it's working.
WELLES	What about the 48th Street?
ROSENTHAL	In fact, you ask me, it's working too good.
HOUSEMAN	Mr. Pratt, the 48th Street?
WELLES	What's that, Jeannie?
ROSENTHAL	People are gettin' antsy. Gettin' dark now and we're no closer to finding a theatre than we were when we started this cockamamie exercise.
HOUSEMAN	In cash?
WELLES	Why don't you go out and calm them down, Howard, you've got mass appeal.
DA SILVA	Finish the trick.
HOUSEMAN	Hold on a minute. *(to the others)* How much cash have we got?
DA SILVA	Five bucks.
WELLES	Which are about to be mine.
HOUSEMAN	We need a hundred.

ROSENTHAL   Forget it. The Chinaman's got it all.

HOUSEMAN   *(in phone)* Would you take a five-dollar down payment?

WELLES   *(producing a card)* Would this be your card?

HOUSEMAN   Well, we simply don't have that kind of...

DA SILVA   Son of a *bitch*!

HOUSEMAN   Mr. Pratt, surely you understand our circumstances.

WELLES   The first principle of magic: misdirection.

DA SILVA   No wonder you're so good at it.

WELLES   I'll take that fiver now.

HOUSEMAN   Yes, yes, I understand your circumstances as well. Mr. Pratt, so far you have offered us three theatres that no longer exist, two that are being renovated, and one that is being picketed, now I—

    Phone rings.

ROSENTHAL   Orson?

HOUSEMAN   Because we're doing a play about a union drive and I don't think it would be prudent of us to cross a picket line in order to put it on.

ROSENTHAL   Orson, don't you think we oughta do something?

HOUSEMAN   Yes, Mr. Pratt, it is my problem. It is, however, also yours. Get that will you, Jeannie?

ROSENTHAL   Sure.

HOUSEMAN   Now please, Mr. Pratt, we've been at it since early this morning, it is now...

ROSENTHAL   *(answering second phone)* 891.

HOUSEMAN Nearly six in the evening and...

ROSENTHAL This is the stage manager, who's this?

HOUSEMAN Thank you, Mr. Pratt. I appreciate it.

    Hangs up.

DA SILVA I oughta check on the cast.

HOUSEMAN He's checking the Apollo, and I'm going to lie down for a minute.

ROSENTHAL Sure, one second. Mr. Houseman?

HOUSEMAN Yes.

ROSENTHAL Musicians' union.

    Long pause.

WELLES Here come the vultures.

BLITZSTEIN Who is it?

ROSENTHAL Petrillo.

HOUSEMAN Right.

BLITZSTEIN You want me to talk to him?

HOUSEMAN No no.

BLITZSTEIN If anybody ought to talk to him, it's—

HOUSEMAN It's the producer.

WELLES You tell him what's going on.

HOUSEMAN I will.

DA SILVA You hear from Actors' Equity yet?

HOUSEMAN   Let me deal with one union at a time, thank you.

WELLES   You tell him the Cossacks took away everything but—

HOUSEMAN   *(taking the phone)* John Houseman... Yes, hello... yes, that's right... that's right, Orson and I have taken over the— Sorry?... well, we, we intend to do the show... that has yet to be determined, but we're looking into a number of—mm hm... yes... oh really... is that a fact?... is that right... well, Mr. Petrillo, you must know that that would make it diff—yes, yes—difficult for us to— ...yes... yes, I understand... thank you. Good afternoon.

     Hangs up.

     A moment.

BLITZSTEIN   What'd he say?

HOUSEMAN   If we move to another theatre...

WELLES   When we—

HOUSEMAN   Yes, when we move to another theatre, we're to pay for extra rehearsal time.

WELLES   What?

HOUSEMAN   At Broadway rates.

WELLES   Bullshit.

HOUSEMAN   No, actually, it's clause seven. And that's not all. We're to add extra musicians.

WELLES   Oh for...

HOUSEMAN   Due to the "operatic" nature of the show, you see.

WELLES   Is that right? Marc, is that—

BLITZSTEIN   Yes, that's right. *(to WELLES)* "Opera!"

WELLES   Well that's absurd.

BLITZSTEIN	Union rules.
WELLES	Oh really. Well to hell with their rules, let's make our own.
ROSENTHAL	Sure, and wake up with a tuba up your ass.
BLITZSTEIN	Thanks for making that clear, Jeannie.
HOUSEMAN	You're all missing the point.
WELLES	Enlighten us.
HOUSEMAN	This has nothing to do with "rules." The simple and delicious fact is that the musicians' union doesn't like your show.
BLITZSTEIN	Come on!
HOUSEMAN	Hasn't from the beginning. They're affiliated with the American Federation of Labor, yes?
BLITZSTEIN	Yes.
HOUSEMAN	The American Federation of Labor is not running the steel strike—the Congress of Industrial Organizations is.
BLITZSTEIN	I don't see what—
HOUSEMAN	Our opera is about a steel strike, and therefore, in the eyes of the American Federation of Labor, is nothing more than propaganda for the Congress of Industrial Organizations!
BLITZSTEIN	This show is pro union.
HOUSEMAN	But your union is not.
WELLES	Jesus Christ. Are you telling me I can't have my musicians?
HOUSEMAN	I'm relaying that information.

Pause.

BLITZSTEIN	We don't need the musicians. Not all of them.

Everyone turns to him.

We can call it a concert, and have just a few. Or one.

WELLES   One?

BLITZSTEIN   Me.

WELLES   You?

BLITZSTEIN   Yes. Me, on the piano, just as I was in rehearsal.

WELLES   Marc, there's a slight difference between rehearsing and performing.

BLITZSTEIN   I'm aware of that. I have performed—many times.

HOUSEMAN   I don't think it'll work.

BLITZSTEIN   Why not, Jack?

HOUSEMAN   Petrillo will see right through it. And in the future, when we go to him for favours, he'll—

DA SILVA   Spoken like a true boss.

BLITZSTEIN   Howard...

DA SILVA   You think he cares if this show ever goes up? There's only one thing he's thinking about—saving his own skin.

BLITZSTEIN   Howard, please...

DA SILVA   He's been on the other side all the way through this. Yeah, that's right. Give you a perfect example. When the WPA started making their cuts, and we all wanted to do something about it, who said, "No sit-downs, strikes, or protests of any kind."

HOUSEMAN   You know why I—

WELLES   Cheap shot, Howard.

HOUSEMAN   I think I can defend myself.

ROSENTHAL   Can we stop eating away at each other for two seconds?

HOUSEMAN   I said that be—to hell with it. I don't need to defend myself to you.

DA SILVA   Course not. I'm just an employee.

HOUSEMAN   I need some air.

ROSENTHAL   You leave now the Cossacks won't let you back in.

HOUSEMAN   I'm not so sure I'm wanted back in.

WELLES   Course you are, Jack. Howard's going to apologize for that insensitive remark. Aren't you, Howard? Aren't you—Howard?

DA SILVA   Yeah. I'm sorry.

> HOUSEMAN *tries to leave but the door won't open.*

WELLES   Jack? Padlocks?

HOUSEMAN   I'm going for a lie down. *(to* ROSENTHAL*)* Jeannie... you'd better start calling around for a piano.

ROSENTHAL   Sure.

> HOUSEMAN *goes.*

BLITZSTEIN *(going to the piano)* Jeannie, get me the score, would you?

ROSENTHAL   Uh huh.

BLITZSTEIN And have the actors come up, I'd like to start going over the songs.

DA SILVA   Forget it. Not till we get a ruling from Equity.

WELLES   You can't scare Howard—he's stickin' with the union, stickin' with the union, stickin' with the union!

SCENE 13

Several days earlier. Rehearsing the finale. Moll *and* Larry *are in jail.*

Olive	*(as* Moll*)* Go on, Larry! Give it to him!
Da Silva	You think you got me licked? Well, you ain't... you got it all wrong, Mr.— Fuck me... you got it all wrong, Mr. Mister... it's... yes?
Rosenthal	"You got it all wrong, Mr. Mister. It's your time's comin'"—
Da Silva	It's your time comin' to an end, Mr.—
Rosenthal	"Time's."
Da Silva	What?
Rosenthal	"It's your time's comin' to"—
Da Silva	Did I ask for a line?
Rosenthal	No.
Da Silva	Then don't fuckin' give it to me.
Welles	Howard.
Da Silva	You got it all wrong, Mr. Mister. It's your time com—time's—comin' to an end, not mine, brother! You can't beat me—buy me...
Welles	Howard...
Da Silva	You can't buy me out, not for all the steel in steeltown. *(pause)* line!
Rosenthal	"See, we got a new way"—
Da Silva	We got a new way of thinkin' around here—it's called revolution! The workers' revolution!... And it... wait!... it... goddammit!

        Long pause.

WELLES   All right, Howard, forget it, forget it for now.

DA SILVA   Forget it? That's all I'm doin'.

WELLES   That's all right, don't worry about it, that was terrific. It'll be fine.

DA SILVA   Orson, it will not be "fine." We open in a week and we still haven't figured out a way to work with these wagons. They keep movin' around—I'm afraid I'm gonna fall.

WELLES   I have an idea.

DA SILVA   Christ.

WELLES   I want to fly you.

DA SILVA   Fly me?

        HOUSEMAN enters, unseen by WELLES, goes to ROSENTHAL.

        Look, Orson, I think there's enough going on here without...

WELLES   Maybe you could climb the bars.

DA SILVA   I don't...

WELLES   Look. Yes, yes, yes! When you say, what is it you say, when you hear the fifes and drums?

DA SILVA   Uhh...

OLIVE   "It's the machinists."

WELLES   "It's the machinists..." right?—you start to climb the bars, to get to the window.

DA SILVA   Orson, hold on, is not the stage going to be rocking at this point?

WELLES   I sure as hell hope so.

DA SILVA   You want me up on the bars while the stage is—

WELLES	Don't worry.
DA SILVA	Nuts!
WELLES	Now, Olive, what are you feeling during Howard's big speech?
OLIVE	Feeling?
WELLES	Yes, you've just heard how everyone else in the jail—all these fine upstanding citizens—how they've all sold out—except for this man, our hero. Now what is it you're feeling for him?
OLIVE	I thought I wasn't supposed to feel anything... for him.
WELLES	Of course you're supposed to— *(sees HOUSEMAN)* What are you doing in here?
HOUSEMAN	I need a word.
WELLES	You'll wait till after rehearsal.
ROSENTHAL	Company meeting. Mr. Houseman's got something to say. Let's go, let's go, gather round. *(to a cast member)* What are you, special? Sit! Go ahead, Mr. Houseman.
HOUSEMAN	Thank you, Jeannie. Sorry for interrupting your work, everyone. It's rather unusual for me, for any producer, to step in at a time like this, a week before our first preview and address the company. But there are a few things I wanted to let you know. First of all, I had the opportunity to watch a few moments of rehearsal just now, and I want to let you know how excited I am by what I saw. It confirms for me what I felt when I first heard this powerful story. I really think we have something very special here, and I applaud all your work. And lest you think I'm a lone voice, you ought to know that as of this morning, we have sold, for the run, nearly 18,000 tickets.

Company members cheer.

Yes... yes, which, by the way, represents a high watermark for Project 891. Now, a number of these tickets have been purchased by organizations on the Left.

DA SILVA   You better believe it!

HOUSEMAN   Yes, including the Downtown Music Club, which has in fact
            bought the house for the first preview.

            More cheering.

            Yes, absolutely. Wonderful. Now, on a somewhat less joyous
            note, it is my sad duty to pass along some rather disquieting
            news, regarding cuts to the WPA, specifically to the arts projects.
            We all knew this day would come, and I can tell you that some
            of us, some of us believed that the news would be much worse.
            The initial rumour was that we were to be wiped out altogeth-
            er. Well I am here to tell you that we have not been wiped out,
            that we are to be permitted to continue with our work. No one
            in this room is to be affected by the news I am about to relate.

DA SILVA   Would you just get to it?

HOUSEMAN   The WPA has announced a cut of 30% to the New York Theatre
            Project. That is effective immediately. Again, I stress that no
            one in this room is to be affected. I think we should all take a
            moment to reflect on our good fortune, let the news sink in,
            and then go on. Again I thank you for your work. And I thank
            you for listening.

            HOUSEMAN *starts to go.*

DA SILVA   Wait a second.

HOUSEMAN   Yes, Howard.

DA SILVA   I'm not too good at math. You mind telling me, you mind tell-
            ing us, just exactly what a 30% cut means—I mean in people
            numbers?

HOUSEMAN   Well I would be hard pressed to name an exact figure.

DA SILVA   Well you're pretty good at naming exact figures for our atten-
            dance, so how's about giving it a try with this? How many?

BLITZSTEIN How many, Jack? We need to know.

HOUSEMAN	Seventeen hundred.

A gasp from OLIVE.

DA SILVA	Ah, Christ.

BLITZSTEIN	So much for "rumours."

DA SILVA	Seventeen hundred?

HOUSEMAN	Please...

DA SILVA	Those are our friends we're talking about. And you're telling us nobody in here's gonna be affected by that?

HOUSEMAN	Not directly.

DA SILVA	So this is a victory. Is that what you're saying?

HOUSEMAN	In a sense.

DA SILVA	You think that way, you've already given up. You think that way, you're gonna let 'em steamroll you from here till doomsday. Well, that's fine, mister, but I got a different outlook. I say they ain't gonna stop at 1,700. I say this is just the beginning—pretty soon, who knows, in a month, maybe two, maybe sooner—they're gonna kill the whole thing altogether and there is not one person in this room who is not gonna be affected by that. Now I say we stop work right now and do something about this, 'cause we don't, we're gonna have nobody to blame but ourselves.

WELLES	What do you propose doing about it, Mr. Da Silva.

DA SILVA	Anything we can. Protests, strikes, sit-downs, something, anything to make 'em hear us.

HOUSEMAN	It seems to me that was the aim of your famous march to city hall—a march you were all given the afternoon off to attend. And what did that accomplish? *(holds up the paper)* Seventeen hundred of your friends—our friends—gone.

DA SILVA	Don't you pretend to care about those people—they're just numbers to you, numbers!

WELLES	Christ sake.
DA SILVA	Oh yeah, he's a real regular Mr. Mister. Only his game wasn't steel, it was wheat, and when it all came crashing down… *(to* HOUSEMAN*)* how many lives did you ruin?
HOUSEMAN	Many. My own included.
DA SILVA	You seem to come out all right!
HOUSEMAN	Yes, by working.
DA SILVA	Oh, now he's a worker! Well, let's see your hands, Mr. Worker. Let's see the cuts and bruises. I bet they're not as deep as the ones on the hands of the farmers you destroyed, yeah destroyed, with your inflated prices and your trading in futures. Well I got news for you, that's all over with. From here on in, we decide how things are gonna be.
HOUSEMAN	There will be no strikes, sit-downs, or protests of any kind, not from this company. If you want to change the world, you'll do it from inside this room.
DA SILVA	Don't listen to this bureaucrat! All he's thinkin' about is his own future. Now I say we take a vote. Everybody in this room gets a say in this. Now I want to see a show of hands. Who is for—
WELLES	Just a second, Howard. Shouldn't we see if anyone else would like to speak? Jeannie? Olive? Marc?
BLITZSTEIN	Yes. Yes, I would like to say something. *(beat)* I've been thinking about this for some time and… it seems to me that we have a chance here, and from the sounds of things maybe the last chance we're going to have for a long while to… to make things change. Therefore, I think the last thing we ought do is stop our work.
DA SILVA	What?
BLITZSTEIN	Yes.
DA SILVA	You don't really—

BLITZSTEIN   Yes, stop it to... to go on another march or... a march that prob-
              ably won't make a difference. That's just what Washington
              wants, Howard, you see, that's exactly what it wants, for us to
              waste our energy fighting the battle on their terms. Well, I say
              we fight it on our terms, in here. And if you don't agree with
              me—if there's anyone who doesn't agree with me—I mean
              anyone!—who doesn't believe that what we do in this room
              will make a difference, then goddammit, leave. Leave now.

              Silence.

OLIVE   Clap if you believe in fairies everyone... Sorry.

ROSENTHAL   Okay, people, we're broken.

              ROSENTHAL and OLIVE go; ORSON follows HOUSEMAN off.

BLITZSTEIN   I'm sorry, Howard. There's too much work to be done.

DA SILVA   Sure. You don't have to explain it to me. I get it now. What
              you really want is a big Broadway hit.

BLITZSTEIN   That isn't fair.

DA SILVA   Maybe you're just another Odets.

BLITZSTEIN   That isn't true.

DA SILVA   But what you just done, that was "fair"? That was "true"? Tell
              me something, brother, why did you give your play to Welles?
              You knew all about his bag of tricks. You knew what he'd do.
              I tried to steer you clear, but you didn't pay me no attention.
              You let him suck you in with his "vision."

BLITZSTEIN   Your argument's with Orson, not me.

DA SILVA   Oh, I got an argument with Orson, all right. But so have you.
              You got any idea what's been goin' on lately? I don't see you
              in rehearsals so much, so let me fill you in. The scene we just
              worked on? The big climax of the show, where the workers
              come on stage, and we all raise our fists in solidarity? You re-
              member that scene? I'm asking you.

BLITZSTEIN   Of course I remember it.

DA SILVA   Good. 'Cause nobody else is gonna. He cut the workers. Cut 'em!

EVA appears.

Look up here. Look at it. Is this what you saw when you wrote this thing? We open this show the way it is now, you are gonna be through. 'Cause it's your name, brother. Welles, he's already got a reputation, and a bright future. All he ever cared about was doing a musical. He don't believe in this show. And just about now, I'm wondering if you do.

SCENE 14

HOUSEMAN and WELLES by the stage door—in the dark.

HOUSEMAN   I can't do it. I just can't.

WELLES   You can, and you will.

HOUSEMAN   Standing up there, knowing the truth, looking into the eyes of… it's ridiculous… ridiculous! I'm tired of being at the mercy of forces outside my control. Seventeen hundred jobs gone at the stroke of a pen. I felt like I was back at the exchange, watching the numbers fall on the wheat-futures board, knowing there wasn't a damned thing I could do about it. The life I'd built was disappearing before my eyes. Then I found myself hoping it would disappear. I wanted it to be over. I'd been living a lie, and now, the world was freeing me of it. All around me was terror and fear, and I sat there, released of a burden.

WELLES   That's right, Jack. You went on.

HOUSEMAN   To another illusion, it turns out.

WELLES   How long have we got?

HOUSEMAN   *The Cradle* will be our last show here.

WELLES   Wish I could start again. Those goddamn wagons—why didn't you talk me out of them?

HOUSEMAN   It's not the wagons.

WELLES   No.

HOUSEMAN   It's the play. Don't know what you saw in it. *Waiting for Lefty*— with songs. Not very original songs at that.

WELLES   It's the characters, Jack. We just don't care about them.

HOUSEMAN   Well. You spent so much time working on those wagons, you forgot about the people on them.

WELLES   ...Christ, it's not that bad, is it?

Beat.

WELLES &
HOUSEMAN   The lighting's nice.

They laugh.

HOUSEMAN   Beautiful moon tonight.

WELLES   Yes.

WELLES slips away under:

HOUSEMAN   When we go on, I want more say. Not going to lie anymore, not to myself. Not to anyone. You know what I think of you, Orson. We're going to do wonderful things. Don't you think so, Orson?... Orson?

SCENE 15

The stage. OLIVE sits there. DA SILVA enters, thinks about leaving again, comes in.

DA SILVA   Olive.

Olive stiffens.

Look, I... I got no right to talk to you, I guess. I just wanted to tell ya... I figured I owed it to ya to explain what happened.

She shakes her head.

It was Orson. He found out about us. Told me if I didn't stop seeing you, he'd fire you. That's the truth. It's been eating away at me. I ain't sleeping. I just...

OLIVE   You got no shame, do you, Howard? Making up a story like that.

DA SILVA   But...

Enter WELLES and ROSENTHAL.

ROSENTHAL   Places, everyone.

DA SILVA and OLIVE take their places.

WELLES   All right, folks, let's try to put the bad news behind us. I think the best we can—

DA SILVA   Stow it.

Pause.

WELLES   Let's play nice. Now look, I have an idea about this scene. It's been missing something.

BLITZSTEIN enters.

BLITZSTEIN   Yes, what's that?

WELLES   Marc!

BLITZSTEIN   We need to talk.

WELLES   Of course. Let me just show you this first. Olive, "Give it to him."

OLIVE   Huh?

WELLES	Your line, darling.
OLIVE	Oh. *(as MOLL)* Give it to him, Larry!
DA SILVA	*(as LARRY)* You think you got me licked? Well you ain't—it's your... time's comin' to an end, not mine, brother! You can't buy me out, not for all the steel in steeltown! Say, what's that? You hear that, doll? It's the machinists. Ha ha! They're gonna join us! We won, we won, I tell ya!
WELLES	Yes! All right, Jeannie, I want moonlight here.
ROSENTHAL	Moonlight?
WELLES	Yes. It fades up when Larry starts the song. It strikes the floor, here, cuts across the wagons, across the moll's body... and Larry, he sees it, and it reminds him of the first time he saw her, of the promises he made to her.
BLITZSTEIN	"Moonlight," is it?
WELLES	Yes. You do like that, don't you?
BLITZSTEIN	Yes, it's marvellous.
DA SILVA	*(sings)* "Listen to that, what do you hear?"
WELLES	Just a second, Howard. Well, Marc?
BLITZSTEIN	Yes, I... when do the workers come in?
WELLES	I cut them.
BLITZSTEIN	*Cut* them.
WELLES	Well, we can have them offstage if you like. But this is what it comes down to—just two people, alone, marching toward the future.
BLITZSTEIN	I suppose the stage is still rocking, is it? You haven't cut that, have you?
WELLES	Well...

BLITZSTEIN   That should be very entertaining. "Let's go see that show about... oh, those two people marching toward the future. Well, what are they marching for, Mildred? I don't know, but the seats rock! Why, it's like Coney Island—without the hot dogs!" This is... This is!... What do you think we're doing here, a bedroom farce? This isn't about two people, Orson, it's about *the* people! "Moonlight"! How dare you? You may have no love in your life, but you certainly don't have the right to steal it from mine! You'll put those workers back in.

WELLES   Get out of my rehearsal. Get out!

Pause. The actors look to WELLES.

Howard.

DA SILVA   I uh...

WELLES   Howard.

As DA SILVA *sings,* BLITZSTEIN *leaves.*

DA SILVA   Listen to that, what do you hear?/Footsteps! A million footsteps marching...

The door slams.

SCENE 16

Outside stage door:

VIRGINIA   *(out of a laugh)* Banished?

BLITZSTEIN   Hello, Virginia. What brings you here?

VIRGINIA   I formed a secret alliance with the stage manager—she's about to declare a state of emergency; art must stop so that life may go on.

BLITZSTEIN   There's not much of either going on at the moment.

VIRGINIA   Should make for a lively dinner.

Trying to pass.

If you don't mind.

BLITZSTEIN   Actually, I've been meaning to ask you something. About the night we met. We talked about my play. You told me you didn't like it.

VIRGINIA   Oh dear. In vino veritas.

BLITZSTEIN   I see.

VIRGINIA   I don't apologize for my opinion.

BLITZSTEIN   Nor should you—as long as it's yours.

VIRGINIA   That's a bit too cryptic for me.

BLITZSTEIN   I was wondering if perhaps Orson put you up to it. To suss me out. Because he was afraid that if he talked to me about it himself, he'd betray the fact that he didn't understand the play at all.

VIRGINIA   Oh, you rat! You've ruined our game! Come out, everyone, he's got it figured. What shall we play next, pin the tail on the horse's ass? Thanks for the laugh. *(tries to pass)* Would you mind?

BLITZSTEIN   Course. Enjoy your dinner. What's on the menu? Pickles, oysters? Do you indulge, or do you just prefer to watch?

VIRGINIA   I'm not going to talk to you. I'll say something mean. And then we'll both feel bad.

BLITZSTEIN   It's true, isn't it? He put you up to it.

VIRGINIA   Of course it's true, every awful thought you've ever had. Have you ever had a good thought? Ever been happy? Or in love?

BLITZSTEIN   Depends on your definition. I suppose yours involves begging.

VIRGINIA   Begging!

BLITZSTEIN   Well, that's what you're doing here, isn't it?

VIRGINIA   Get out of my way.

BLITZSTEIN   Yes, go on. He's in there. There's nothing between you and the man you love but a wall of bricks and a question you've never asked yourself. How long are you going to wait, Virginia, for a future that'll never come? He'll never give you what you want. He can't. He told me so. One day he may even get around to telling you. And on that day, when you're left with nothing but your "darlings" and cigarettes, you'll wonder why you waited so long to hear it. But don't let me stop you. The man you love is waiting for you.

        Pause.

VIRGINIA   At least I had it, and for real—not like you, you fucking queer.

        VIRGINIA goes.

        EVA appears.

EVA   Useless. Don't deserve to eat. Light me a smoke, you joke. My body filled with disease. They cut off my tits—do you like me better now? You can pretend I'm what you want. Kneel before me—I'm your queen.

        He starts to go.

Sentimental boy. Go fuck your men! They're the ones you want and you'd love them too if you had the courage to be anything but a fine talker of talking, talking, go on, then... go on... on your knees, filthy boy... if we can't have truth, let's at least have joy.

SCENE 17

        ORSON, half asleep, at the theatre.

WELLES   ...Devils... ugly hell... one bare hour... Ah Mephistophilis!

HOUSEMAN enters.

HOUSEMAN   Orson... Orson...

WELLES   What is it?

HOUSEMAN   Did you sleep here all night?

WELLES   Thinking about the show.

HOUSEMAN   Well you can stop thinking. I've just received a cable from Harry Hopkins. We're not to open.

WELLES   So we stop?

HOUSEMAN   Unless you'd like to go to Washington and beg Harry for an exemption. Shall I cancel the dress rehearsal?

HOUSEMAN stays in his spot. BLITZSTEIN enters.

BLITZSTEIN   Magician... magician? I know you're here! You've got nowhere else to go.

WELLES   Did you drink all night?

BLITZSTEIN   No, no. I stopped once or twice to puke. And I thought. I thought and I thought and I thought... about... I forget. No, I remember now. Love.

WELLES   Listen, Marc.

BLITZSTEIN   You're right! There's no love in this show. So let's put some in.

WELLES   Marc.

BLITZSTEIN   You know that tune I had the other day? I thought of the lyrics. They came to me... in an alleyway.

Goes to piano.

Eva Eva, I'll never leave ya/you'll always be my girl.
Eva Eva, I did deceive ya/so you'd always be my girl.
You asked me to hurt you/Not in so many words.

You saved those for your novels.
That'll go unread/Long after you're dead/
and... something... something... grovels.

Pause.

Not very good, is it? That's what happens when I write about
love. To hell with it. When you fall into it, you can't eat, or sleep,
or think, and when you fall out of it, you still can't. Either way,
you can't function. You're useless. No good to the revolution.
So let's not have love. Let's just have... a good fuck—and get
on with it, and if you want to call that love, be my guest. I used
to call it moonlight, now I call it a financial transaction. Less
sentimental that way. Now you listen to me. You do this play
the way I wrote it. They're not my words, they're hers. And just
because you don't believe in them, doesn't give you the right
to get rid of them... or me... because I'm not going to disappear, no matter how much you wish I would... O wouldn't it
be wonderful if I did. Go on, magician. Make a wish. Make me
disappear... Still here. You see? I told you it wasn't so easy. We
have to do it the way I wrote it, you see. Or I'll never be rid of
her. I have to get rid of her. Won't you help me... magician?

BLITZSTEIN is next to WELLES now.

WELLES Jesus, what happened to you? There's blood on your face.

BLITZSTEIN Oh... just my brain leaking out my ears.

WELLES Come here.

WELLES starts to clean him off.

BLITZSTEIN No, I, I know what it was. I was, I was walking along the street.
I saw a light on in a house. Went inside, there was a... a blackjack game going on.

WELLES Blackjack, was it?

BLITZSTEIN Yes, blackjack and... I played and... when I asked the dealer
to hit me, he, he did. Very hard. Several times. I'm not very
good at cards. Not very good at... anything, really. I'm just
generally...

WELLES — But you are. You're a brilliant writer, Mr. Blitzstein. And I'm going to put all your words back. I'm going to give you everything you want.

BLITZSTEIN — But no moonlight?

WELLES — No moonlight.

> BLITZSTEIN *stays in place.* VIRGINIA, *at home.*

VIRGINIA — Orson?

WELLES — Not disturbing anyone, am I?

> *Pause.*

VIRGINIA — How was Washington?

WELLES — How did you know?

VIRGINIA — Harry Hopkins's office called. Said to tell you if you wanted *The Cradle*, it was all yours. But not in his theatre.

WELLES — Well...

VIRGINIA — What are you going to do?

WELLES — Carry on. I called Jack. We're going to do the dress tonight.

VIRGINIA — And tomorrow? Why are you doing this?

WELLES — For Marc.

VIRGINIA — Yes. You wouldn't want to lose a friend. You love this theatre, Orson. You know they'll take it away from you if you go ahead.

WELLES — They'll take it away from me one way or the other. It's all coming to an end.

VIRGINIA — It's a frightening thing, isn't it? To give up what you've known, what you've depended on, to walk away from it, start over.

WELLES — Not when the thing you depended on betrays you.

VIRGINIA	No.
WELLES	Anyway, I don't see as we have any choice.
VIRGINIA	We don't. *(pause)* Why did you come back?
WELLES	I'd say for a clean shirt, but you wouldn't—
VIRGINIA	Stop being clever, would you, for one second?
WELLES	What else is there?
VIRGINIA	Are you afraid to find out?

Pause.

WELLES	I missed you.
VIRGINIA	Is that true?
WELLES	It is. I was thinking, on the plane, "I miss her, I'll forgive her if she asks me to."
VIRGINIA	You'll forgive me.
WELLES	Well?
VIRGINIA	*(putting his hands on her throat)* Here... tell me you love me. Squeeze... harder... tell me you love me. *(WELLES breaks away.)* I've already packed.
WELLES	Virginia...
VIRGINIA	I'll tell you something. You haven't got a single friend in the world, just a lot of hangers-on, fair-weather nobodies, like me, who need you 'cause you're on a roll, you're going places. All right, drop me a line when you get there, let me know how many warm bodies you see lying around. And try to remember the one that wanted your arms around her.

Pause.

WELLES	*(looking to HOUSEMAN, who now leaves)* Don't go.

VIRGINIA   Say it like you mean it.

WELLES   *(ditto BLITZSTEIN)* Don't go.

VIRGINIA   Try it again.

WELLES   *(to VIRGINIA)* DON'T GO!

VIRGINIA   Fake.

ACT THREE
SCENE 18

The present. WELLES, BLITZSTEIN, ROSENTHAL (on phone), and HOUSEMAN (on phone).

ROSENTHAL   Orson? Orson?

WELLES   What is it, Jeannie?

ROSENTHAL   That was the piano place. The guy says he can—

DA SILVA enters.

DA SILVA   Oh brother, was that amazing. Holy shit, I never felt anything like it. There's gotta be two thousand people out there, it's a fuckin' mob scene, guys handin' out flyers, cops all over the place, then Blitz, Blitz, I do the jail speech, just launch into it, see? "Now listen, Mr. Mister, you think you got me licked? Well, you ain't. It's your time's comin' to an end, not mine, brother! You can't buy me out—no, sir! Not for all the steel in steeltown!" You shoulda seen 'em. I was right with 'em, working the crowd like it was a real demonstration, goin' up to people, right in their faces—and the thing of it is, they didn't pretend like I wasn't there like they normally do—I never felt that, no sir, not from any stage.

HOUSEMAN puts phone down.

HOUSEMAN   You certainly won't be feeling it from any stage in this city. That was Equity. It seems that actors who've been receiving pay from one producer cannot work on the same show for another producer without—

BLITZSTEIN What?

HOUSEMAN Without permission of the first, that being the United States government.

BLITZSTEIN Well, what, what...

DA SILVA He made it up!

BLITZSTEIN What does that—?

HOUSEMAN Howard.

DA SILVA He made it up!

HOUSEMAN That is the decision.

DA SILVA You call that son of a bitch back and tell him what to do with his fuckin' decision!

HOUSEMAN Be my guest. It's your union.

BLITZSTEIN Are you telling me the union is preventing our actors from—

HOUSEMAN I'm telling you we have no actors.

BLITZSTEIN I don't understand.

HOUSEMAN Effectively.

BLITZSTEIN Why would they do that? Somebody... somebody explain to me why... why the union would... when it's a play about unions... about... about... goddammit!

Pause.

WELLES Well, look at it this way. They can't take anything else from us.

The phone rings. HOUSEMAN lets it ring a few times, then warily picks it up.

Houseman	891... Hello, Harry, I've been expecting your call... How's Washington?... Raining, is it?... Don't know, haven't been able to—get outside... Yes... Yes... Of course... No need to apologize, I understand perfectly... Thank you for calling. *(hangs up)* Orson. We've been relieved of our duties... with Project 891.

Pause. WELLES starts to laugh.

Blitzstein	Glad you find it funny.

BLITZSTEIN starts to go.

Welles	Where are you going?
Blitzstein	There's nothing left here. I'm going home.
Welles	You're not.
Blitzstein	It's over. They've beaten us. They finally got what they wanted.
Welles	We still have the music... Oh come on, Marc. You have to laugh! That really is all we have left.
Blitzstein	You set me up. You, the government, those chickenshit artists' unions. This is exactly what you've wanted. You've lied to me all day. "You were worried enough, Marc, about the show." Bullshit! You were complicit. That's why you didn't tell me about the cable! You kept it from me—kept it all from me! "Campaigned for Roosevelt!" And you wouldn't want to embarrass your friend, would you? Patsy! You and your friend Hausmann! Go on, then, back to your putty noses and floating pigs. Nothing but a fraud.
Welles	Fake! That's me. We can't all live our lives as honestly as you do, Marc. You're a man of courage. Why, you have so much courage, you're going to walk out just when things get tough. Is this how you're going to change the world, Marc? By running out on the people who love you? Take a look around. Everyone in this room gave something up for you. Jack and I just gave up this theatre. Jeannie, all she does is give. Howard—you know what he gave up. All right, go—finish the job the government and the unions started—go on! Look Howard in the eye—tell him he never believed. Tell Jeannie. Jack. Me.

A pause. BLITZSTEIN looks around. Then down.

You know why you're doing this.

EVA appears.

Me, I put on little shows, pretending to be what I'm not, hoping to figure out what I am. I'm searching for something. Something to help me through the darkness. What shall we call it, this thing that helps us? Faith? Love? Friendship? It's in this room, padlocked in here with the rest of us, it's been in here all day, laughing at us, floating in the air, and I mean to pull it down, I mean to take it in my hands and wrestle it to the ground, stare into its smiling eyes and demand to know: What are you? Why am I so afraid? I don't want to be afraid anymore. I want to live my life honestly. To be real. And if you leave, it's going to leave with you. If I could close my eyes, make a wish, bring it all back—but I can't. So I'm begging you, Marc—my friend—don't go.

The phone rings.

HOUSEMAN   Project 89— John Houseman here... Hello, Mr. Pratt... You have?... Just a minute. *(to the group)* He thinks he has a theatre. I take it we're not interested?

WELLES   *(to BLITZSTEIN)* Are we?

EVA disappears.

BLITZSTEIN   *(looks around)* I'm sorry, everyone... About what I said... Please forgive me. Forgive me for not believing in you. *(turns to HOUSEMAN)* Are you going to ask Pratt about that goddamned theatre?

HOUSEMAN   Go ahead, Mr. Pratt.

WELLES   All right. We don't have sets, or musicians...

DA SILVA   But we got Blitzstein.

HOUSEMAN   Where is it?

WELLES   Yes, we do have Blitzstein.

HOUSEMAN   Is it proscenium?

WELLES   What about that piano? Jeannie?

ROSENTHAL   *(from the house)* Yeah, Orson. All set.

HOUSEMAN   How many seats?

ROSENTHAL   Course we don't have actors.

HOUSEMAN   How much?

WELLES   No. *(staring out at* ROSENTHAL*)* Not on stage. Not on stage.

DA SILVA   What?

HOUSEMAN   What's that, Mr. Pratt?

WELLES   Last time I checked, Equity had nothing to say about audience members standing in their seats and singing, am I right?

WELLES and DA SILVA *share a huge laugh.*

HOUSEMAN   Would you be quiet for fuck's sake?... Um, no—not you, Mr. Pratt. Sorry, awful commotion in here. Go ahead, Mr. Pratt... I see... well can you get hold of him?... All right, thank you. *(hangs up)* The Venice.

WELLES   Never heard of it.

ROSENTHAL   Straight up 7th, about twenty blocks.

HOUSEMAN   Yes, used only on weekends.

DA SILVA   By little old ladies.

HOUSEMAN   Amateur Italians, in fact. He's calling the owner to see if he'll take a cheque.

WELLES   Jeannie, find a way to get that piano to—

ROSENTHAL   On my way.

BLITZSTEIN	I'll need the score.
ROSENTHAL	*(producing it from beneath her clothes)* Thoughta that.
WELLES	Good girl. All right, let's go talk to the actors.
HOUSEMAN	About what?
WELLES	Singing from their seats.
HOUSEMAN	From their—!
WELLES	Yes. We'll put them in the house, we'll spread them all around, and when their turn comes—
HOUSEMAN	Are you mad?
DA SILVA	We got every right.
HOUSEMAN	You do *not.*
ROSENTHAL	*(heading out)* Let's move, let's move.
HOUSEMAN	You'd better think this through.
WELLES	No time to think, Jack, just do.
HOUSEMAN	That's fine for you. You're pulling in a thousand a week as the voice of the Shadow and My-T-Fine pudding, but what about the rest of the company?
WELLES	What about the rest of the company?
HOUSEMAN	If they do this...
WELLES	Yes?
HOUSEMAN	They'll lose their jobs.
WELLES	We don't know that.
HOUSEMAN	We certainly do.

DA SILVA   We're fighting for a principle now, Jack.

HOUSEMAN   Bully for that! Try paying the rent with principles. Try buying a loaf of bread with nothing in your pocket but a handful of dust and the shreds of your worthless stock! Twenty-three sixty a week, that's all they get. You have no right to force those people to defy the government when Orson and I were just fired for doing the same.

WELLES   Those people will not lose their jobs.

HOUSEMAN   No? Well you go down to those dressing rooms and tell them that. You tell them precisely what's at stake!

DA SILVA   We know what's at stake, and we're saying screw the government, screw the government and screw the unions, screw 'em for—

        He sees OLIVE.

OLIVE   Hello, Mr. Welles. Mr. Houseman. Mr. Blitzstein.

WELLES   Hello, Olive.

HOUSEMAN   How long have you been...

OLIVE   Long enough.

WELLES   Well?

OLIVE   You're saying we'd sing from the audience?

WELLES   That's it.

OLIVE   Without the WPA knowing about it?

HOUSEMAN   Oh, they'd know about it, Olive.

OLIVE   I see.

WELLES   Listen, Olive, I can't ask you to—

OLIVE   No you can't, so you might as well not even try. I hope you can understand.

WELLES   Of course, Olive.

OLIVE   Do you, Mr. Blitzstein? No. I can see it you don't. You don't understand it at all. I can see how important this is for you. Yeah, it's important for me too, honest it is. And you'll never understand how much it hurts for me to walk away from this, but I've got no choice in it. Really, I don't. I'm not saying it's easier for you, just different. I never got into this for the politics of it, Mr. Blitzstein. You know that better than anybody in the room. My whole life I've been waiting for the chance to do something I could be proud of, to stand up and do something where people could see I was good.

         The phone rings. All but OLIVE turn to it.

     I think I was good, and it kills me to have to walk away from it. But I'm walking, Mr. Blitzstein.

HOUSEMAN   *(picking up)* Houseman.

OLIVE   Twenty-three sixty-*eight* a week.

HOUSEMAN   Yes.

OLIVE   I got three kids.

HOUSEMAN   I see.

OLIVE   I'm sorry f-for being afraid.

HOUSEMAN   You're sure?

OLIVE   Don't hate me, all right? You don't have to hate me. I got enough of that myself for the both of us.

HOUSEMAN   *(hanging up)* I hesitate to inject a note of... enthusiasm... the Venice is ours.

DA SILVA   What?

HOUSEMAN   Yes. Yes.

DA SILVA   We got a house. Blitz, we got a house. We got a fuckin' house!

        A small celebration, Olive goes.

WELLES   Two songs, that's all, you'll cover 'em both. And if the rest of the cast walks, you'll do every song! Now let's go see who else is with us.

        Blitzstein, Da Silva, and Welles start off.

HOUSEMAN   Orson... don't you want to take one last look?

DA SILVA   *(off)* Orson, come on!

WELLES   *(beat)* No time for sentiment.

        He goes.

        The phone rings. Houseman picks it up, hangs up, takes off the receiver, takes the receiver off the second phone, has one last look around the theatre, and leaves.

SCENE 19

        Backstage at the Venice.

BLITZSTEIN   This is my piano?

ROSENTHAL   What's wrong with it?

BLITZSTEIN   Take a look at this place. Big. Take a look at that. Small.

ROSENTHAL   Hey, I phoned all over this goddamn city looking for—

BLITZSTEIN   I'm just saying nobody's gonna hear this thing.

ROSENTHAL   Press the keys harder. Honest to God.

WELLES   How's my spot coming?

HOUSEMAN   Your spot?

WELLES   You know what I mean.

HOUSEMAN   Sadly, yes.

As ROSENTHAL *readies a spotlight.*

Right, have a listen to this, would you?

WELLES   What is it?

HOUSEMAN   Jotted down a few notes for my speech.

WELLES   Your speech?

HOUSEMAN   The one I'm going to make before I introduce you.

WELLES   Oh all right.

HOUSEMAN   I'm going to say that this is an artistic act, not a political one.

BLITZSTEIN   Orson, can we lose the backdrop?

WELLES   What is it?

BLITZSTEIN   Vesuvius... I think.

WELLES   We're gonna have to live with it.

HOUSEMAN   Then I'm going to thank Harry.

WELLES   You're not!

HOUSEMAN   Yes, for allowing us to do a new American work when no private producer would.

Loud booing and hissing.

BLITZSTEIN   What's that for?

WELLES   *(peering through a rip in the curtain)* The spot's fallen on the Italian flag. Wait a second: Howard's climbing up to it. *(cheering)* He's ripping it down! *(another cheer)* How's that for a curtain raiser?

HOUSEMAN   Then I'll introduce Orson. Thank you for listening.

BLITZSTEIN   See any other actors, Orson?

WELLES   A handful in the front row. A couple in the balcony.

BLITZSTEIN   Is that all?

WELLES   Don't worry. It's packed, Marc. They're standing at the back... lined up against the walls on the side aisles. You've got to see this.

Rhythmic clapping begins outside.

HOUSEMAN   Midnight, gentlemen. We ought to begin.

BLITZSTEIN   Oh Christ.

HOUSEMAN   I'm going to talk to front of house. Good luck, Marc.

HOUSEMAN goes, WELLES turns back to BLITZSTEIN.

BLITZSTEIN   I can't get my breath.

WELLES   Here. *(puts a hand on BLITZSTEIN's stomach)* Breathe into my hand. Go on. Nice deep breaths. That's the boy. That's right. Better?

BLITZSTEIN nods. They embrace.

WELLES goes. Applause.

BLITZSTEIN takes EVA's Phi Beta Kappa ring from his pocket, puts it on.

EVA   Who's this fairy coming?

BLITZSTEIN   Please, Eva.

EVA   What have you done?

BLITZSTEIN   Wrote something for you.

EVA   For yourself, you mean.

BLITZSTEIN   Yes.

EVA   You won't forget me so easily.

BLITZSTEIN   I know.

EVA   Give me a drink. Light me a smoke. The moon will never come. Hold me in your—

WELLES   Curtain!

BLITZSTEIN moves to the piano. Sits. Turns to the audience.

BLITZSTEIN   Scene one. Alleyway. Enter the moll. She walks to the lamppost. Enter the stranger.

DA SILVA as LARRY stands up in audience. The spotlight hits him.

They look each other over. *(pause)* She sings. *(sings)* "Are you the man I'm going to love..."

OLIVE   *(joining BLITZSTEIN)* ...tonight?

BLITZSTEIN and DA SILVA look out as a spotlight catches OLIVE standing in the audience. She walks toward DA SILVA as she sings. BLITZSTEIN plays.

Light me a smoke, honey,
but don't pay for that drink.
Don't want you thinking the worst,
my father was a sailor,
my mother was a gypsy,
the whole damn bunch of us are cursed... are cursed... are cursed!

WELLES joins BLITZSTEIN on stage. Looking out at OLIVE:

WELLES   Magic.

The end.

ACKNOWLEDGEMENTS

My deepest thanks to all the playwrights in this anthology whose work has inspired me onstage and continues to do so on the page.

I'm grateful to Annie Gibson, publisher of Playwrights Canada Press, for entertaining my initial and unfocused pitches for a theatre-specific anthology like this one. PLCN's support and commitment to this project (and many others) form an essential and rarely acknowledged part in preserving and annotating this country's theatrical history. Blake Sproule has been a sharp, gentle, and accommodating editor and I couldn't have pulled off this anthology without his help (and patience) in the final stages of the manuscript.

The team at the Tarragon Theatre has always made me feel at home—as a critic, a theatregoer, a researcher, and, once as a favour to the always-gracious front-of-house manager Natasha Parsons, an usher. My thanks go first and foremost to Kirk Thomson, the theatre's indefatigable and loveable former director of marketing and publicity; Camilla Holland, its super-organized (and also former) general manager; literary manager Andrea Romaldi for allowing me to pick her brain at the early stages of this anthology; and the nimble director of marketing Amanda Kennedy for too many favours to list here. Captain Richard Rose continues to steer the Tarragon ship through calm and turbulent waters. An early conversation in 2009 with him about this book helped shape many of my early concepts as an editor.

Colleagues and staff members at the School of Journalism and the Faculty of Communication & Design deserve a special thanks for checking in regularly on the progress of this book for almost two years and for allowing me to run some of my editorial decisions by them in a research seminar in April 2010. I'm grateful to Dean Gerd Hauck for his continued support of my research and to past, interim (2010-'11), and current chairs of the School of Journalism: Paul Knox, Suanne Kelman, and Ivor Shapiro, respectively. Don Rubin from York University's Department of Theatre has been my mentor and role model for many, many years and I'm truly grateful for his support of this book and with all things related to Canadian theatre and criticism. Thanks also go to fellow members of the Canadian Theatre Critics Association for keeping criticism on the theatrical agenda.

On a personal note, I'm indebted to my many insightful and supportive friends in the worlds of theatre, arts, and journalism for emotional and professional support. I'd like to single out my dearest pal (and theatre lover despite his exclusive film and TV work) Laurie Lynd for being my family in Toronto, and Shane Smith for his beautiful friendship. Thanks go to the following in no particular order but with particular love and gratitude: Liz Millward, Richard Leblanc, Rachel Giese, Erika Ritter, Terry Finn, Florence Gibson MacDonald, Leonard McHardy, John Harvey, Joel Greenberg, Rory McKeown, Robert Gray, George Gillis, Victor Dwyer, John Pearce, Jim Gifford, Noreen Flanagan, Bill Flanagan, David Eggleston, Nada Ristich, Elizabeth Comper, Tony Comper, Tim Gray, Alex Boyd, Joe Fantetti, Harry Wiebe, Alex Kade, Leonard Schlichting, Garth Norbraten, Sue Andrew, John Daly, Andy Ryan, Judith Killoran, Denise Ashby, Kate Taylor, Elle Flanders, Jennifer Kawaja, Christopher Harris, Trish Wilson, Brad Wheeler, Maryam Sanati, Vanessa Wyse, Judith Pereira, Clare Jordan, Richard Ouzounian, Dorene Saltzer, Elizabeth Renzetti, Gordon Bowness, Kevin Connolly, Doug Cudmore, Odette Yazbeck.

Finally, my eternal gratitude and love to all my students, past and present.

BIBLIOGRAPHY

Al-Solaylee, Kamal. "A drama about the power of forgetting." *Globe and Mail*, March 1, 2005.

———. "Generational journey tries to fill in gaps." *Globe and Mail*, March 4, 2004.

———. "German political comedy? That's about as funny as it gets." *Globe and Mail*, April 29, 2004.

———. "Rolling the dice for love." *Globe and Mail*, February 13, 2004.

———. "Too Poor to Send Flowers: The State of Canadian Theatre," *Best Canadian Essays 2009*, edited by Alex Boyd and Carmine Starnino. Toronto: Tightrope Books, 2009.

Barton, Bruce, ed. *Developing Nation: New Play Creation in English-Speaking Canada*. Toronto: Playwrights Canada Press, 2008.

Benson, Eugene and L.W. Conolly. *English-Canadian Theatre*. Toronto: Oxford University Press, 1987.

Breon, Robin. "Tarragon Flavoured Memories." *Canadian Theatre Review* 112 (2003).

Carson, Neil. *Harlequin in Hogtown: George Luscombe and Toronto Workshop Productions*. Toronto, University of Toronto Press, 1995.

Clark, Bob. "Junction scores with Optimists." *Calgary Herald*, February 7, 2004.

Connolly, Kevin. "Sherman's mark." *Eye Weekly*, January 7, 1999.

Conolly, L.W., ed. *Canadian Drama and the Critics* (Revised Edition). Vancouver, Talonbooks, 1995.

Coulbourn, John. "Just a few reservations." *Toronto Sun*, April 19, 2000.

———. "Pessimistic view of *The Optimists*." *Toronto Sun*, September 22, 2005.

———. "Play leaves family in Rune." *Toronto Sun*, March 4, 2004.

Cushman, Robert. "She, Claudia, has a few thoughts on the subject." *National Post*, April 5, 2001.

Filewod, Alan. *Theatre Histories*. (Critical Perspectives on Canadian Theatre in English, Vol. 13.) Toronto: Playwrights Canada Press, 2009.

Giese, Rachel. "Thomson's Claudia needs no distractions." *Eye Weekly*, April 5, 2001.

Glaap, Albert-Reiner, ed. *Voices from Canada: Focus on Thirty Plays*. Toronto: Playwrights Canada Press, 2003.

Gould, Allan. "*Drawer Boy* author brings new play to Tarragon." *Post City Magazine*, March 2004.

Hood, Sarah B. "A memorable play: Award-winning playwright explores the nature of identity." *Tandem/Corriere Canadese*, February 27, 2005.

Isaacs, Paul. "On Stage: *The Optimists*." *Eye Weekly*, September 29, 2005.

Johnston, Denis W. *Up the Mainstream: The Rise of Toronto's Alternative Theatres*. Toronto: University of Toronto Press, 1991.

Kaplan, Jon. "It's never too late." *NOW Magazine*, February 24, 2005.

———. "Rune's tune." *NOW Magazine*, February 27, 2004.

Kareda, Urjo. "Canada's new playwrights have found a home at home." *The New York Times*, November 23, 1974.

———. "A Former Life." In *Theatre Memories: On the Occasion of the Canadian Theatre Conference*. Toronto, Playwrights Union of Canada, 1998.

———. "An Introduction." In *Jason Sherman: Six Plays*. Toronto: Playwrights Canada Press, 2001.

Knowles, Ric. "Reading Judith Thompson." In *Late 20th Century Plays: 1980–2000*. Toronto: Playwrights Canada Press, 2003.

Knowles, Richard Paul and Jennifer Fletcher. "Towards a Materialist Performance Analysis: The Case of Tarragon Theatre." In *The Performance Text*, edited by Domenico Pietropaolo. Toronto: Legas, 1999.

McKinnie, Michael. *City Stages: Theatre and Urban Space in a Global City*. Toronto: University of Toronto Press, 2007.

Offman, Craig. "Everything's relative." *Time*, February 1, 1999.

Ouzounian, Richard. "Claudia is masked for success." *Toronto Star*, April 5, 2001.

———. "Cottage tale makes merry and drowns." *Toronto Star*, March 3, 2004.

Posner, Michael. "Things are all write in Brebner's world." *Globe and Mail*, September 20, 2005.

Rubin, Don, ed. *Canadian Theatre History: Selected Readings*. Toronto: Playwrights Canada Press, 2004.

Sumi, Glenn. "Spidell smokin'." *NOW Magazine*, April 19, 2000.

Taylor, Kate. "Character that's bred in the bone." *Globe and Mail*, April 16, 2001.

———. "Playing with voyeurism may cause queasiness." *Globe and Mail*, April 19, 2000.

———. "Truly, it's a night of magic." *Globe and Mail*, October 18, 1999.

———. "Twenty seasons at the Tarragon." *Globe and Mail*, September 15, 2001.

Usmiani, Renate. *Second Stage: The Alternative Theatre Movement in Canada*. Vancouver, University of British Columbia Press, 1983.

Wagner, Anton, ed. *Contemporary Canadian Theatre: New World Visions*. Toronto: Simon & Pierre, 1985.

————, ed. *Establishing Our Boundaries: English-Canadian Theatre Criticism*. Toronto: University of Toronto Press, 1999.

Wallace, Robert. *Producing Marginality: Theatre and Criticism in Canada*. Saskatoon: Fifth House Publishers, 1990.

————. *Theatre and Transformation in Contemporary Canada*. Toronto: Robarts Centre for Canadian Studies, 1999.

Wilson, Ann, ed. "Urjo Kareda." Special issue, *Canadian Theatre Review* 113 (2003).

Younger, Sharon. "Working-class poetry accents drama." *National Post*, April 15, 2000.

Kamal Al-Solaylee is a former theatre critic for the *Globe and Mail* and currently an assistant professor and undergraduate program director at the School of Journalism in the Faculty of Communication & Design, Ryerson University. Based in Toronto, he started his career as a theatre critic and feature writer at *Eye Weekly* in 1998 and since then contributed to the *National Post*, the *Toronto Star*, *The Walrus*, *Toronto Life*, *Report on Business* magazine, *Elle Canada*, *Canadian Notes & Queries*, *Literary Review of Canada* and *Xtra!*, among others, on different aspects of Canadian arts and culture. He holds a Ph.D. in Victorian literature from the University of Nottingham, England. He's the co-editor (with Alex Boyd) of *Best Canadian Essays 2010* (Tightrope Books) and the author of *Intolerable: A Memoir of Extremes* (HarperCollins Canada, 2012).